STAR WARS

THE LAST COMMAND

SCRIPT
MIKE BARON

PENCILS
EDVIN BIUKOVIC

INKS
ERIC SHANOWER

COLORS
PAM RAMBO & DAN BROWN

SEPARATIONS
DIGITAL CHAMELEON

LETTERING
ELLIE DEVILLE

COVER ART
MATHIEU LAUFFRAY

BASED ON THE NOVEL BY
TIMOTHY ZAHN

STAR WARS®

THE LAST COMMAND

DARK HORSE COMICS®

Grand Admiral Thrawn to throw a big ol' monkey wrench into the Alliance's gears. By the time *The Last Command* cranks up, Luke, Leia, Han, and the rest of the gang are in peril to their eyebrows, about to have new additions to their family, and a well-deserved rest is simply out of the question.

Chances are real good that if you are reading this, you also read *Heir to the Empire* and *Dark Force Rising*, and if you haven't, you should. Tim Zahn set the bar pretty high for the rest of us who later joined up to work in George Lucas' universe, and I have to say, I never expected to see a graphic novelization of this trilogy. Why do I say that? Because so much of what goes on in Tim's books is very complex. The novels are political, introspective, loaded with intrigue, and weighted with complicated tactical setups. With Tim's stories, you get the feeling you are behind the scenes of the battles, that you know not only how they are fought, but why. You get a long-range view, the big picture, and a sense of what makes his characters and the entire *Star Wars* galaxy tick.

You can't toss this off in a couple of lines.

This is not to say you can't express complex ideas in a comic book, for certainly you can. But when you write a novel, you have all this *room* to explain these things; when you write a comic book, you run into your limits pretty fast. When you condense a three- or four-hundred-page novel into six comics, you have to lose a lot of material, no two ways about it.

For those of you who think that writing or drawing comics is a snap, I am here to tell you that it ain't so easy. I discovered this the hard way when I ventured into these waters with my *Star Wars* series, *Shadows of the Empire: Evolution*.

Creating original material is hard enough. Taking a well-known and much-loved series of novels and turning them into comics is harder in some ways than creating comics from scratch, because you have a whole lot of people looking over your shoulder, ready to whap you when you make a mistake. That the creative team who adapted Zahn's trilogy managed to do it at all is a major accomplishment. That they managed to do it so well is amazing. I could rattle off their names, but all you have to do is flip over the page and see who they are. Do that. You should always read the credits; you ought to know who wrote and edited the words, who drew and inked and colored and painted the pictures.

I could go off here and tell you about my initial experiences with *Star Wars*, how I felt when I first saw the first movie, but I won't. I saw it, I liked it, it was great—what else is there to say? No, I'd rather ramble a little bit about the *Star Wars* worlds and the friendly folks who bring you the stories you have come to love.

Or, in some cases, the stories you positively hate.

As it happens, many of the folks who write the *Star Wars* novels live in the Pacific Northwest. Six of us are in Washington or Oregon, and a couple of us live in the same towns. A lot of the folks who play with the comics live around here, too, but since Dark Horse is in Milwaukie, Oregon, maybe that's not such a surprise.

As a result, most of us know each other, and most of us respect each other. Some of us even work together now and then—in fact, the guy editing this collection collaborated with me on a screenplay! Those of us who write and draw and all like that know what it takes to do this stuff, we know how hard it is, and as a result, we generally wish each other good luck when we get our turns on the firing line.

And it sometimes does get to be a firing line. *Star Wars* fans hold strong, (sometimes positively *rabid*) opinions about their favorite literature and movies, and they are quick to tell you what they don't like. This is as it should be, because the fans keep this series going and growing. But fans also love to compare: there are those who love Tim and hate Kevin—or vice-versa; who think Vonda wrote the best book—or the worst. And there are some who think I ought to be taken out and shot for taking Leia's clothes off in *Shadows of the Empire.* I got my very first death threat as a writer from a demented *Star Wars* fan. I felt pretty good about that until I talked to K. W. Jeter, another *Star Wars* writer, who said he received death threats all the time.

Aw, gee.

My point here is that the writers and artists are pros, and they do what they do for love as well as money, and they, by and large, do it well. We all want to please fans, but from where we sit, contrasting Zahn against Anderson against Stackpole, or Randall against Biukovic against Plunkett, is a lot like comparing vanilla to chocolate to strawberry. Different flavors please different folks, and one isn't better than the other, just . . . well, *different.*

Whatever your favorite, you have to admit that Tim Zahn took the scoop from George Lucas and worked well with it, so we all owe him. He gave us a flavor we hadn't tasted in the movies, and a villain who was a worthy adversary for the *Star Wars* heroes. Not even to mention the deadly-but-lovely Mara Jade. By the time you read this, Mara will have spun off into her own series, and rightfully so.

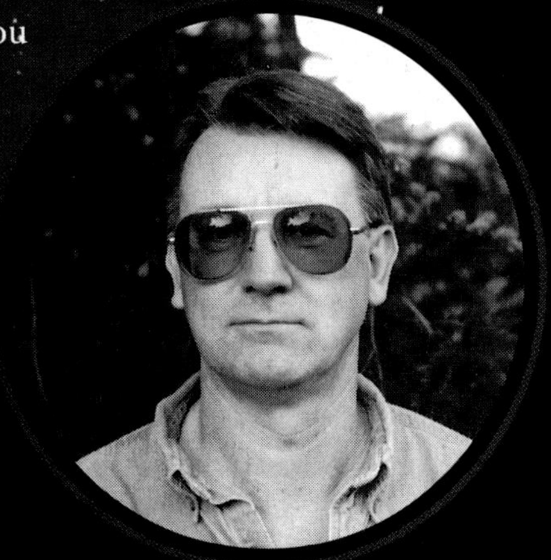

So, come along and enjoy the final loops on this particular ride. You are in good hands here.

Steve Perry
Beaverton, Oregon
August 1998

PUBLISHER
MIKE RICHARDSON

SERIES EDITORS
BOB COOPER & PEET JANES

COLLECTION EDITOR
CHRIS WARNER

COLLECTION DESIGNER
KRISTEN BURDA

ART DIRECTOR
MARK COX

SPECIAL THANKS TO ALLAN KAUSCH &
LUCY AUTREY WILSON AT LUCAS LICENSING.

STAR WARS® THE LAST COMMAND

This book collects issues 1-6 of the Dark Horse comic-book series
Star Wars®: The Last Command.

Published by
Dark Horse Comics, Inc.
10956 SE Main Street
Milwaukie, OR 97222

First edition: June 1999
ISBN:1-56971-378-2

1 3 5 7 9 10 8 6 4 2

Printed in Canada

A long time ago in a galaxy far, far away. . . .

The Last Command

The struggle for power over the galaxy continues in the wake of the Emperor's death. With the help of Jedi Master C'Baoth, Admiral Thrawn has seized control of the fabled Katana Fleet. The balance of power has been tipped against the New Republic. Infighting between the Republican councilors has ceased as aggressions are turned toward a common foe — Admiral Thrawn.

In addition to the Katana Fleet, it has been discovered that Thrawn is now in control of new cloning technology. With an unlimited supply of clones, the Empire's ranks will grow to enormous proportions and become more of a threat than ever before.

Having escaped the clutches of Jedi Master C'Baoth, Luke Skywalker goes in search of the cloning cylinders which are swelling the ranks of Thrawn's army. Despite having lost Skywalker, Master C'Baoth continues to pursue Luke's sister — Leia Organa Solo. Once in control of Leia and her unborn children C'Baoth believes he will become the undisputed master of the Empire. Thrawn, however, has different plans for C'Baoth . . .

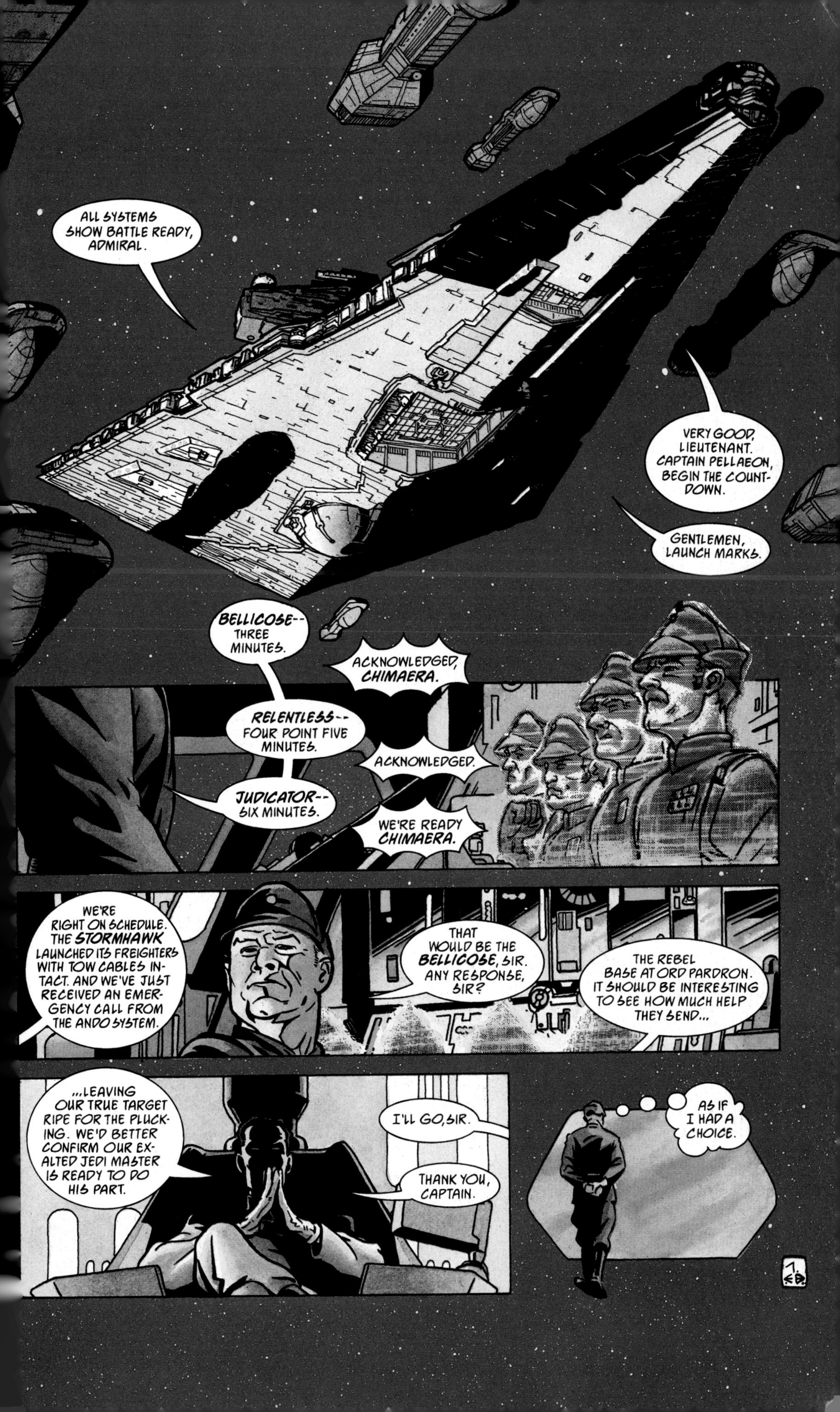
ALL SYSTEMS SHOW BATTLE READY, ADMIRAL.
VERY GOOD, LIEUTENANT. CAPTAIN PELLAEON, BEGIN THE COUNT-DOWN.
GENTLEMEN, LAUNCH MARKS.
BELLICOSE-- THREE MINUTES.
ACKNOWLEDGED, CHIMAERA.
RELENTLESS-- FOUR POINT FIVE MINUTES.
ACKNOWLEDGED.
JUDICATOR-- SIX MINUTES.
WE'RE READY CHIMAERA.
WE'RE RIGHT ON SCHEDULE. THE STORMHAWK LAUNCHED ITS FREIGHTERS WITH TOW CABLES IN-TACT. AND WE'VE JUST RECEIVED AN EMER-GENCY CALL FROM THE ANDO SYSTEM.
THAT WOULD BE THE BELLICOSE, SIR. ANY RESPONSE, SIR?
THE REBEL BASE AT ORD PARDRON. IT SHOULD BE INTERESTING TO SEE HOW MUCH HELP THEY SEND...
...LEAVING OUR TRUE TARGET RIPE FOR THE PLUCK-ING. WE'D BETTER CONFIRM OUR EX-ALTED JEDI MASTER IS READY TO DO HIS PART.
I'LL GO, SIR.
THANK YOU, CAPTAIN.
AS IF I HAD A CHOICE.

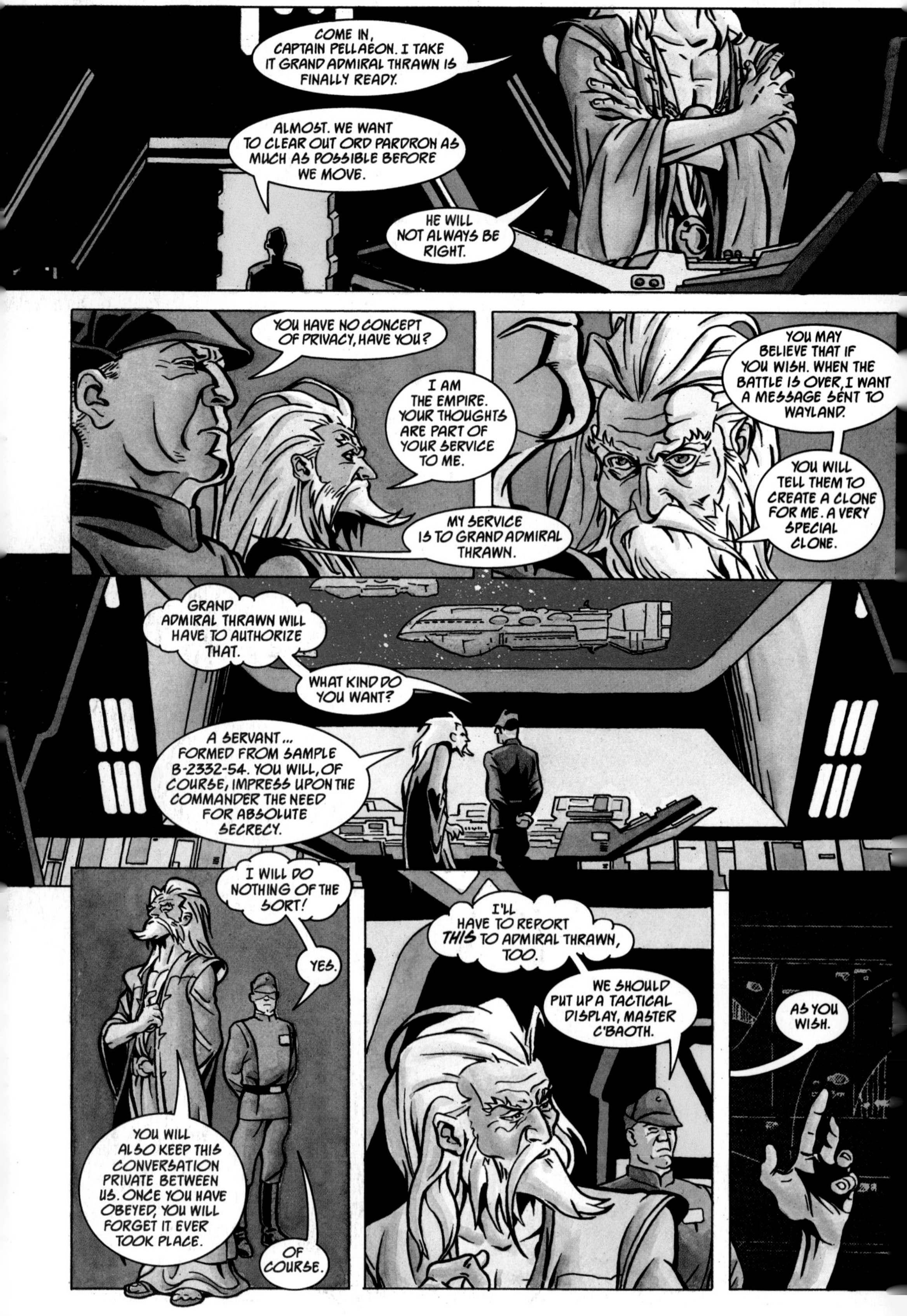
COME IN, CAPTAIN PELLAEON. I TAKE IT GRAND ADMIRAL THRAWN IS FINALLY READY.
ALMOST. WE WANT TO CLEAR OUT ORD PARDRON AS MUCH AS POSSIBLE BEFORE WE MOVE.
HE WILL NOT ALWAYS BE RIGHT.
YOU HAVE NO CONCEPT OF PRIVACY, HAVE YOU?
I AM THE EMPIRE. YOUR THOUGHTS ARE PART OF YOUR SERVICE TO ME.
MY SERVICE IS TO GRAND ADMIRAL THRAWN.
YOU MAY BELIEVE THAT IF YOU WISH. WHEN THE BATTLE IS OVER, I WANT A MESSAGE SENT TO WAYLAND.
YOU WILL TELL THEM TO CREATE A CLONE FOR ME. A VERY SPECIAL CLONE.
GRAND ADMIRAL THRAWN WILL HAVE TO AUTHORIZE THAT.
WHAT KIND DO YOU WANT?
A SERVANT... FORMED FROM SAMPLE B-2332-54. YOU WILL, OF COURSE, IMPRESS UPON THE COMMANDER THE NEED FOR ABSOLUTE SECRECY.
I WILL DO NOTHING OF THE SORT!
YES.
YOU WILL ALSO KEEP THIS CONVERSATION PRIVATE BETWEEN US. ONCE YOU HAVE OBEYED, YOU WILL FORGET IT EVER TOOK PLACE.
OF COURSE.
I'LL HAVE TO REPORT THIS TO ADMIRAL THRAWN, TOO.
WE SHOULD PUT UP A TACTICAL DISPLAY, MASTER C'BAOTH.
AS YOU WISH.

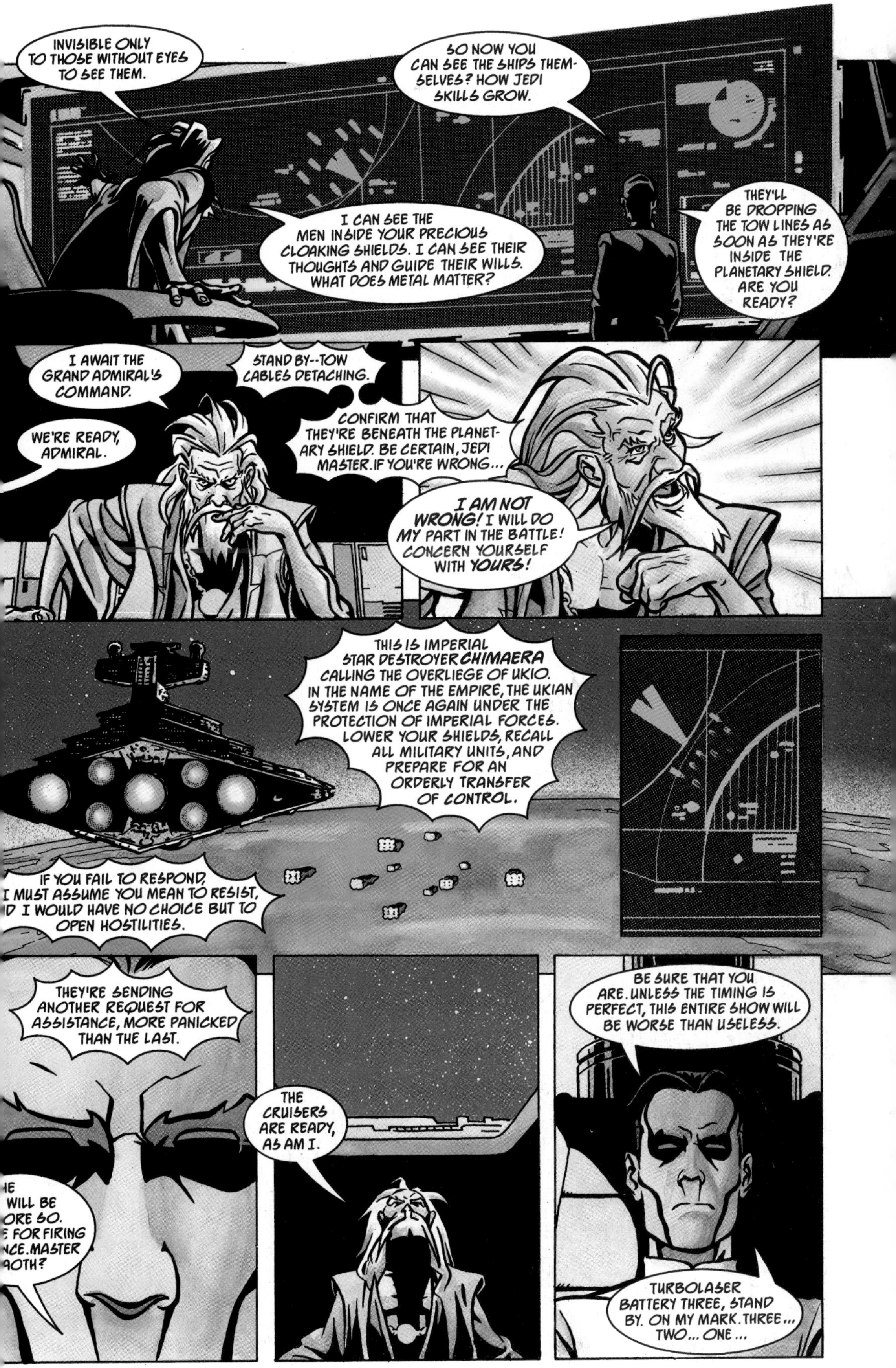
INVISIBLE ONLY TO THOSE WITHOUT EYES TO SEE THEM.
SO NOW YOU CAN SEE THE SHIPS THEMSELVES? HOW JEDI SKILLS GROW.
I CAN SEE THE MEN INSIDE YOUR PRECIOUS CLOAKING SHIELDS. I CAN SEE THEIR THOUGHTS AND GUIDE THEIR WILLS. WHAT DOES METAL MATTER?
THEY'LL BE DROPPING THE TOW LINES AS SOON AS THEY'RE INSIDE THE PLANETARY SHIELD. ARE YOU READY?
I AWAIT THE GRAND ADMIRAL'S COMMAND.
STAND BY--TOW CABLES DETACHING.
WE'RE READY, ADMIRAL.
CONFIRM THAT THEY'RE BENEATH THE PLANETARY SHIELD. BE CERTAIN, JEDI MASTER. IF YOU'RE WRONG...
I AM NOT WRONG! I WILL DO MY PART IN THE BATTLE! CONCERN YOURSELF WITH YOURS!
THIS IS IMPERIAL STAR DESTROYER CHIMAERA CALLING THE OVERLIEGE OF UKIO. IN THE NAME OF THE EMPIRE, THE UKIAN SYSTEM IS ONCE AGAIN UNDER THE PROTECTION OF IMPERIAL FORCES. LOWER YOUR SHIELDS, RECALL ALL MILITARY UNITS, AND PREPARE FOR AN ORDERLY TRANSFER OF CONTROL.
IF YOU FAIL TO RESPOND, I MUST ASSUME YOU MEAN TO RESIST, D I WOULD HAVE NO CHOICE BUT TO OPEN HOSTILITIES.
THEY'RE SENDING ANOTHER REQUEST FOR ASSISTANCE, MORE PANICKED THAN THE LAST.
HE WILL BE ORE SO. E FOR FIRING NCE. MASTER AOTH?
THE CRUISERS ARE READY, AS AM I.
BE SURE THAT YOU ARE. UNLESS THE TIMING IS PERFECT, THIS ENTIRE SHOW WILL BE WORSE THAN USELESS.
TURBOLASER BATTERY THREE, STAND BY. ON MY MARK. THREE... TWO... ONE...

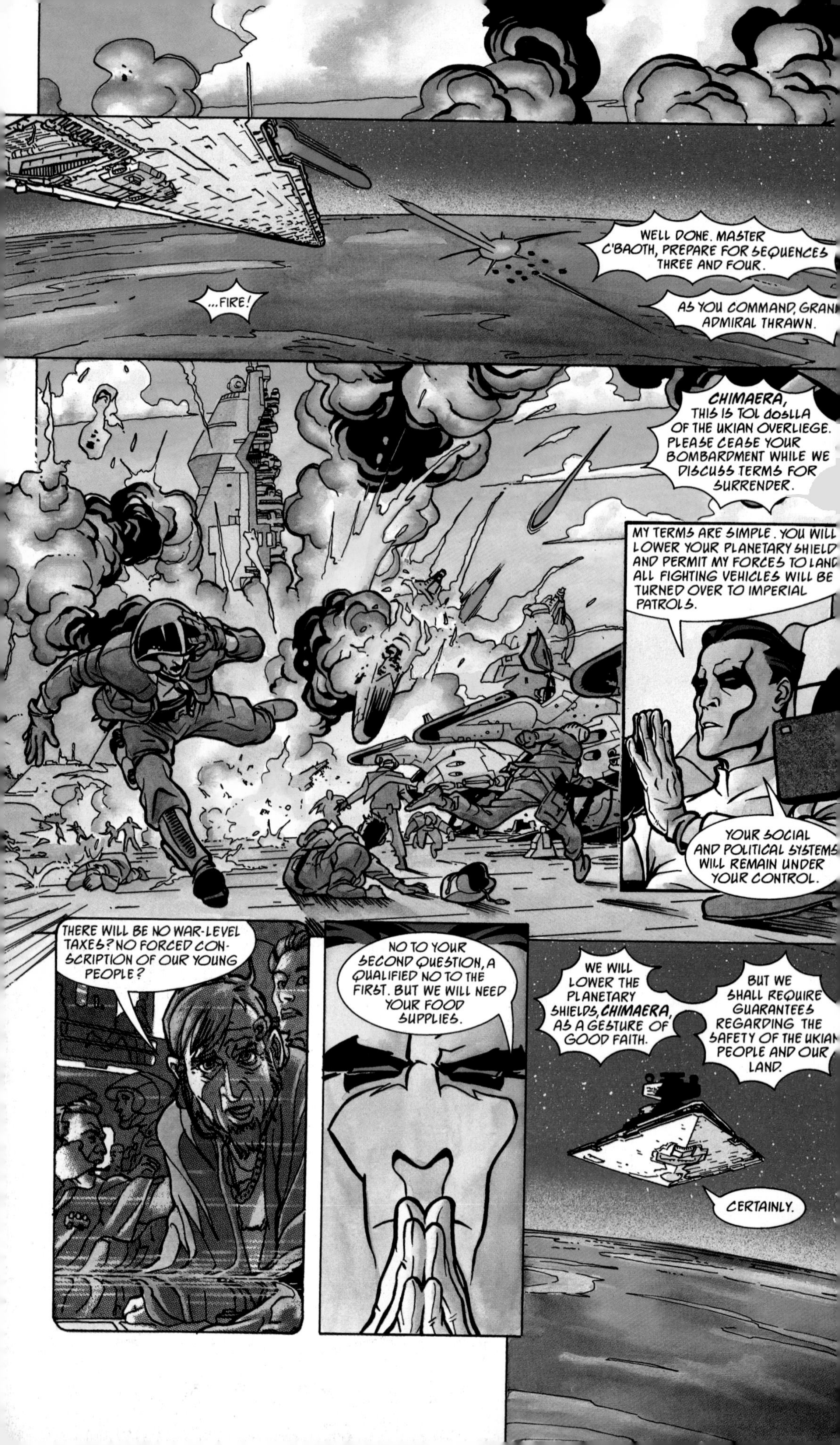
WELL DONE. MASTER C'BAOTH, PREPARE FOR SEQUENCES THREE AND FOUR.
...FIRE!
AS YOU COMMAND, GRAN ADMIRAL THRAWN.
CHIMAERA, THIS IS TOL DOSLLA OF THE UKIAN OVERLIEGE. PLEASE CEASE YOUR BOMBARDMENT WHILE WE DISCUSS TERMS FOR SURRENDER.
MY TERMS ARE SIMPLE. YOU WILL LOWER YOUR PLANETARY SHIELD AND PERMIT MY FORCES TO LAND. ALL FIGHTING VEHICLES WILL BE TURNED OVER TO IMPERIAL PATROLS.
YOUR SOCIAL AND POLITICAL SYSTEMS WILL REMAIN UNDER YOUR CONTROL.
THERE WILL BE NO WAR-LEVEL TAXES? NO FORCED CONSCRIPTION OF OUR YOUNG PEOPLE?
NO TO YOUR SECOND QUESTION, A QUALIFIED NO TO THE FIRST. BUT WE WILL NEED YOUR FOOD SUPPLIES.
WE WILL LOWER THE PLANETARY SHIELDS, CHIMAERA, AS A GESTURE OF GOOD FAITH.
BUT WE SHALL REQUIRE GUARANTEES REGARDING THE SAFETY OF THE UKIAN PEOPLE AND OUR LAND.
CERTAINLY.

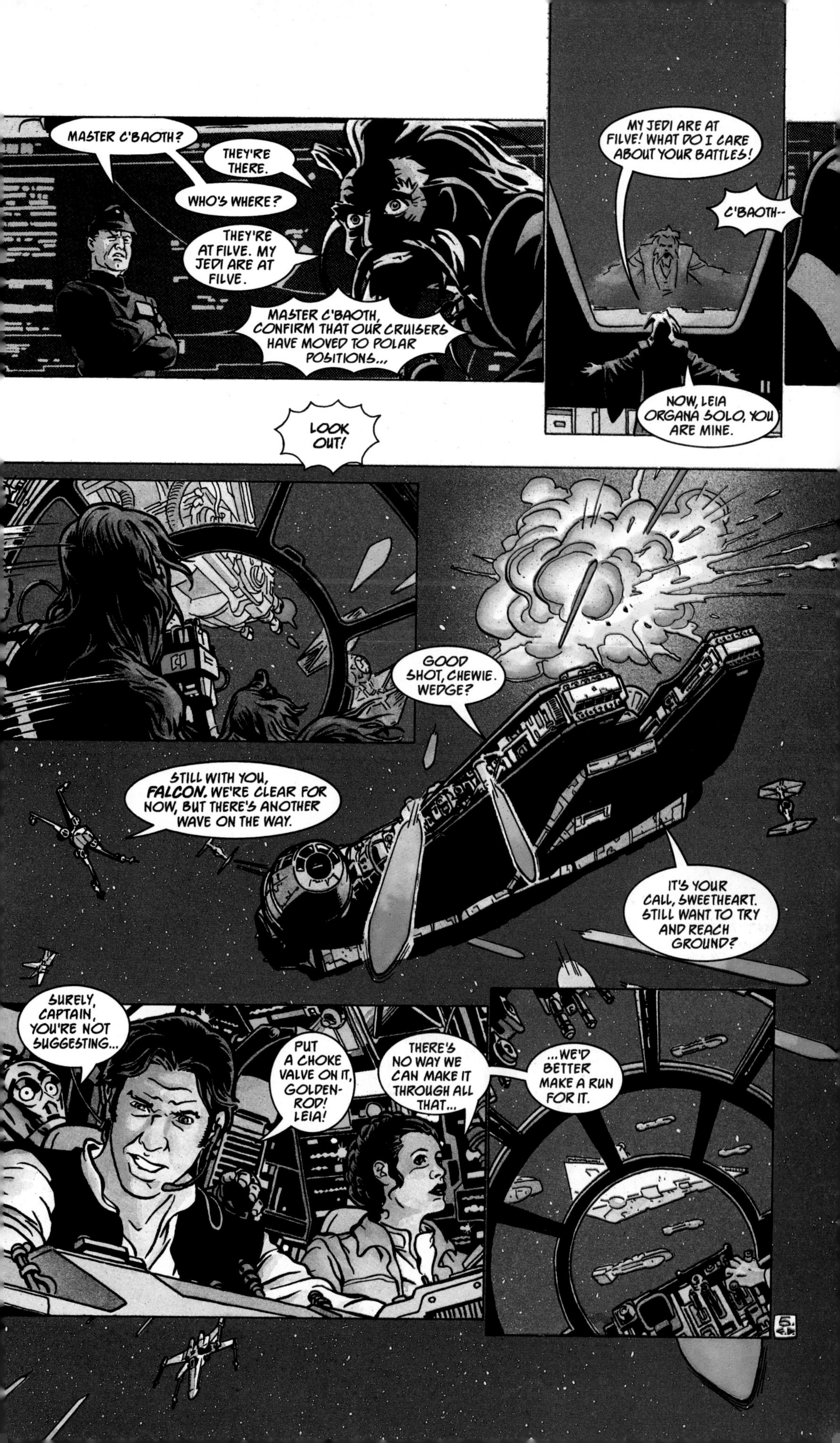
MASTER C'BAOTH?
THEY'RE THERE.
WHO'S WHERE?
THEY'RE AT FILVE. MY JEDI ARE AT FILVE.
MASTER C'BAOTH, CONFIRM THAT OUR CRUISERS HAVE MOVED TO POLAR POSITIONS...
MY JEDI ARE AT FILVE! WHAT DO I CARE ABOUT YOUR BATTLES!
C'BAOTH--
NOW, LEIA ORGANA SOLO, YOU ARE MINE.
LOOK OUT!
GOOD SHOT, CHEWIE. WEDGE?
STILL WITH YOU, FALCON. WE'RE CLEAR FOR NOW, BUT THERE'S ANOTHER WAVE ON THE WAY.
IT'S YOUR CALL, SWEETHEART. STILL WANT TO TRY AND REACH GROUND?
SURELY, CAPTAIN, YOU'RE NOT SUGGESTING...
PUT A CHOKE VALVE ON IT, GOLDENROD! LEIA!
THERE'S NO WAY WE CAN MAKE IT THROUGH ALL THAT...
...WE'D BETTER MAKE A RUN FOR IT.

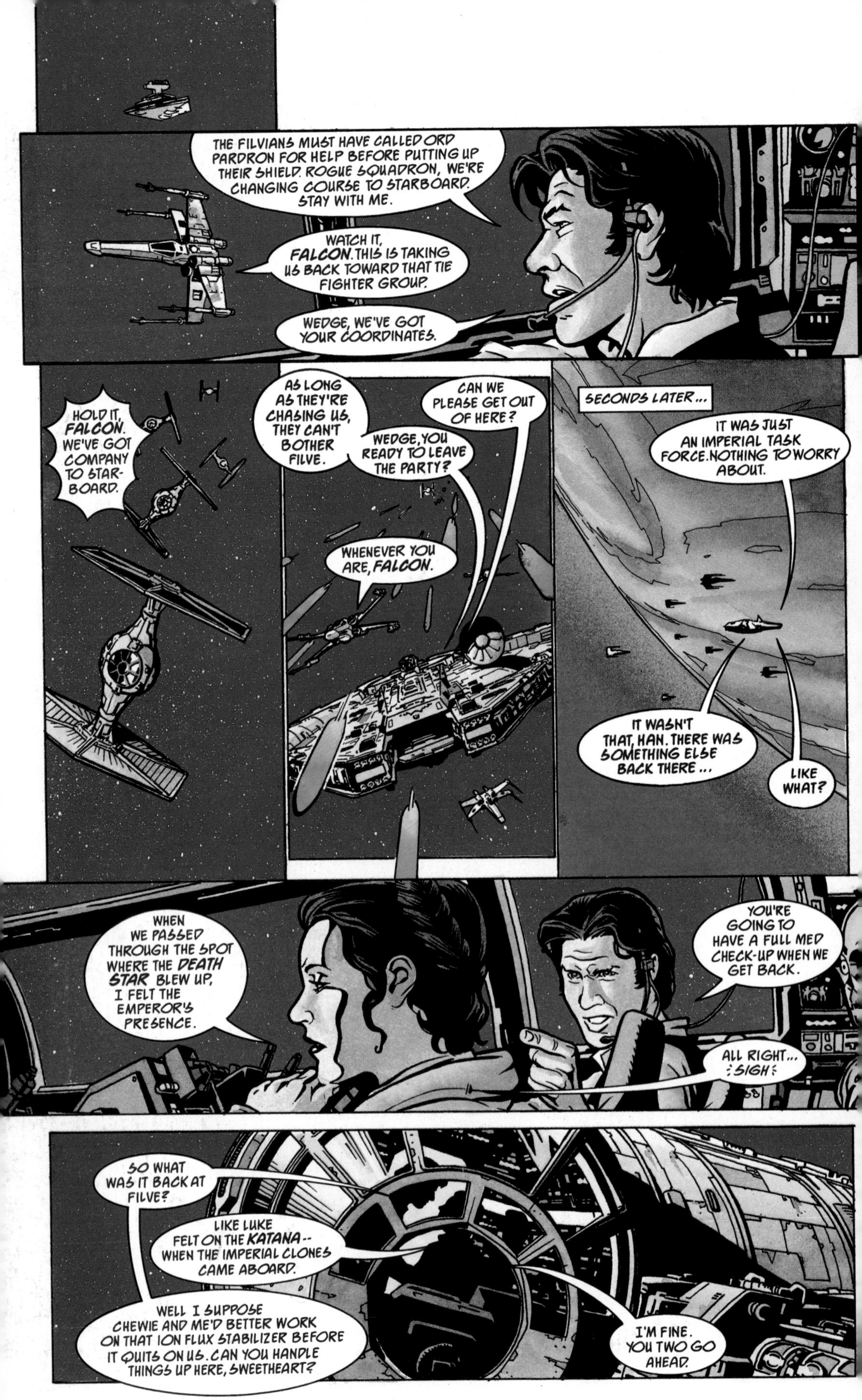
THE FILVIANS MUST HAVE CALLED ORD PARDRON FOR HELP BEFORE PUTTING UP THEIR SHIELD. ROGUE SQUADRON, WE'RE CHANGING COURSE TO STARBOARD. STAY WITH ME.
WATCH IT, FALCON. THIS IS TAKING US BACK TOWARD THAT TIE FIGHTER GROUP.
WEDGE, WE'VE GOT YOUR COORDINATES.
HOLD IT, FALCON. WE'VE GOT COMPANY TO STAR-BOARD.
AS LONG AS THEY'RE CHASING US, THEY CAN'T BOTHER FILVE.
CAN WE PLEASE GET OUT OF HERE?
WEDGE, YOU READY TO LEAVE THE PARTY?
WHENEVER YOU ARE, FALCON.
SECONDS LATER...
IT WAS JUST AN IMPERIAL TASK FORCE. NOTHING TO WORRY ABOUT.
IT WASN'T THAT, HAN. THERE WAS SOMETHING ELSE BACK THERE...
LIKE WHAT?
WHEN WE PASSED THROUGH THE SPOT WHERE THE DEATH STAR BLEW UP, I FELT THE EMPEROR'S PRESENCE.
YOU'RE GOING TO HAVE A FULL MED CHECK-UP WHEN WE GET BACK.
ALL RIGHT... SIGH
SO WHAT WAS IT BACK AT FILVE?
LIKE LUKE FELT ON THE KATANA -- WHEN THE IMPERIAL CLONES CAME ABOARD.
WELL I SUPPOSE CHEWIE AND ME'D BETTER WORK ON THAT ION FLUX STABILIZER BEFORE IT QUITS ON US. CAN YOU HANDLE THINGS UP HERE, SWEETHEART?
I'M FINE. YOU TWO GO AHEAD.

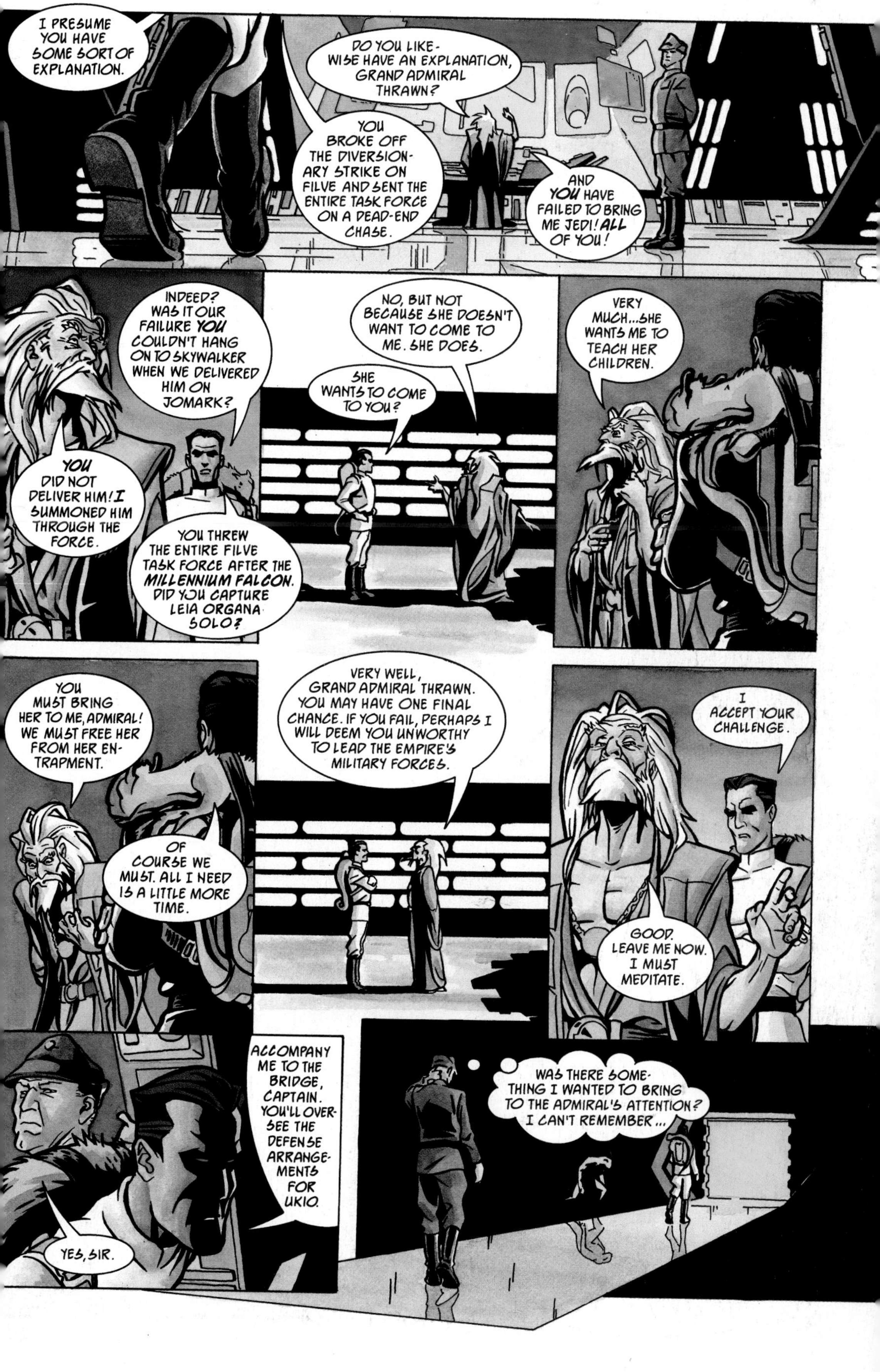

I PRESUME YOU HAVE SOME SORT OF EXPLANATION.
DO YOU LIKE-WISE HAVE AN EXPLANATION, GRAND ADMIRAL THRAWN?
YOU BROKE OFF THE DIVERSION-ARY STRIKE ON FILVE AND SENT THE ENTIRE TASK FORCE ON A DEAD-END CHASE.
AND YOU HAVE FAILED TO BRING ME JEDI! ALL OF YOU!
INDEED? WAS IT OUR FAILURE YOU COULDN'T HANG ON TO SKYWALKER WHEN WE DELIVERED HIM ON JOMARK?
YOU DID NOT DELIVER HIM! I SUMMONED HIM THROUGH THE FORCE.
YOU THREW THE ENTIRE FILVE TASK FORCE AFTER THE MILLENNIUM FALCON. DID YOU CAPTURE LEIA ORGANA SOLO?
NO, BUT NOT BECAUSE SHE DOESN'T WANT TO COME TO ME. SHE DOES.
SHE WANTS TO COME TO YOU?
VERY MUCH...SHE WANTS ME TO TEACH HER CHILDREN.
YOU MUST BRING HER TO ME, ADMIRAL! WE MUST FREE HER FROM HER EN-TRAPMENT.
OF COURSE WE MUST. ALL I NEED IS A LITTLE MORE TIME.
VERY WELL, GRAND ADMIRAL THRAWN. YOU MAY HAVE ONE FINAL CHANCE. IF YOU FAIL, PERHAPS I WILL DEEM YOU UNWORTHY TO LEAD THE EMPIRE'S MILITARY FORCES.
I ACCEPT YOUR CHALLENGE.
GOOD. LEAVE ME NOW. I MUST MEDITATE.
ACCOMPANY ME TO THE BRIDGE, CAPTAIN. YOU'LL OVER-SEE THE DEFENSE ARRANGE-MENTS FOR UKIO.
YES, SIR.
WAS THERE SOME-THING I WANTED TO BRING TO THE ADMIRAL'S ATTENTION? I CAN'T REMEMBER...

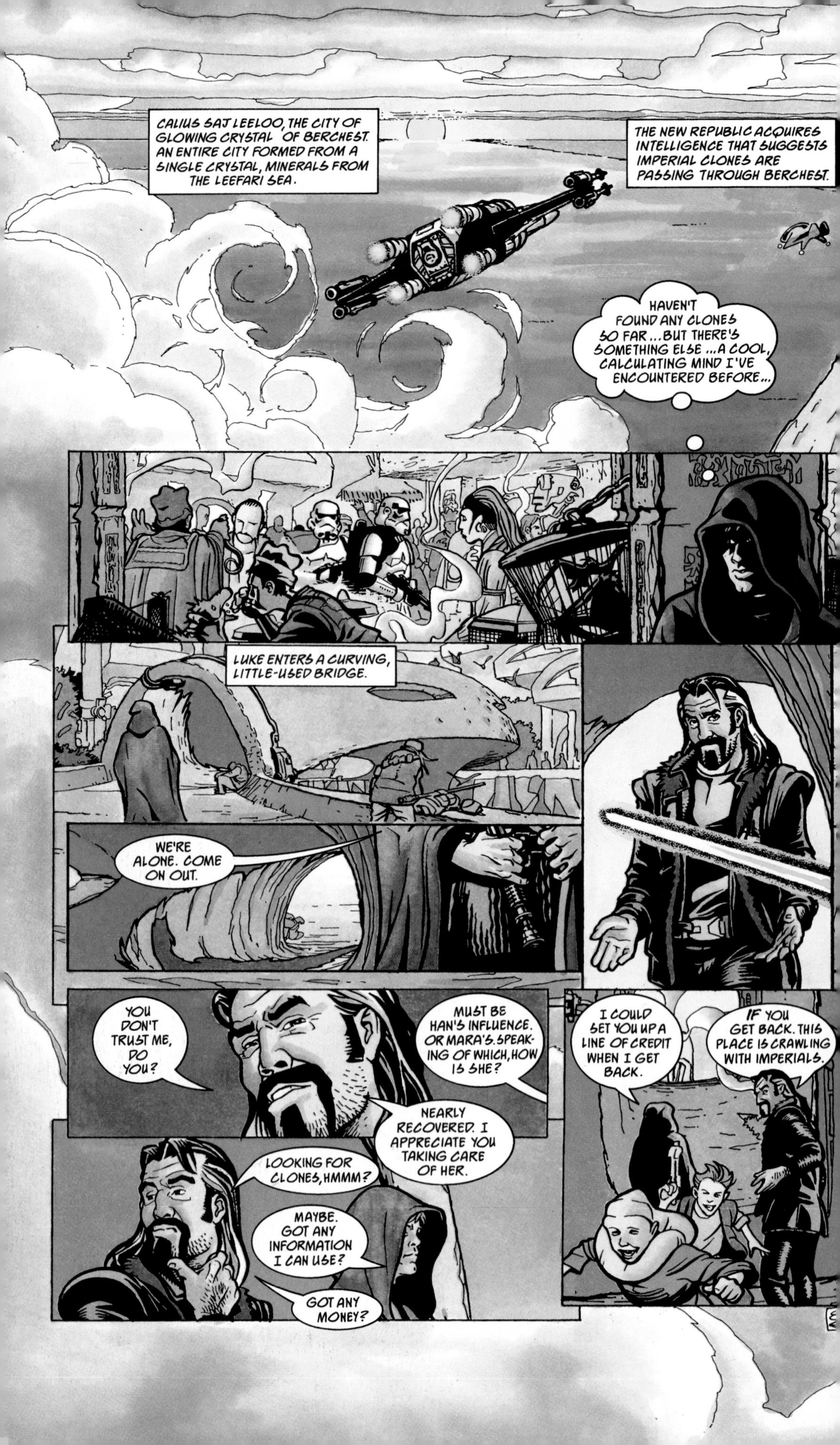

CALIUS SAJ LEELOO, THE CITY OF GLOWING CRYSTAL OF BERCHEST. AN ENTIRE CITY FORMED FROM A SINGLE CRYSTAL, MINERALS FROM THE LEEFARI SEA.
THE NEW REPUBLIC ACQUIRES INTELLIGENCE THAT SUGGESTS IMPERIAL CLONES ARE PASSING THROUGH BERCHEST.
HAVEN'T FOUND ANY CLONES SO FAR... BUT THERE'S SOMETHING ELSE... A COOL, CALCULATING MIND I'VE ENCOUNTERED BEFORE...
LUKE ENTERS A CURVING, LITTLE-USED BRIDGE.
WE'RE ALONE. COME ON OUT.
YOU DON'T TRUST ME, DO YOU?
MUST BE HAN'S INFLUENCE. OR MARA'S. SPEAKING OF WHICH, HOW IS SHE?
NEARLY RECOVERED. I APPRECIATE YOU TAKING CARE OF HER.
LOOKING FOR CLONES, HMMM?
MAYBE. GOT ANY INFORMATION I CAN USE?
GOT ANY MONEY?
I COULD SET YOU UP A LINE OF CREDIT WHEN I GET BACK.
IF YOU GET BACK. THIS PLACE IS CRAWLING WITH IMPERIALS.

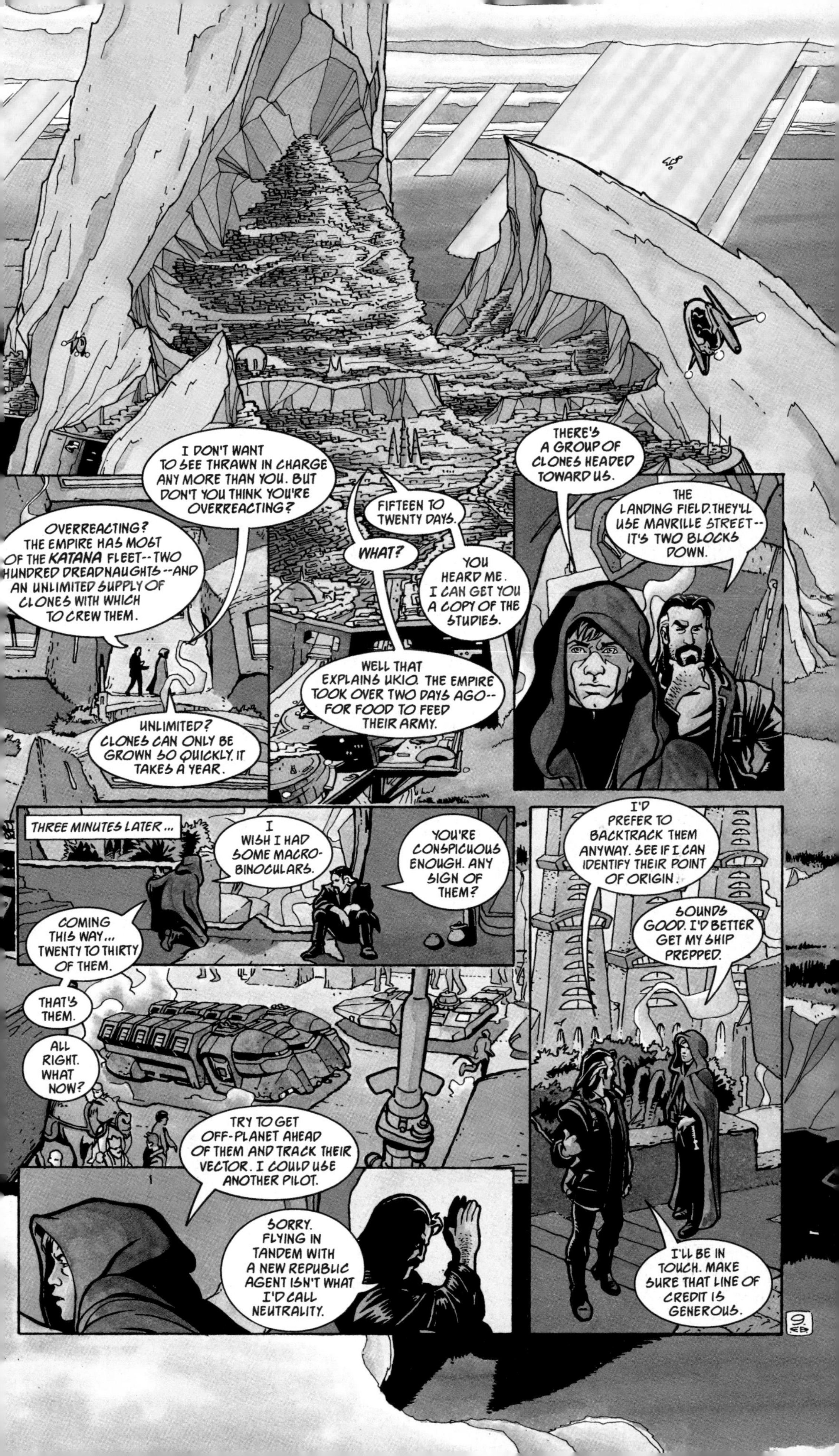
I DON'T WANT TO SEE THRAWN IN CHARGE ANY MORE THAN YOU. BUT DON'T YOU THINK YOU'RE OVERREACTING?
OVERREACTING? THE EMPIRE HAS MOST OF THE KATANA FLEET-- TWO HUNDRED DREADNAUGHTS--AND AN UNLIMITED SUPPLY OF CLONES WITH WHICH TO CREW THEM.
UNLIMITED? CLONES CAN ONLY BE GROWN SO QUICKLY. IT TAKES A YEAR.
FIFTEEN TO TWENTY DAYS.
WHAT?
YOU HEARD ME. I CAN GET YOU A COPY OF THE STUDIES.
WELL THAT EXPLAINS UKIO. THE EMPIRE TOOK OVER TWO DAYS AGO-- FOR FOOD TO FEED THEIR ARMY.
THERE'S A GROUP OF CLONES HEADED TOWARD US.
THE LANDING FIELD. THEY'LL USE MAVRILLE STREET-- IT'S TWO BLOCKS DOWN.
THREE MINUTES LATER...
I WISH I HAD SOME MACRO-BINOCULARS.
YOU'RE CONSPICUOUS ENOUGH. ANY SIGN OF THEM?
COMING THIS WAY... TWENTY TO THIRTY OF THEM.
THAT'S THEM.
ALL RIGHT. WHAT NOW?
TRY TO GET OFF-PLANET AHEAD OF THEM AND TRACK THEIR VECTOR. I COULD USE ANOTHER PILOT.
SORRY. FLYING IN TANDEM WITH A NEW REPUBLIC AGENT ISN'T WHAT I'D CALL NEUTRALITY.
I'D PREFER TO BACKTRACK THEM ANYWAY. SEE IF I CAN IDENTIFY THEIR POINT OF ORIGIN.
SOUNDS GOOD. I'D BETTER GET MY SHIP PREPPED.
I'LL BE IN TOUCH. MAKE SURE THAT LINE OF CREDIT IS GENEROUS.
9

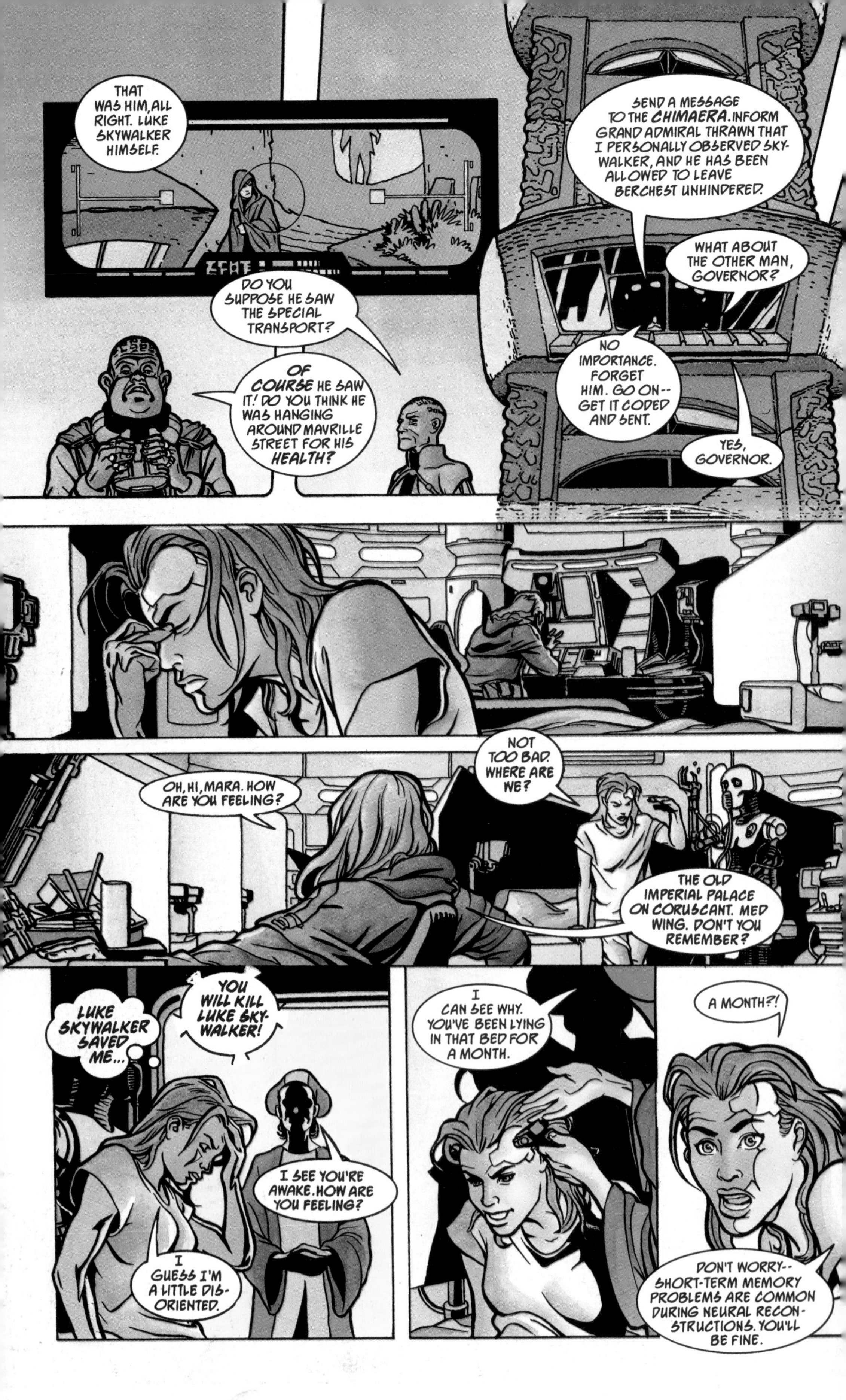

THAT WAS HIM, ALL RIGHT. LUKE SKYWALKER HIMSELF.
DO YOU SUPPOSE HE SAW THE SPECIAL TRANSPORT?
OF COURSE HE SAW IT! DO YOU THINK HE WAS HANGING AROUND MAVRILLE STREET FOR HIS HEALTH?
SEND A MESSAGE TO THE CHIMAERA. INFORM GRAND ADMIRAL THRAWN THAT I PERSONALLY OBSERVED SKY-WALKER, AND HE HAS BEEN ALLOWED TO LEAVE BERCHEST UNHINDERED.
WHAT ABOUT THE OTHER MAN, GOVERNOR?
NO IMPORTANCE. FORGET HIM. GO ON-- GET IT CODED AND SENT.
YES, GOVERNOR.
OH, HI, MARA. HOW ARE YOU FEELING?
NOT TOO BAD. WHERE ARE WE?
THE OLD IMPERIAL PALACE ON CORUSCANT. MED WING. DON'T YOU REMEMBER?
LUKE SKYWALKER SAVED ME...
YOU WILL KILL LUKE SKY-WALKER!
I SEE YOU'RE AWAKE. HOW ARE YOU FEELING?
I GUESS I'M A LITTLE DIS-ORIENTED.
I CAN SEE WHY. YOU'VE BEEN LYING IN THAT BED FOR A MONTH.
A MONTH?!
DON'T WORRY-- SHORT-TERM MEMORY PROBLEMS ARE COMMON DURING NEURAL RECON-STRUCTIONS. YOU'LL BE FINE.

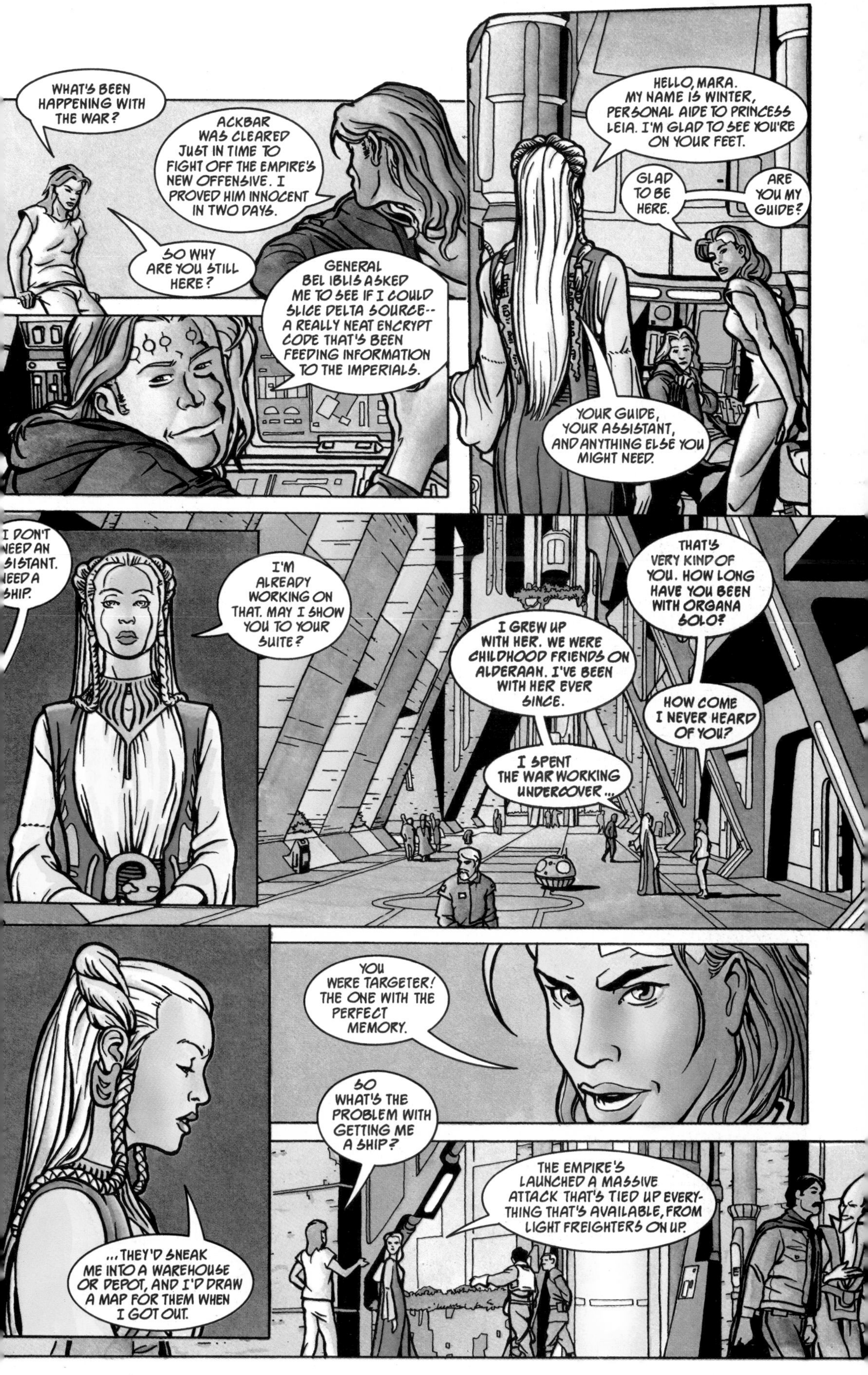
WHAT'S BEEN HAPPENING WITH THE WAR?
ACKBAR WAS CLEARED JUST IN TIME TO FIGHT OFF THE EMPIRE'S NEW OFFENSIVE. I PROVED HIM INNOCENT IN TWO DAYS.
SO WHY ARE YOU STILL HERE?
GENERAL BEL IBLIS ASKED ME TO SEE IF I COULD SLICE DELTA SOURCE-- A REALLY NEAT ENCRYPT CODE THAT'S BEEN FEEDING INFORMATION TO THE IMPERIALS.
HELLO, MARA. MY NAME IS WINTER, PERSONAL AIDE TO PRINCESS LEIA. I'M GLAD TO SEE YOU'RE ON YOUR FEET.
GLAD TO BE HERE.
ARE YOU MY GUIDE?
YOUR GUIDE, YOUR ASSISTANT, AND ANYTHING ELSE YOU MIGHT NEED.
I DON'T NEED AN SISTANT. NEED A SHIP.
I'M ALREADY WORKING ON THAT. MAY I SHOW YOU TO YOUR SUITE?
THAT'S VERY KIND OF YOU. HOW LONG HAVE YOU BEEN WITH ORGANA SOLO?
I GREW UP WITH HER. WE WERE CHILDHOOD FRIENDS ON ALDERAAN. I'VE BEEN WITH HER EVER SINCE.
HOW COME I NEVER HEARD OF YOU?
I SPENT THE WAR WORKING UNDERCOVER...
...THEY'D SNEAK ME INTO A WAREHOUSE OR DEPOT, AND I'D DRAW A MAP FOR THEM WHEN I GOT OUT.
YOU WERE TARGETER! THE ONE WITH THE PERFECT MEMORY.
SO WHAT'S THE PROBLEM WITH GETTING ME A SHIP?
THE EMPIRE'S LAUNCHED A MASSIVE ATTACK THAT'S TIED UP EVERY-THING THAT'S AVAILABLE, FROM LIGHT FREIGHTERS ON UP.

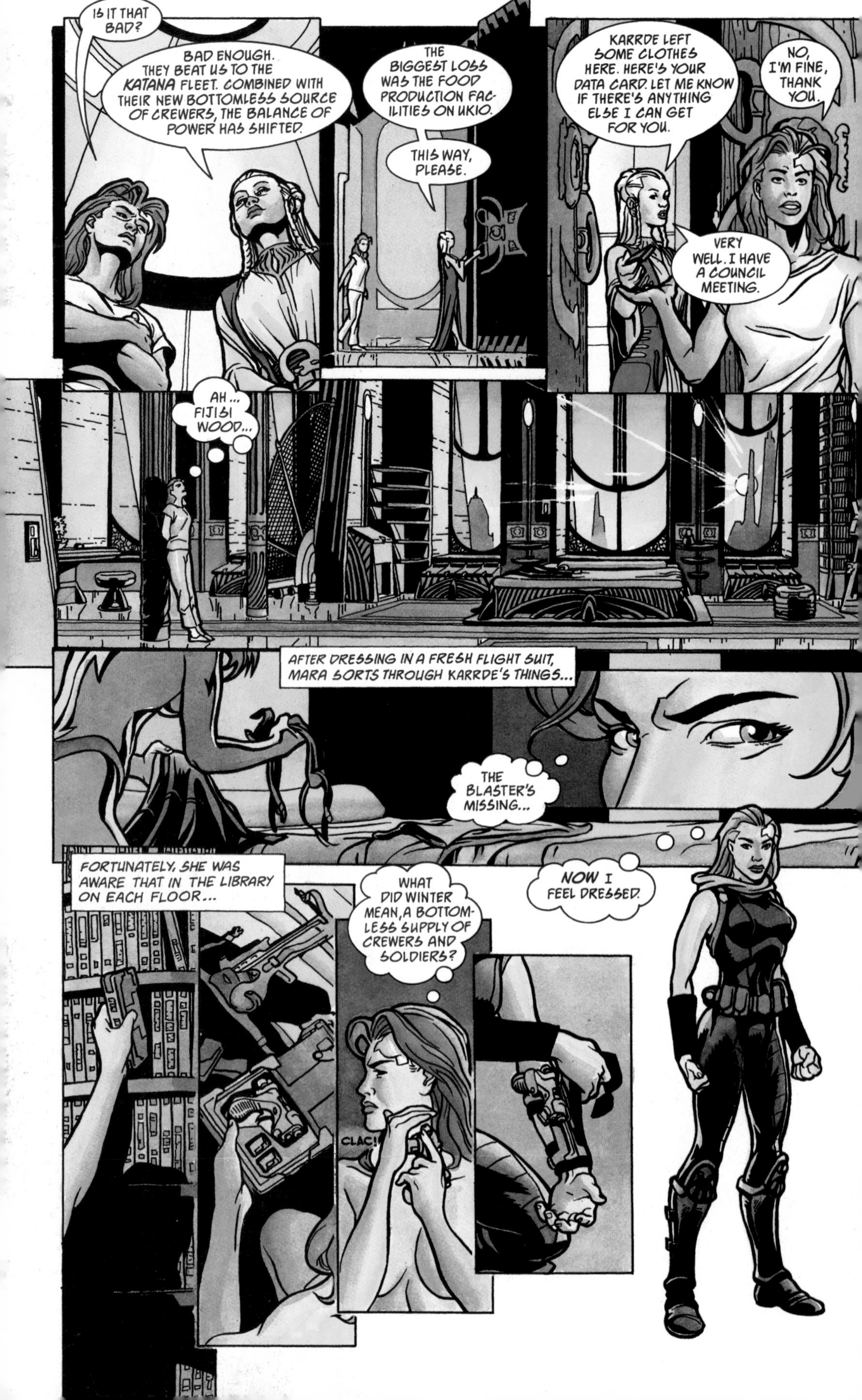
IS IT THAT BAD?
BAD ENOUGH. THEY BEAT US TO THE KATANA FLEET. COMBINED WITH THEIR NEW BOTTOMLESS SOURCE OF CREWERS, THE BALANCE OF POWER HAS SHIFTED.
THE BIGGEST LOSS WAS THE FOOD PRODUCTION FACILITIES ON UKIO.
THIS WAY, PLEASE.
KARRDE LEFT SOME CLOTHES HERE. HERE'S YOUR DATA CARD. LET ME KNOW IF THERE'S ANYTHING ELSE I CAN GET FOR YOU.
NO, I'M FINE, THANK YOU.
VERY WELL. I HAVE A COUNCIL MEETING.
AH... FIJISI WOOD...
AFTER DRESSING IN A FRESH FLIGHT SUIT, MARA SORTS THROUGH KARRDE'S THINGS...
THE BLASTER'S MISSING...
FORTUNATELY, SHE WAS AWARE THAT IN THE LIBRARY ON EACH FLOOR...
WHAT DID WINTER MEAN, A BOTTOMLESS SUPPLY OF CREWERS AND SOLDIERS?
CLAC!
NOW I FEEL DRESSED.

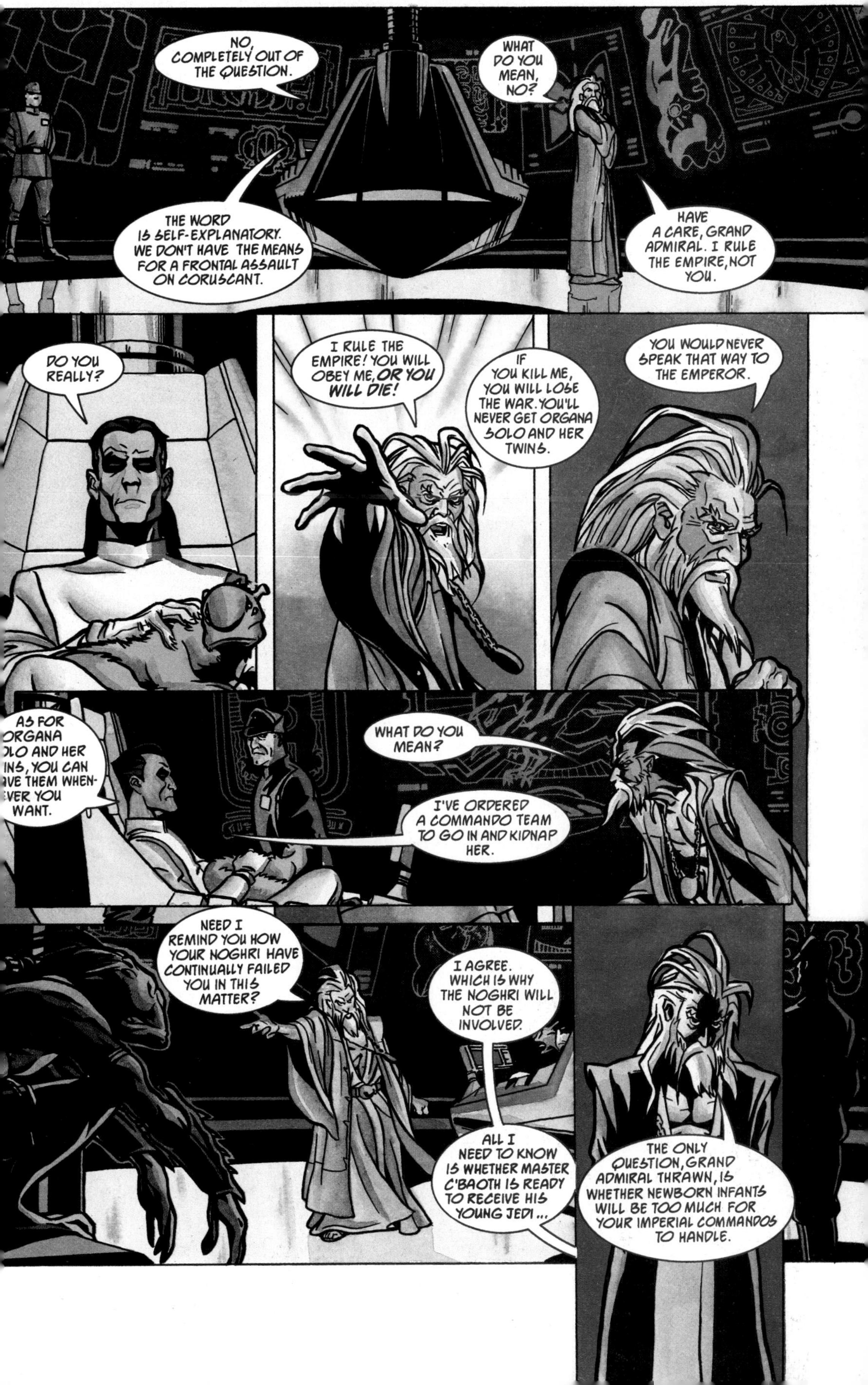
NO, COMPLETELY OUT OF THE QUESTION.
WHAT DO YOU MEAN, NO?
THE WORD IS SELF-EXPLANATORY. WE DON'T HAVE THE MEANS FOR A FRONTAL ASSAULT ON CORUSCANT.
HAVE A CARE, GRAND ADMIRAL. I RULE THE EMPIRE, NOT YOU.
DO YOU REALLY?
I RULE THE EMPIRE! YOU WILL OBEY ME, OR YOU WILL DIE!
IF YOU KILL ME, YOU WILL LOSE THE WAR. YOU'LL NEVER GET ORGANA SOLO AND HER TWINS.
YOU WOULD NEVER SPEAK THAT WAY TO THE EMPEROR.
AS FOR ORGANA OLO AND HER INS, YOU CAN AVE THEM WHEN- EVER YOU WANT.
WHAT DO YOU MEAN?
I'VE ORDERED A COMMANDO TEAM TO GO IN AND KIDNAP HER.
NEED I REMIND YOU HOW YOUR NOGHRI HAVE CONTINUALLY FAILED YOU IN THIS MATTER?
I AGREE. WHICH IS WHY THE NOGHRI WILL NOT BE INVOLVED.
ALL I NEED TO KNOW IS WHETHER MASTER C'BAOTH IS READY TO RECEIVE HIS YOUNG JEDI...
THE ONLY QUESTION, GRAND ADMIRAL THRAWN, IS WHETHER NEWBORN INFANTS WILL BE TOO MUCH FOR YOUR IMPERIAL COMMANDOS TO HANDLE.

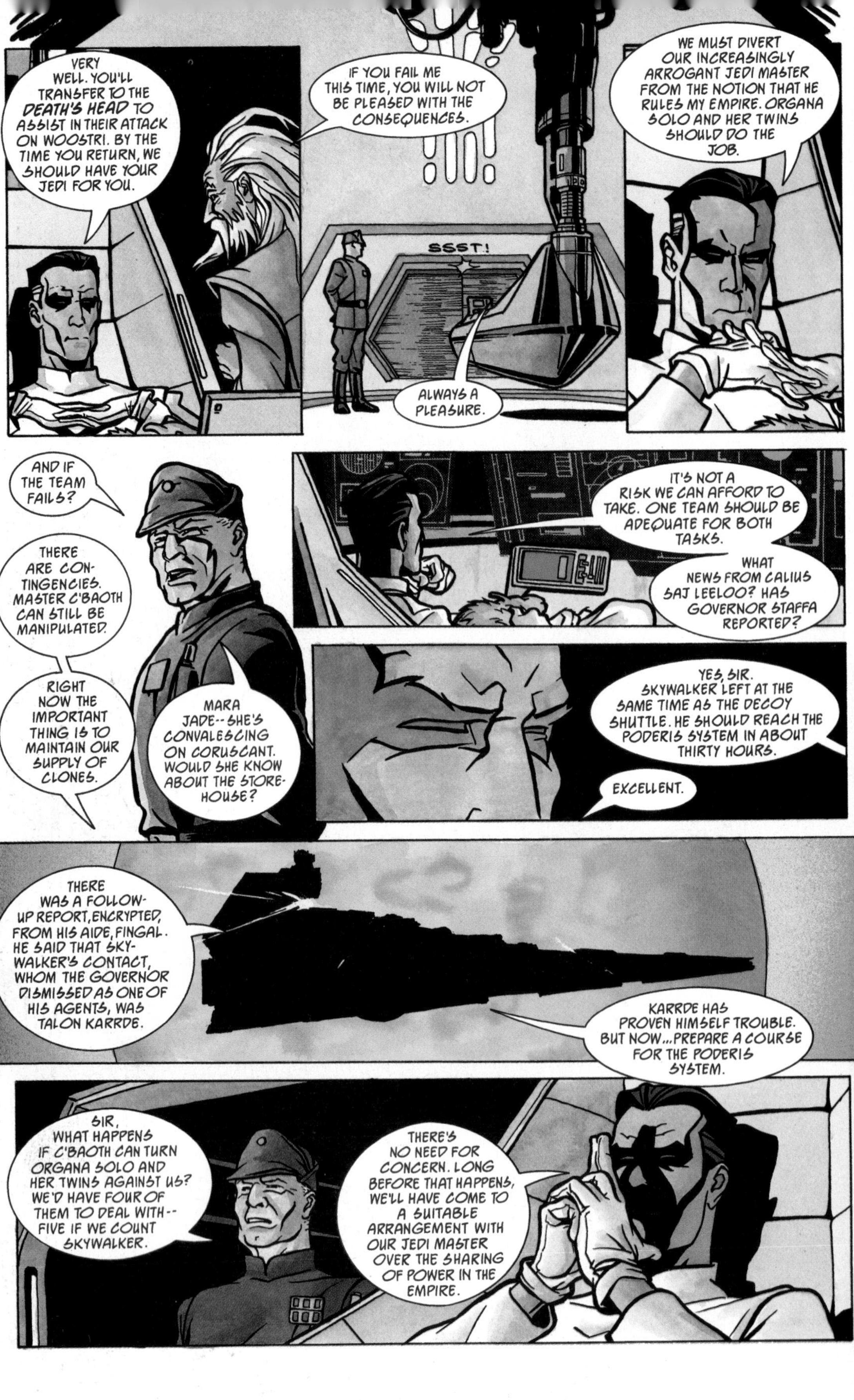
VERY WELL. YOU'LL TRANSFER TO THE DEATH'S HEAD TO ASSIST IN THEIR ATTACK ON WOOSTRI. BY THE TIME YOU RETURN, WE SHOULD HAVE YOUR JEDI FOR YOU.
IF YOU FAIL ME THIS TIME, YOU WILL NOT BE PLEASED WITH THE CONSEQUENCES.
SSST!
ALWAYS A PLEASURE.
WE MUST DIVERT OUR INCREASINGLY ARROGANT JEDI MASTER FROM THE NOTION THAT HE RULES MY EMPIRE. ORGANA SOLO AND HER TWINS SHOULD DO THE JOB.
AND IF THE TEAM FAILS?
THERE ARE CONTINGENCIES. MASTER C'BAOTH CAN STILL BE MANIPULATED.
RIGHT NOW THE IMPORTANT THING IS TO MAINTAIN OUR SUPPLY OF CLONES.
MARA JADE--SHE'S CONVALESCING ON CORUSCANT. WOULD SHE KNOW ABOUT THE STOREHOUSE?
IT'S NOT A RISK WE CAN AFFORD TO TAKE. ONE TEAM SHOULD BE ADEQUATE FOR BOTH TASKS.
WHAT NEWS FROM CALIUS SAJ LEELOO? HAS GOVERNOR STAFFA REPORTED?
YES, SIR. SKYWALKER LEFT AT THE SAME TIME AS THE DECOY SHUTTLE. HE SHOULD REACH THE PODERIS SYSTEM IN ABOUT THIRTY HOURS.
EXCELLENT.
THERE WAS A FOLLOW-UP REPORT, ENCRYPTED, FROM HIS AIDE, FINGAL. HE SAID THAT SKYWALKER'S CONTACT, WHOM THE GOVERNOR DISMISSED AS ONE OF HIS AGENTS, WAS TALON KARRDE.
KARRDE HAS PROVEN HIMSELF TROUBLE. BUT NOW...PREPARE A COURSE FOR THE PODERIS SYSTEM.
SIR, WHAT HAPPENS IF C'BAOTH CAN TURN ORGANA SOLO AND HER TWINS AGAINST US? WE'D HAVE FOUR OF THEM TO DEAL WITH--FIVE IF WE COUNT SKYWALKER.
THERE'S NO NEED FOR CONCERN. LONG BEFORE THAT HAPPENS, WE'LL HAVE COME TO A SUITABLE ARRANGEMENT WITH OUR JEDI MASTER OVER THE SHARING OF POWER IN THE EMPIRE.

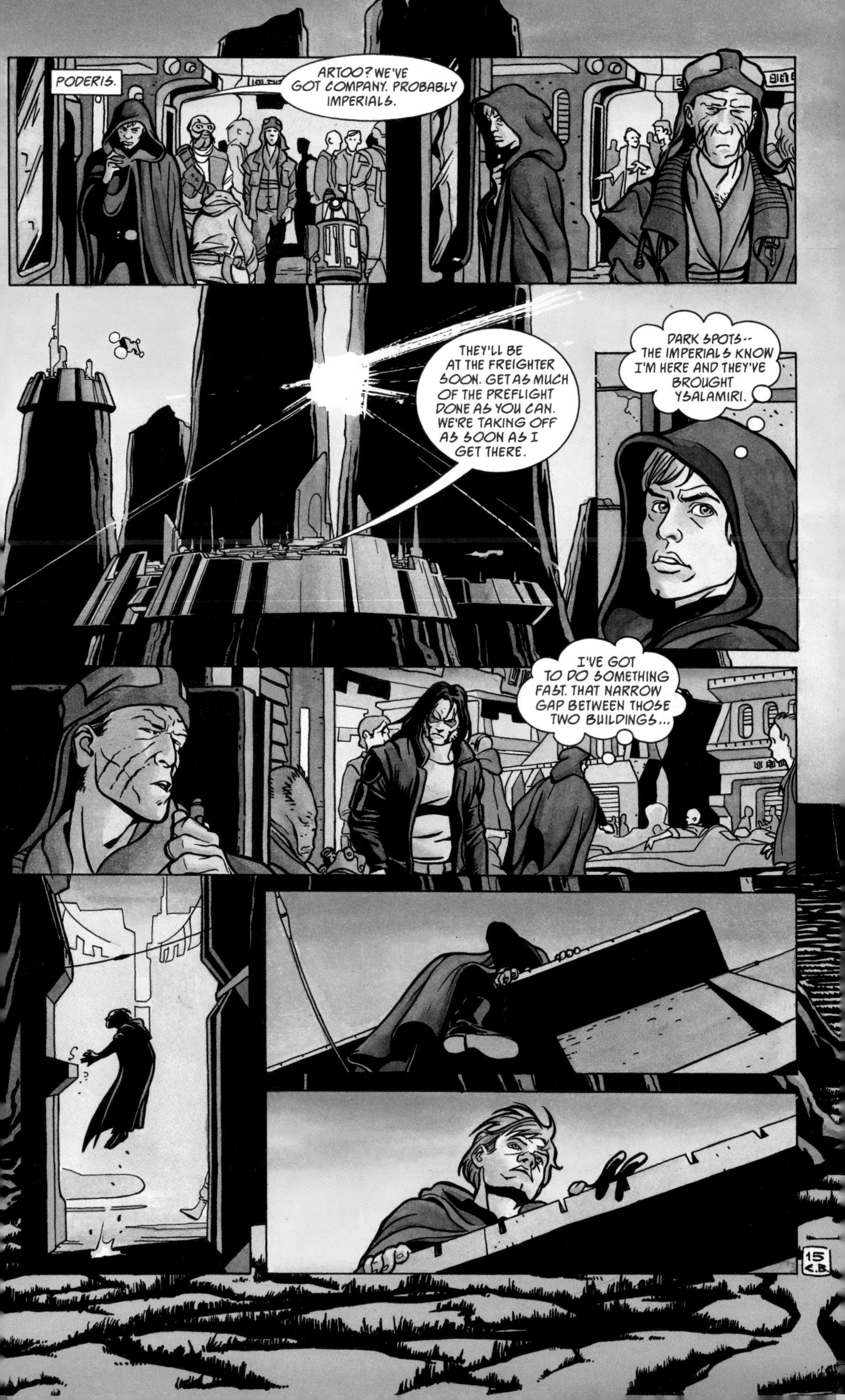
PODERIS.
ARTOO? WE'VE GOT COMPANY. PROBABLY IMPERIALS.
THEY'LL BE AT THE FREIGHTER SOON. GET AS MUCH OF THE PREFLIGHT DONE AS YOU CAN. WE'RE TAKING OFF AS SOON AS I GET THERE.
DARK SPOTS-- THE IMPERIALS KNOW I'M HERE AND THEY'VE BROUGHT YSALAMIRI.
I'VE GOT TO DO SOMETHING FAST. THAT NARROW GAP BETWEEN THOSE TWO BUILDINGS...
15
C.B.

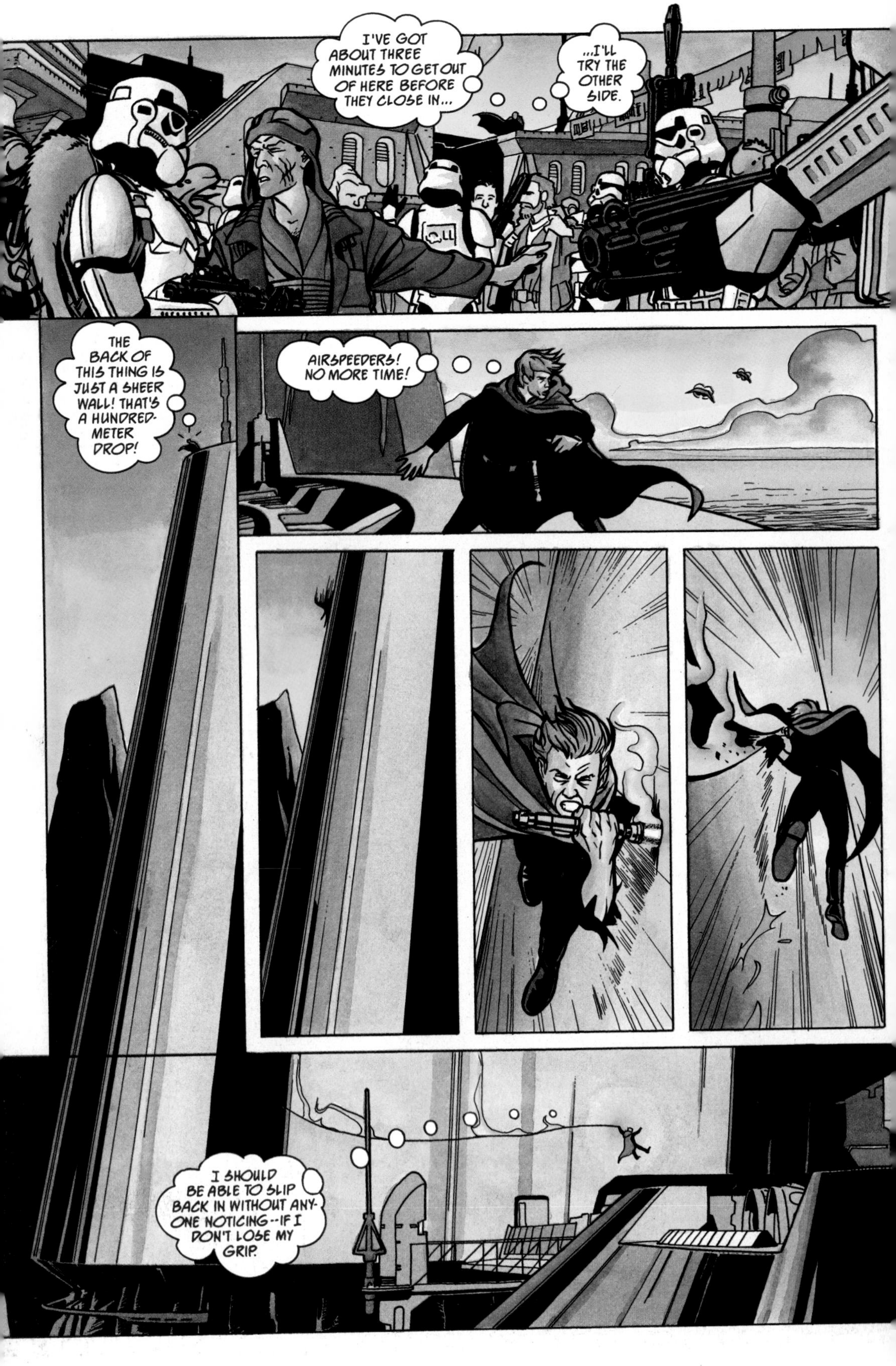
I'VE GOT ABOUT THREE MINUTES TO GET OUT OF HERE BEFORE THEY CLOSE IN...
...I'LL TRY THE OTHER SIDE.
THE BACK OF THIS THING IS JUST A SHEER WALL! THAT'S A HUNDRED-METER DROP!
AIRSPEEDERS! NO MORE TIME!
I SHOULD BE ABLE TO SLIP BACK IN WITHOUT ANY-ONE NOTICING--IF I DON'T LOSE MY GRIP.

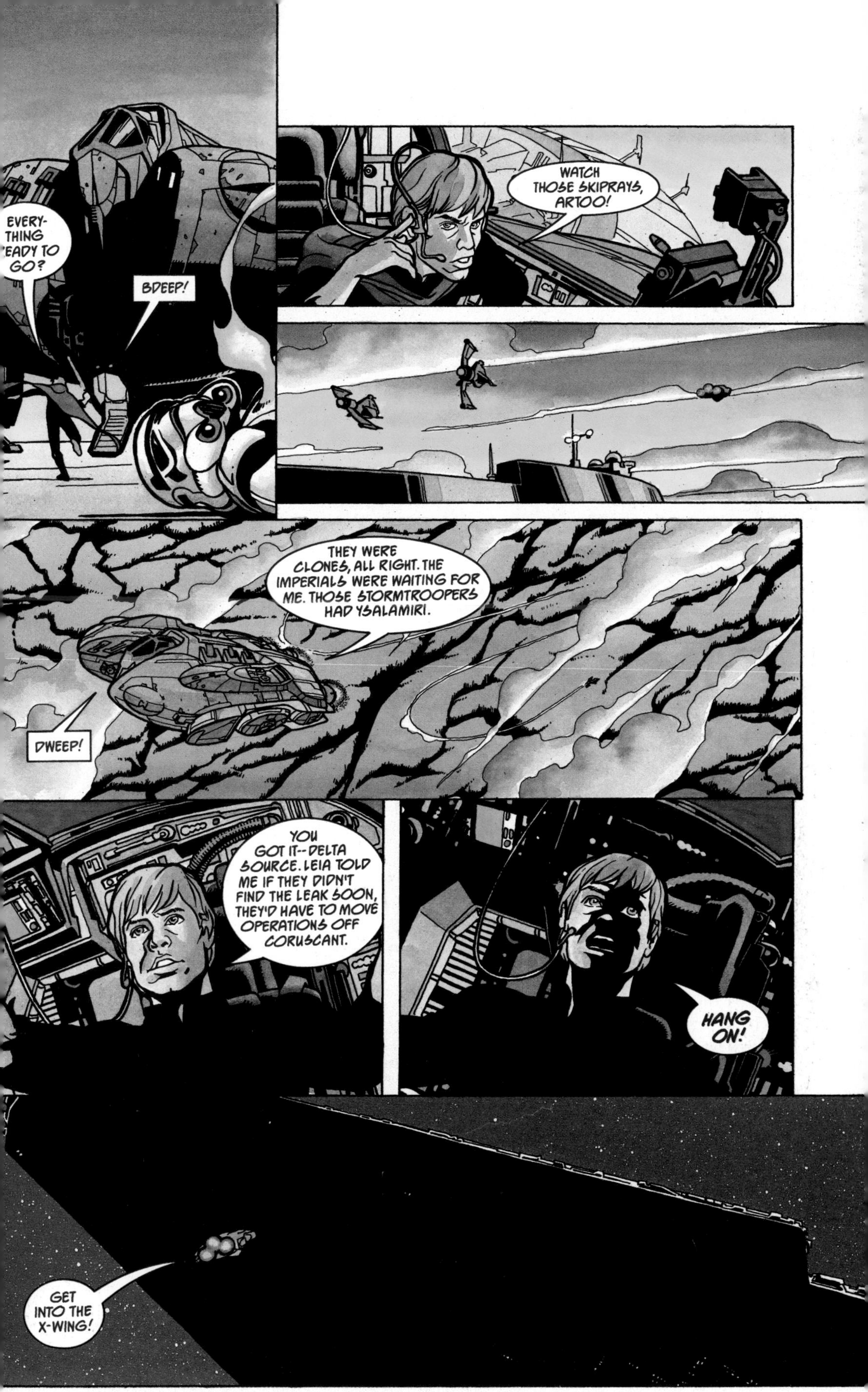
EVERY-THING 'EADY TO GO?
BDEEP!
WATCH THOSE SKIPRAYS, ARTOO!
THEY WERE CLONES, ALL RIGHT. THE IMPERIALS WERE WAITING FOR ME. THOSE STORMTROOPERS HAD YSALAMIRI.
DWEEP!
YOU GOT IT--DELTA SOURCE. LEIA TOLD ME IF THEY DIDN'T FIND THE LEAK SOON, THEY'D HAVE TO MOVE OPERATIONS OFF CORUSCANT.
HANG ON!
GET INTO THE X-WING!

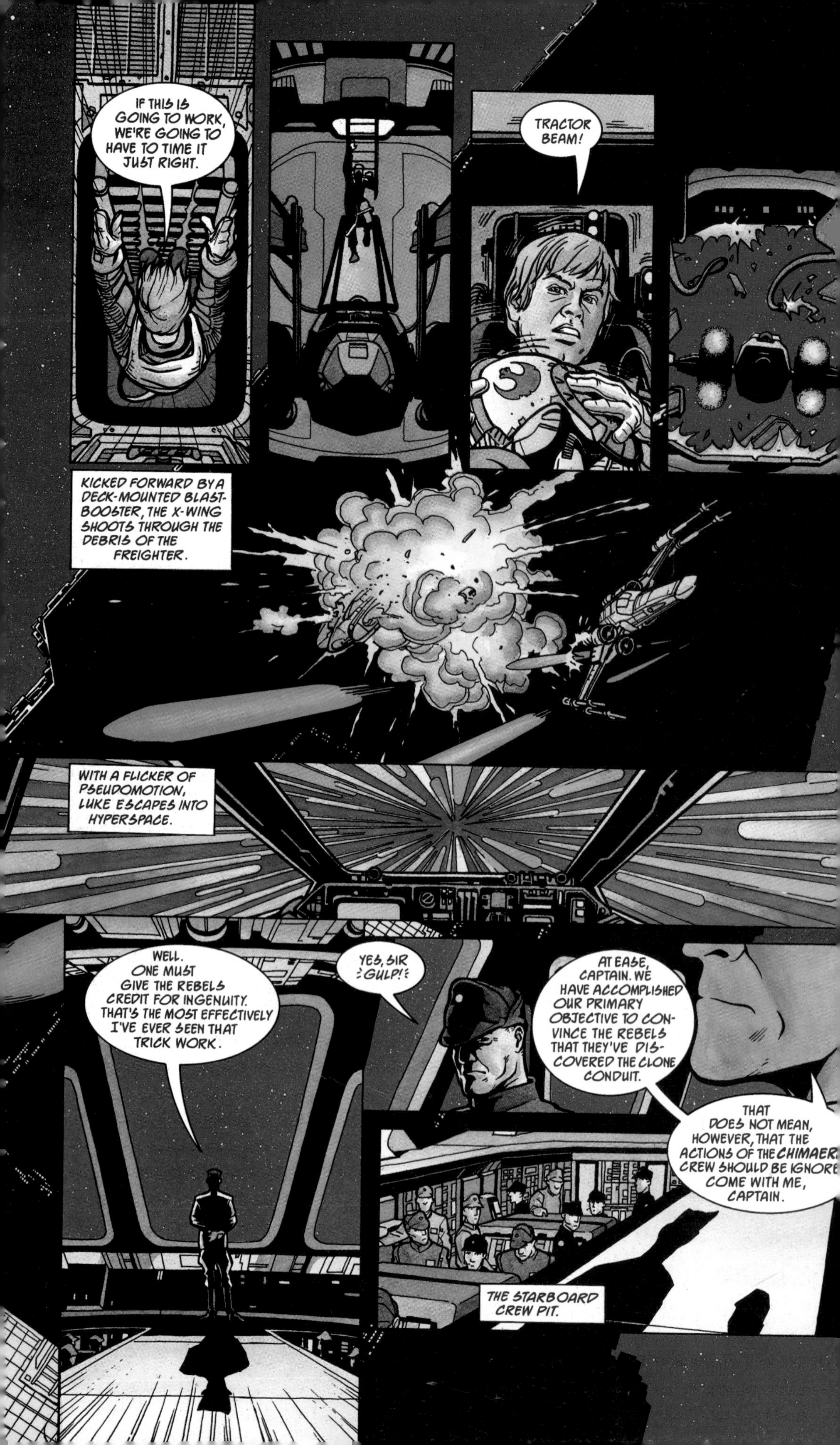
IF THIS IS GOING TO WORK, WE'RE GOING TO HAVE TO TIME IT JUST RIGHT.
TRACTOR BEAM!
KICKED FORWARD BY A DECK-MOUNTED BLAST-BOOSTER, THE X-WING SHOOTS THROUGH THE DEBRIS OF THE FREIGHTER.
WITH A FLICKER OF PSEUDOMOTION, LUKE ESCAPES INTO HYPERSPACE.
WELL. ONE MUST GIVE THE REBELS CREDIT FOR INGENUITY. THAT'S THE MOST EFFECTIVELY I'VE EVER SEEN THAT TRICK WORK.
YES, SIR *GULP!*
AT EASE, CAPTAIN. WE HAVE ACCOMPLISHED OUR PRIMARY OBJECTIVE TO CONVINCE THE REBELS THAT THEY'VE DISCOVERED THE CLONE CONDUIT.
THAT DOES NOT MEAN, HOWEVER, THAT THE ACTIONS OF THE CHIMAER CREW SHOULD BE IGNORE COME WITH ME, CAPTAIN.
THE STARBOARD CREW PIT.

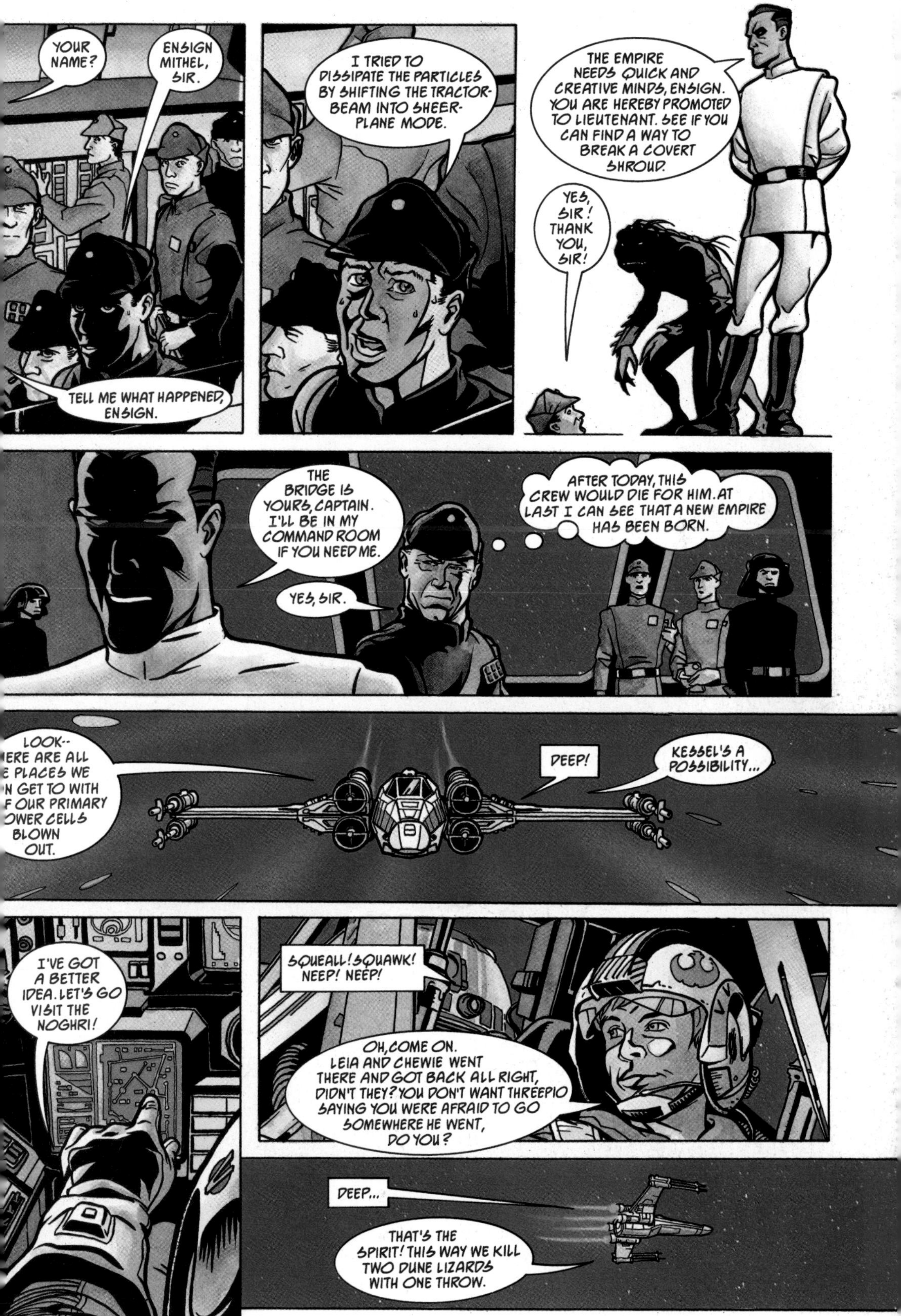
YOUR NAME?
ENSIGN MITHEL, SIR.
TELL ME WHAT HAPPENED, ENSIGN.
I TRIED TO DISSIPATE THE PARTICLES BY SHIFTING THE TRACTOR-BEAM INTO SHEER-PLANE MODE.
THE EMPIRE NEEDS QUICK AND CREATIVE MINDS, ENSIGN. YOU ARE HEREBY PROMOTED TO LIEUTENANT. SEE IF YOU CAN FIND A WAY TO BREAK A COVERT SHROUD.
YES, SIR! THANK YOU, SIR!
THE BRIDGE IS YOURS, CAPTAIN. I'LL BE IN MY COMMAND ROOM IF YOU NEED ME.
YES, SIR.
AFTER TODAY, THIS CREW WOULD DIE FOR HIM. AT LAST I CAN SEE THAT A NEW EMPIRE HAS BEEN BORN.
LOOK-- ERE ARE ALL E PLACES WE N GET TO WITH F OUR PRIMARY OWER CELLS BLOWN OUT.
DEEP!
KESSEL'S A POSSIBILITY...
I'VE GOT A BETTER IDEA. LET'S GO VISIT THE NOGHRI!
SQUEALL! SQUAWK! NEEP! NEEP!
OH, COME ON. LEIA AND CHEWIE WENT THERE AND GOT BACK ALL RIGHT, DIDN'T THEY? YOU DON'T WANT THREEPIO SAYING YOU WERE AFRAID TO GO SOMEWHERE HE WENT, DO YOU?
DEEP...
THAT'S THE SPIRIT! THIS WAY WE KILL TWO DUNE LIZARDS WITH ONE THROW.

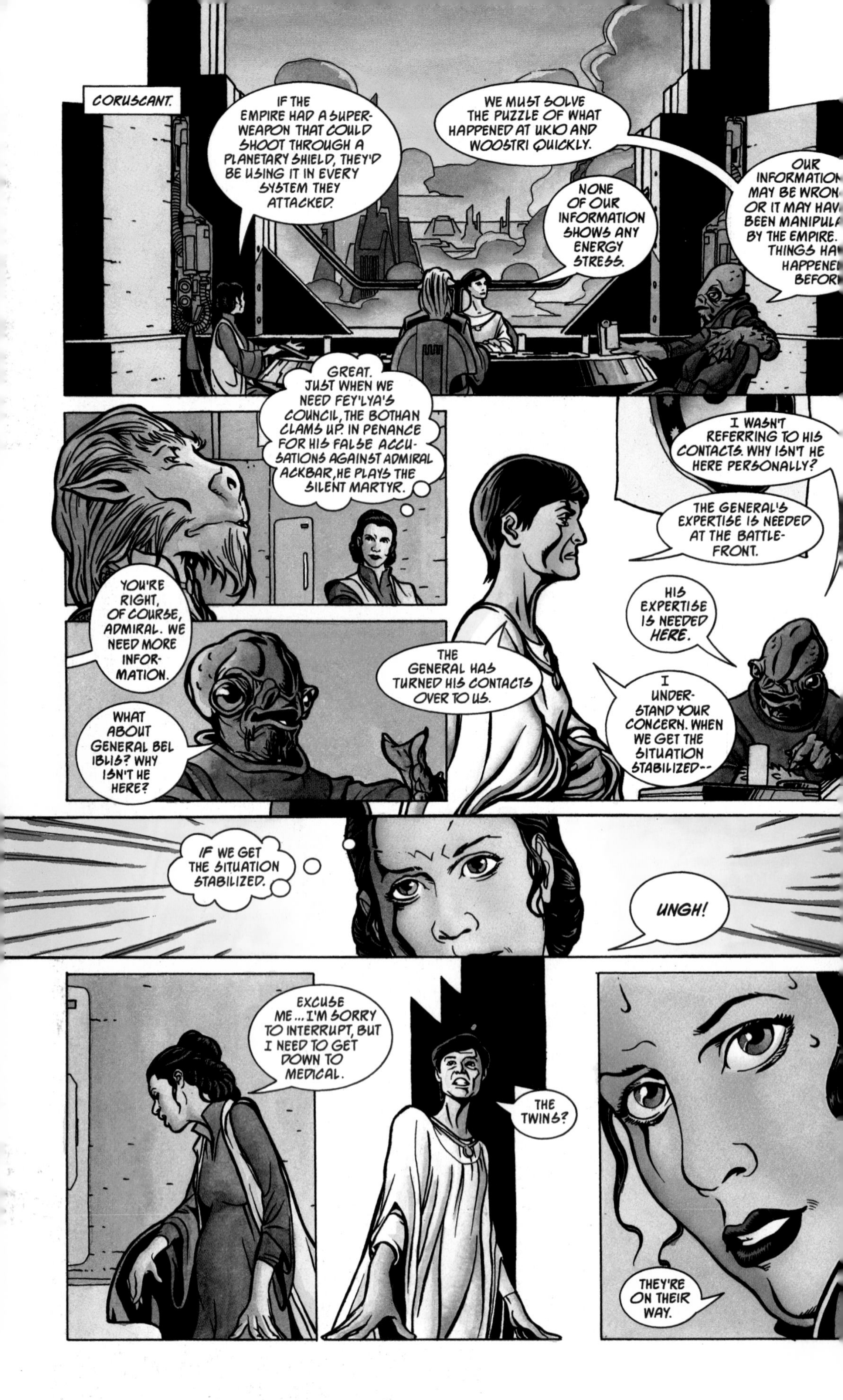
CORUSCANT.
IF THE EMPIRE HAD A SUPER-WEAPON THAT COULD SHOOT THROUGH A PLANETARY SHIELD, THEY'D BE USING IT IN EVERY SYSTEM THEY ATTACKED.
WE MUST SOLVE THE PUZZLE OF WHAT HAPPENED AT UKIO AND WOOSTRI QUICKLY.
NONE OF OUR INFORMATION SHOWS ANY ENERGY STRESS.
OUR INFORMATIO MAY BE WRON OR IT MAY HAV BEEN MANIPULA BY THE EMPIRE. THINGS HA HAPPENE BEFOR
GREAT. JUST WHEN WE NEED FEY'LYA'S COUNCIL, THE BOTHAN CLAMS UP. IN PENANCE FOR HIS FALSE ACCU-SATIONS AGAINST ADMIRAL ACKBAR, HE PLAYS THE SILENT MARTYR.
YOU'RE RIGHT, OF COURSE, ADMIRAL. WE NEED MORE INFOR-MATION.
WHAT ABOUT GENERAL BEL IBLIS? WHY ISN'T HE HERE?
THE GENERAL HAS TURNED HIS CONTACTS OVER TO US.
I WASN'T REFERRING TO HIS CONTACTS. WHY ISN'T HE HERE PERSONALLY?
THE GENERAL'S EXPERTISE IS NEEDED AT THE BATTLE-FRONT.
HIS EXPERTISE IS NEEDED *HERE*.
I UNDER-STAND YOUR CONCERN. WHEN WE GET THE SITUATION STABILIZED--
IF WE GET THE SITUATION STABILIZED.
UNGH!
EXCUSE ME... I'M SORRY TO INTERRUPT, BUT I NEED TO GET DOWN TO MEDICAL.
THE TWINS?
THEY'RE ON THEIR WAY.

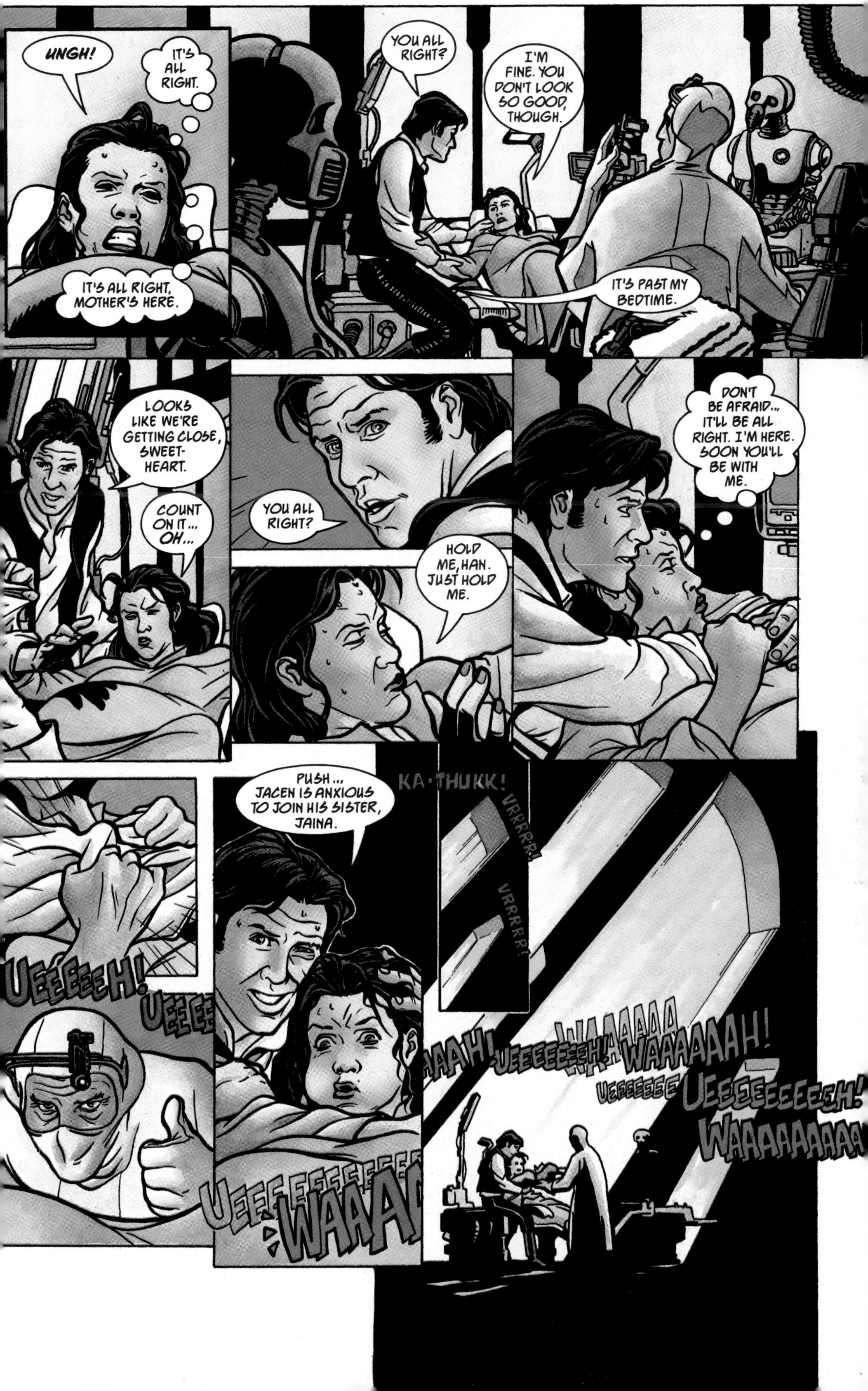
UNGH!
IT'S ALL RIGHT.
IT'S ALL RIGHT, MOTHER'S HERE.
YOU ALL RIGHT?
I'M FINE. YOU DON'T LOOK SO GOOD, THOUGH.
IT'S PAST MY BEDTIME.
LOOKS LIKE WE'RE GETTING CLOSE, SWEET-HEART.
COUNT ON IT... OH...
YOU ALL RIGHT?
HOLD ME, HAN. JUST HOLD ME.
DON'T BE AFRAID... IT'LL BE ALL RIGHT. I'M HERE. SOON YOU'LL BE WITH ME.
UEEEEEH!
PUSH... JACEN IS ANXIOUS TO JOIN HIS SISTER, JAINA.
KA-THUKK!
VRRRRR!
VRRRRR!
WAAAAAAAAH!
UEEEEEEEH!
UEEEEEEEEEEH!
WAAAAAAAA

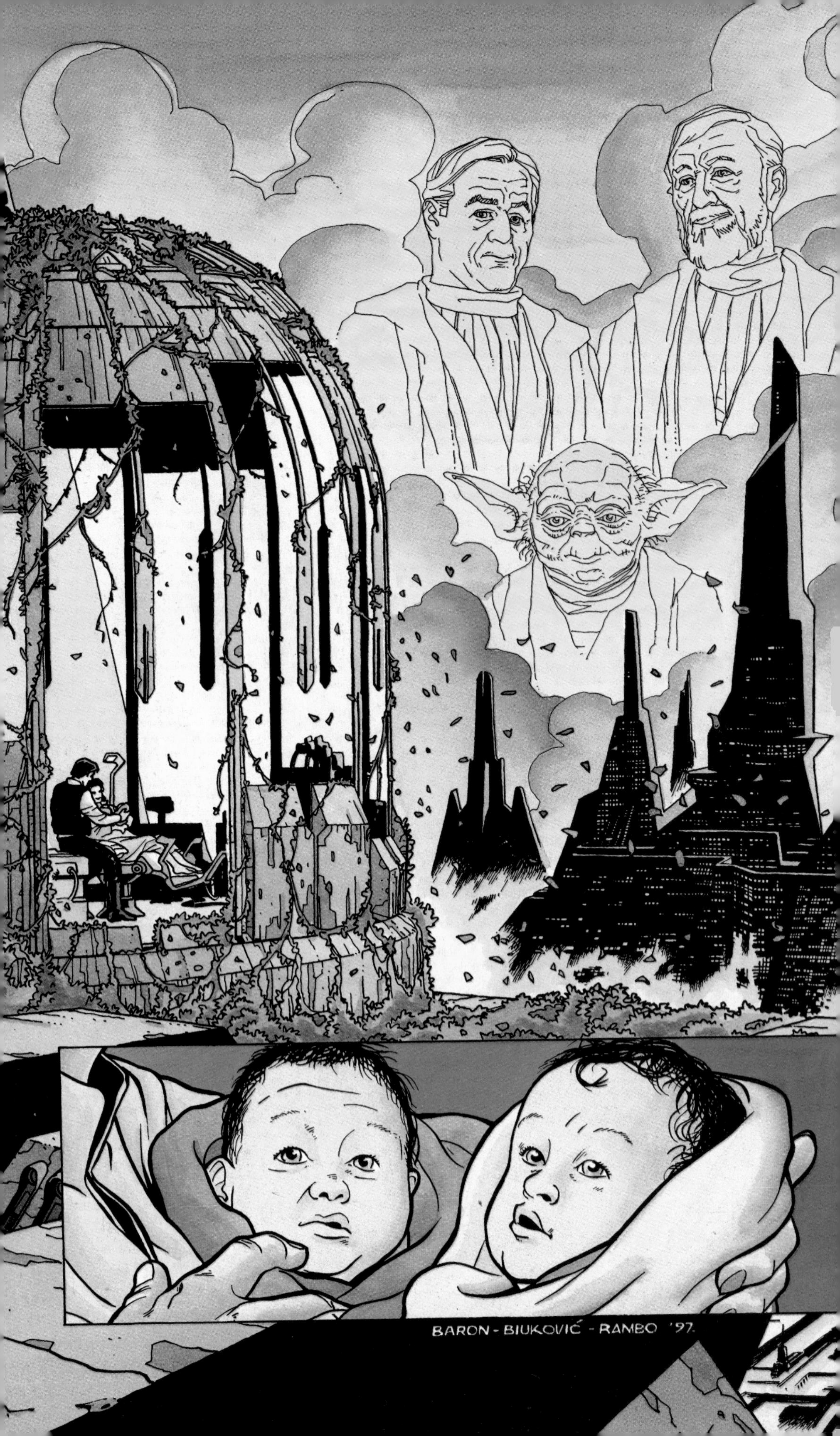
BARON - BIUKOVIĆ - RAMBO '97.

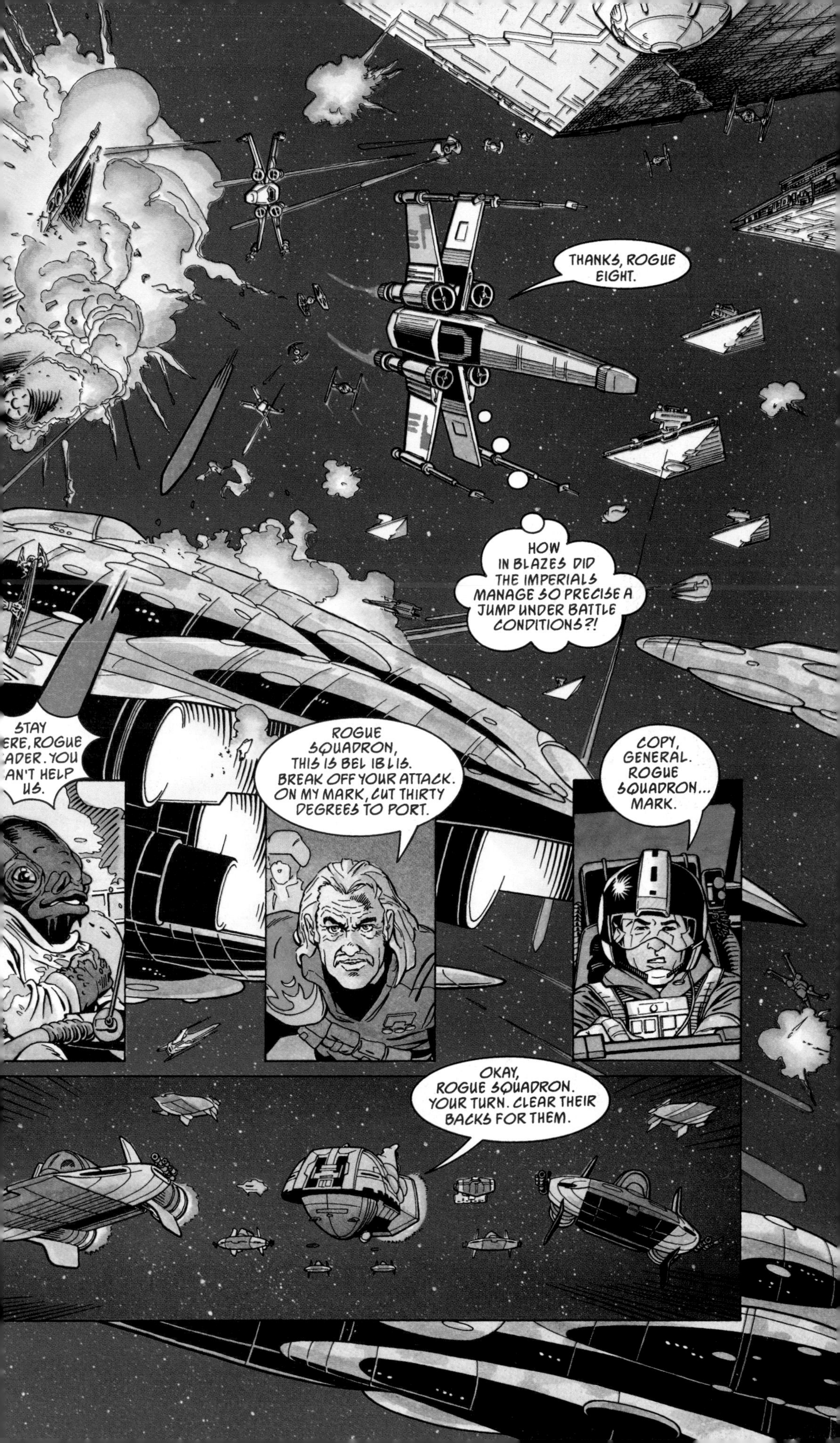
THANKS, ROGUE EIGHT.
HOW IN BLAZES DID THE IMPERIALS MANAGE SO PRECISE A JUMP UNDER BATTLE CONDITIONS?!
STAY ERE, ROGUE ADER. YOU AN'T HELP US.
ROGUE SQUADRON, THIS IS BEL IBLIS. BREAK OFF YOUR ATTACK. ON MY MARK, CUT THIRTY DEGREES TO PORT.
COPY, GENERAL. ROGUE SQUADRON... MARK.
OKAY, ROGUE SQUADRON. YOUR TURN. CLEAR THEIR BACKS FOR THEM.

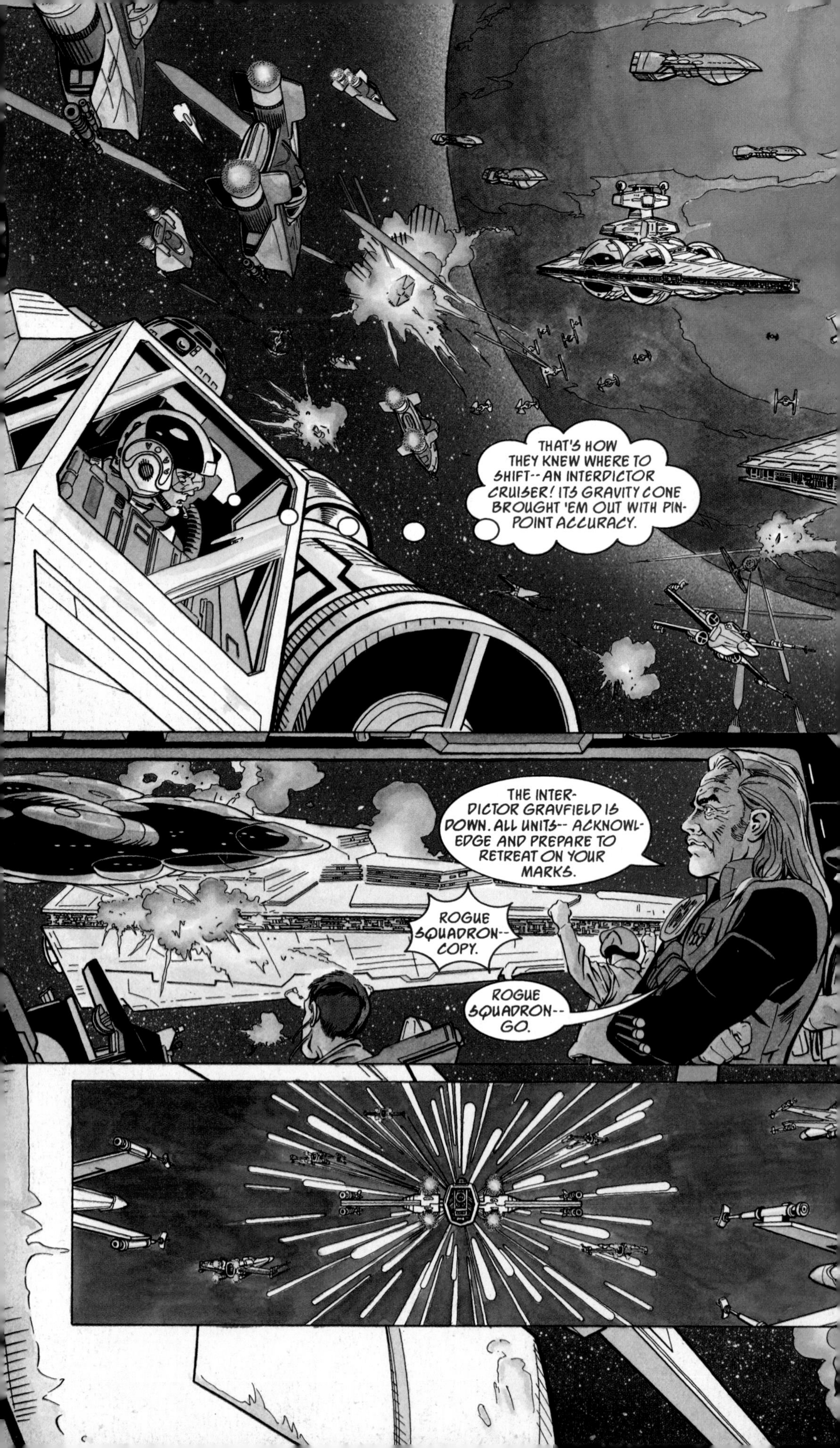
THAT'S HOW THEY KNEW WHERE TO SHIFT-- AN INTERDICTOR CRUISER! ITS GRAVITY CONE BROUGHT 'EM OUT WITH PIN-POINT ACCURACY.
THE INTER-DICTOR GRAVFIELD IS DOWN. ALL UNITS-- ACKNOWL-EDGE AND PREPARE TO RETREAT ON YOUR MARKS.
ROGUE SQUADRON-- COPY.
ROGUE SQUADRON-- GO.

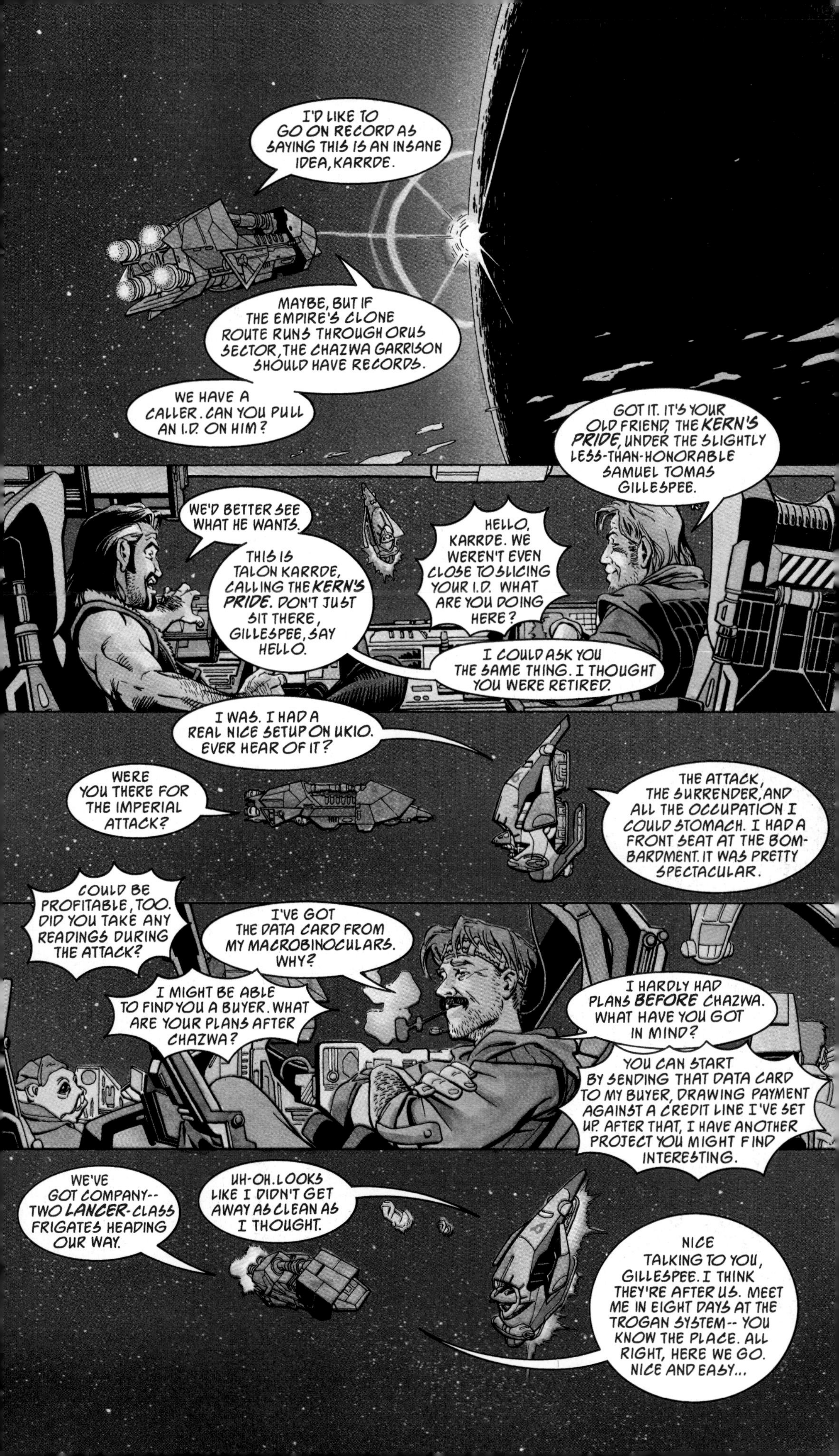
I'D LIKE TO GO ON RECORD AS SAYING THIS IS AN INSANE IDEA, KARRDE.
MAYBE, BUT IF THE EMPIRE'S CLONE ROUTE RUNS THROUGH ORUS SECTOR, THE CHAZWA GARRISON SHOULD HAVE RECORDS.
WE HAVE A CALLER. CAN YOU PULL AN I.D. ON HIM?
GOT IT. IT'S YOUR OLD FRIEND, THE KERN'S PRIDE, UNDER THE SLIGHTLY LESS-THAN-HONORABLE SAMUEL TOMAS GILLESPEE.
WE'D BETTER SEE WHAT HE WANTS.
THIS IS TALON KARRDE, CALLING THE KERN'S PRIDE. DON'T JUST SIT THERE, GILLESPEE, SAY HELLO.
HELLO, KARRDE. WE WEREN'T EVEN CLOSE TO SLICING YOUR I.D. WHAT ARE YOU DOING HERE?
I COULD ASK YOU THE SAME THING. I THOUGHT YOU WERE RETIRED.
I WAS. I HAD A REAL NICE SETUP ON UKIO. EVER HEAR OF IT?
WERE YOU THERE FOR THE IMPERIAL ATTACK?
THE ATTACK, THE SURRENDER, AND ALL THE OCCUPATION I COULD STOMACH. I HAD A FRONT SEAT AT THE BOMBARDMENT. IT WAS PRETTY SPECTACULAR.
COULD BE PROFITABLE, TOO. DID YOU TAKE ANY READINGS DURING THE ATTACK?
I'VE GOT THE DATA CARD FROM MY MACROBINOCULARS. WHY?
I MIGHT BE ABLE TO FIND YOU A BUYER. WHAT ARE YOUR PLANS AFTER CHAZWA?
I HARDLY HAD PLANS BEFORE CHAZWA. WHAT HAVE YOU GOT IN MIND?
YOU CAN START BY SENDING THAT DATA CARD TO MY BUYER, DRAWING PAYMENT AGAINST A CREDIT LINE I'VE SET UP. AFTER THAT, I HAVE ANOTHER PROJECT YOU MIGHT FIND INTERESTING.
WE'VE GOT COMPANY-- TWO LANCER-CLASS FRIGATES HEADING OUR WAY.
UH-OH. LOOKS LIKE I DIDN'T GET AWAY AS CLEAN AS I THOUGHT.
NICE TALKING TO YOU, GILLESPEE. I THINK THEY'RE AFTER US. MEET ME IN EIGHT DAYS AT THE TROGAN SYSTEM-- YOU KNOW THE PLACE. ALL RIGHT, HERE WE GO. NICE AND EASY...

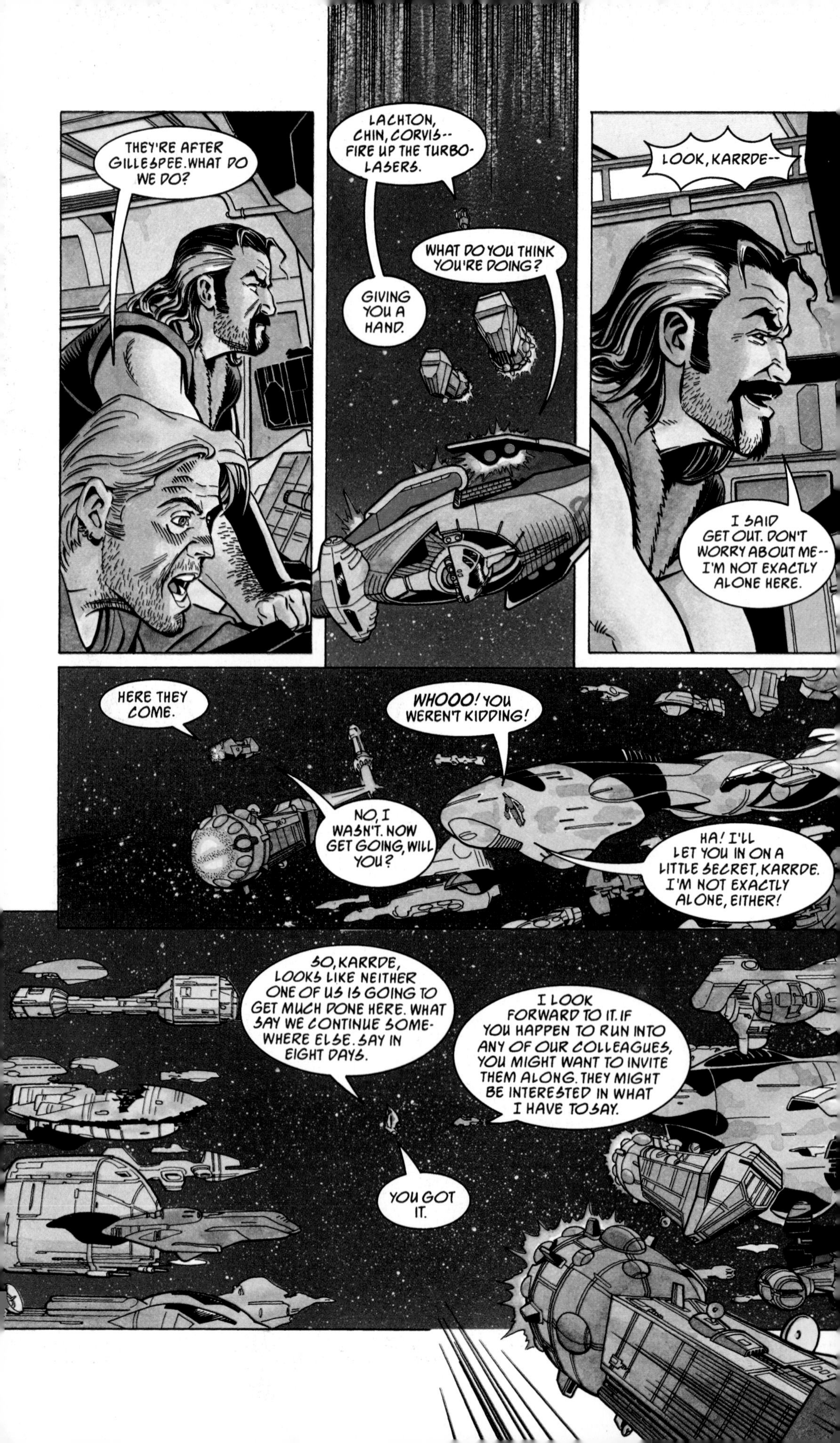
THEY'RE AFTER GILLESPEE. WHAT DO WE DO?
LACHTON, CHIN, CORVIS-- FIRE UP THE TURBO-LASERS.
GIVING YOU A HAND.
WHAT DO YOU THINK YOU'RE DOING?
LOOK, KARRDE--
I SAID GET OUT. DON'T WORRY ABOUT ME-- I'M NOT EXACTLY ALONE HERE.
HERE THEY COME.
WHOOO! YOU WEREN'T KIDDING!
NO, I WASN'T. NOW GET GOING, WILL YOU?
HA! I'LL LET YOU IN ON A LITTLE SECRET, KARRDE. I'M NOT EXACTLY ALONE, EITHER!
SO, KARRDE, LOOKS LIKE NEITHER ONE OF US IS GOING TO GET MUCH DONE HERE. WHAT SAY WE CONTINUE SOME-WHERE ELSE. SAY IN EIGHT DAYS.
I LOOK FORWARD TO IT. IF YOU HAPPEN TO RUN INTO ANY OF OUR COLLEAGUES, YOU MIGHT WANT TO INVITE THEM ALONG. THEY MIGHT BE INTERESTED IN WHAT I HAVE TO SAY.
YOU GOT IT.

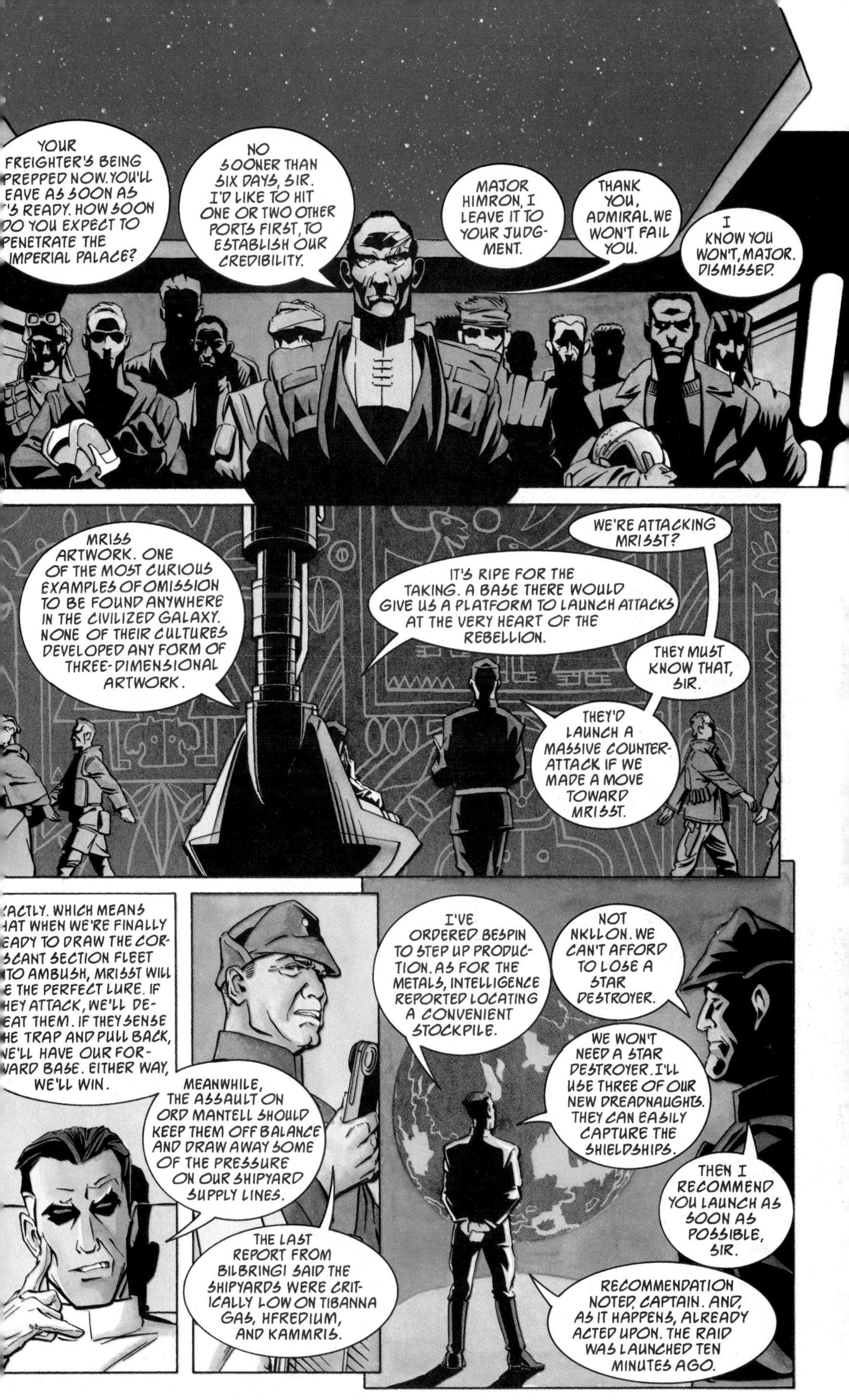
YOUR FREIGHTER'S BEING PREPPED NOW. YOU'LL EAVE AS SOON AS 'S READY. HOW SOON DO YOU EXPECT TO PENETRATE THE IMPERIAL PALACE?
NO SOONER THAN SIX DAYS, SIR. I'D LIKE TO HIT ONE OR TWO OTHER PORTS FIRST, TO ESTABLISH OUR CREDIBILITY.
MAJOR HIMRON, I LEAVE IT TO YOUR JUDGMENT.
THANK YOU, ADMIRAL. WE WON'T FAIL YOU.
I KNOW YOU WON'T, MAJOR. DISMISSED.
MRISS ARTWORK. ONE OF THE MOST CURIOUS EXAMPLES OF OMISSION TO BE FOUND ANYWHERE IN THE CIVILIZED GALAXY. NONE OF THEIR CULTURES DEVELOPED ANY FORM OF THREE-DIMENSIONAL ARTWORK.
WE'RE ATTACKING MRISST?
IT'S RIPE FOR THE TAKING. A BASE THERE WOULD GIVE US A PLATFORM TO LAUNCH ATTACKS AT THE VERY HEART OF THE REBELLION.
THEY MUST KNOW THAT, SIR.
THEY'D LAUNCH A MASSIVE COUNTER-ATTACK IF WE MADE A MOVE TOWARD MRISST.
XACTLY. WHICH MEANS HAT WHEN WE'RE FINALLY EADY TO DRAW THE CORSCANT SECTION FLEET TO AMBUSH, MRISST WILL E THE PERFECT LURE. IF HEY ATTACK, WE'LL DEEAT THEM. IF THEY SENSE HE TRAP AND PULL BACK, VE'LL HAVE OUR FORVARD BASE. EITHER WAY, WE'LL WIN.
MEANWHILE, THE ASSAULT ON ORD MANTELL SHOULD KEEP THEM OFF BALANCE AND DRAW AWAY SOME OF THE PRESSURE ON OUR SHIPYARD SUPPLY LINES.
THE LAST REPORT FROM BILBRINGI SAID THE SHIPYARDS WERE CRITICALLY LOW ON TIBANNA GAS, HFREDIUM, AND KAMMRIS.
I'VE ORDERED BESPIN TO STEP UP PRODUCTION. AS FOR THE METALS, INTELLIGENCE REPORTED LOCATING A CONVENIENT STOCKPILE.
NOT NKLLON. WE CAN'T AFFORD TO LOSE A STAR DESTROYER.
WE WON'T NEED A STAR DESTROYER. I'LL USE THREE OF OUR NEW DREADNAUGHTS. THEY CAN EASILY CAPTURE THE SHIELDSHIPS.
THEN I RECOMMEND YOU LAUNCH AS SOON AS POSSIBLE, SIR.
RECOMMENDATION NOTED, CAPTAIN. AND, AS IT HAPPENS, ALREADY ACTED UPON. THE RAID WAS LAUNCHED TEN MINUTES AGO.

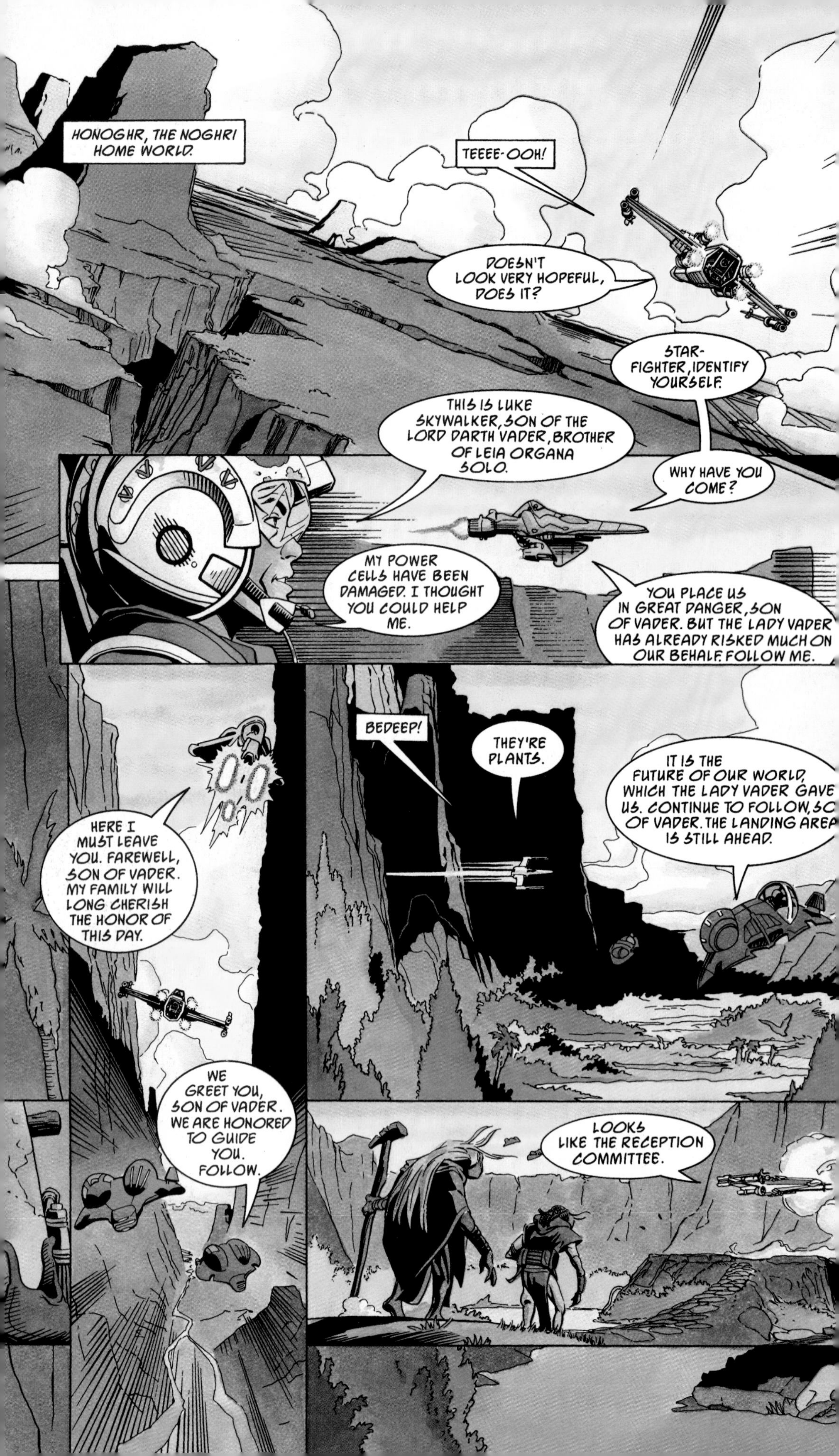
HONOGHR, THE NOGHRI HOME WORLD.
TEEEE-OOH!
DOESN'T LOOK VERY HOPEFUL, DOES IT?
STAR-FIGHTER, IDENTIFY YOURSELF.
THIS IS LUKE SKYWALKER, SON OF THE LORD DARTH VADER, BROTHER OF LEIA ORGANA SOLO.
WHY HAVE YOU COME?
MY POWER CELLS HAVE BEEN DAMAGED. I THOUGHT YOU COULD HELP ME.
YOU PLACE US IN GREAT DANGER, SON OF VADER. BUT THE LADY VADER HAS ALREADY RISKED MUCH ON OUR BEHALF. FOLLOW ME.
HERE I MUST LEAVE YOU. FAREWELL, SON OF VADER. MY FAMILY WILL LONG CHERISH THE HONOR OF THIS DAY.
BEDEEP!
THEY'RE PLANTS.
IT IS THE FUTURE OF OUR WORLD, WHICH THE LADY VADER GAVE US. CONTINUE TO FOLLOW, SO OF VADER. THE LANDING AREA IS STILL AHEAD.
WE GREET YOU, SON OF VADER. WE ARE HONORED TO GUIDE YOU. FOLLOW.
LOOKS LIKE THE RECEPTION COMMITTEE.

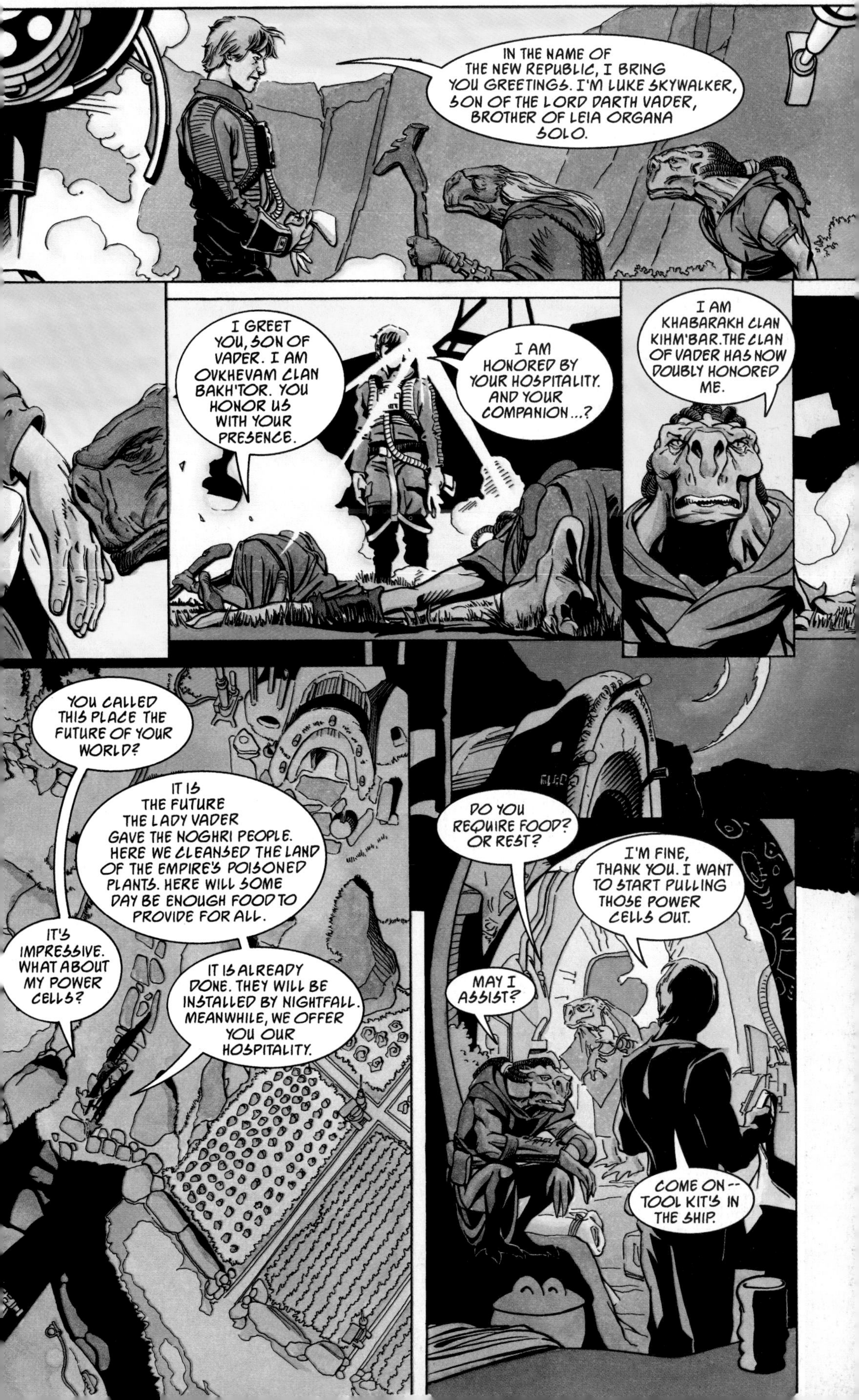
IN THE NAME OF THE NEW REPUBLIC, I BRING YOU GREETINGS. I'M LUKE SKYWALKER, SON OF THE LORD DARTH VADER, BROTHER OF LEIA ORGANA SOLO.
I GREET YOU, SON OF VADER. I AM OVKHEVAM CLAN BAKH'TOR. YOU HONOR US WITH YOUR PRESENCE.
I AM HONORED BY YOUR HOSPITALITY. AND YOUR COMPANION...?
I AM KHABARAKH CLAN KIHM'BAR. THE CLAN OF VADER HAS NOW DOUBLY HONORED ME.
YOU CALLED THIS PLACE THE FUTURE OF YOUR WORLD?
IT IS THE FUTURE THE LADY VADER GAVE THE NOGHRI PEOPLE. HERE WE CLEANSED THE LAND OF THE EMPIRE'S POISONED PLANTS. HERE WILL SOME DAY BE ENOUGH FOOD TO PROVIDE FOR ALL.
IT'S IMPRESSIVE. WHAT ABOUT MY POWER CELLS?
IT IS ALREADY DONE. THEY WILL BE INSTALLED BY NIGHTFALL. MEANWHILE, WE OFFER YOU OUR HOSPITALITY.
DO YOU REQUIRE FOOD? OR REST?
I'M FINE, THANK YOU. I WANT TO START PULLING THOSE POWER CELLS OUT.
MAY I ASSIST?
COME ON -- TOOL KIT'S IN THE SHIP.

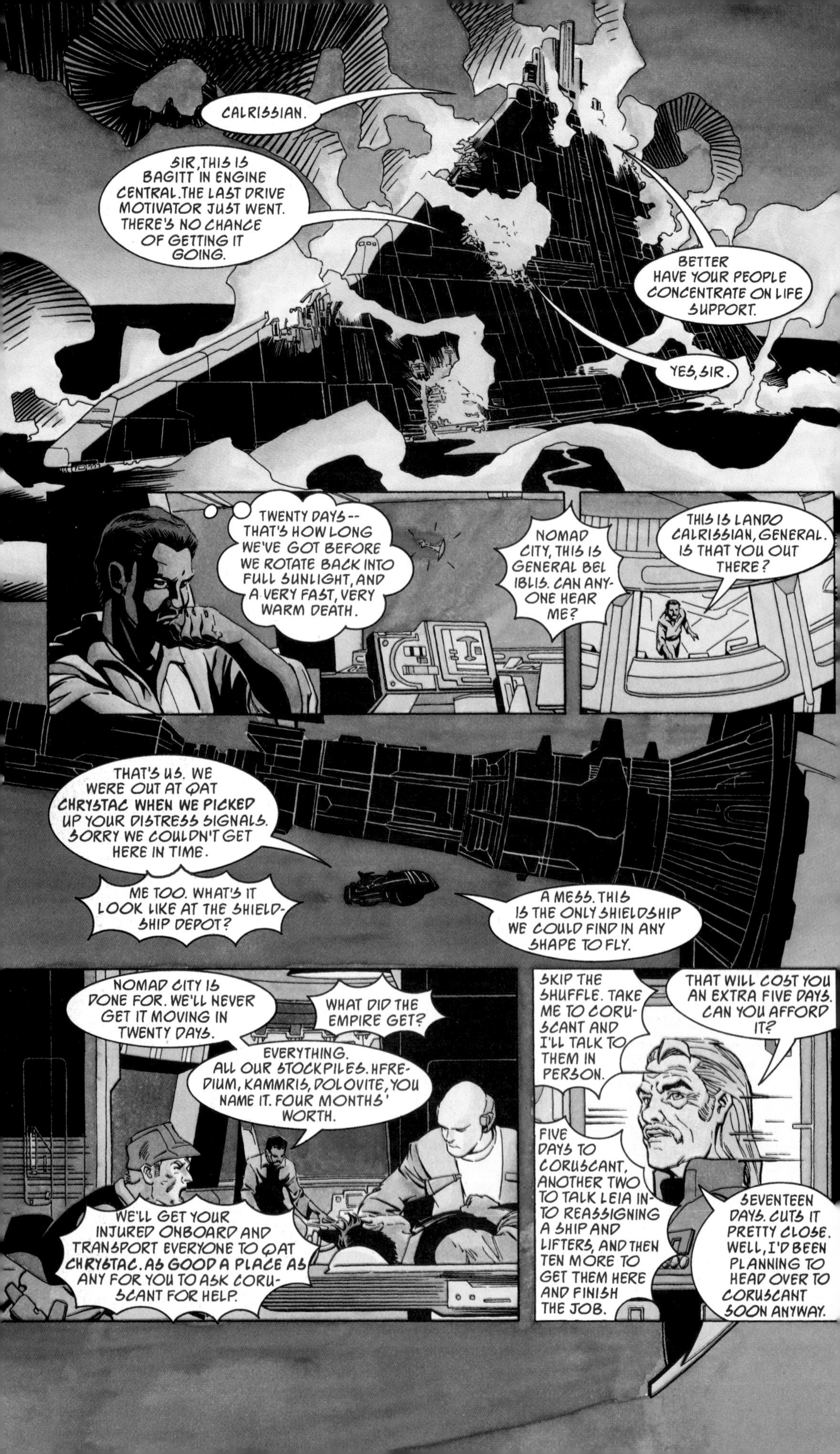
CALRISSIAN.
SIR, THIS IS BAGITT IN ENGINE CENTRAL. THE LAST DRIVE MOTIVATOR JUST WENT. THERE'S NO CHANCE OF GETTING IT GOING.
BETTER HAVE YOUR PEOPLE CONCENTRATE ON LIFE SUPPORT.
YES, SIR.
TWENTY DAYS -- THAT'S HOW LONG WE'VE GOT BEFORE WE ROTATE BACK INTO FULL SUNLIGHT, AND A VERY FAST, VERY WARM DEATH.
NOMAD CITY, THIS IS GENERAL BEL IBLIS. CAN ANYONE HEAR ME?
THIS IS LANDO CALRISSIAN, GENERAL. IS THAT YOU OUT THERE?
THAT'S US. WE WERE OUT AT QAT CHRYSTAC WHEN WE PICKED UP YOUR DISTRESS SIGNALS. SORRY WE COULDN'T GET HERE IN TIME.
ME TOO. WHAT'S IT LOOK LIKE AT THE SHIELDSHIP DEPOT?
A MESS. THIS IS THE ONLY SHIELDSHIP WE COULD FIND IN ANY SHAPE TO FLY.
NOMAD CITY IS DONE FOR. WE'LL NEVER GET IT MOVING IN TWENTY DAYS.
WHAT DID THE EMPIRE GET?
EVERYTHING. ALL OUR STOCKPILES. HFREDIUM, KAMMRIS, DOLOVITE, YOU NAME IT. FOUR MONTHS' WORTH.
WE'LL GET YOUR INJURED ONBOARD AND TRANSPORT EVERYONE TO QAT CHRYSTAC. AS GOOD A PLACE AS ANY FOR YOU TO ASK CORUSCANT FOR HELP.
SKIP THE SHUFFLE. TAKE ME TO CORUSCANT AND I'LL TALK TO THEM IN PERSON.
THAT WILL COST YOU AN EXTRA FIVE DAYS. CAN YOU AFFORD IT?
FIVE DAYS TO CORUSCANT, ANOTHER TWO TO TALK LEIA INTO REASSIGNING A SHIP AND LIFTERS, AND THEN TEN MORE TO GET THEM HERE AND FINISH THE JOB.
SEVENTEEN DAYS. CUTS IT PRETTY CLOSE. WELL, I'D BEEN PLANNING TO HEAD OVER TO CORUSCANT SOON ANYWAY.

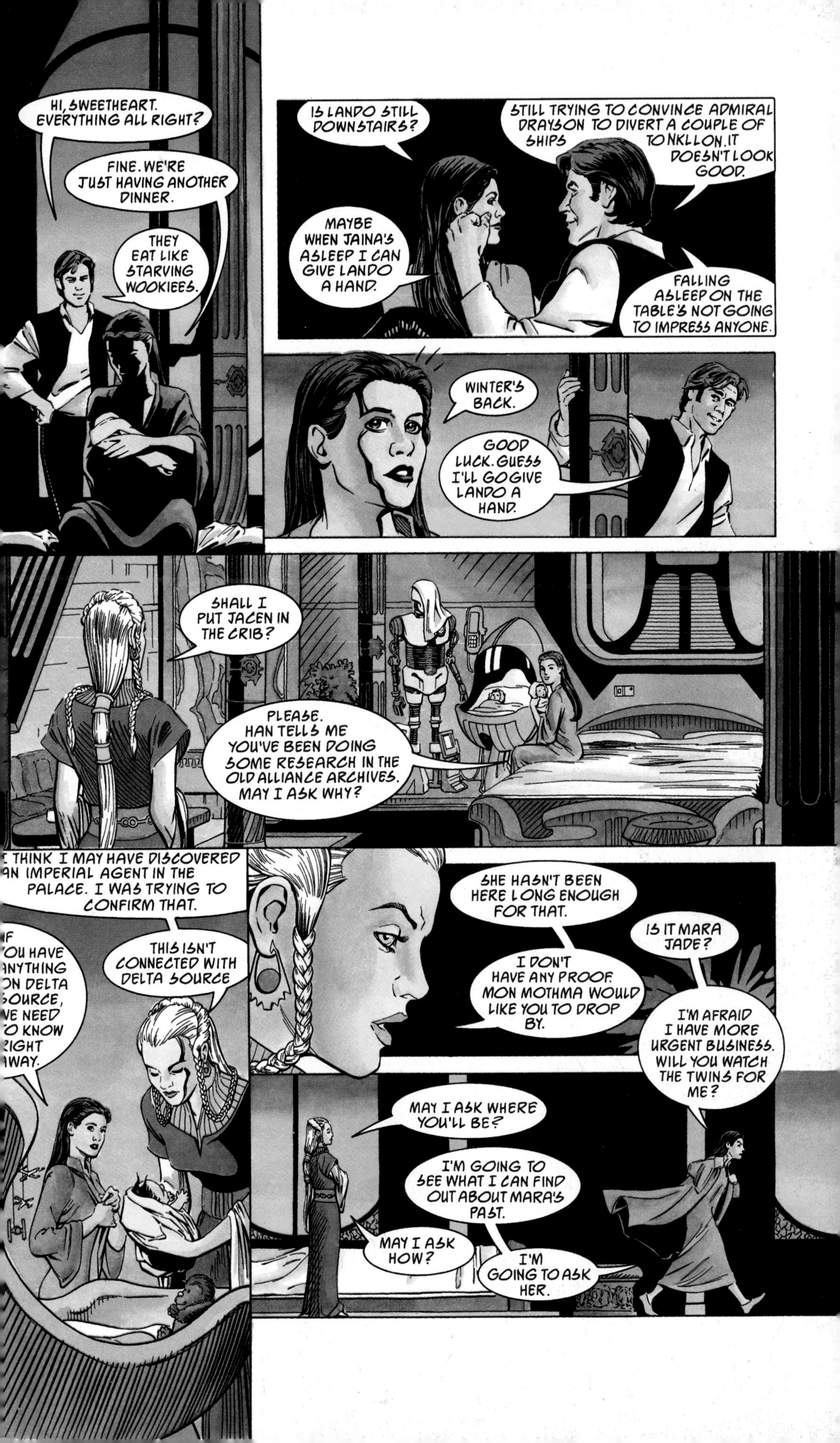
HI, SWEETHEART. EVERYTHING ALL RIGHT?
FINE. WE'RE JUST HAVING ANOTHER DINNER.
THEY EAT LIKE STARVING WOOKIEES.
IS LANDO STILL DOWNSTAIRS?
STILL TRYING TO CONVINCE ADMIRAL DRAYSON TO DIVERT A COUPLE OF SHIPS TO NKLLON. IT DOESN'T LOOK GOOD.
MAYBE WHEN JAINA'S ASLEEP I CAN GIVE LANDO A HAND.
FALLING ASLEEP ON THE TABLE'S NOT GOING TO IMPRESS ANYONE.
WINTER'S BACK.
GOOD LUCK. GUESS I'LL GO GIVE LANDO A HAND.
SHALL I PUT JACEN IN THE CRIB?
PLEASE. HAN TELLS ME YOU'VE BEEN DOING SOME RESEARCH IN THE OLD ALLIANCE ARCHIVES. MAY I ASK WHY?
I THINK I MAY HAVE DISCOVERED AN IMPERIAL AGENT IN THE PALACE. I WAS TRYING TO CONFIRM THAT.
IF YOU HAVE ANYTHING ON DELTA SOURCE, WE NEED TO KNOW RIGHT AWAY.
THIS ISN'T CONNECTED WITH DELTA SOURCE
SHE HASN'T BEEN HERE LONG ENOUGH FOR THAT.
IS IT MARA JADE?
I DON'T HAVE ANY PROOF. MON MOTHMA WOULD LIKE YOU TO DROP BY.
I'M AFRAID I HAVE MORE URGENT BUSINESS. WILL YOU WATCH THE TWINS FOR ME?
MAY I ASK WHERE YOU'LL BE?
I'M GOING TO SEE WHAT I CAN FIND OUT ABOUT MARA'S PAST.
MAY I ASK HOW?
I'M GOING TO ASK HER.

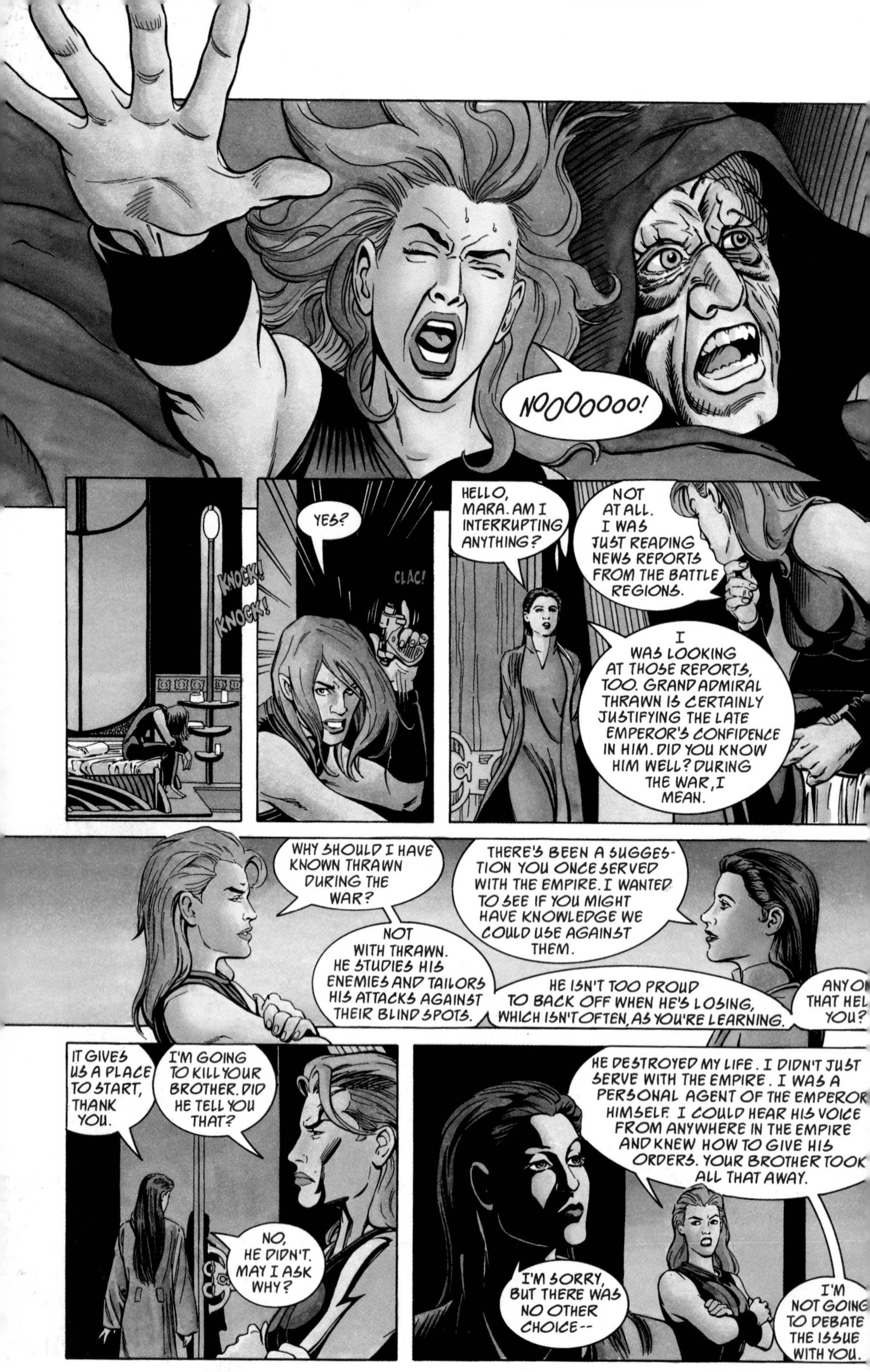
NOOOOOOO!
KNOCK! KNOCK!
YES?
CLAC!
HELLO, MARA. AM I INTERRUPTING ANYTHING?
NOT AT ALL. I WAS JUST READING NEWS REPORTS FROM THE BATTLE REGIONS.
I WAS LOOKING AT THOSE REPORTS, TOO. GRAND ADMIRAL THRAWN IS CERTAINLY JUSTIFYING THE LATE EMPEROR'S CONFIDENCE IN HIM. DID YOU KNOW HIM WELL? DURING THE WAR, I MEAN.
WHY SHOULD I HAVE KNOWN THRAWN DURING THE WAR?
THERE'S BEEN A SUGGESTION YOU ONCE SERVED WITH THE EMPIRE. I WANTED TO SEE IF YOU MIGHT HAVE KNOWLEDGE WE COULD USE AGAINST THEM.
NOT WITH THRAWN. HE STUDIES HIS ENEMIES AND TAILORS HIS ATTACKS AGAINST THEIR BLIND SPOTS.
HE ISN'T TOO PROUD TO BACK OFF WHEN HE'S LOSING, WHICH ISN'T OFTEN, AS YOU'RE LEARNING.
IT GIVES US A PLACE TO START, THANK YOU.
I'M GOING TO KILL YOUR BROTHER. DID HE TELL YOU THAT?
NO, HE DIDN'T. MAY I ASK WHY?
HE DESTROYED MY LIFE. I DIDN'T JUST SERVE WITH THE EMPIRE. I WAS A PERSONAL AGENT OF THE EMPEROR HIMSELF. I COULD HEAR HIS VOICE FROM ANYWHERE IN THE EMPIRE AND KNEW HOW TO GIVE HIS ORDERS. YOUR BROTHER TOOK ALL THAT AWAY.
I'M SORRY, BUT THERE WAS NO OTHER CHOICE--
I'M NOT GOING TO DEBATE THE ISSUE WITH YOU.

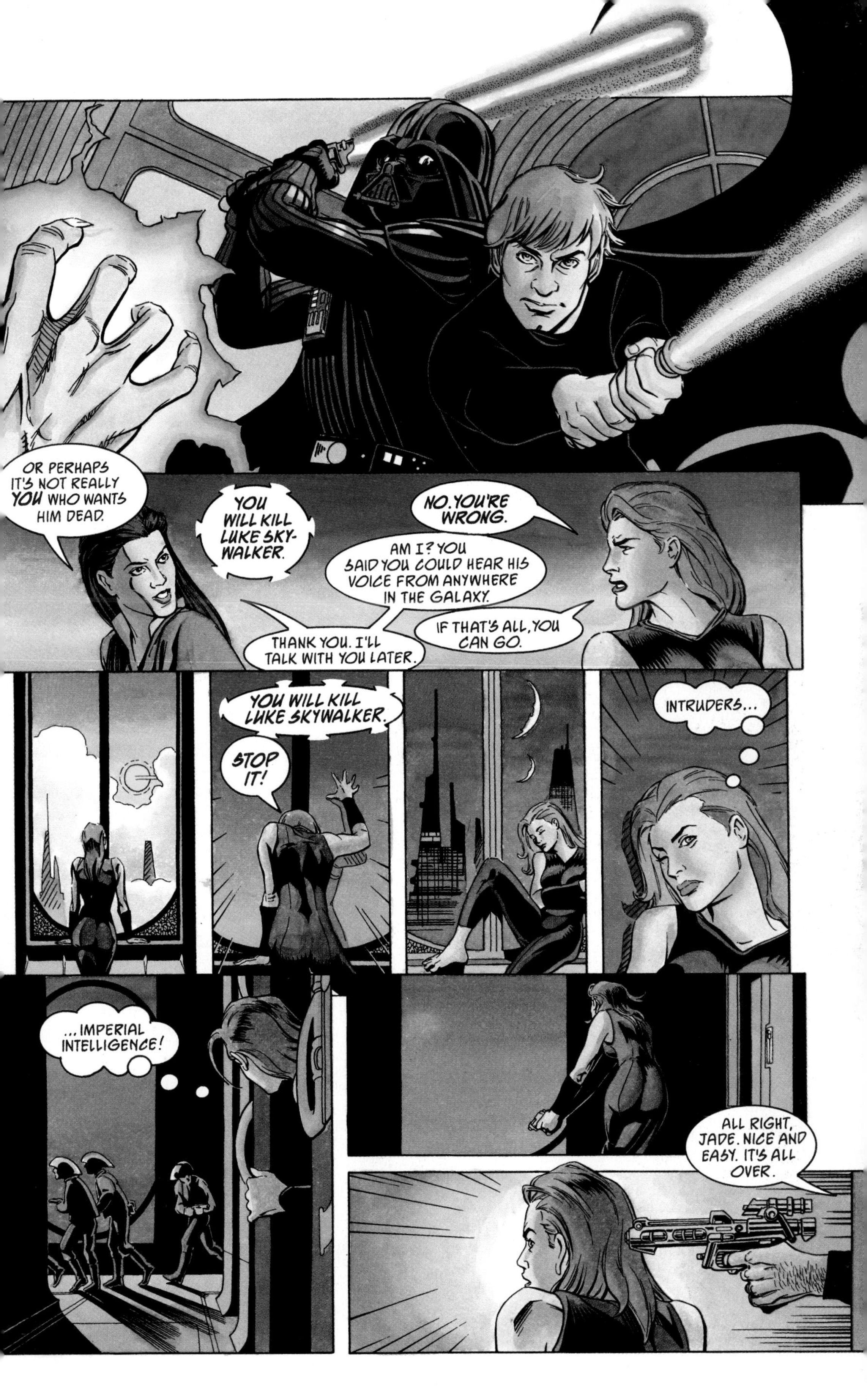
OR PERHAPS IT'S NOT REALLY YOU WHO WANTS HIM DEAD.
YOU WILL KILL LUKE SKY-WALKER.
NO. YOU'RE WRONG.
AM I? YOU SAID YOU COULD HEAR HIS VOICE FROM ANYWHERE IN THE GALAXY.
THANK YOU. I'LL TALK WITH YOU LATER.
IF THAT'S ALL, YOU CAN GO.
YOU WILL KILL LUKE SKYWALKER.
STOP IT!
INTRUDERS...
...IMPERIAL INTELLIGENCE!
ALL RIGHT, JADE. NICE AND EASY. IT'S ALL OVER.

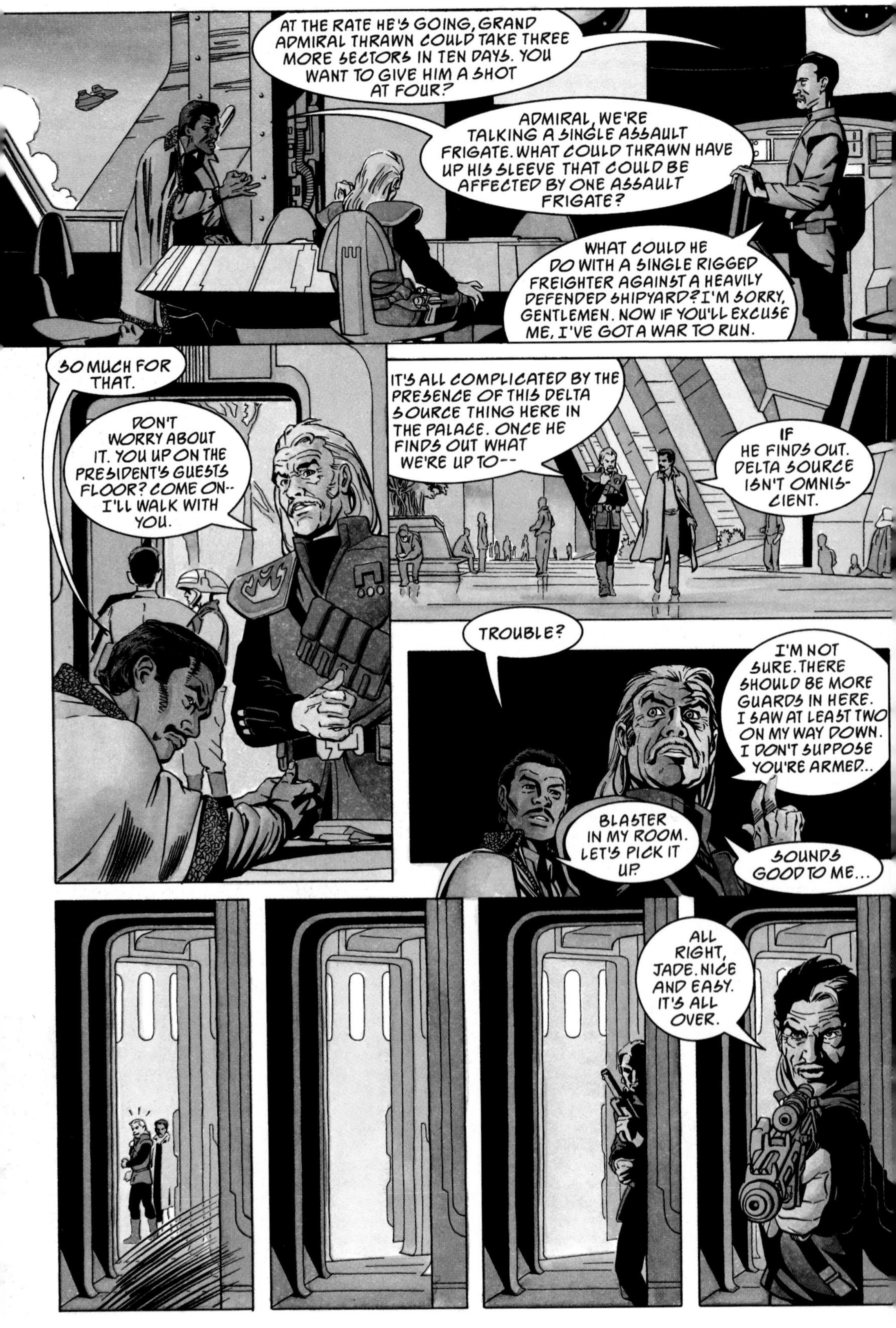
AT THE RATE HE'S GOING, GRAND ADMIRAL THRAWN COULD TAKE THREE MORE SECTORS IN TEN DAYS. YOU WANT TO GIVE HIM A SHOT AT FOUR?
ADMIRAL, WE'RE TALKING A SINGLE ASSAULT FRIGATE. WHAT COULD THRAWN HAVE UP HIS SLEEVE THAT COULD BE AFFECTED BY ONE ASSAULT FRIGATE?
WHAT COULD HE DO WITH A SINGLE RIGGED FREIGHTER AGAINST A HEAVILY DEFENDED SHIPYARD? I'M SORRY, GENTLEMEN. NOW IF YOU'LL EXCUSE ME, I'VE GOT A WAR TO RUN.
SO MUCH FOR THAT.
DON'T WORRY ABOUT IT. YOU UP ON THE PRESIDENT'S GUESTS FLOOR? COME ON-- I'LL WALK WITH YOU.
IT'S ALL COMPLICATED BY THE PRESENCE OF THIS DELTA SOURCE THING HERE IN THE PALACE. ONCE HE FINDS OUT WHAT WE'RE UP TO--
IF HE FINDS OUT. DELTA SOURCE ISN'T OMNISCIENT.
TROUBLE?
I'M NOT SURE. THERE SHOULD BE MORE GUARDS IN HERE. I SAW AT LEAST TWO ON MY WAY DOWN. I DON'T SUPPOSE YOU'RE ARMED...
BLASTER IN MY ROOM. LET'S PICK IT UP.
SOUNDS GOOD TO ME...
ALL RIGHT, JADE. NICE AND EASY. IT'S ALL OVER.

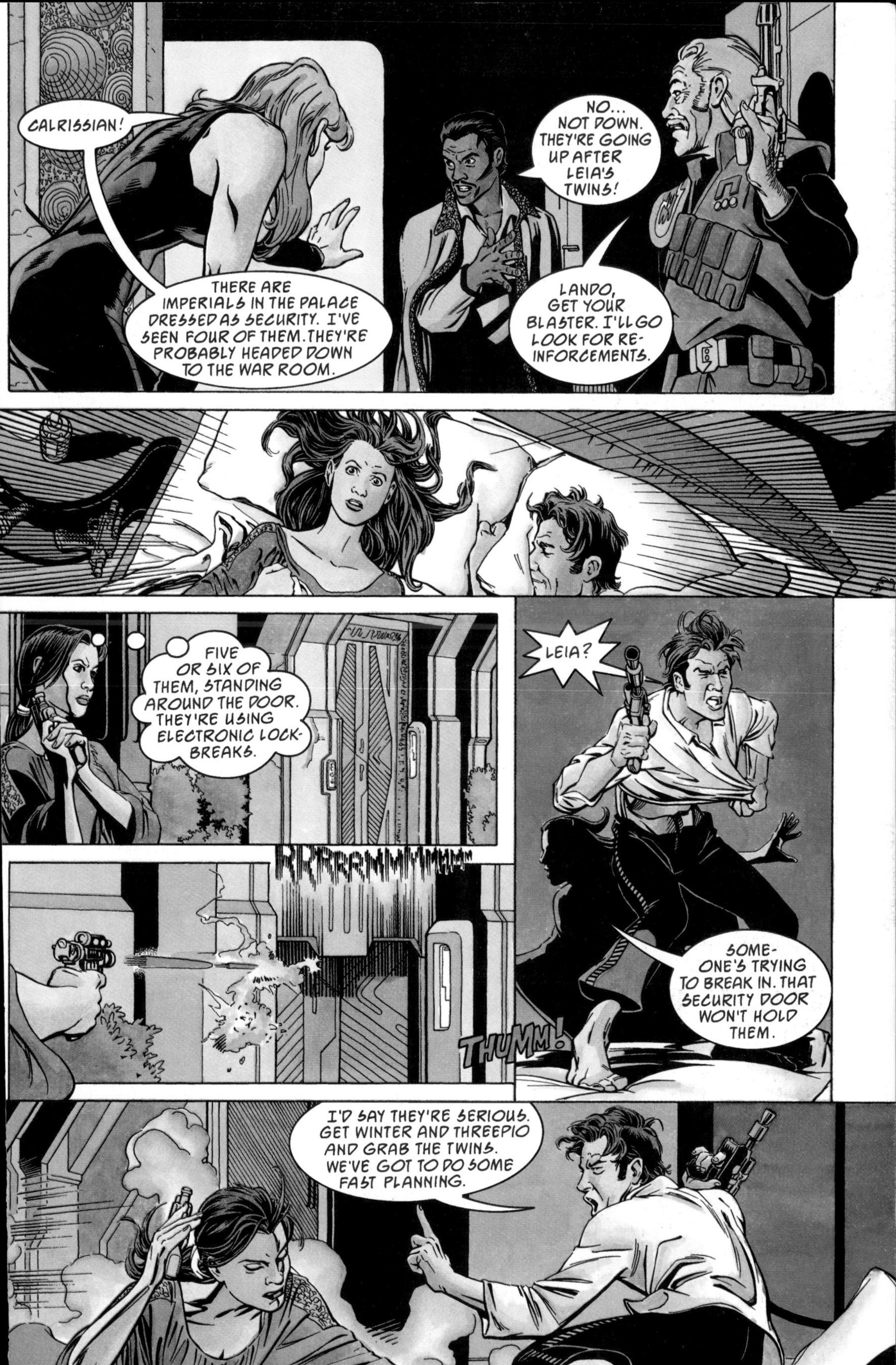
CALRISSIAN!
THERE ARE IMPERIALS IN THE PALACE DRESSED AS SECURITY. I'VE SEEN FOUR OF THEM. THEY'RE PROBABLY HEADED DOWN TO THE WAR ROOM.
NO... NOT DOWN. THEY'RE GOING UP AFTER LEIA'S TWINS!
LANDO, GET YOUR BLASTER. I'LL GO LOOK FOR RE-INFORCEMENTS.
FIVE OR SIX OF THEM, STANDING AROUND THE DOOR. THEY'RE USING ELECTRONIC LOCK-BREAKS.
LEIA?
RRRRRRMMMMMMM
SOME-ONE'S TRYING TO BREAK IN. THAT SECURITY DOOR WON'T HOLD THEM.
THUMM!
I'D SAY THEY'RE SERIOUS. GET WINTER AND THREEPIO AND GRAB THE TWINS. WE'VE GOT TO DO SOME FAST PLANNING.

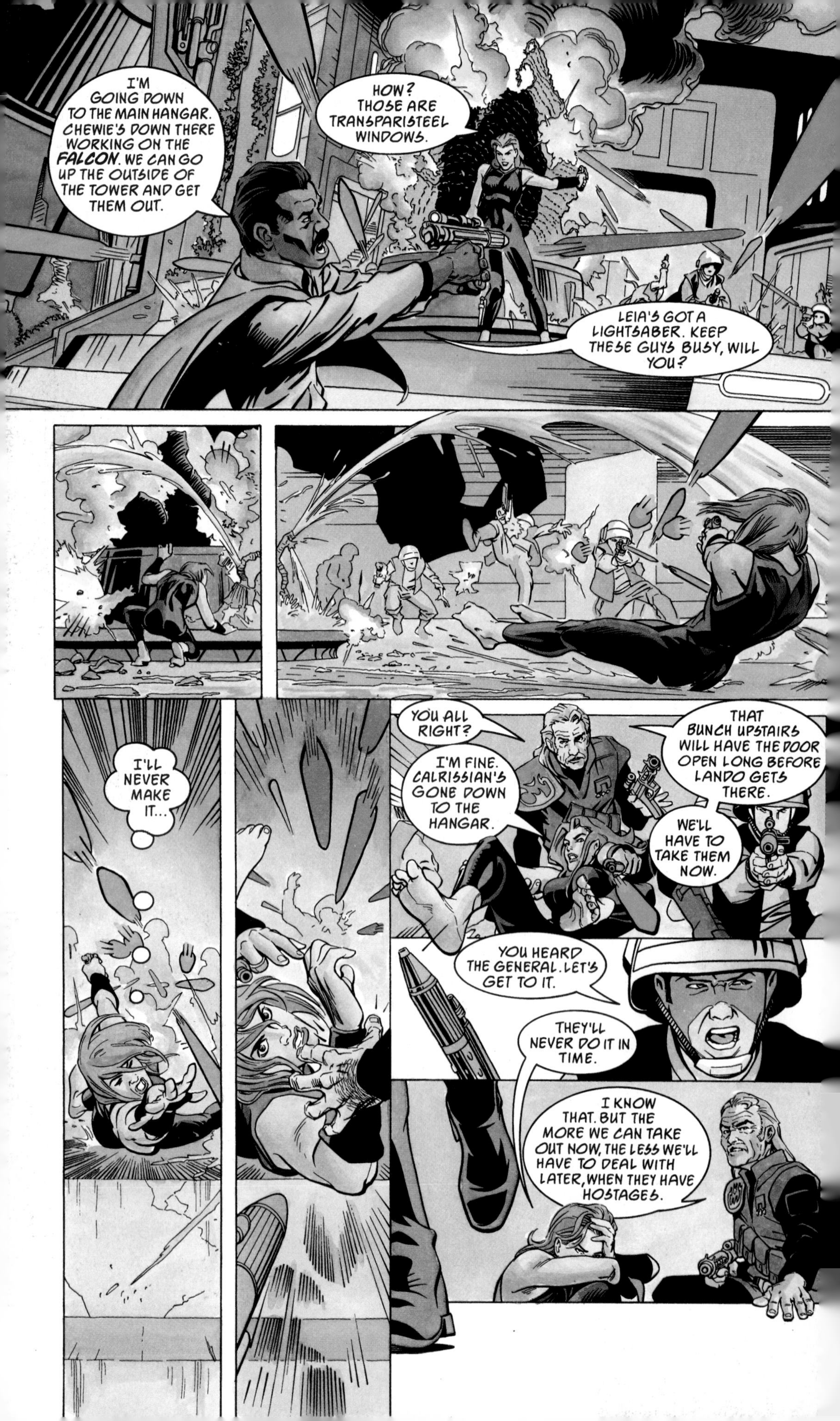

I'M GOING DOWN TO THE MAIN HANGAR. CHEWIE'S DOWN THERE WORKING ON THE FALCON. WE CAN GO UP THE OUTSIDE OF THE TOWER AND GET THEM OUT.
HOW? THOSE ARE TRANSPARISTEEL WINDOWS.
LEIA'S GOT A LIGHTSABER. KEEP THESE GUYS BUSY, WILL YOU?
I'LL NEVER MAKE IT...
YOU ALL RIGHT?
I'M FINE. CALRISSIAN'S GONE DOWN TO THE HANGAR.
THAT BUNCH UPSTAIRS WILL HAVE THE DOOR OPEN LONG BEFORE LANDO GETS THERE.
WE'LL HAVE TO TAKE THEM NOW.
YOU HEARD THE GENERAL. LET'S GET TO IT.
THEY'LL NEVER DO IT IN TIME.
I KNOW THAT. BUT THE MORE WE CAN TAKE OUT NOW, THE LESS WE'LL HAVE TO DEAL WITH LATER, WHEN THEY HAVE HOSTAGES.

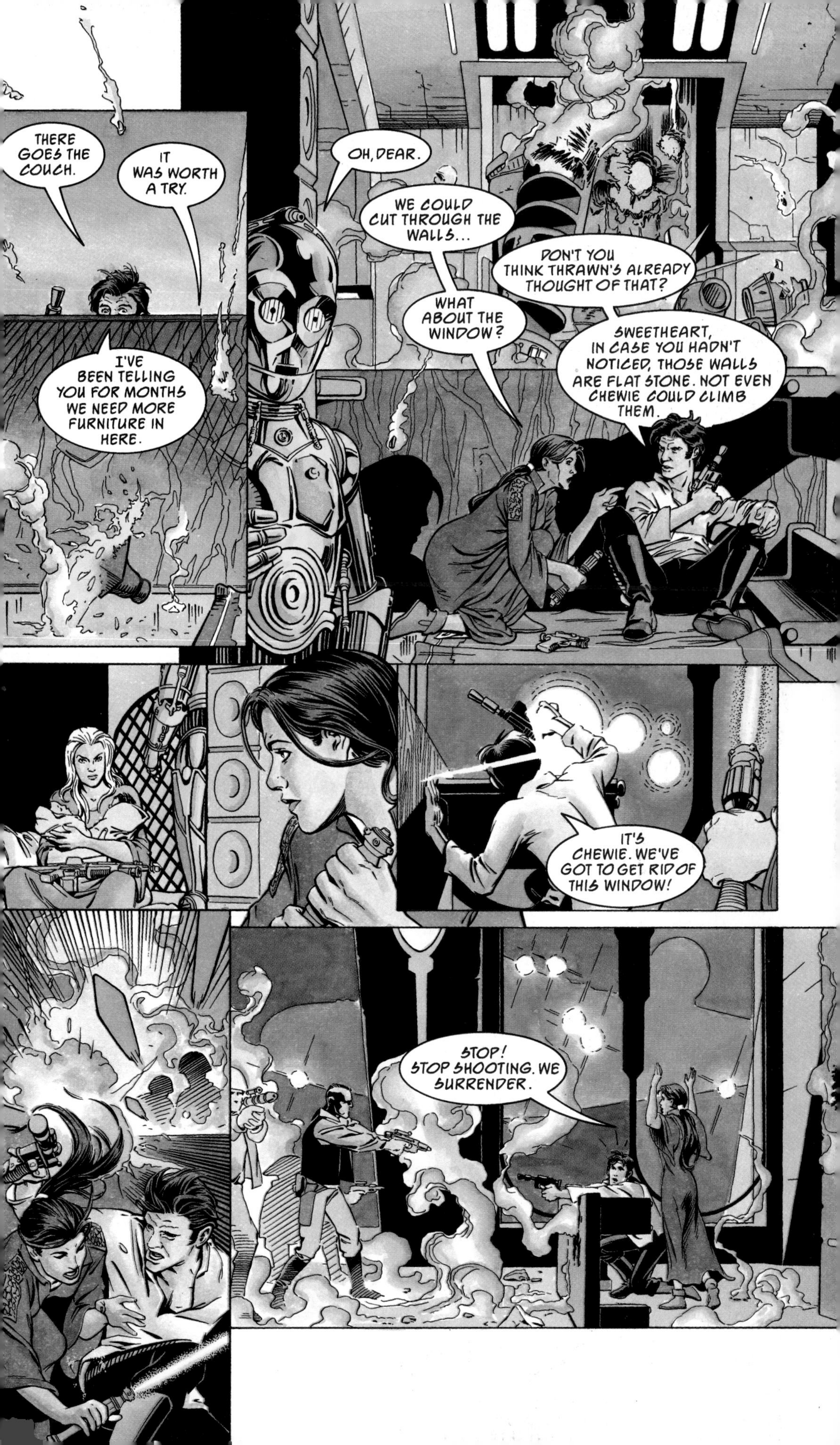
THERE GOES THE COUCH.
IT WAS WORTH A TRY.
I'VE BEEN TELLING YOU FOR MONTHS WE NEED MORE FURNITURE IN HERE.
OH, DEAR.
WE COULD CUT THROUGH THE WALLS...
DON'T YOU THINK THRAWN'S ALREADY THOUGHT OF THAT?
WHAT ABOUT THE WINDOW?
SWEETHEART, IN CASE YOU HADN'T NOTICED, THOSE WALLS ARE FLAT STONE. NOT EVEN CHEWIE COULD CLIMB THEM.
IT'S CHEWIE. WE'VE GOT TO GET RID OF THIS WINDOW!
STOP! STOP SHOOTING. WE SURRENDER.

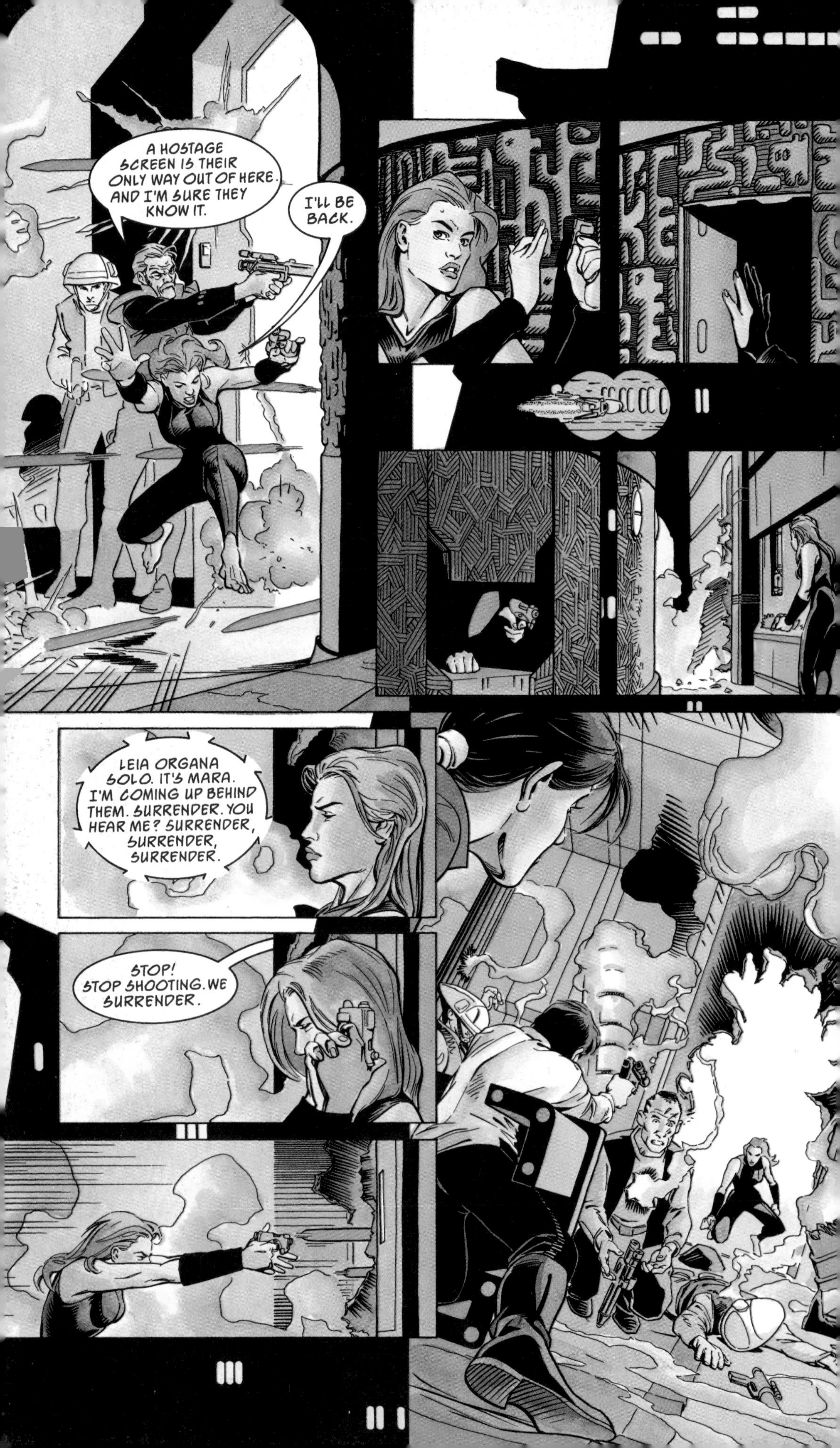
A HOSTAGE SCREEN IS THEIR ONLY WAY OUT OF HERE. AND I'M SURE THEY KNOW IT.
I'LL BE BACK.
LEIA ORGANA SOLO. IT'S MARA. I'M COMING UP BEHIND THEM. SURRENDER. YOU HEAR ME? SURRENDER, SURRENDER, SURRENDER.
STOP! STOP SHOOTING. WE SURRENDER.

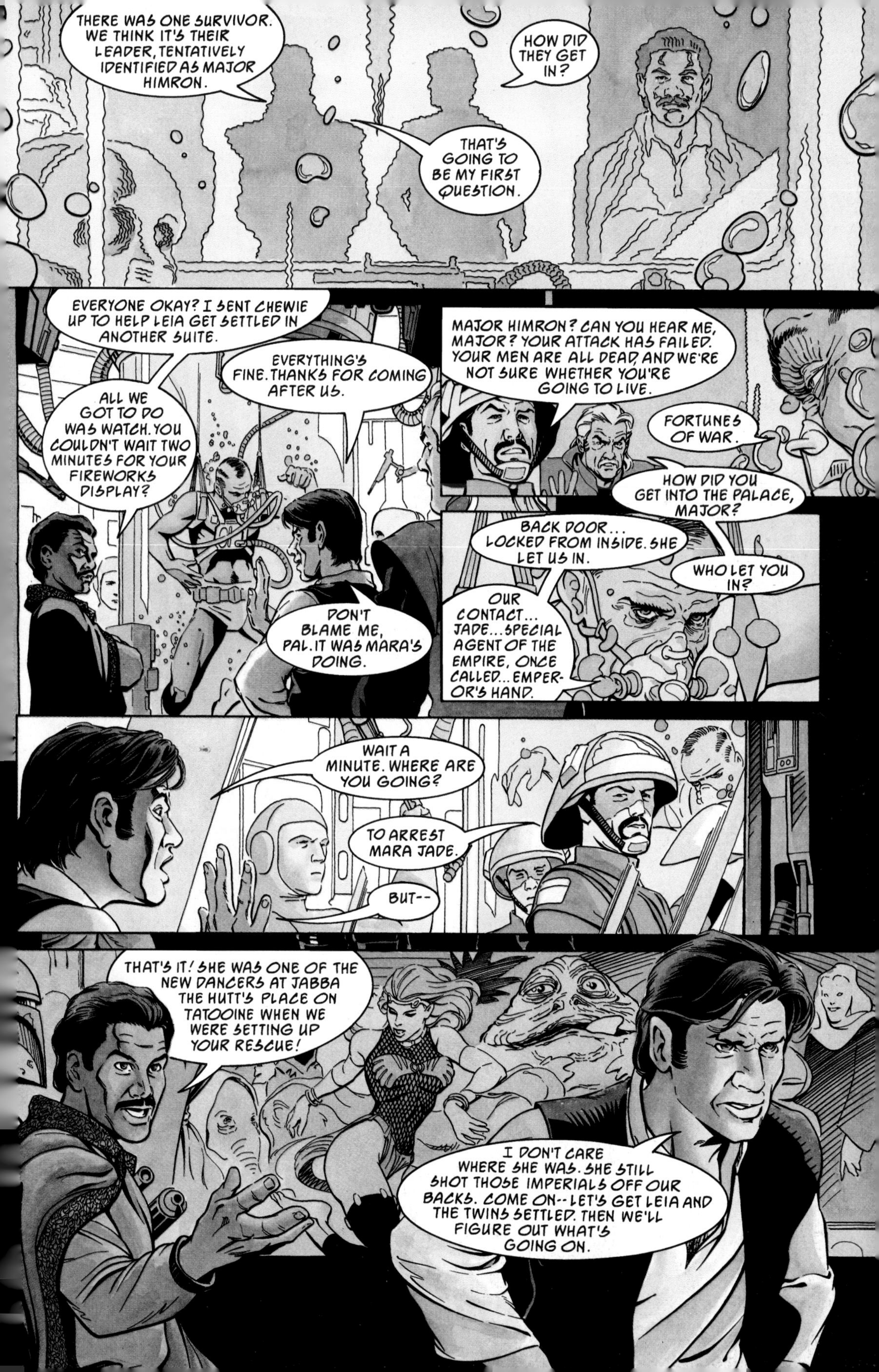
THERE WAS ONE SURVIVOR. WE THINK IT'S THEIR LEADER, TENTATIVELY IDENTIFIED AS MAJOR HIMRON.
HOW DID THEY GET IN?
THAT'S GOING TO BE MY FIRST QUESTION.
EVERYONE OKAY? I SENT CHEWIE UP TO HELP LEIA GET SETTLED IN ANOTHER SUITE.
EVERYTHING'S FINE. THANKS FOR COMING AFTER US.
ALL WE GOT TO DO WAS WATCH. YOU COULDN'T WAIT TWO MINUTES FOR YOUR FIREWORKS DISPLAY?
DON'T BLAME ME, PAL. IT WAS MARA'S DOING.
MAJOR HIMRON? CAN YOU HEAR ME, MAJOR? YOUR ATTACK HAS FAILED. YOUR MEN ARE ALL DEAD, AND WE'RE NOT SURE WHETHER YOU'RE GOING TO LIVE.
FORTUNES OF WAR.
HOW DID YOU GET INTO THE PALACE, MAJOR?
BACK DOOR... LOCKED FROM INSIDE. SHE LET US IN.
WHO LET YOU IN?
OUR CONTACT... JADE... SPECIAL AGENT OF THE EMPIRE, ONCE CALLED... EMPEROR'S HAND.
WAIT A MINUTE. WHERE ARE YOU GOING?
TO ARREST MARA JADE.
BUT--
THAT'S IT! SHE WAS ONE OF THE NEW DANCERS AT JABBA THE HUTT'S PLACE ON TATOOINE WHEN WE WERE SETTING UP YOUR RESCUE!
I DON'T CARE WHERE SHE WAS. SHE STILL SHOT THOSE IMPERIALS OFF OUR BACKS. COME ON-- LET'S GET LEIA AND THE TWINS SETTLED. THEN WE'LL FIGURE OUT WHAT'S GOING ON.

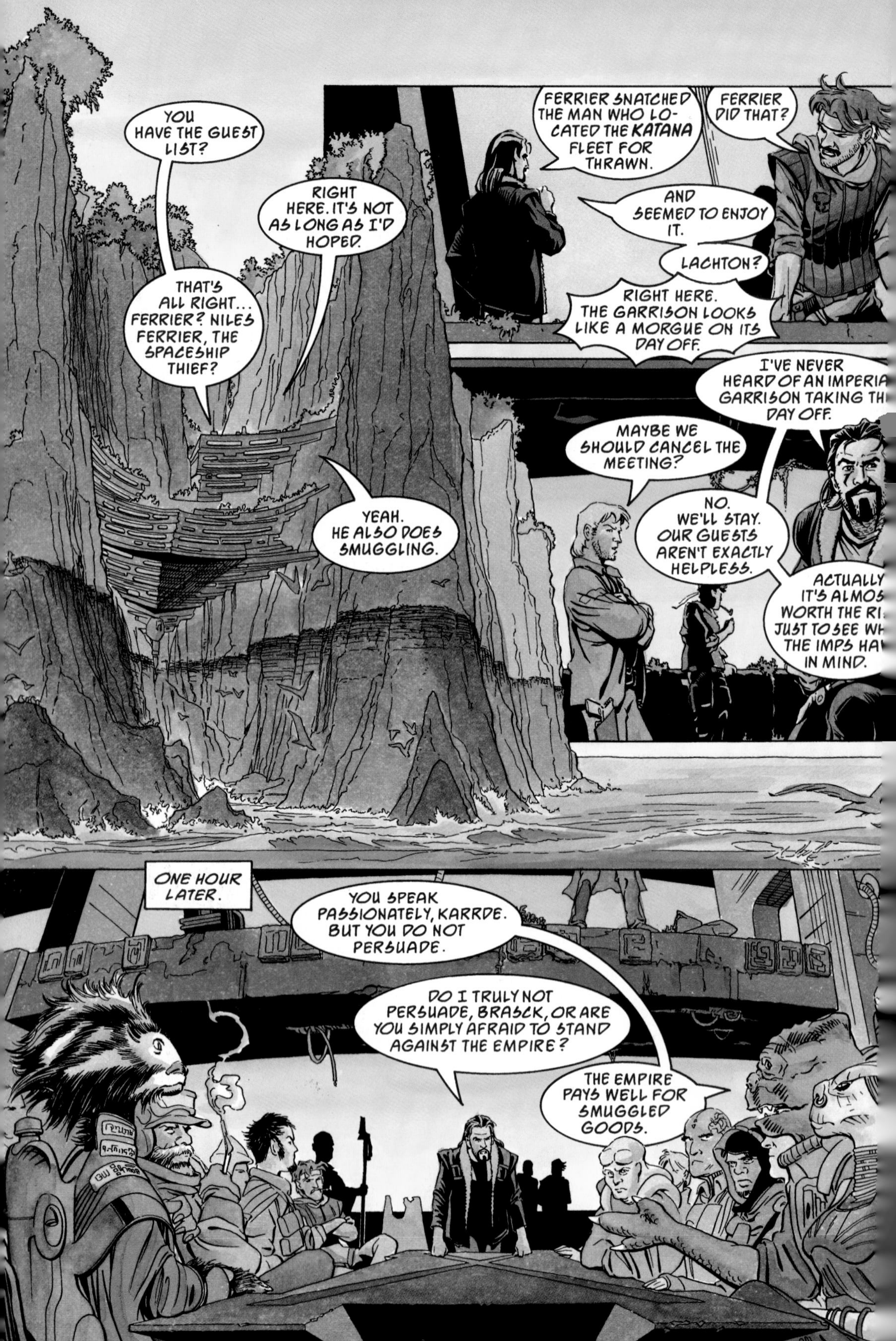
YOU HAVE THE GUEST LIST?
RIGHT HERE. IT'S NOT AS LONG AS I'D HOPED.
THAT'S ALL RIGHT... FERRIER? NILES FERRIER, THE SPACESHIP THIEF?
YEAH. HE ALSO DOES SMUGGLING.
FERRIER SNATCHED THE MAN WHO LOCATED THE KATANA FLEET FOR THRAWN.
FERRIER DID THAT?
AND SEEMED TO ENJOY IT.
LACHTON?
RIGHT HERE. THE GARRISON LOOKS LIKE A MORGUE ON ITS DAY OFF.
I'VE NEVER HEARD OF AN IMPERIA GARRISON TAKING TH DAY OFF.
MAYBE WE SHOULD CANCEL THE MEETING?
NO. WE'LL STAY. OUR GUESTS AREN'T EXACTLY HELPLESS.
ACTUALLY IT'S ALMOS WORTH THE RI JUST TO SEE WH THE IMPS HA IN MIND.
ONE HOUR LATER.
YOU SPEAK PASSIONATELY, KARRDE. BUT YOU DO NOT PERSUADE.
DO I TRULY NOT PERSUADE, BRASCK, OR ARE YOU SIMPLY AFRAID TO STAND AGAINST THE EMPIRE?
THE EMPIRE PAYS WELL FOR SMUGGLED GOODS.

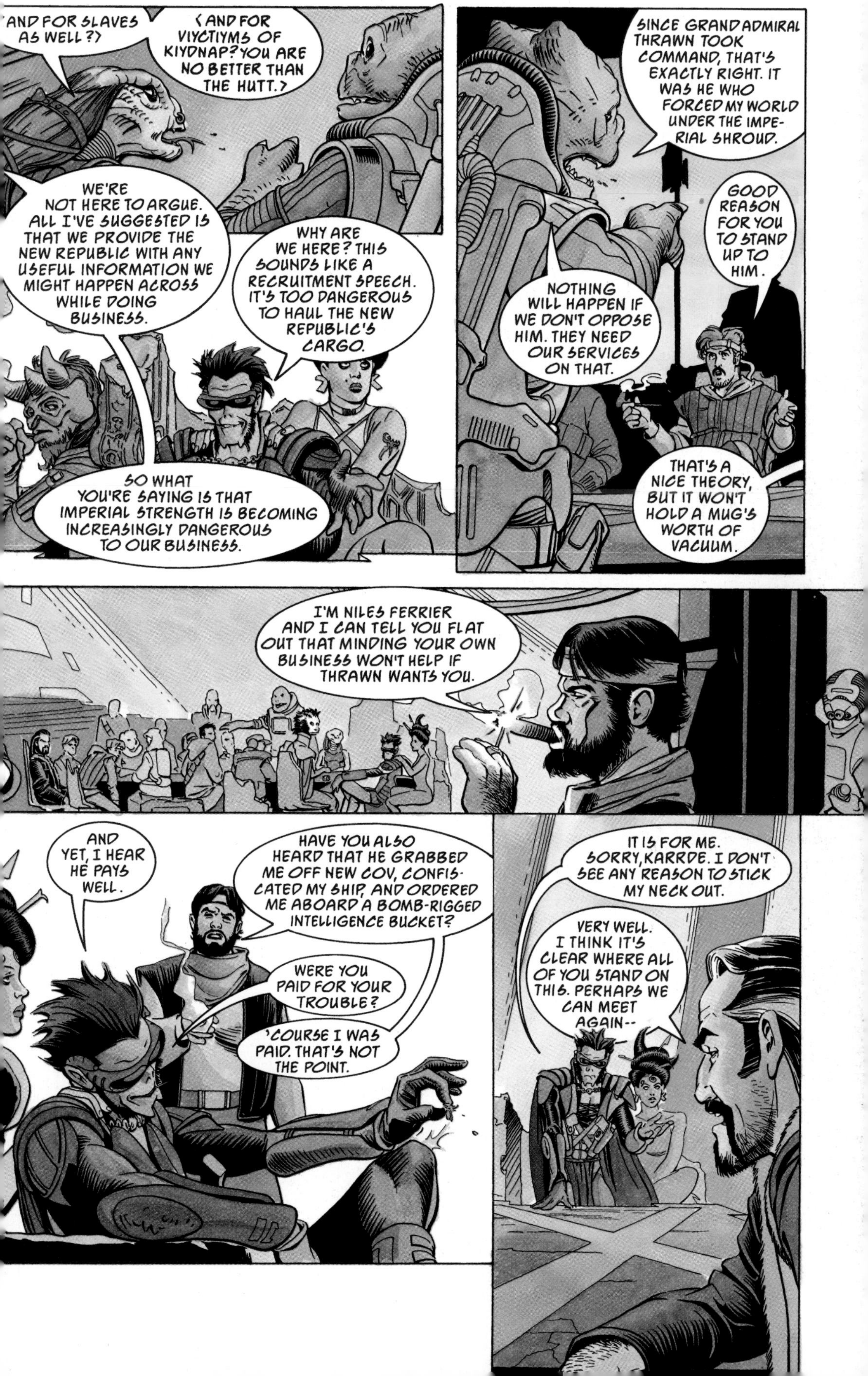

<AND FOR SLAVES AS WELL?>
<AND FOR VIYCTIYMS OF KIYDNAP? YOU ARE NO BETTER THAN THE HUTT.>
WE'RE NOT HERE TO ARGUE. ALL I'VE SUGGESTED IS THAT WE PROVIDE THE NEW REPUBLIC WITH ANY USEFUL INFORMATION WE MIGHT HAPPEN ACROSS WHILE DOING BUSINESS.
WHY ARE WE HERE? THIS SOUNDS LIKE A RECRUITMENT SPEECH. IT'S TOO DANGEROUS TO HAUL THE NEW REPUBLIC'S CARGO.
SO WHAT YOU'RE SAYING IS THAT IMPERIAL STRENGTH IS BECOMING INCREASINGLY DANGEROUS TO OUR BUSINESS.
SINCE GRAND ADMIRAL THRAWN TOOK COMMAND, THAT'S EXACTLY RIGHT. IT WAS HE WHO FORCED MY WORLD UNDER THE IMPERIAL SHROUD.
GOOD REASON FOR YOU TO STAND UP TO HIM.
NOTHING WILL HAPPEN IF WE DON'T OPPOSE HIM. THEY NEED OUR SERVICES ON THAT.
THAT'S A NICE THEORY, BUT IT WON'T HOLD A MUG'S WORTH OF VACUUM.
I'M NILES FERRIER AND I CAN TELL YOU FLAT OUT THAT MINDING YOUR OWN BUSINESS WON'T HELP IF THRAWN WANTS YOU.
AND YET, I HEAR HE PAYS WELL.
HAVE YOU ALSO HEARD THAT HE GRABBED ME OFF NEW COV, CONFISCATED MY SHIP, AND ORDERED ME ABOARD A BOMB-RIGGED INTELLIGENCE BUCKET?
WERE YOU PAID FOR YOUR TROUBLE?
'COURSE I WAS PAID. THAT'S NOT THE POINT.
IT IS FOR ME. SORRY, KARRDE. I DON'T SEE ANY REASON TO STICK MY NECK OUT.
VERY WELL. I THINK IT'S CLEAR WHERE ALL OF YOU STAND ON THIS. PERHAPS WE CAN MEET AGAIN--

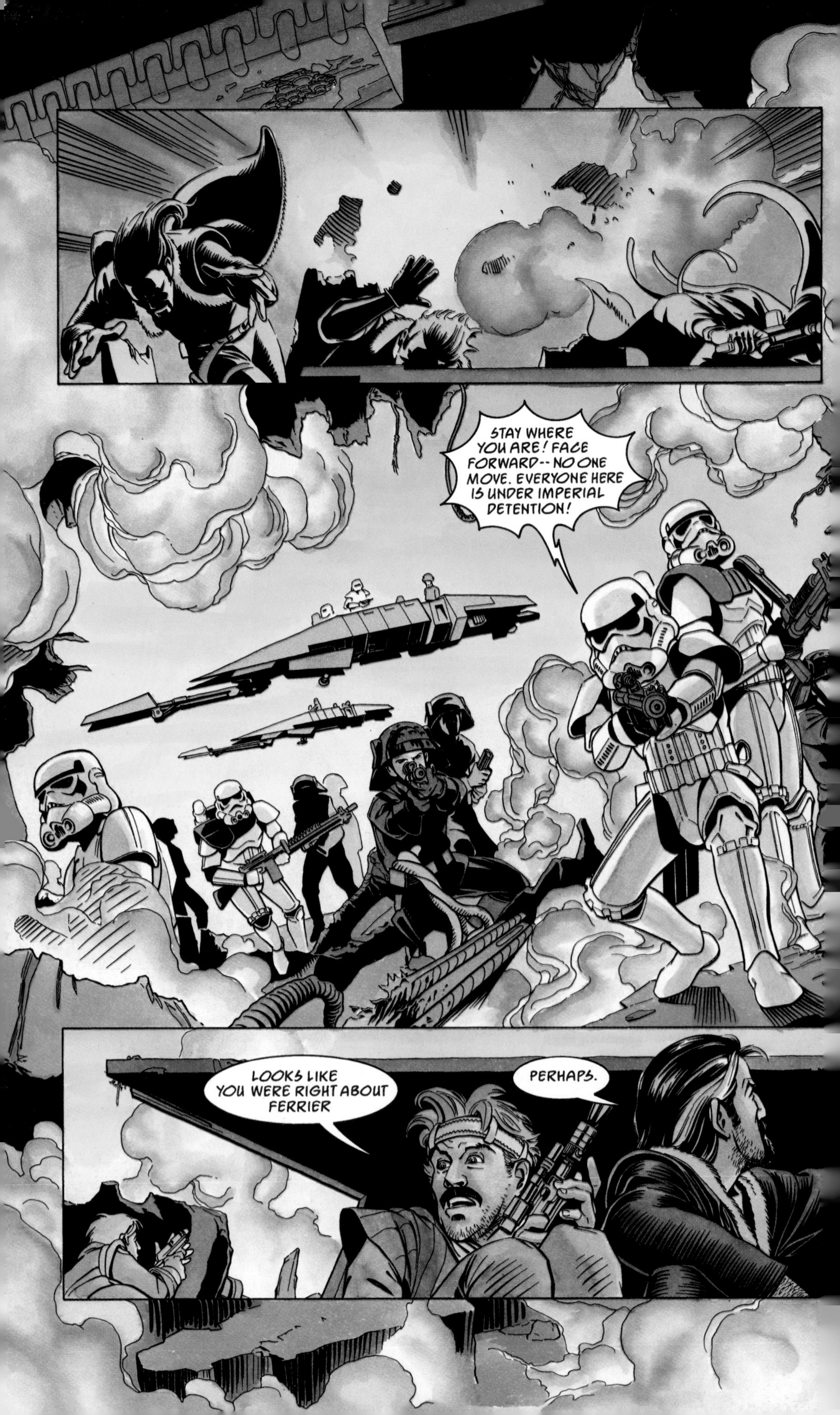
STAY WHERE YOU ARE! FACE FORWARD-- NO ONE MOVE. EVERYONE HERE IS UNDER IMPERIAL DETENTION!
LOOKS LIKE YOU WERE RIGHT ABOUT FERRIER
PERHAPS.

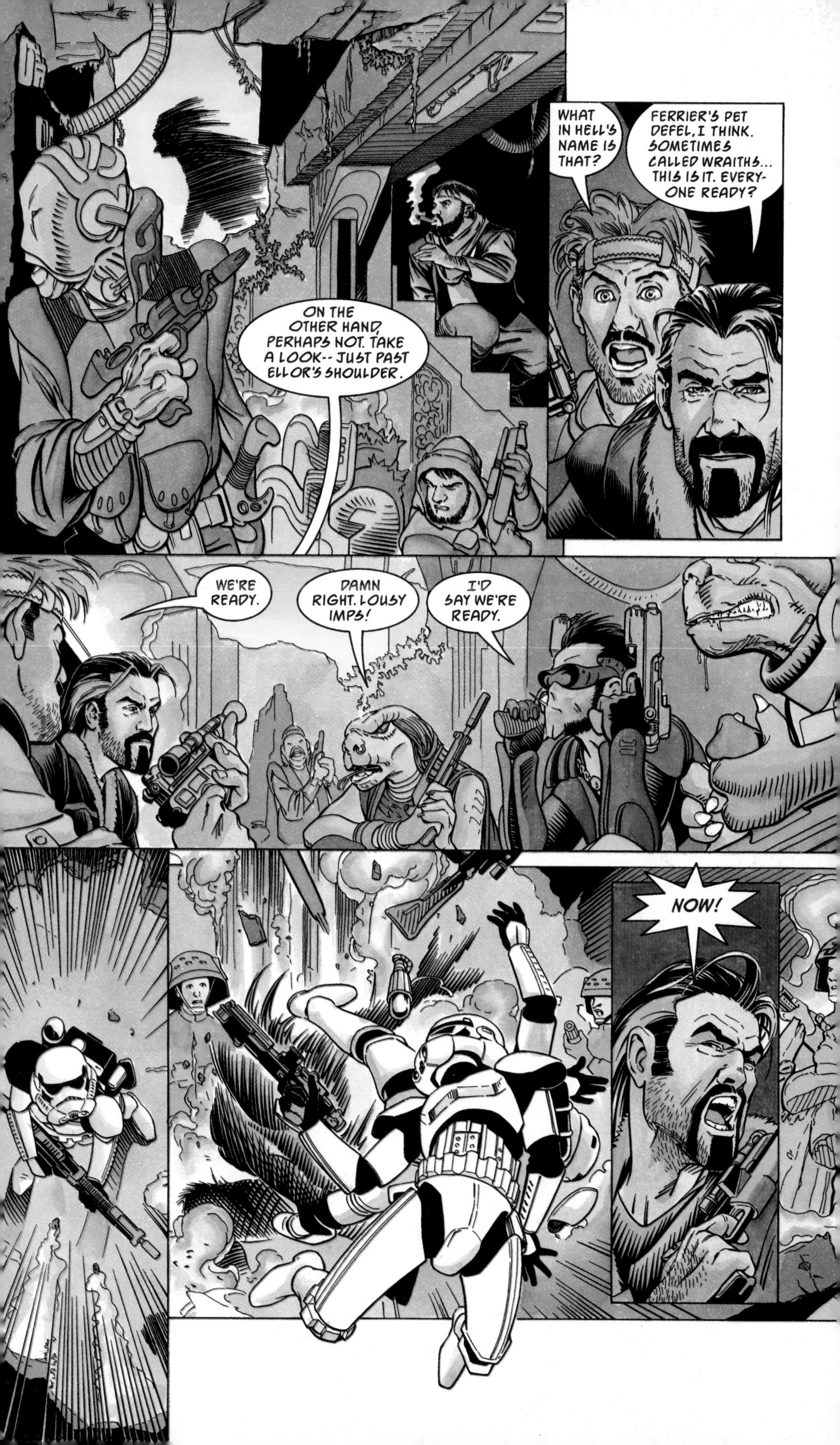
ON THE OTHER HAND, PERHAPS NOT. TAKE A LOOK-- JUST PAST ELLOR'S SHOULDER.
WHAT IN HELL'S NAME IS THAT?
FERRIER'S PET DEFEL, I THINK. SOMETIMES CALLED WRAITHS... THIS IS IT. EVERY-ONE READY?
WE'RE READY.
DAMN RIGHT. LOUSY IMPS!
I'D SAY WE'RE READY.
NOW!

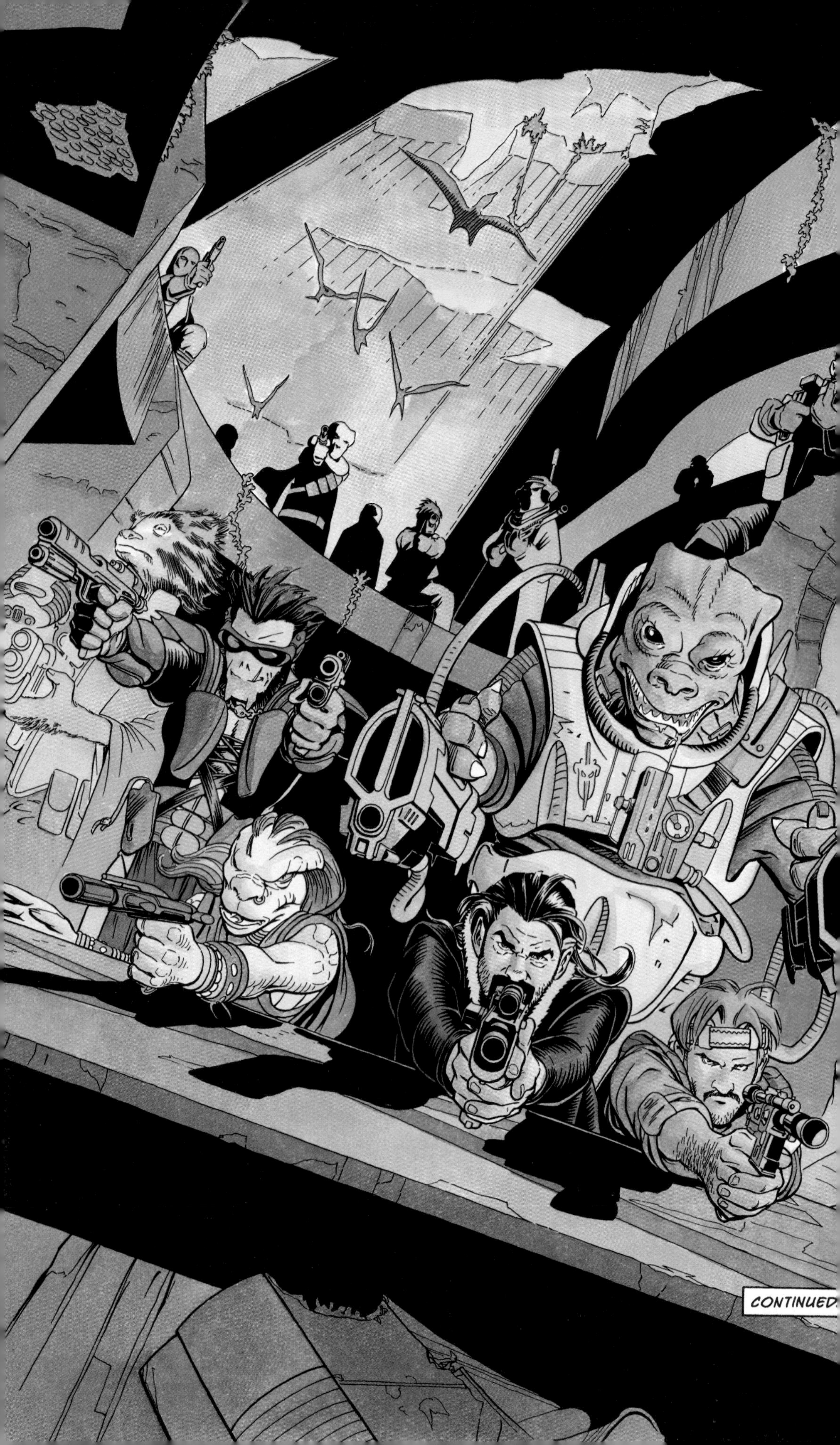
CONTINUED

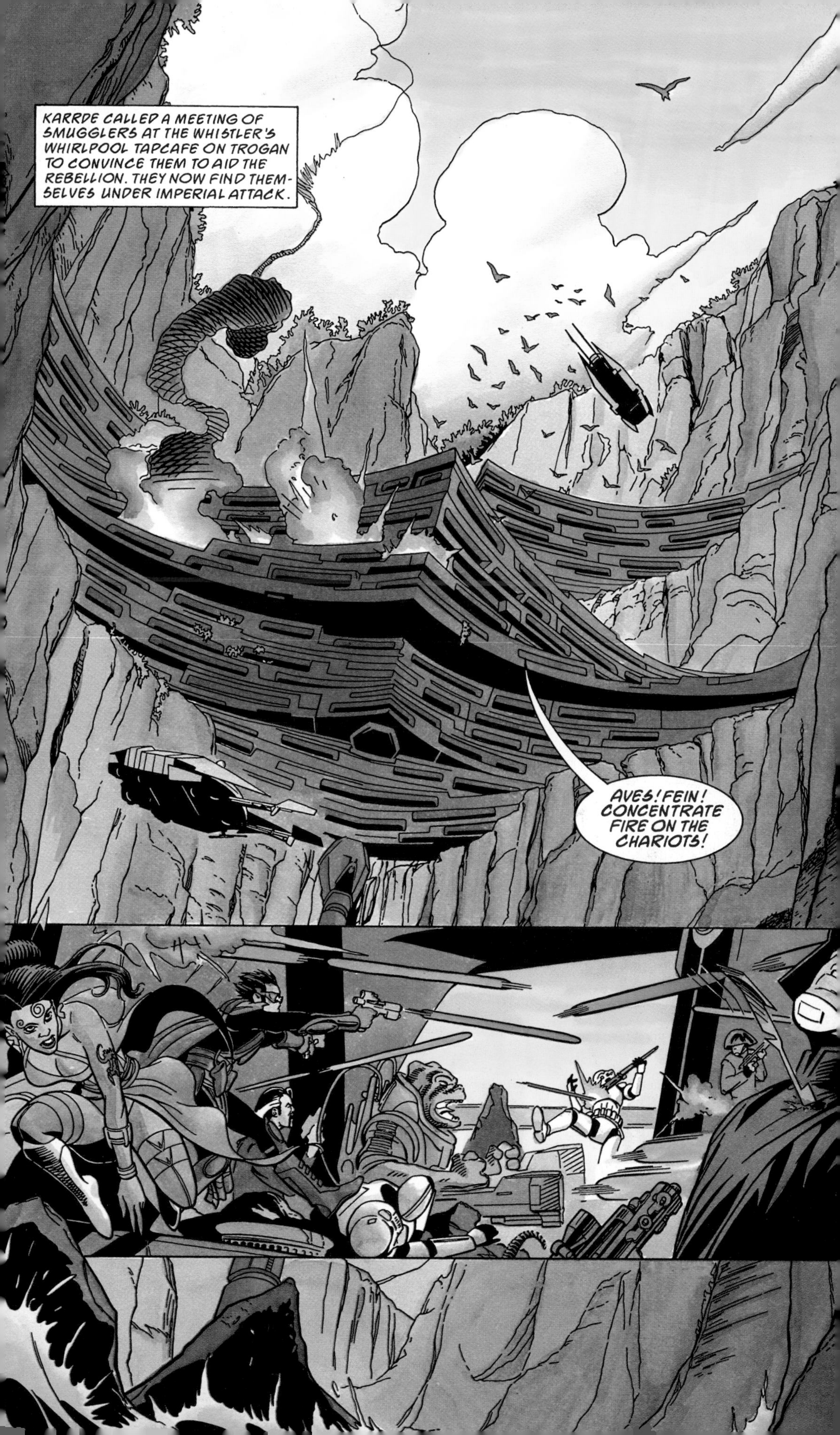
KARRDE CALLED A MEETING OF SMUGGLERS AT THE WHISTLER'S WHIRLPOOL TAPCAFE ON TROGAN TO CONVINCE THEM TO AID THE REBELLION. THEY NOW FIND THEMSELVES UNDER IMPERIAL ATTACK.
AVES! FEIN! CONCENTRATE FIRE ON THE CHARIOTS!

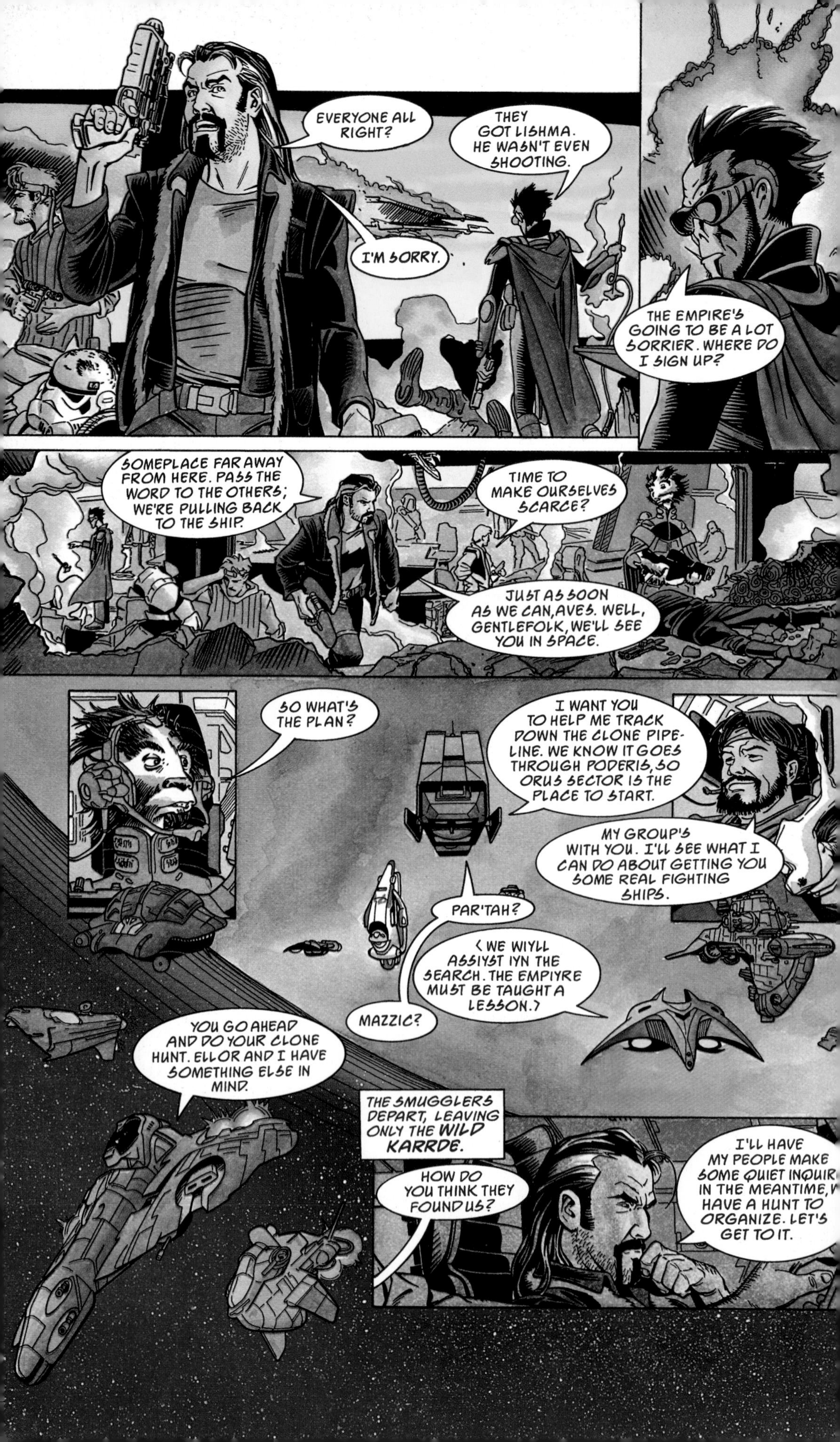
EVERYONE ALL RIGHT?
THEY GOT LISHMA. HE WASN'T EVEN SHOOTING.
I'M SORRY.
THE EMPIRE'S GOING TO BE A LOT SORRIER. WHERE DO I SIGN UP?
SOMEPLACE FAR AWAY FROM HERE. PASS THE WORD TO THE OTHERS; WE'RE PULLING BACK TO THE SHIP.
TIME TO MAKE OURSELVES SCARCE?
JUST AS SOON AS WE CAN, AVES. WELL, GENTLEFOLK, WE'LL SEE YOU IN SPACE.
SO WHAT'S THE PLAN?
I WANT YOU TO HELP ME TRACK DOWN THE CLONE PIPE-LINE. WE KNOW IT GOES THROUGH PODERIS, SO ORUS SECTOR IS THE PLACE TO START.
MY GROUP'S WITH YOU. I'LL SEE WHAT I CAN DO ABOUT GETTING YOU SOME REAL FIGHTING SHIPS.
PAR'TAH?
< WE WIYLL ASSIYST IYN THE SEARCH. THE EMPIYRE MUST BE TAUGHT A LESSON. >
MAZZIC?
YOU GO AHEAD AND DO YOUR CLONE HUNT. ELLOR AND I HAVE SOMETHING ELSE IN MIND.
THE SMUGGLERS DEPART, LEAVING ONLY THE WILD KARRDE.
HOW DO YOU THINK THEY FOUND US?
I'LL HAVE MY PEOPLE MAKE SOME QUIET INQUIR IN THE MEANTIME, W HAVE A HUNT TO ORGANIZE. LET'S GET TO IT.

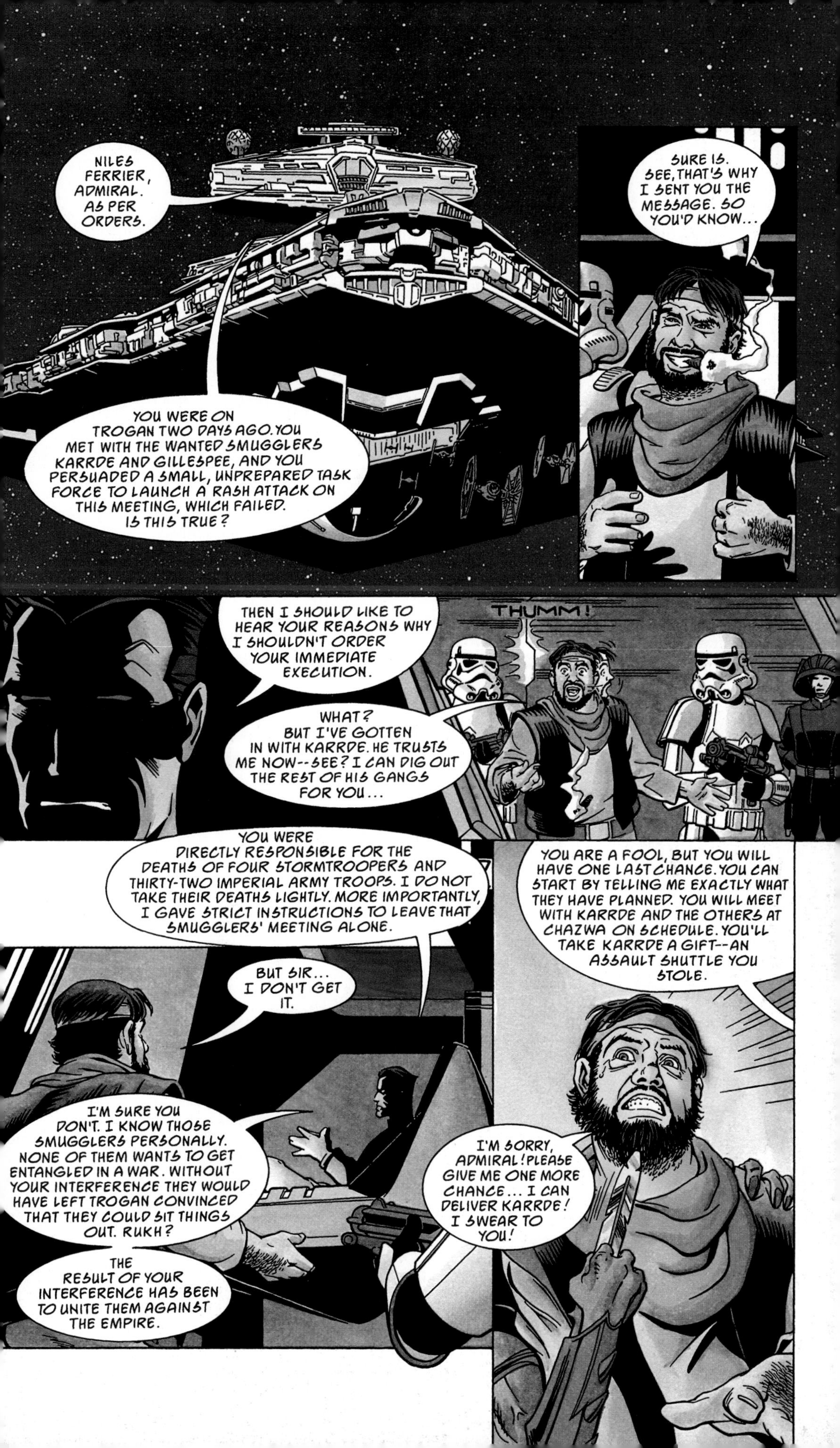
NILES FERRIER, ADMIRAL. AS PER ORDERS.
SURE IS. SEE, THAT'S WHY I SENT YOU THE MESSAGE. SO YOU'D KNOW...
YOU WERE ON TROGAN TWO DAYS AGO. YOU MET WITH THE WANTED SMUGGLERS KARRDE AND GILLESPEE, AND YOU PERSUADED A SMALL, UNPREPARED TASK FORCE TO LAUNCH A RASH ATTACK ON THIS MEETING, WHICH FAILED. IS THIS TRUE?
THEN I SHOULD LIKE TO HEAR YOUR REASONS WHY I SHOULDN'T ORDER YOUR IMMEDIATE EXECUTION.
THUMM!
WHAT? BUT I'VE GOTTEN IN WITH KARRDE. HE TRUSTS ME NOW--SEE? I CAN DIG OUT THE REST OF HIS GANGS FOR YOU...
YOU WERE DIRECTLY RESPONSIBLE FOR THE DEATHS OF FOUR STORMTROOPERS AND THIRTY-TWO IMPERIAL ARMY TROOPS. I DO NOT TAKE THEIR DEATHS LIGHTLY. MORE IMPORTANTLY, I GAVE STRICT INSTRUCTIONS TO LEAVE THAT SMUGGLERS' MEETING ALONE.
BUT SIR... I DON'T GET IT.
I'M SURE YOU DON'T. I KNOW THOSE SMUGGLERS PERSONALLY. NONE OF THEM WANTS TO GET ENTANGLED IN A WAR. WITHOUT YOUR INTERFERENCE THEY WOULD HAVE LEFT TROGAN CONVINCED THAT THEY COULD SIT THINGS OUT. RUKH?
THE RESULT OF YOUR INTERFERENCE HAS BEEN TO UNITE THEM AGAINST THE EMPIRE.
YOU ARE A FOOL, BUT YOU WILL HAVE ONE LAST CHANCE. YOU CAN START BY TELLING ME EXACTLY WHAT THEY HAVE PLANNED. YOU WILL MEET WITH KARRDE AND THE OTHERS AT CHAZWA ON SCHEDULE. YOU'LL TAKE KARRDE A GIFT--AN ASSAULT SHUTTLE YOU STOLE.
I'M SORRY, ADMIRAL! PLEASE GIVE ME ONE MORE CHANCE... I CAN DELIVER KARRDE! I SWEAR TO YOU!

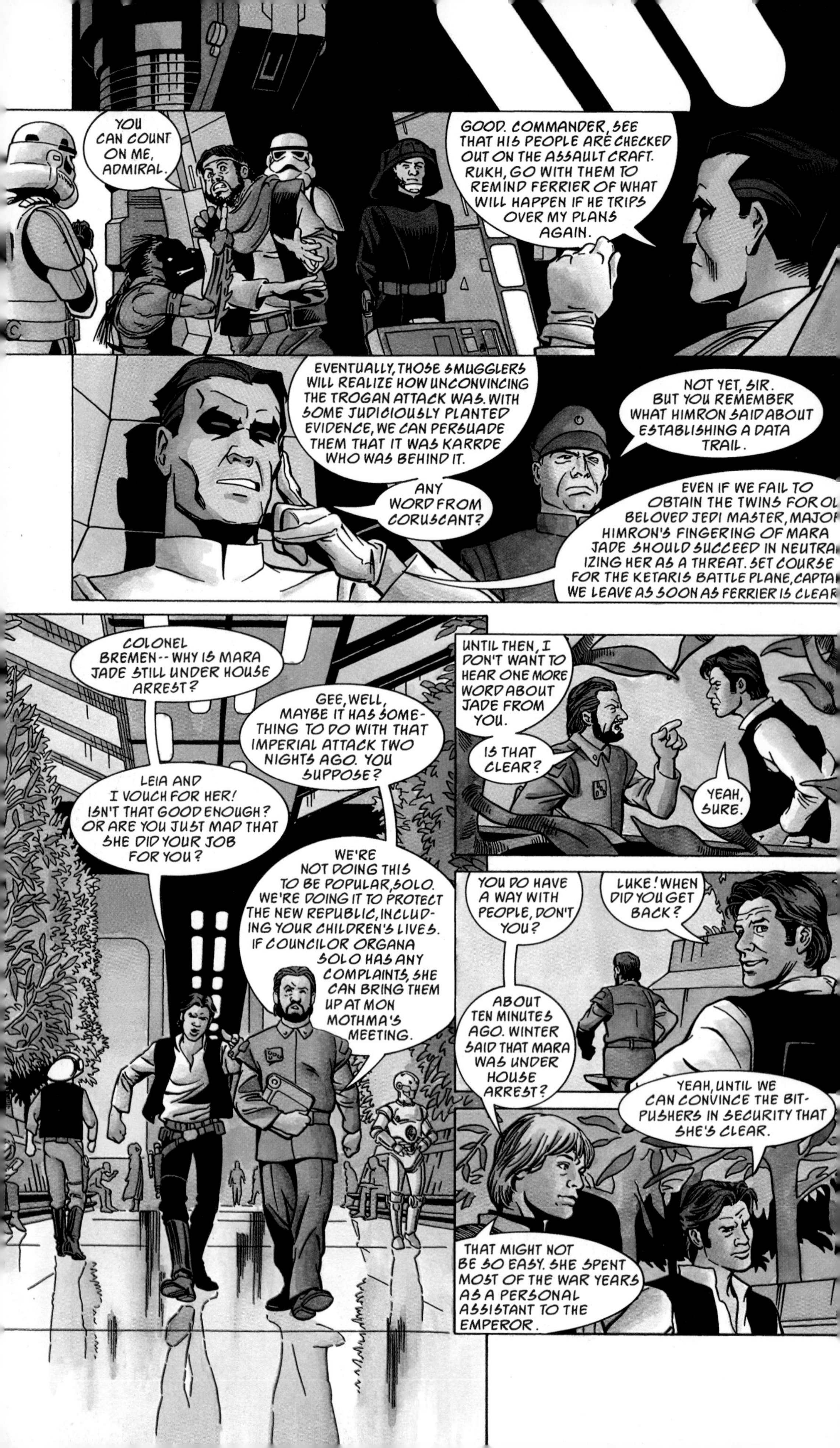
YOU CAN COUNT ON ME, ADMIRAL.
GOOD. COMMANDER, SEE THAT HIS PEOPLE ARE CHECKED OUT ON THE ASSAULT CRAFT. RUKH, GO WITH THEM TO REMIND FERRIER OF WHAT WILL HAPPEN IF HE TRIPS OVER MY PLANS AGAIN.
EVENTUALLY, THOSE SMUGGLERS WILL REALIZE HOW UNCONVINCING THE TROGAN ATTACK WAS. WITH SOME JUDICIOUSLY PLANTED EVIDENCE, WE CAN PERSUADE THEM THAT IT WAS KARRDE WHO WAS BEHIND IT.
ANY WORD FROM CORUSCANT?
NOT YET, SIR. BUT YOU REMEMBER WHAT HIMRON SAID ABOUT ESTABLISHING A DATA TRAIL.
EVEN IF WE FAIL TO OBTAIN THE TWINS FOR OU BELOVED JEDI MASTER, MAJOR HIMRON'S FINGERING OF MARA JADE SHOULD SUCCEED IN NEUTRA IZING HER AS A THREAT. SET COURSE FOR THE KETARIS BATTLE PLANE, CAPTA WE LEAVE AS SOON AS FERRIER IS CLEAR
COLONEL BREMEN-- WHY IS MARA JADE STILL UNDER HOUSE ARREST?
GEE, WELL, MAYBE IT HAS SOMETHING TO DO WITH THAT IMPERIAL ATTACK TWO NIGHTS AGO. YOU SUPPOSE?
LEIA AND I VOUCH FOR HER! ISN'T THAT GOOD ENOUGH? OR ARE YOU JUST MAD THAT SHE DID YOUR JOB FOR YOU?
WE'RE NOT DOING THIS TO BE POPULAR, SOLO. WE'RE DOING IT TO PROTECT THE NEW REPUBLIC, INCLUDING YOUR CHILDREN'S LIVES. IF COUNCILOR ORGANA SOLO HAS ANY COMPLAINTS, SHE CAN BRING THEM UP AT MON MOTHMA'S MEETING.
UNTIL THEN, I DON'T WANT TO HEAR ONE MORE WORD ABOUT JADE FROM YOU.
IS THAT CLEAR?
YEAH, SURE.
YOU DO HAVE A WAY WITH PEOPLE, DON'T YOU?
LUKE! WHEN DID YOU GET BACK?
ABOUT TEN MINUTES AGO. WINTER SAID THAT MARA WAS UNDER HOUSE ARREST?
YEAH, UNTIL WE CAN CONVINCE THE BIT-PUSHERS IN SECURITY THAT SHE'S CLEAR.
THAT MIGHT NOT BE SO EASY. SHE SPENT MOST OF THE WAR YEARS AS A PERSONAL ASSISTANT TO THE EMPEROR.

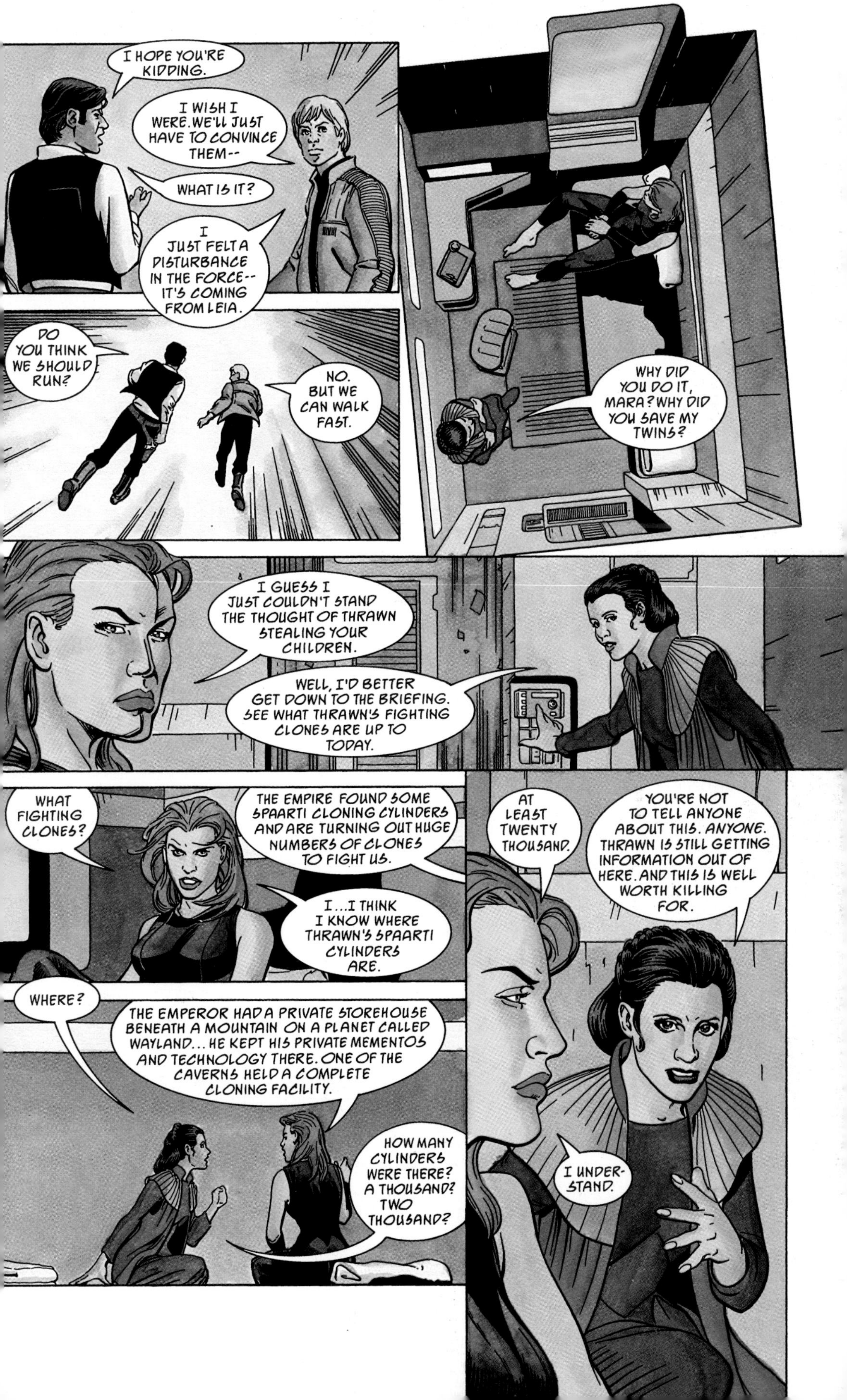
I HOPE YOU'RE KIDDING.
I WISH I WERE. WE'LL JUST HAVE TO CONVINCE THEM--
WHAT IS IT?
I JUST FELT A DISTURBANCE IN THE FORCE-- IT'S COMING FROM LEIA.
DO YOU THINK WE SHOULD RUN?
NO. BUT WE CAN WALK FAST.
WHY DID YOU DO IT, MARA? WHY DID YOU SAVE MY TWINS?
I GUESS I JUST COULDN'T STAND THE THOUGHT OF THRAWN STEALING YOUR CHILDREN.
WELL, I'D BETTER GET DOWN TO THE BRIEFING. SEE WHAT THRAWN'S FIGHTING CLONES ARE UP TO TODAY.
WHAT FIGHTING CLONES?
THE EMPIRE FOUND SOME SPAARTI CLONING CYLINDERS AND ARE TURNING OUT HUGE NUMBERS OF CLONES TO FIGHT US.
I...I THINK I KNOW WHERE THRAWN'S SPAARTI CYLINDERS ARE.
WHERE?
THE EMPEROR HAD A PRIVATE STOREHOUSE BENEATH A MOUNTAIN ON A PLANET CALLED WAYLAND... HE KEPT HIS PRIVATE MEMENTOS AND TECHNOLOGY THERE. ONE OF THE CAVERNS HELD A COMPLETE CLONING FACILITY.
HOW MANY CYLINDERS WERE THERE? A THOUSAND? TWO THOUSAND?
AT LEAST TWENTY THOUSAND.
YOU'RE NOT TO TELL ANYONE ABOUT THIS. ANYONE. THRAWN IS STILL GETTING INFORMATION OUT OF HERE. AND THIS IS WELL WORTH KILLING FOR.
I UNDER-STAND.

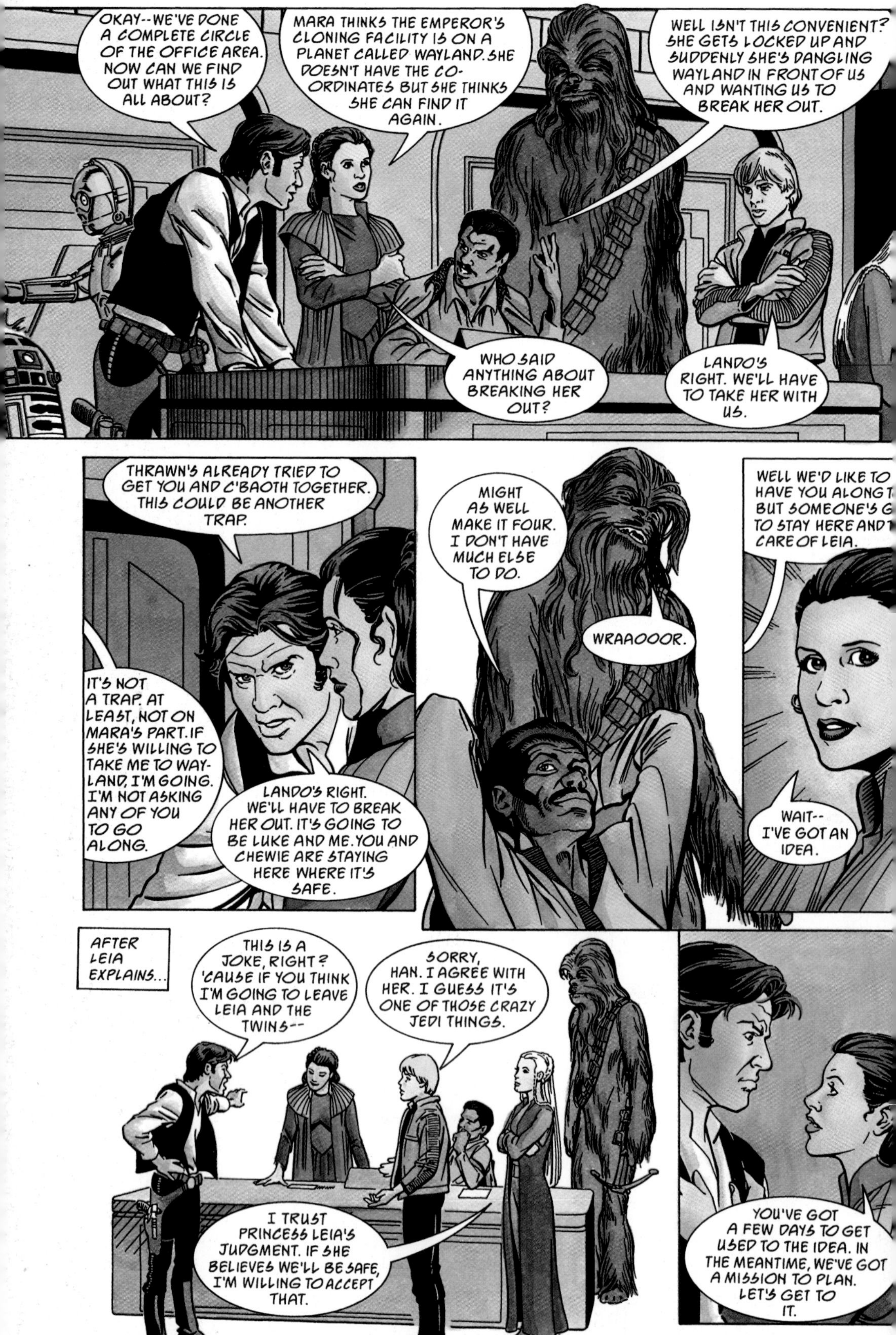
OKAY--WE'VE DONE A COMPLETE CIRCLE OF THE OFFICE AREA. NOW CAN WE FIND OUT WHAT THIS IS ALL ABOUT?
MARA THINKS THE EMPEROR'S CLONING FACILITY IS ON A PLANET CALLED WAYLAND. SHE DOESN'T HAVE THE CO-ORDINATES BUT SHE THINKS SHE CAN FIND IT AGAIN.
WELL ISN'T THIS CONVENIENT? SHE GETS LOCKED UP AND SUDDENLY SHE'S DANGLING WAYLAND IN FRONT OF US AND WANTING US TO BREAK HER OUT.
WHO SAID ANYTHING ABOUT BREAKING HER OUT?
LANDO'S RIGHT. WE'LL HAVE TO TAKE HER WITH US.
THRAWN'S ALREADY TRIED TO GET YOU AND C'BAOTH TOGETHER. THIS COULD BE ANOTHER TRAP.
IT'S NOT A TRAP. AT LEAST, NOT ON MARA'S PART. IF SHE'S WILLING TO TAKE ME TO WAYLAND, I'M GOING. I'M NOT ASKING ANY OF YOU TO GO ALONG.
LANDO'S RIGHT. WE'LL HAVE TO BREAK HER OUT. IT'S GOING TO BE LUKE AND ME. YOU AND CHEWIE ARE STAYING HERE WHERE IT'S SAFE.
MIGHT AS WELL MAKE IT FOUR. I DON'T HAVE MUCH ELSE TO DO.
WRAAOOOR.
WAIT-- I'VE GOT AN IDEA.
AFTER LEIA EXPLAINS...
THIS IS A JOKE, RIGHT? 'CAUSE IF YOU THINK I'M GOING TO LEAVE LEIA AND THE TWINS--
SORRY, HAN. I AGREE WITH HER. I GUESS IT'S ONE OF THOSE CRAZY JEDI THINGS.
I TRUST PRINCESS LEIA'S JUDGMENT. IF SHE BELIEVES WE'LL BE SAFE, I'M WILLING TO ACCEPT THAT.
YOU'VE GOT A FEW DAYS TO GET USED TO THE IDEA. IN THE MEANTIME, WE'VE GOT A MISSION TO PLAN. LET'S GET TO IT.

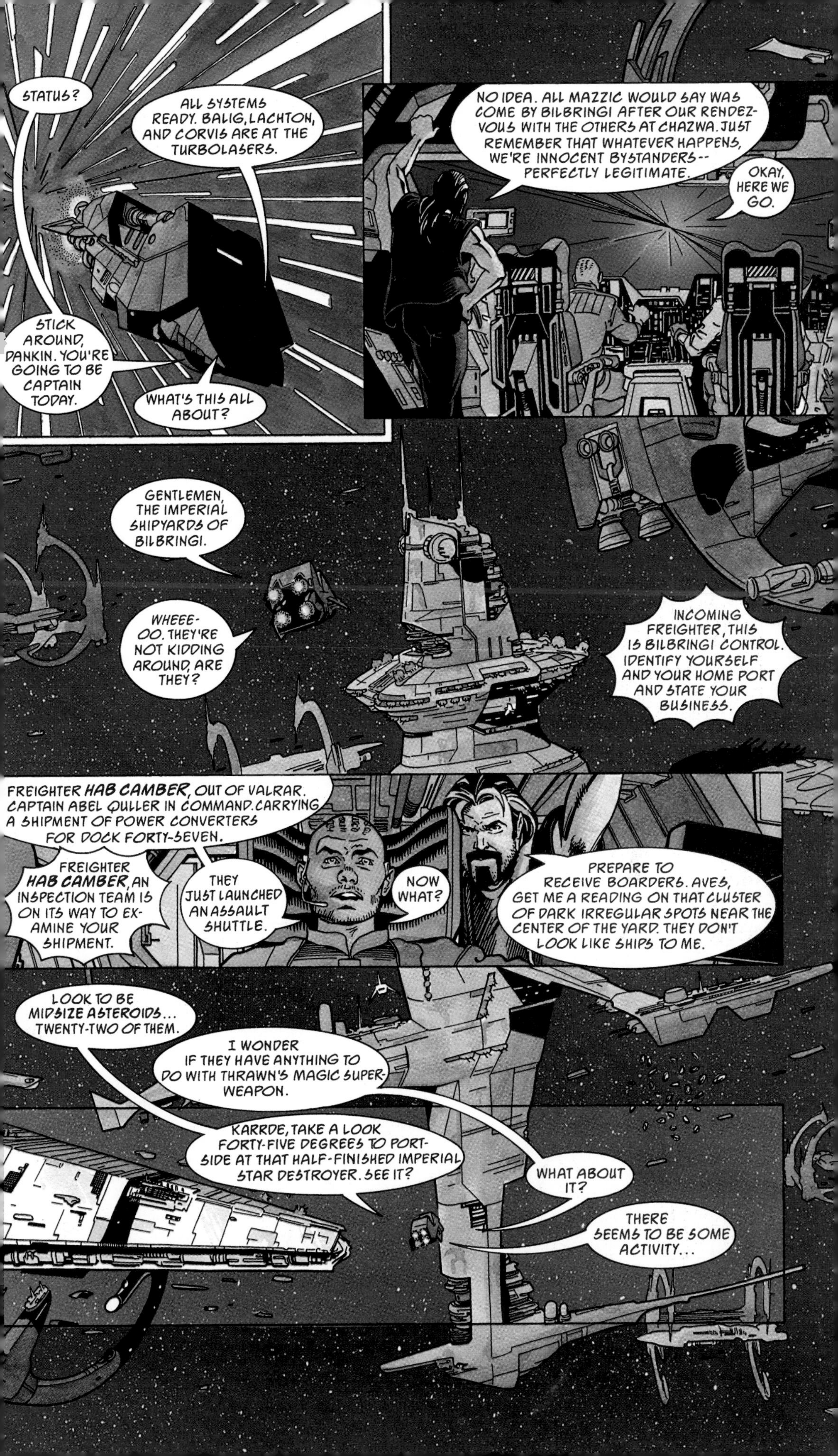
STATUS?
ALL SYSTEMS READY. BALIG, LACHTON, AND CORVIS ARE AT THE TURBOLASERS.
STICK AROUND, DANKIN. YOU'RE GOING TO BE CAPTAIN TODAY.
WHAT'S THIS ALL ABOUT?
NO IDEA. ALL MAZZIC WOULD SAY WAS COME BY BILBRINGI AFTER OUR RENDEZVOUS WITH THE OTHERS AT CHAZWA. JUST REMEMBER THAT WHATEVER HAPPENS, WE'RE INNOCENT BYSTANDERS -- PERFECTLY LEGITIMATE.
OKAY, HERE WE GO.
GENTLEMEN, THE IMPERIAL SHIPYARDS OF BILBRINGI.
WHEEE-OO. THEY'RE NOT KIDDING AROUND, ARE THEY?
INCOMING FREIGHTER, THIS IS BILBRINGI CONTROL. IDENTIFY YOURSELF AND YOUR HOME PORT AND STATE YOUR BUSINESS.
FREIGHTER HAB CAMBER, OUT OF VALRAR. CAPTAIN ABEL QULLER IN COMMAND. CARRYING A SHIPMENT OF POWER CONVERTERS FOR DOCK FORTY-SEVEN.
FREIGHTER HAB CAMBER, AN INSPECTION TEAM IS ON ITS WAY TO EXAMINE YOUR SHIPMENT.
THEY JUST LAUNCHED AN ASSAULT SHUTTLE.
NOW WHAT?
PREPARE TO RECEIVE BOARDERS. AVES, GET ME A READING ON THAT CLUSTER OF DARK IRREGULAR SPOTS NEAR THE CENTER OF THE YARD. THEY DON'T LOOK LIKE SHIPS TO ME.
LOOK TO BE MIDSIZE ASTEROIDS... TWENTY-TWO OF THEM.
I WONDER IF THEY HAVE ANYTHING TO DO WITH THRAWN'S MAGIC SUPER-WEAPON.
KARRDE, TAKE A LOOK FORTY-FIVE DEGREES TO PORTSIDE AT THAT HALF-FINISHED IMPERIAL STAR DESTROYER. SEE IT?
WHAT ABOUT IT?
THERE SEEMS TO BE SOME ACTIVITY...

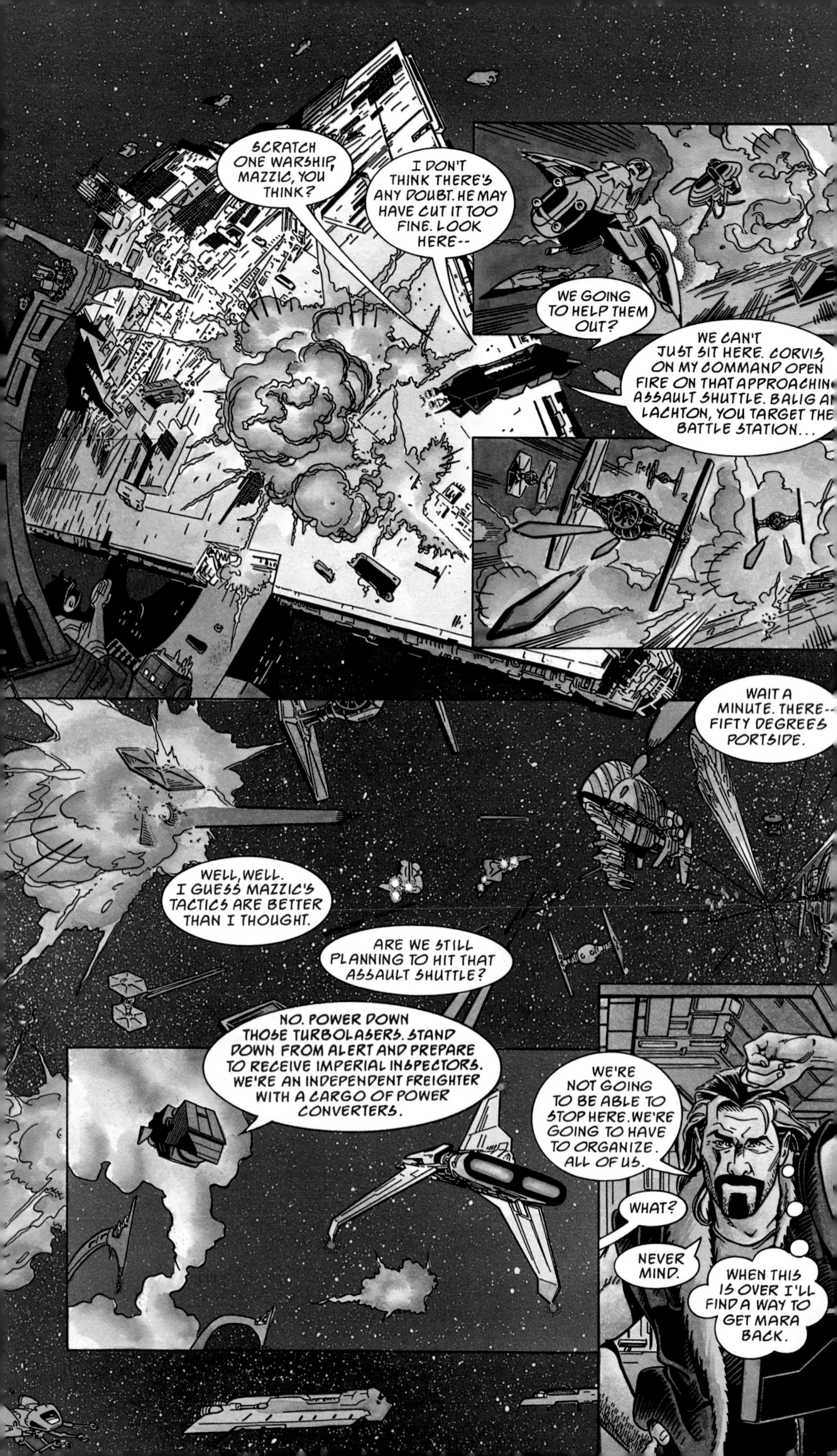
SCRATCH ONE WARSHIP, MAZZIC, YOU THINK?
I DON'T THINK THERE'S ANY DOUBT. HE MAY HAVE CUT IT TOO FINE. LOOK HERE--
WE GOING TO HELP THEM OUT?
WE CAN'T JUST SIT HERE. CORVIS, ON MY COMMAND OPEN FIRE ON THAT APPROACHIN ASSAULT SHUTTLE. BALIG AI LACHTON, YOU TARGET THE BATTLE STATION...
WAIT A MINUTE. THERE-- FIFTY DEGREES PORTSIDE.
WELL, WELL. I GUESS MAZZIC'S TACTICS ARE BETTER THAN I THOUGHT.
ARE WE STILL PLANNING TO HIT THAT ASSAULT SHUTTLE?
NO. POWER DOWN THOSE TURBOLASERS. STAND DOWN FROM ALERT AND PREPARE TO RECEIVE IMPERIAL INSPECTORS. WE'RE AN INDEPENDENT FREIGHTER WITH A CARGO OF POWER CONVERTERS.
WE'RE NOT GOING TO BE ABLE TO STOP HERE. WE'RE GOING TO HAVE TO ORGANIZE. ALL OF US.
WHAT?
NEVER MIND.
WHEN THIS IS OVER I'LL FIND A WAY TO GET MARA BACK.

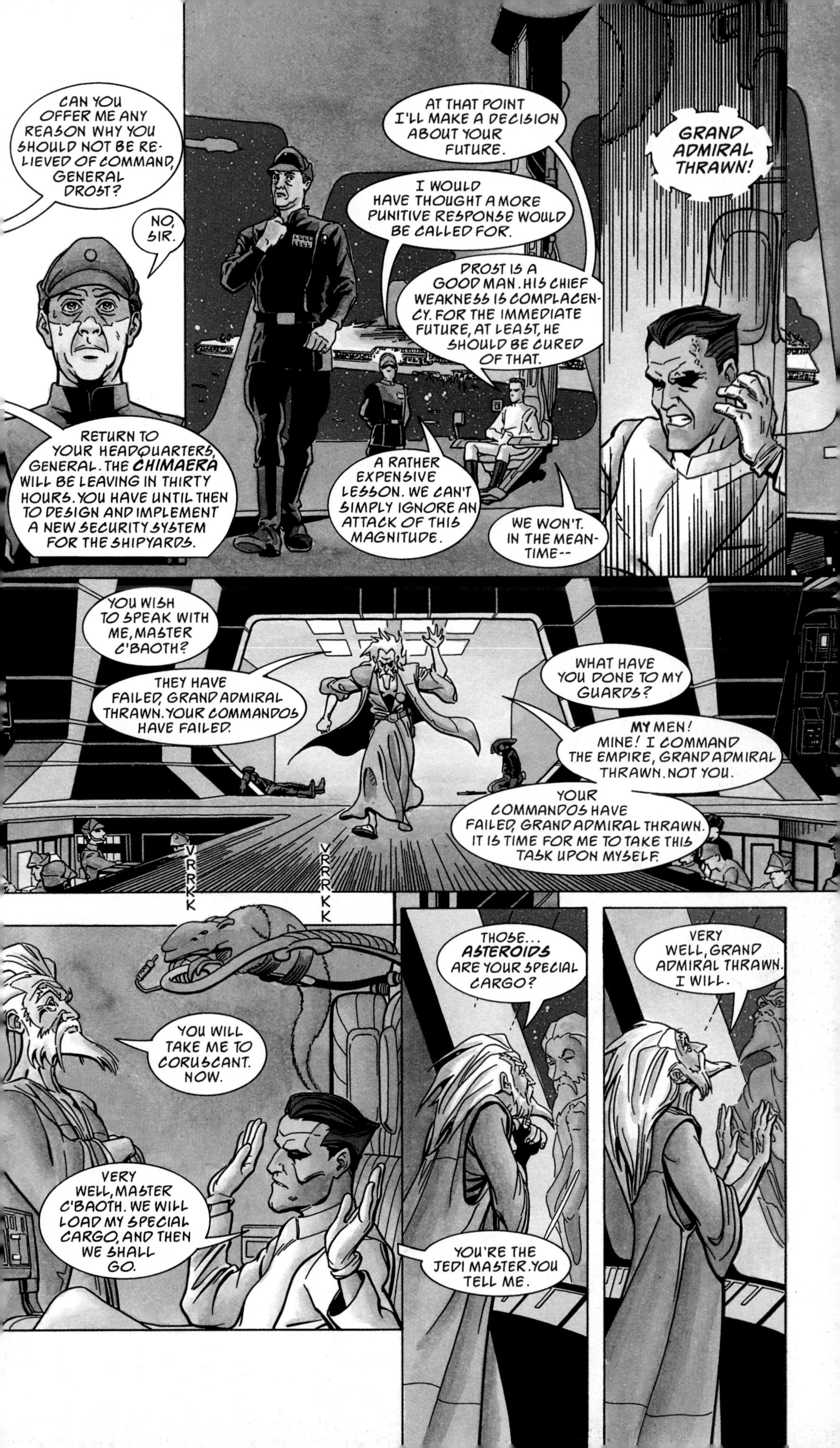
CAN YOU OFFER ME ANY REASON WHY YOU SHOULD NOT BE RELIEVED OF COMMAND, GENERAL DROST?
NO, SIR.
AT THAT POINT I'LL MAKE A DECISION ABOUT YOUR FUTURE.
I WOULD HAVE THOUGHT A MORE PUNITIVE RESPONSE WOULD BE CALLED FOR.
DROST IS A GOOD MAN. HIS CHIEF WEAKNESS IS COMPLACENCY. FOR THE IMMEDIATE FUTURE, AT LEAST, HE SHOULD BE CURED OF THAT.
GRAND ADMIRAL THRAWN!
RETURN TO YOUR HEADQUARTERS, GENERAL. THE CHIMAERA WILL BE LEAVING IN THIRTY HOURS. YOU HAVE UNTIL THEN TO DESIGN AND IMPLEMENT A NEW SECURITY SYSTEM FOR THE SHIPYARDS.
A RATHER EXPENSIVE LESSON. WE CAN'T SIMPLY IGNORE AN ATTACK OF THIS MAGNITUDE.
WE WON'T. IN THE MEANTIME--
YOU WISH TO SPEAK WITH ME, MASTER C'BAOTH?
THEY HAVE FAILED, GRAND ADMIRAL THRAWN. YOUR COMMANDOS HAVE FAILED.
WHAT HAVE YOU DONE TO MY GUARDS?
MY MEN! MINE! I COMMAND THE EMPIRE, GRAND ADMIRAL THRAWN. NOT YOU.
YOUR COMMANDOS HAVE FAILED, GRAND ADMIRAL THRAWN. IT IS TIME FOR ME TO TAKE THIS TASK UPON MYSELF.
VRRRKK
VRRRKK
YOU WILL TAKE ME TO CORUSCANT. NOW.
VERY WELL, MASTER C'BAOTH. WE WILL LOAD MY SPECIAL CARGO, AND THEN WE SHALL GO.
THOSE... ASTEROIDS ARE YOUR SPECIAL CARGO?
YOU'RE THE JEDI MASTER. YOU TELL ME.
VERY WELL, GRAND ADMIRAL THRAWN. I WILL.

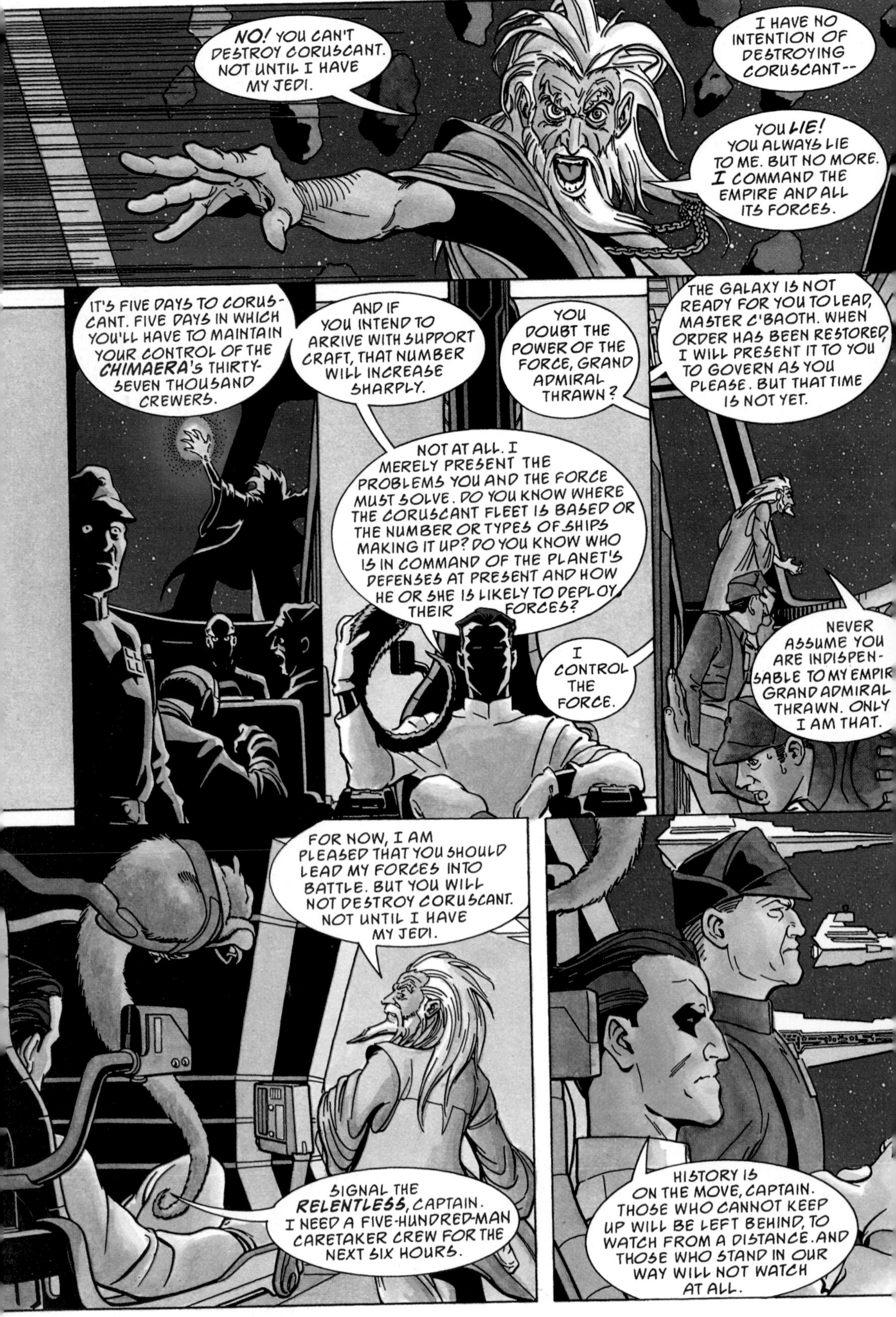
NO! YOU CAN'T DESTROY CORUSCANT. NOT UNTIL I HAVE MY JEDI.
I HAVE NO INTENTION OF DESTROYING CORUSCANT--
YOU LIE! YOU ALWAYS LIE TO ME. BUT NO MORE. I COMMAND THE EMPIRE AND ALL ITS FORCES.
IT'S FIVE DAYS TO CORUSCANT. FIVE DAYS IN WHICH YOU'LL HAVE TO MAINTAIN YOUR CONTROL OF THE CHIMAERA'S THIRTY-SEVEN THOUSAND CREWERS.
AND IF YOU INTEND TO ARRIVE WITH SUPPORT CRAFT, THAT NUMBER WILL INCREASE SHARPLY.
YOU DOUBT THE POWER OF THE FORCE, GRAND ADMIRAL THRAWN?
NOT AT ALL. I MERELY PRESENT THE PROBLEMS YOU AND THE FORCE MUST SOLVE. DO YOU KNOW WHERE THE CORUSCANT FLEET IS BASED OR THE NUMBER OR TYPES OF SHIPS MAKING IT UP? DO YOU KNOW WHO IS IN COMMAND OF THE PLANET'S DEFENSES AT PRESENT AND HOW HE OR SHE IS LIKELY TO DEPLOY THEIR FORCES?
I CONTROL THE FORCE.
THE GALAXY IS NOT READY FOR YOU TO LEAD, MASTER C'BAOTH. WHEN ORDER HAS BEEN RESTORED, I WILL PRESENT IT TO YOU TO GOVERN AS YOU PLEASE. BUT THAT TIME IS NOT YET.
NEVER ASSUME YOU ARE INDISPENSABLE TO MY EMPIRE, GRAND ADMIRAL THRAWN. ONLY I AM THAT.
FOR NOW, I AM PLEASED THAT YOU SHOULD LEAD MY FORCES INTO BATTLE. BUT YOU WILL NOT DESTROY CORUSCANT. NOT UNTIL I HAVE MY JEDI.
SIGNAL THE RELENTLESS, CAPTAIN. I NEED A FIVE-HUNDRED-MAN CARETAKER CREW FOR THE NEXT SIX HOURS.
HISTORY IS ON THE MOVE, CAPTAIN. THOSE WHO CANNOT KEEP UP WILL BE LEFT BEHIND, TO WATCH FROM A DISTANCE. AND THOSE WHO STAND IN OUR WAY WILL NOT WATCH AT ALL.

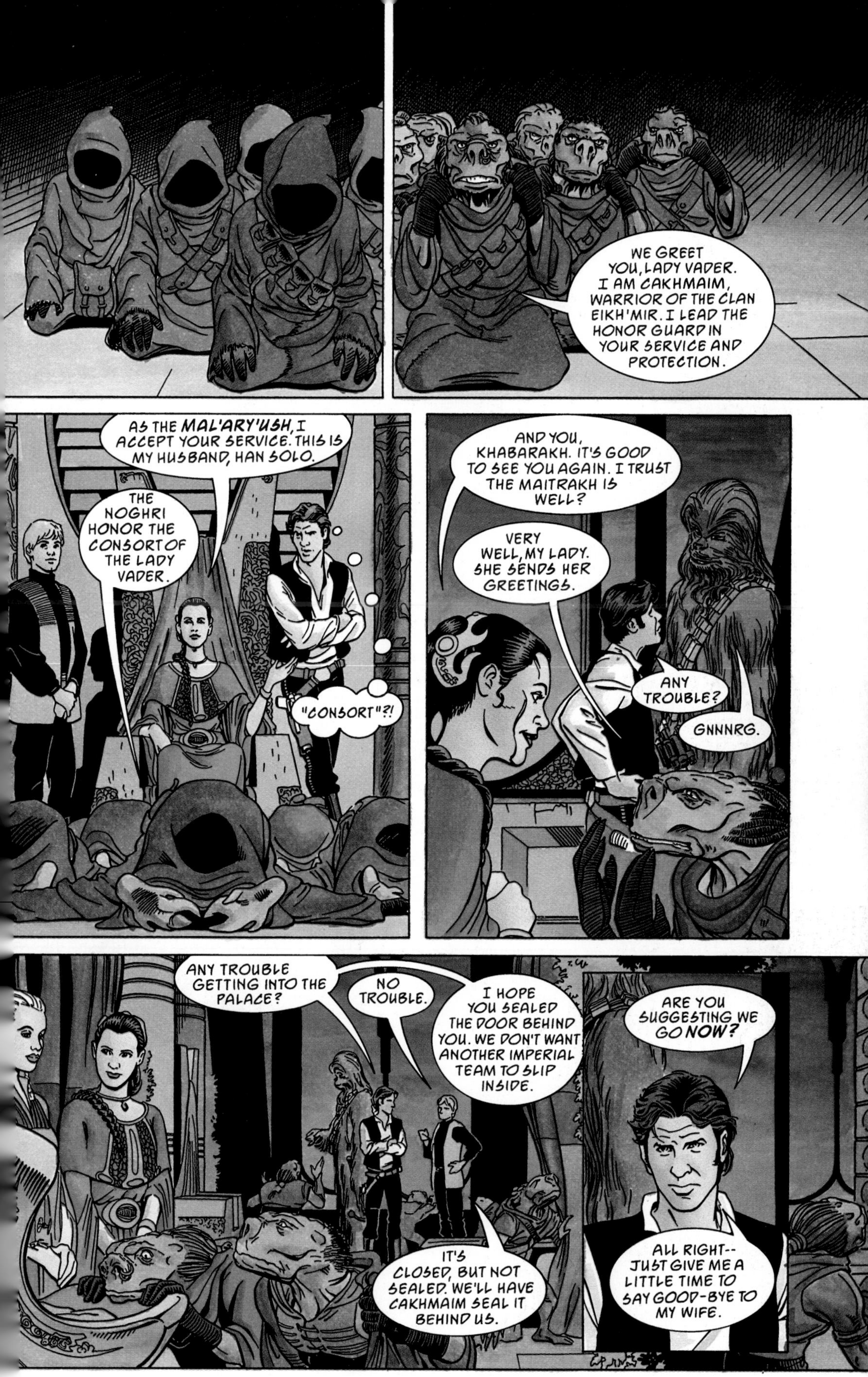

WE GREET YOU, LADY VADER. I AM CAKHMAIM, WARRIOR OF THE CLAN EIKH'MIR. I LEAD THE HONOR GUARD IN YOUR SERVICE AND PROTECTION.
AS THE MAL'ARY'USH, I ACCEPT YOUR SERVICE. THIS IS MY HUSBAND, HAN SOLO.
THE NOGHRI HONOR THE CONSORT OF THE LADY VADER.
"CONSORT"?!
AND YOU, KHABARAKH. IT'S GOOD TO SEE YOU AGAIN. I TRUST THE MAITRAKH IS WELL?
VERY WELL, MY LADY. SHE SENDS HER GREETINGS.
ANY TROUBLE?
GNNNRG.
ANY TROUBLE GETTING INTO THE PALACE?
NO TROUBLE.
I HOPE YOU SEALED THE DOOR BEHIND YOU. WE DON'T WANT ANOTHER IMPERIAL TEAM TO SLIP INSIDE.
IT'S CLOSED, BUT NOT SEALED. WE'LL HAVE CAKHMAIM SEAL IT BEHIND US.
ARE YOU SUGGESTING WE GO NOW?
ALL RIGHT-- JUST GIVE ME A LITTLE TIME TO SAY GOOD-BYE TO MY WIFE.

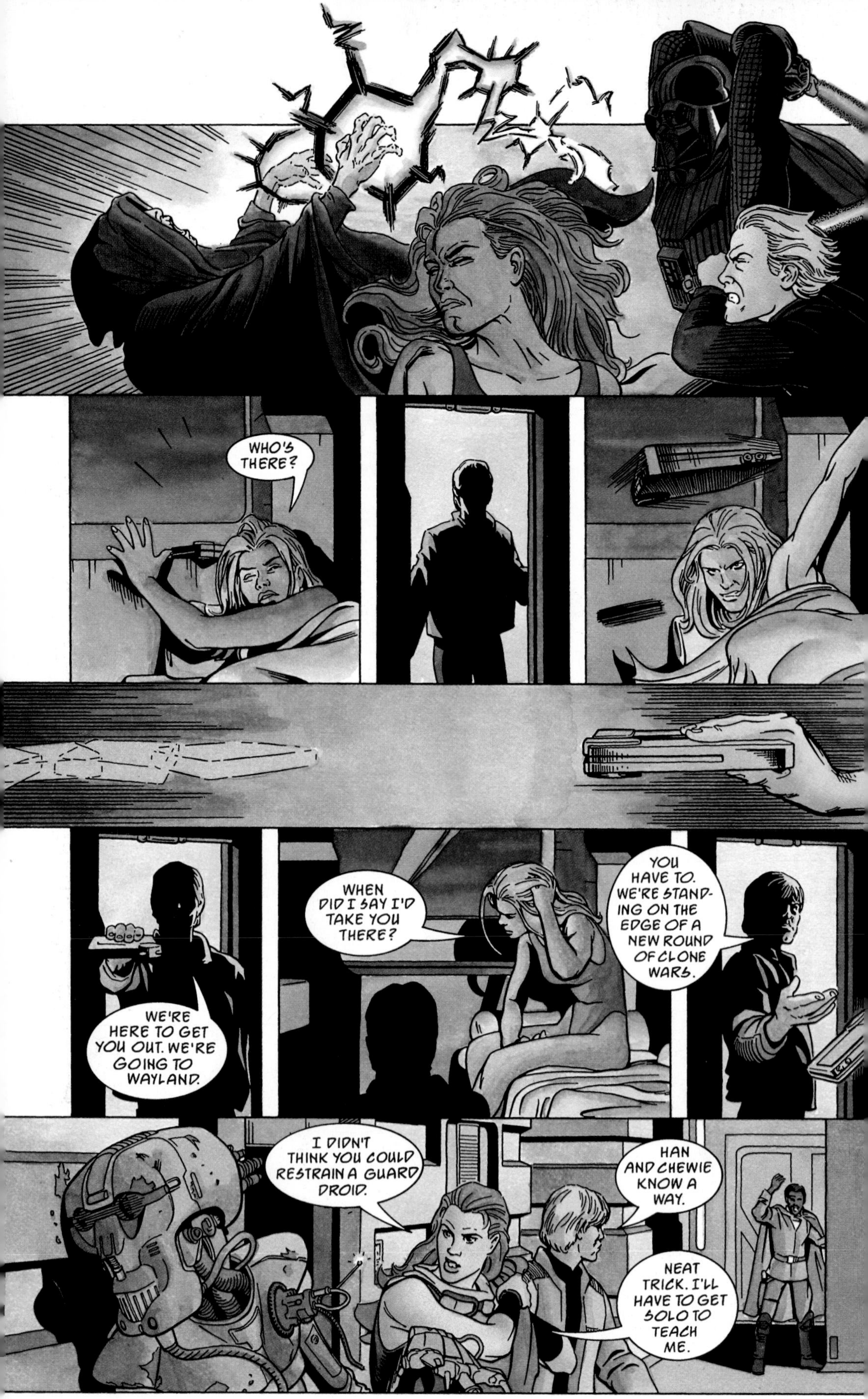
WHO'S THERE?
WHEN DID I SAY I'D TAKE YOU THERE?
WE'RE HERE TO GET YOU OUT. WE'RE GOING TO WAYLAND.
YOU HAVE TO. WE'RE STANDING ON THE EDGE OF A NEW ROUND OF CLONE WARS.
I DIDN'T THINK YOU COULD RESTRAIN A GUARD DROID.
HAN AND CHEWIE KNOW A WAY.
NEAT TRICK. I'LL HAVE TO GET SOLO TO TEACH ME.

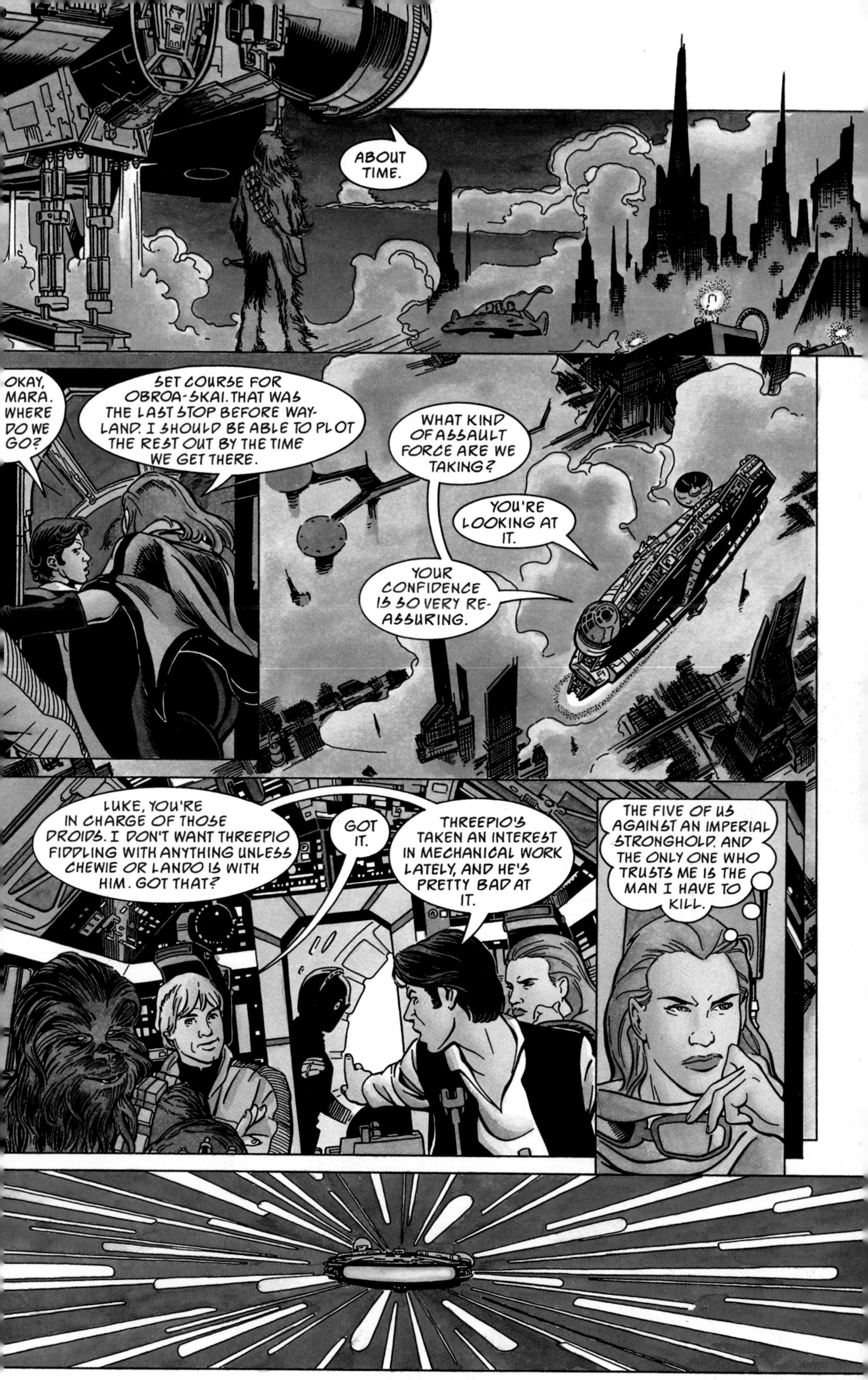
ABOUT TIME.
OKAY, MARA. WHERE DO WE GO?
SET COURSE FOR OBROA-SKAI. THAT WAS THE LAST STOP BEFORE WAY-LAND. I SHOULD BE ABLE TO PLOT THE REST OUT BY THE TIME WE GET THERE.
WHAT KIND OF ASSAULT FORCE ARE WE TAKING?
YOU'RE LOOKING AT IT.
YOUR CONFIDENCE IS SO VERY RE-ASSURING.
LUKE, YOU'RE IN CHARGE OF THOSE DROIDS. I DON'T WANT THREEPIO FIDDLING WITH ANYTHING UNLESS CHEWIE OR LANDO IS WITH HIM. GOT THAT?
GOT IT.
THREEPIO'S TAKEN AN INTEREST IN MECHANICAL WORK LATELY, AND HE'S PRETTY BAD AT IT.
THE FIVE OF US AGAINST AN IMPERIAL STRONGHOLD. AND THE ONLY ONE WHO TRUSTS ME IS THE MAN I HAVE TO KILL.

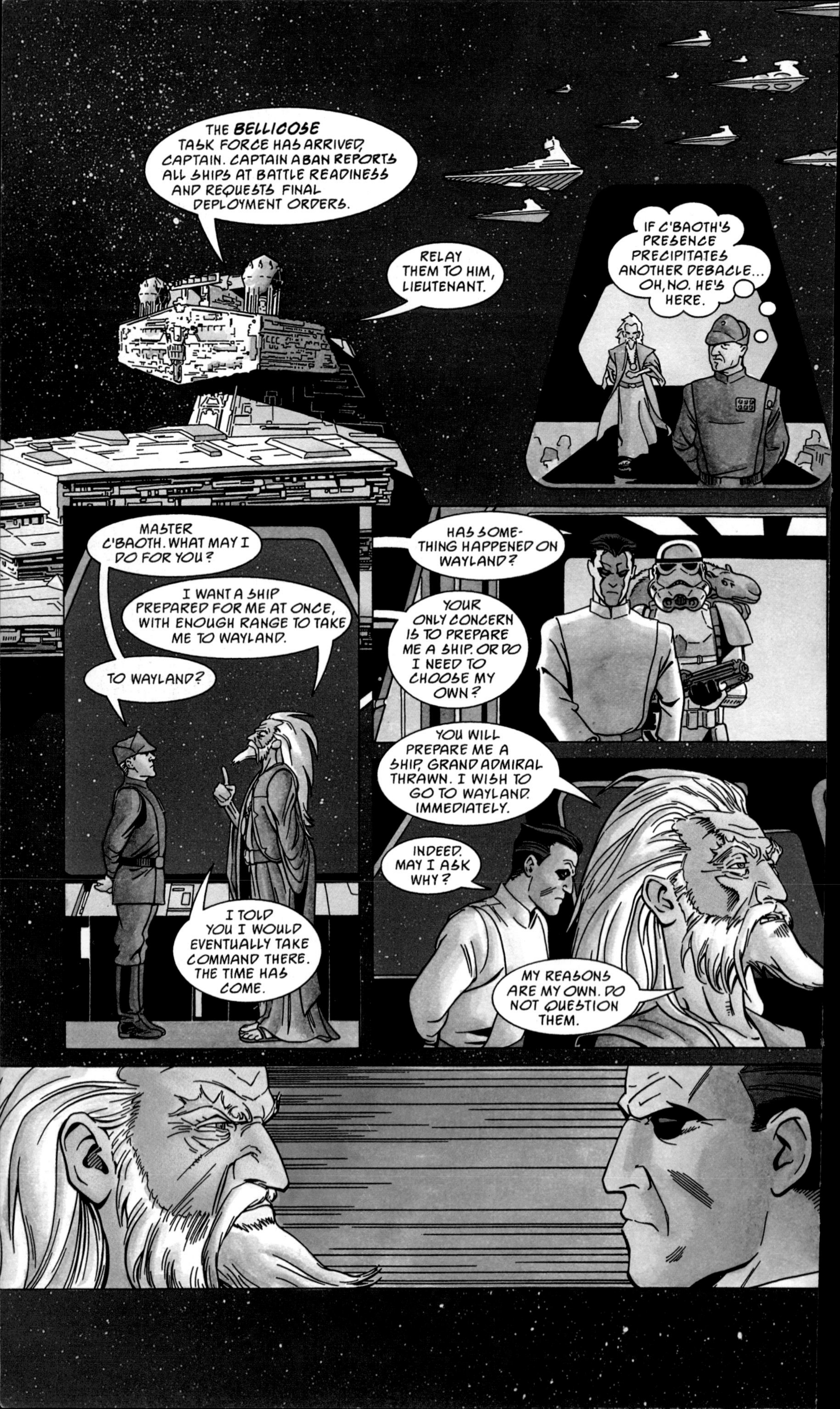
THE BELLICOSE TASK FORCE HAS ARRIVED, CAPTAIN. CAPTAIN ABAN REPORTS ALL SHIPS AT BATTLE READINESS AND REQUESTS FINAL DEPLOYMENT ORDERS.
RELAY THEM TO HIM, LIEUTENANT.
IF C'BAOTH'S PRESENCE PRECIPITATES ANOTHER DEBACLE... OH, NO. HE'S HERE.
MASTER C'BAOTH. WHAT MAY I DO FOR YOU?
I WANT A SHIP PREPARED FOR ME AT ONCE, WITH ENOUGH RANGE TO TAKE ME TO WAYLAND.
TO WAYLAND?
I TOLD YOU I WOULD EVENTUALLY TAKE COMMAND THERE. THE TIME HAS COME.
HAS SOMETHING HAPPENED ON WAYLAND?
YOUR ONLY CONCERN IS TO PREPARE ME A SHIP. OR DO I NEED TO CHOOSE MY OWN?
YOU WILL PREPARE ME A SHIP, GRAND ADMIRAL THRAWN. I WISH TO GO TO WAYLAND. IMMEDIATELY.
INDEED. MAY I ASK WHY?
MY REASONS ARE MY OWN. DO NOT QUESTION THEM.

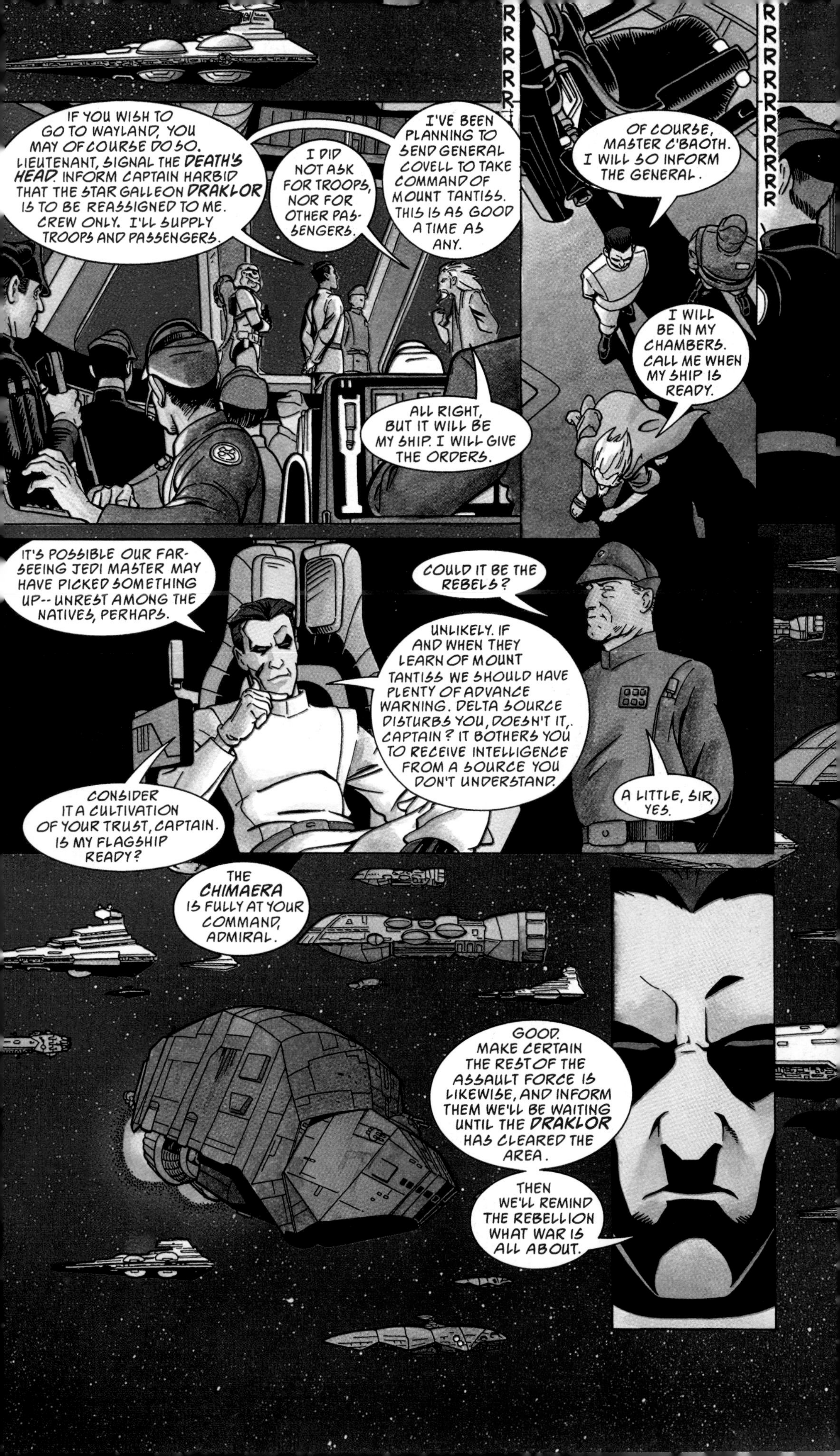
RRRRRR
IF YOU WISH TO GO TO WAYLAND, YOU MAY OF COURSE DO SO. LIEUTENANT, SIGNAL THE DEATH'S HEAD. INFORM CAPTAIN HARBID THAT THE STAR GALLEON DRAKLOR IS TO BE REASSIGNED TO ME. CREW ONLY. I'LL SUPPLY TROOPS AND PASSENGERS.
I DID NOT ASK FOR TROOPS, NOR FOR OTHER PASSENGERS.
I'VE BEEN PLANNING TO SEND GENERAL COVELL TO TAKE COMMAND OF MOUNT TANTISS. THIS IS AS GOOD A TIME AS ANY.
ALL RIGHT, BUT IT WILL BE MY SHIP. I WILL GIVE THE ORDERS.
RRRRRRRRRRR
OF COURSE, MASTER C'BAOTH. I WILL SO INFORM THE GENERAL.
I WILL BE IN MY CHAMBERS. CALL ME WHEN MY SHIP IS READY.
IT'S POSSIBLE OUR FAR-SEEING JEDI MASTER MAY HAVE PICKED SOMETHING UP-- UNREST AMONG THE NATIVES, PERHAPS.
COULD IT BE THE REBELS?
UNLIKELY. IF AND WHEN THEY LEARN OF MOUNT TANTISS WE SHOULD HAVE PLENTY OF ADVANCE WARNING. DELTA SOURCE DISTURBS YOU, DOESN'T IT, CAPTAIN? IT BOTHERS YOU TO RECEIVE INTELLIGENCE FROM A SOURCE YOU DON'T UNDERSTAND.
A LITTLE, SIR, YES.
CONSIDER IT A CULTIVATION OF YOUR TRUST, CAPTAIN. IS MY FLAGSHIP READY?
THE CHIMAERA IS FULLY AT YOUR COMMAND, ADMIRAL.
GOOD. MAKE CERTAIN THE REST OF THE ASSAULT FORCE IS LIKEWISE, AND INFORM THEM WE'LL BE WAITING UNTIL THE DRAKLOR HAS CLEARED THE AREA.
THEN WE'LL REMIND THE REBELLION WHAT WAR IS ALL ABOUT.

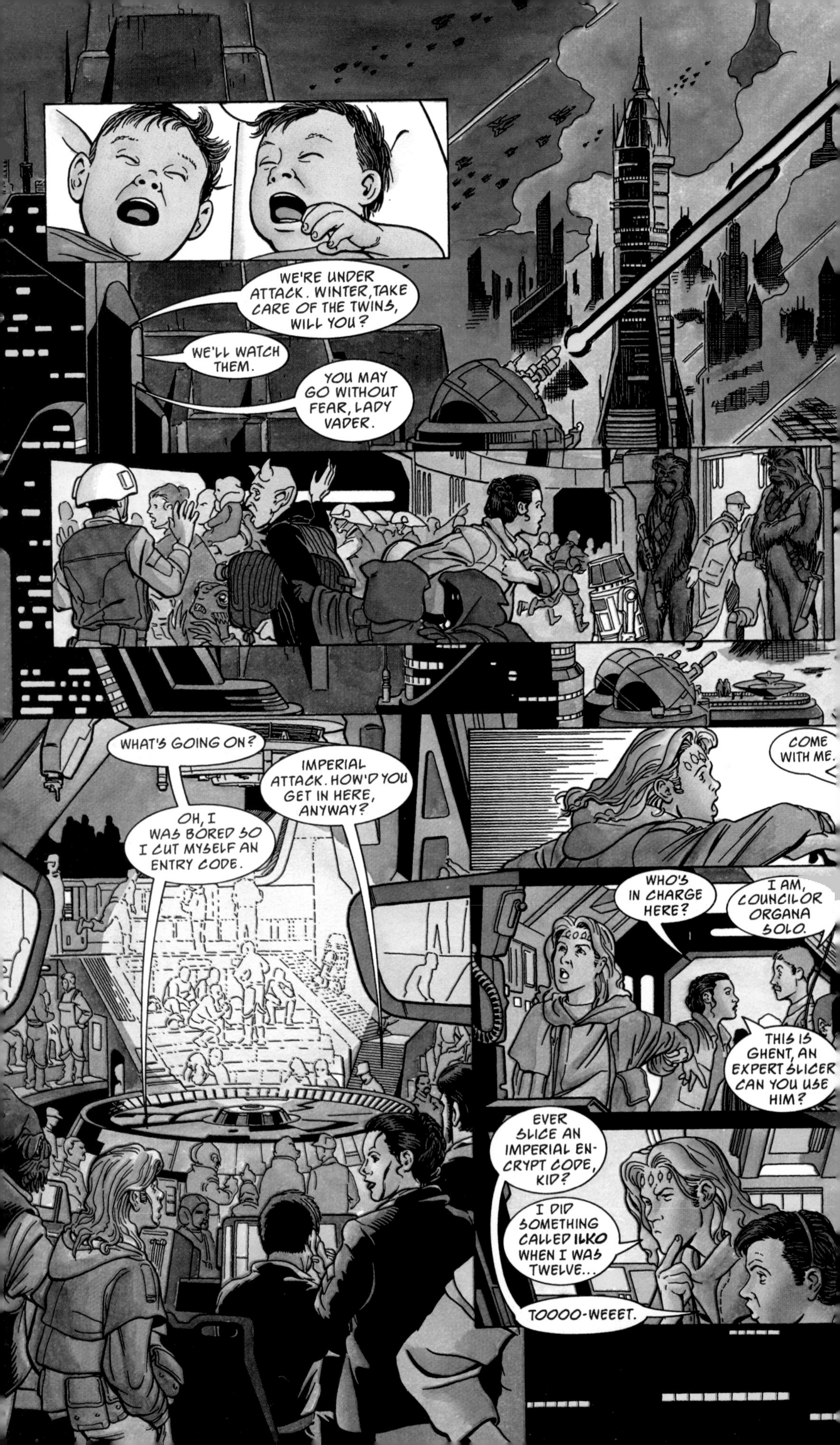
WE'RE UNDER ATTACK. WINTER, TAKE CARE OF THE TWINS, WILL YOU?
WE'LL WATCH THEM.
YOU MAY GO WITHOUT FEAR, LADY VADER.
WHAT'S GOING ON?
IMPERIAL ATTACK. HOW'D YOU GET IN HERE, ANYWAY?
OH, I WAS BORED SO I CUT MYSELF AN ENTRY CODE.
COME WITH ME.
WHO'S IN CHARGE HERE?
I AM, COUNCILOR ORGANA SOLO.
THIS IS GHENT, AN EXPERT SLICER CAN YOU USE HIM?
EVER SLICE AN IMPERIAL EN-CRYPT CODE, KID?
I DID SOMETHING CALLED ILKO WHEN I WAS TWELVE...
TOOOO-WEEET.

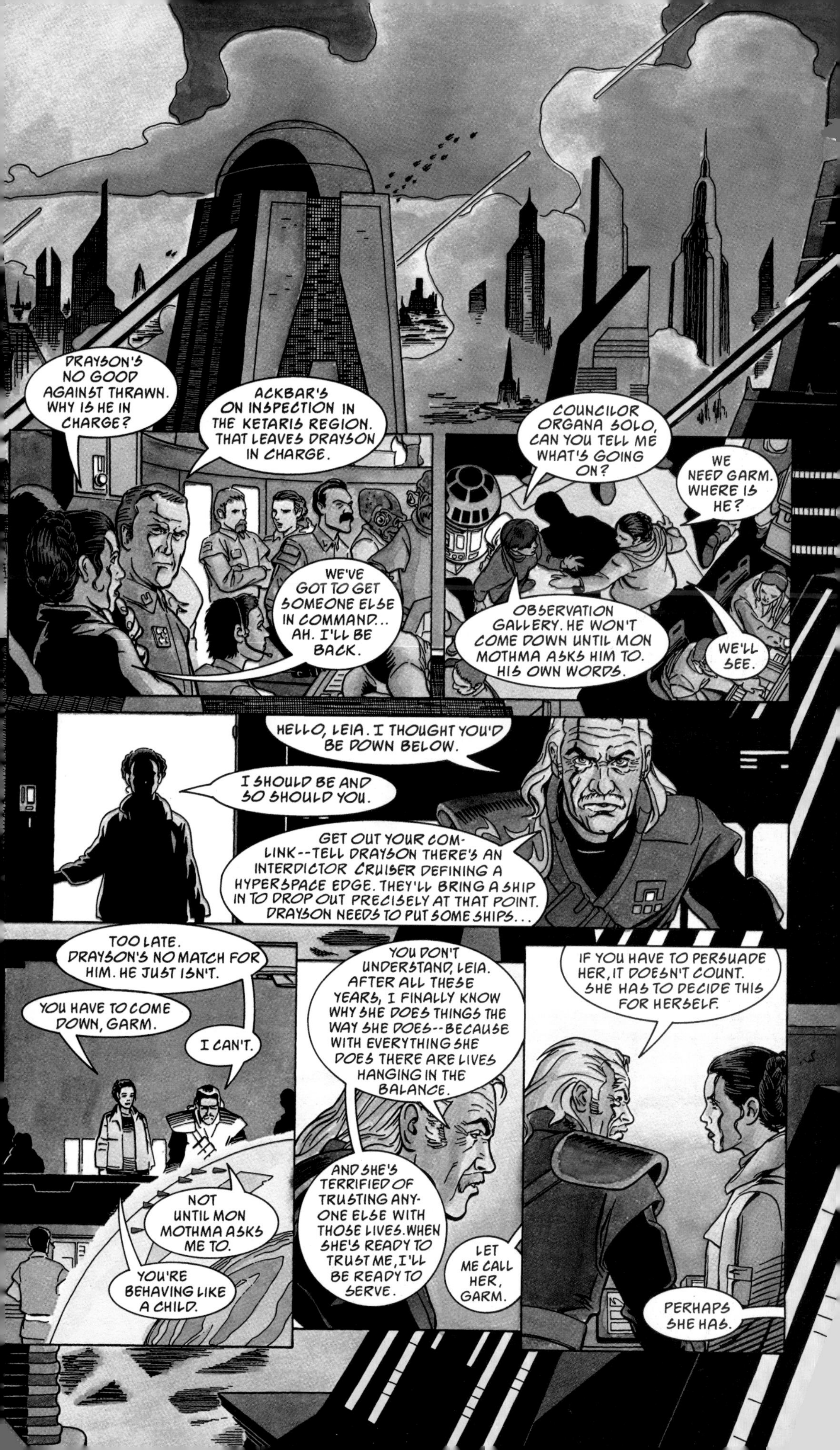
DRAYSON'S NO GOOD AGAINST THRAWN. WHY IS HE IN CHARGE?
ACKBAR'S ON INSPECTION IN THE KETARIS REGION. THAT LEAVES DRAYSON IN CHARGE.
WE'VE GOT TO GET SOMEONE ELSE IN COMMAND... AH. I'LL BE BACK.
COUNCILOR ORGANA SOLO, CAN YOU TELL ME WHAT'S GOING ON?
WE NEED GARM. WHERE IS HE?
OBSERVATION GALLERY. HE WON'T COME DOWN UNTIL MON MOTHMA ASKS HIM TO. HIS OWN WORDS.
WE'LL SEE.
HELLO, LEIA. I THOUGHT YOU'D BE DOWN BELOW.
I SHOULD BE AND SO SHOULD YOU.
GET OUT YOUR COM-LINK--TELL DRAYSON THERE'S AN INTERDICTOR CRUISER DEFINING A HYPERSPACE EDGE. THEY'LL BRING A SHIP IN TO DROP OUT PRECISELY AT THAT POINT. DRAYSON NEEDS TO PUT SOME SHIPS...
TOO LATE. DRAYSON'S NO MATCH FOR HIM. HE JUST ISN'T.
YOU HAVE TO COME DOWN, GARM.
I CAN'T.
NOT UNTIL MON MOTHMA ASKS ME TO.
YOU'RE BEHAVING LIKE A CHILD.
YOU DON'T UNDERSTAND, LEIA. AFTER ALL THESE YEARS, I FINALLY KNOW WHY SHE DOES THINGS THE WAY SHE DOES--BECAUSE WITH EVERYTHING SHE DOES THERE ARE LIVES HANGING IN THE BALANCE.
AND SHE'S TERRIFIED OF TRUSTING ANY-ONE ELSE WITH THOSE LIVES. WHEN SHE'S READY TO TRUST ME, I'LL BE READY TO SERVE.
LET ME CALL HER, GARM.
IF YOU HAVE TO PERSUADE HER, IT DOESN'T COUNT. SHE HAS TO DECIDE THIS FOR HERSELF.
PERHAPS SHE HAS.

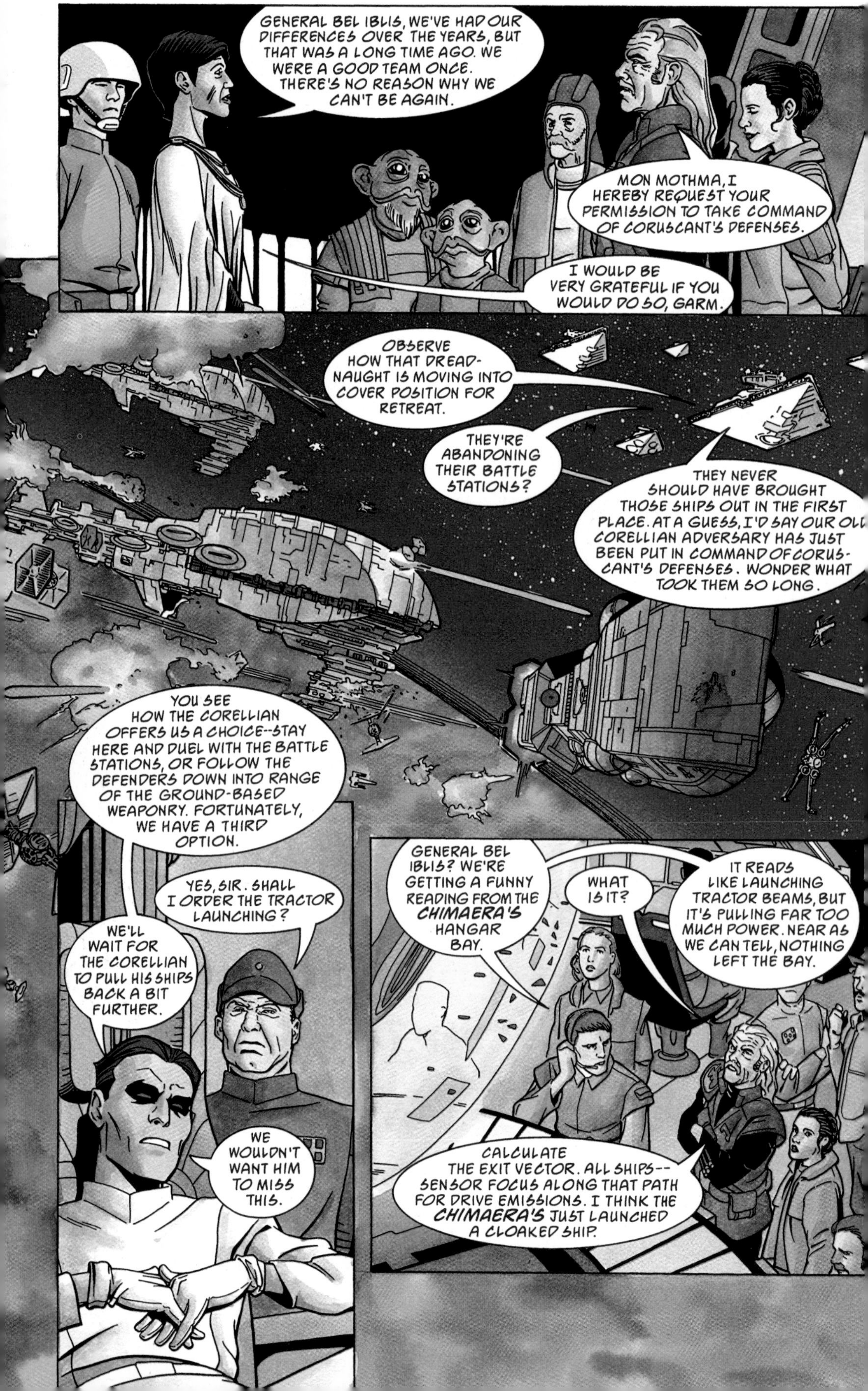
GENERAL BEL IBLIS, WE'VE HAD OUR DIFFERENCES OVER THE YEARS, BUT THAT WAS A LONG TIME AGO. WE WERE A GOOD TEAM ONCE. THERE'S NO REASON WHY WE CAN'T BE AGAIN.
MON MOTHMA, I HEREBY REQUEST YOUR PERMISSION TO TAKE COMMAND OF CORUSCANT'S DEFENSES.
I WOULD BE VERY GRATEFUL IF YOU WOULD DO SO, GARM.
OBSERVE HOW THAT DREAD-NAUGHT IS MOVING INTO COVER POSITION FOR RETREAT.
THEY'RE ABANDONING THEIR BATTLE STATIONS?
THEY NEVER SHOULD HAVE BROUGHT THOSE SHIPS OUT IN THE FIRST PLACE. AT A GUESS, I'D SAY OUR OLD CORELLIAN ADVERSARY HAS JUST BEEN PUT IN COMMAND OF CORUS-CANT'S DEFENSES. WONDER WHAT TOOK THEM SO LONG.
YOU SEE HOW THE CORELLIAN OFFERS US A CHOICE--STAY HERE AND DUEL WITH THE BATTLE STATIONS, OR FOLLOW THE DEFENDERS DOWN INTO RANGE OF THE GROUND-BASED WEAPONRY. FORTUNATELY, WE HAVE A THIRD OPTION.
YES, SIR. SHALL I ORDER THE TRACTOR LAUNCHING?
WE'LL WAIT FOR THE CORELLIAN TO PULL HIS SHIPS BACK A BIT FURTHER.
WE WOULDN'T WANT HIM TO MISS THIS.
GENERAL BEL IBLIS? WE'RE GETTING A FUNNY READING FROM THE CHIMAERA'S HANGAR BAY.
WHAT IS IT?
IT READS LIKE LAUNCHING TRACTOR BEAMS, BUT IT'S PULLING FAR TOO MUCH POWER. NEAR AS WE CAN TELL, NOTHING LEFT THE BAY.
CALCULATE THE EXIT VECTOR. ALL SHIPS-- SENSOR FOCUS ALONG THAT PATH FOR DRIVE EMISSIONS. I THINK THE CHIMAERA'S JUST LAUNCHED A CLOAKED SHIP.

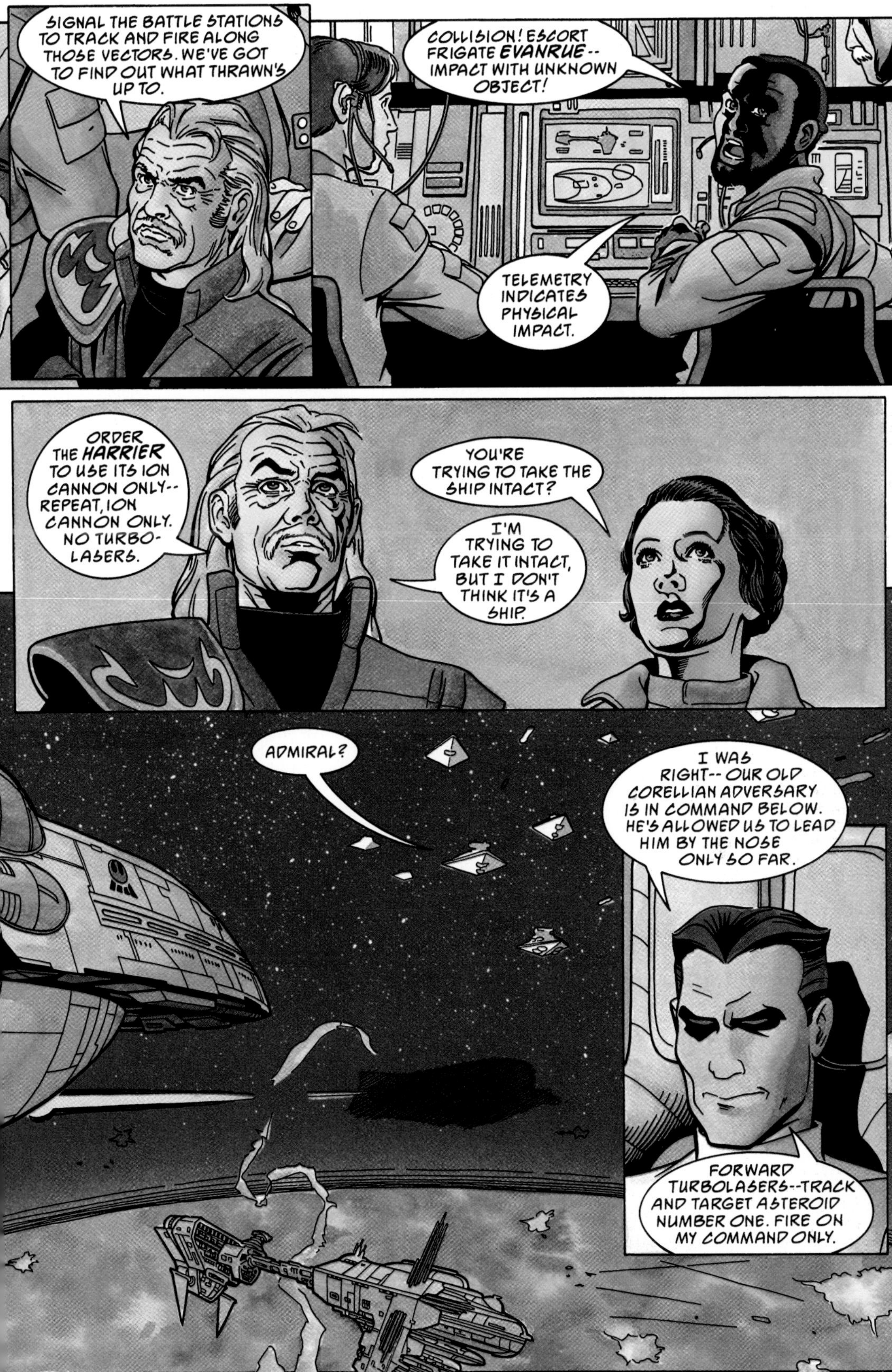
SIGNAL THE BATTLE STATIONS TO TRACK AND FIRE ALONG THOSE VECTORS. WE'VE GOT TO FIND OUT WHAT THRAWN'S UP TO.
COLLISION! ESCORT FRIGATE EVANRUE-- IMPACT WITH UNKNOWN OBJECT!
TELEMETRY INDICATES PHYSICAL IMPACT.
ORDER THE HARRIER TO USE ITS ION CANNON ONLY-- REPEAT, ION CANNON ONLY. NO TURBO-LASERS.
YOU'RE TRYING TO TAKE THE SHIP INTACT?
I'M TRYING TO TAKE IT INTACT, BUT I DON'T THINK IT'S A SHIP.
ADMIRAL?
I WAS RIGHT-- OUR OLD CORELLIAN ADVERSARY IS IN COMMAND BELOW. HE'S ALLOWED US TO LEAD HIM BY THE NOSE ONLY SO FAR.
FORWARD TURBOLASERS--TRACK AND TARGET ASTEROID NUMBER ONE. FIRE ON MY COMMAND ONLY.

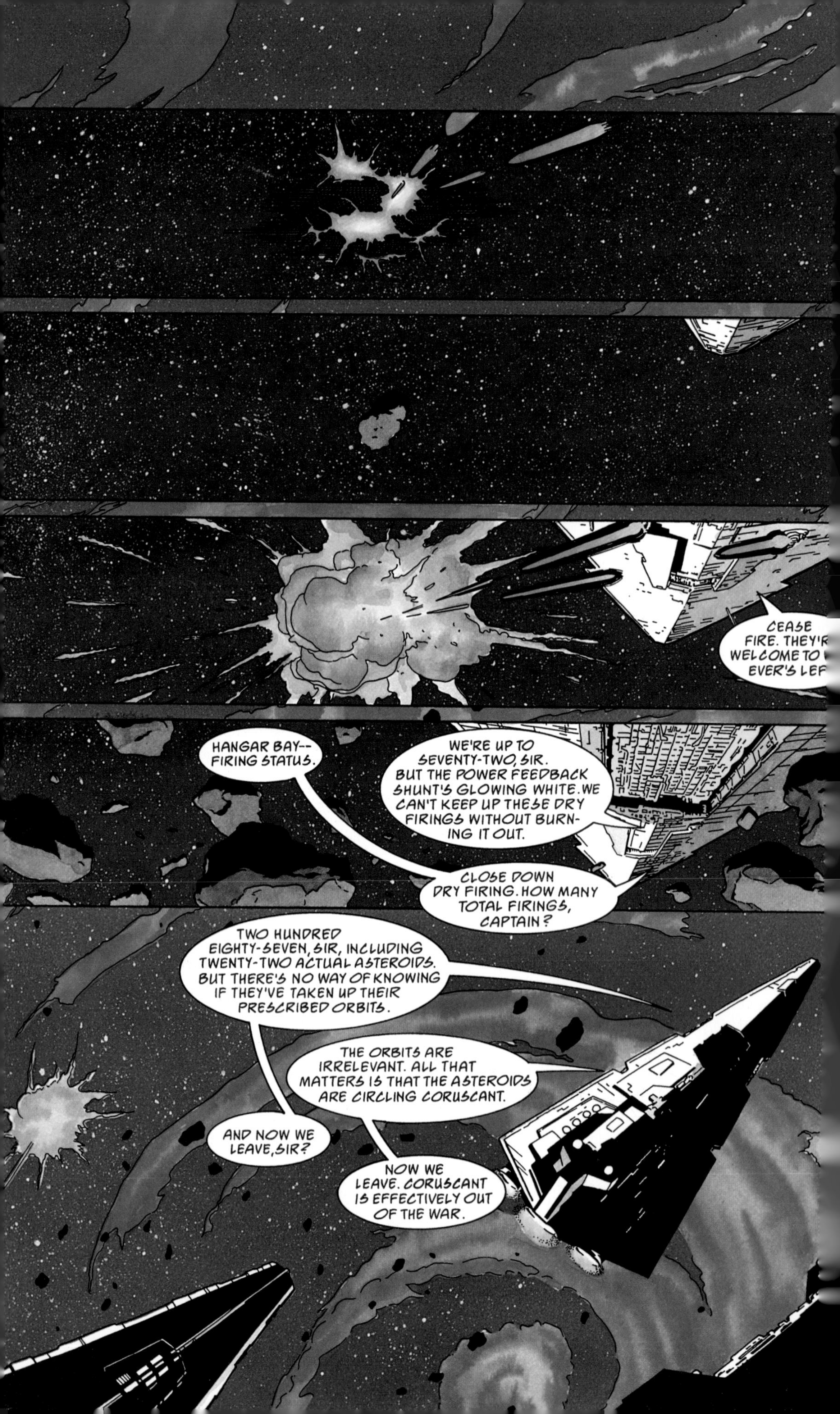
CEASE FIRE. THEY'R WELCOME TO EVER'S LEF
HANGAR BAY-- FIRING STATUS.
WE'RE UP TO SEVENTY-TWO, SIR. BUT THE POWER FEEDBACK SHUNT'S GLOWING WHITE. WE CAN'T KEEP UP THESE DRY FIRINGS WITHOUT BURNING IT OUT.
CLOSE DOWN DRY FIRING. HOW MANY TOTAL FIRINGS, CAPTAIN?
TWO HUNDRED EIGHTY-SEVEN, SIR, INCLUDING TWENTY-TWO ACTUAL ASTEROIDS. BUT THERE'S NO WAY OF KNOWING IF THEY'VE TAKEN UP THEIR PRESCRIBED ORBITS.
THE ORBITS ARE IRRELEVANT. ALL THAT MATTERS IS THAT THE ASTEROIDS ARE CIRCLING CORUSCANT.
AND NOW WE LEAVE, SIR?
NOW WE LEAVE. CORUSCANT IS EFFECTIVELY OUT OF THE WAR.

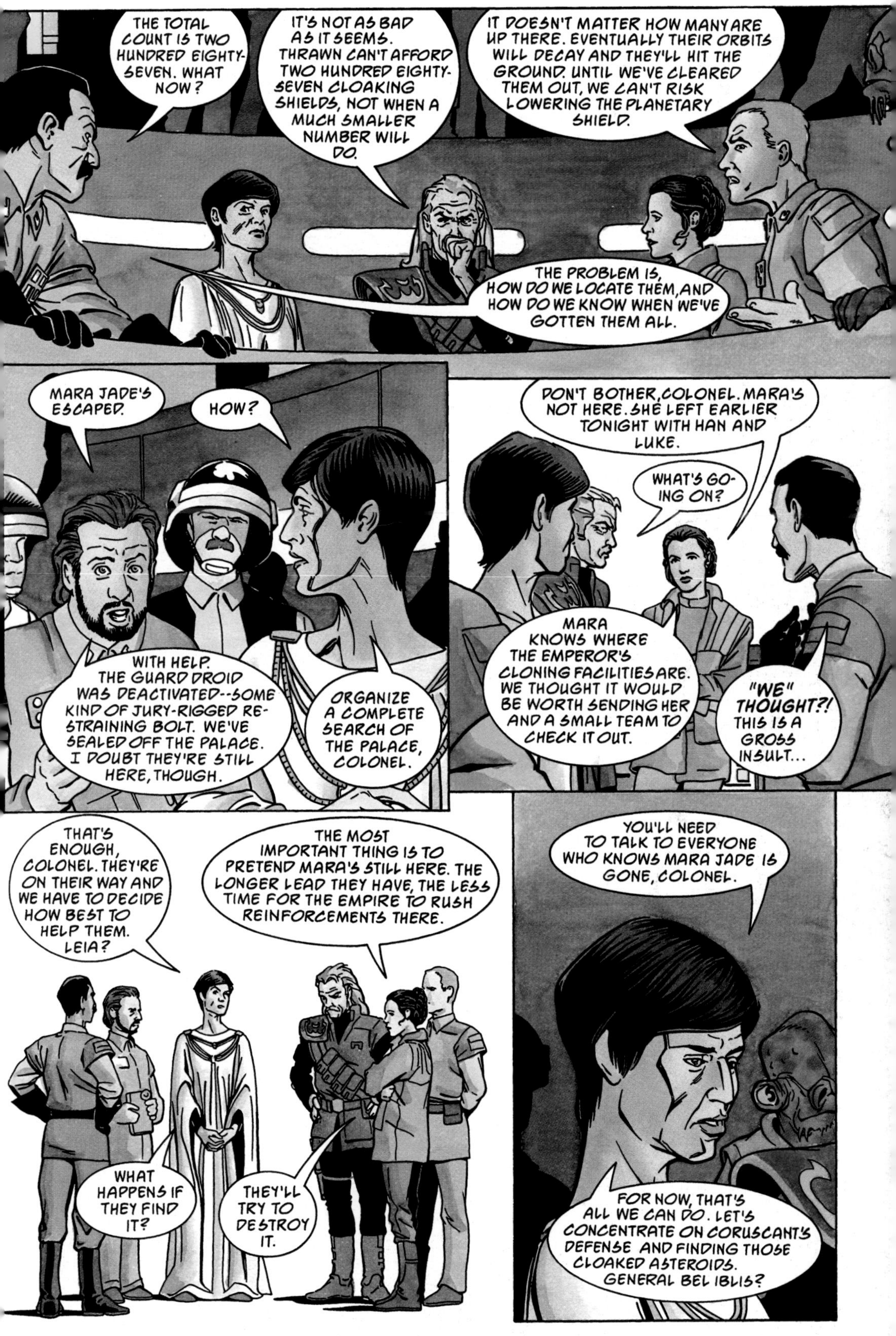
THE TOTAL COUNT IS TWO HUNDRED EIGHTY-SEVEN. WHAT NOW?
IT'S NOT AS BAD AS IT SEEMS. THRAWN CAN'T AFFORD TWO HUNDRED EIGHTY-SEVEN CLOAKING SHIELDS, NOT WHEN A MUCH SMALLER NUMBER WILL DO.
IT DOESN'T MATTER HOW MANY ARE UP THERE. EVENTUALLY THEIR ORBITS WILL DECAY AND THEY'LL HIT THE GROUND. UNTIL WE'VE CLEARED THEM OUT, WE CAN'T RISK LOWERING THE PLANETARY SHIELD.
THE PROBLEM IS, HOW DO WE LOCATE THEM, AND HOW DO WE KNOW WHEN WE'VE GOTTEN THEM ALL.
MARA JADE'S ESCAPED.
HOW?
WITH HELP. THE GUARD DROID WAS DEACTIVATED--SOME KIND OF JURY-RIGGED RESTRAINING BOLT. WE'VE SEALED OFF THE PALACE. I DOUBT THEY'RE STILL HERE, THOUGH.
ORGANIZE A COMPLETE SEARCH OF THE PALACE, COLONEL.
DON'T BOTHER, COLONEL. MARA'S NOT HERE. SHE LEFT EARLIER TONIGHT WITH HAN AND LUKE.
WHAT'S GOING ON?
MARA KNOWS WHERE THE EMPEROR'S CLONING FACILITIES ARE. WE THOUGHT IT WOULD BE WORTH SENDING HER AND A SMALL TEAM TO CHECK IT OUT.
"WE" THOUGHT?! THIS IS A GROSS INSULT...
THAT'S ENOUGH, COLONEL. THEY'RE ON THEIR WAY AND WE HAVE TO DECIDE HOW BEST TO HELP THEM. LEIA?
THE MOST IMPORTANT THING IS TO PRETEND MARA'S STILL HERE. THE LONGER LEAD THEY HAVE, THE LESS TIME FOR THE EMPIRE TO RUSH REINFORCEMENTS THERE.
WHAT HAPPENS IF THEY FIND IT?
THEY'LL TRY TO DESTROY IT.
YOU'LL NEED TO TALK TO EVERYONE WHO KNOWS MARA JADE IS GONE, COLONEL.
FOR NOW, THAT'S ALL WE CAN DO. LET'S CONCENTRATE ON CORUSCANT'S DEFENSE AND FINDING THOSE CLOAKED ASTEROIDS. GENERAL BEL IBLIS?

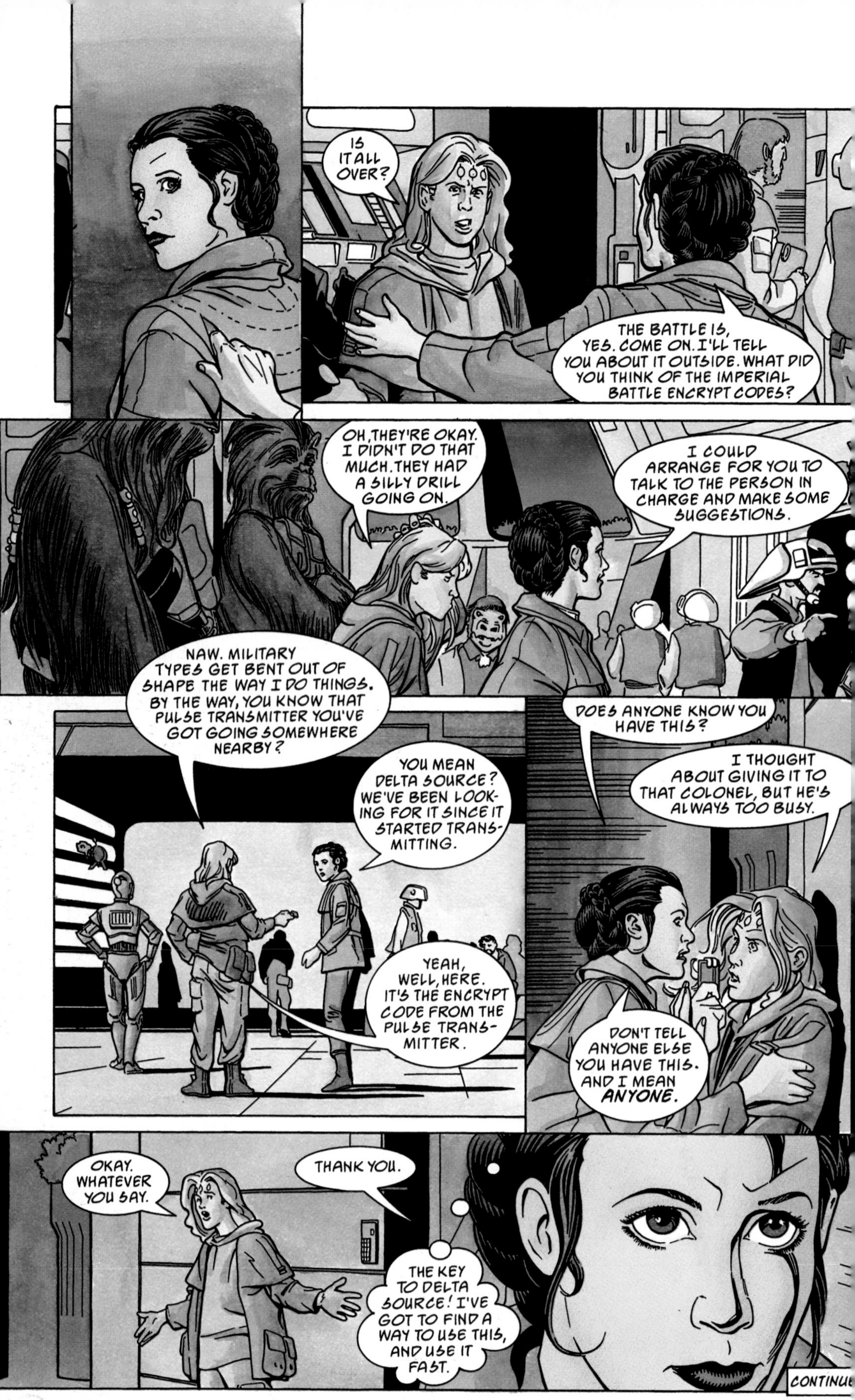
IS IT ALL OVER?
THE BATTLE IS, YES. COME ON. I'LL TELL YOU ABOUT IT OUTSIDE. WHAT DID YOU THINK OF THE IMPERIAL BATTLE ENCRYPT CODES?
OH, THEY'RE OKAY. I DIDN'T DO THAT MUCH. THEY HAD A SILLY DRILL GOING ON.
I COULD ARRANGE FOR YOU TO TALK TO THE PERSON IN CHARGE AND MAKE SOME SUGGESTIONS.
NAW. MILITARY TYPES GET BENT OUT OF SHAPE THE WAY I DO THINGS. BY THE WAY, YOU KNOW THAT PULSE TRANSMITTER YOU'VE GOT GOING SOMEWHERE NEARBY?
YOU MEAN DELTA SOURCE? WE'VE BEEN LOOKING FOR IT SINCE IT STARTED TRANSMITTING.
YEAH, WELL, HERE. IT'S THE ENCRYPT CODE FROM THE PULSE TRANSMITTER.
DOES ANYONE KNOW YOU HAVE THIS?
I THOUGHT ABOUT GIVING IT TO THAT COLONEL, BUT HE'S ALWAYS TOO BUSY.
DON'T TELL ANYONE ELSE YOU HAVE THIS. AND I MEAN ANYONE.
OKAY. WHATEVER YOU SAY.
THANK YOU.
THE KEY TO DELTA SOURCE! I'VE GOT TO FIND A WAY TO USE THIS, AND USE IT FAST.
CONTINU

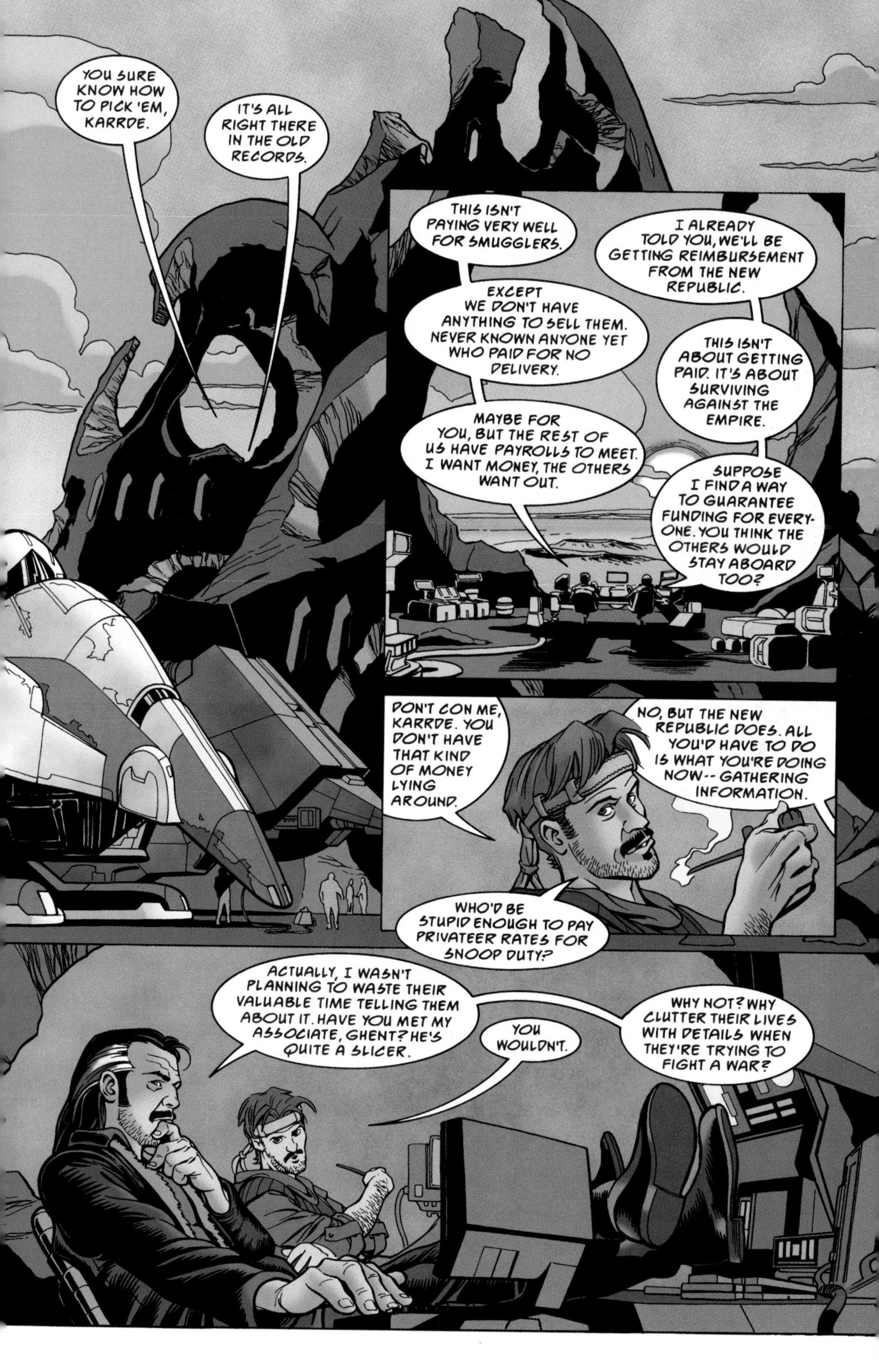
YOU SURE KNOW HOW TO PICK 'EM, KARRDE.
IT'S ALL RIGHT THERE IN THE OLD RECORDS.
THIS ISN'T PAYING VERY WELL FOR SMUGGLERS.
I ALREADY TOLD YOU, WE'LL BE GETTING REIMBURSEMENT FROM THE NEW REPUBLIC.
EXCEPT WE DON'T HAVE ANYTHING TO SELL THEM. NEVER KNOWN ANYONE YET WHO PAID FOR NO DELIVERY.
THIS ISN'T ABOUT GETTING PAID. IT'S ABOUT SURVIVING AGAINST THE EMPIRE.
MAYBE FOR YOU, BUT THE REST OF US HAVE PAYROLLS TO MEET. I WANT MONEY, THE OTHERS WANT OUT.
SUPPOSE I FIND A WAY TO GUARANTEE FUNDING FOR EVERY-ONE. YOU THINK THE OTHERS WOULD STAY ABOARD TOO?
DON'T CON ME, KARRDE. YOU DON'T HAVE THAT KIND OF MONEY LYING AROUND.
NO, BUT THE NEW REPUBLIC DOES. ALL YOU'D HAVE TO DO IS WHAT YOU'RE DOING NOW-- GATHERING INFORMATION.
WHO'D BE STUPID ENOUGH TO PAY PRIVATEER RATES FOR SNOOP DUTY?
ACTUALLY, I WASN'T PLANNING TO WASTE THEIR VALUABLE TIME TELLING THEM ABOUT IT. HAVE YOU MET MY ASSOCIATE, GHENT? HE'S QUITE A SLICER.
YOU WOULDN'T.
WHY NOT? WHY CLUTTER THEIR LIVES WITH DETAILS WHEN THEY'RE TRYING TO FIGHT A WAR?

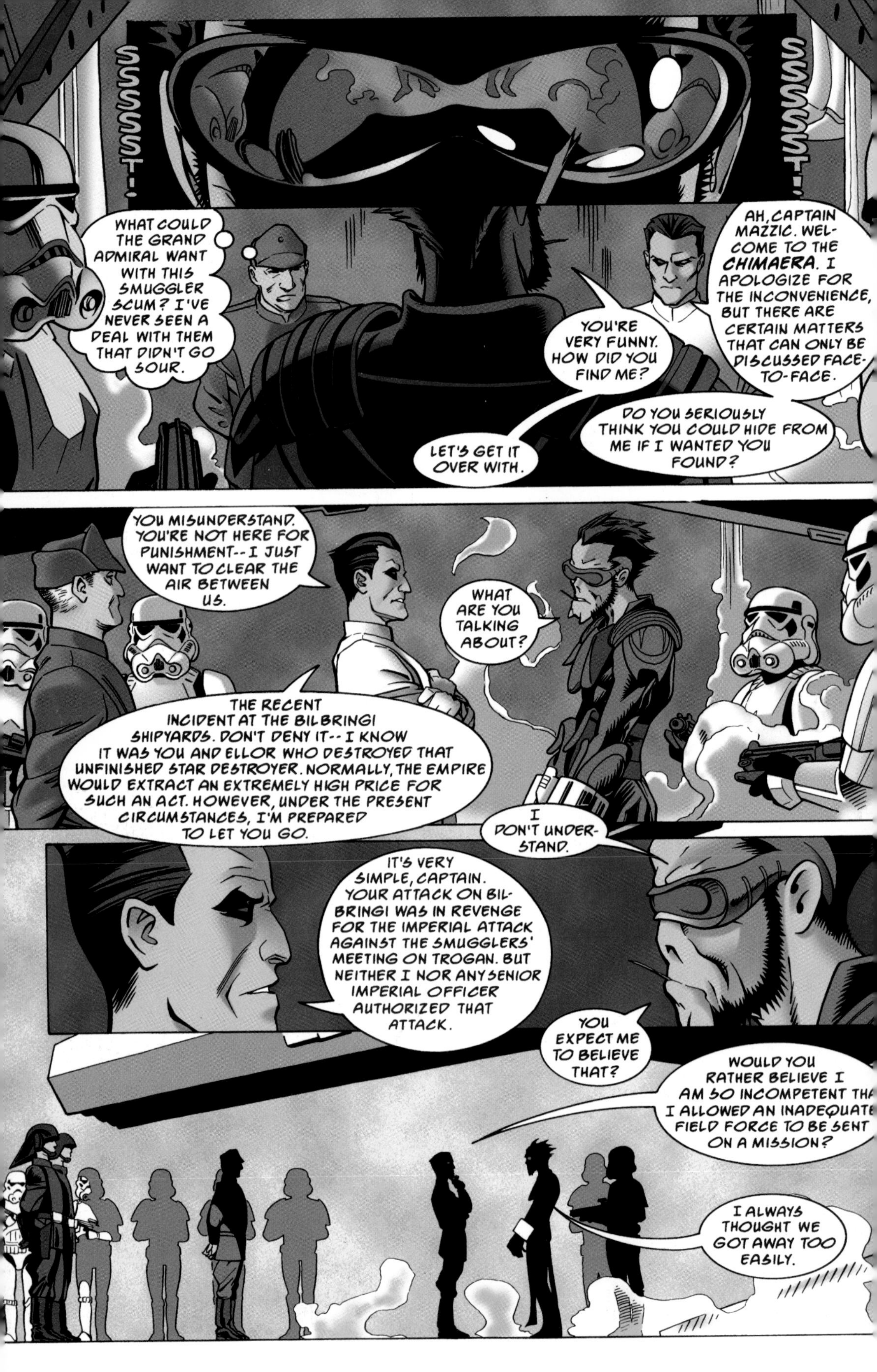
SSSSSST!
SSSSSST!
WHAT COULD THE GRAND ADMIRAL WANT WITH THIS SMUGGLER SCUM? I'VE NEVER SEEN A DEAL WITH THEM THAT DIDN'T GO SOUR.
AH, CAPTAIN MAZZIC. WELCOME TO THE CHIMAERA. I APOLOGIZE FOR THE INCONVENIENCE, BUT THERE ARE CERTAIN MATTERS THAT CAN ONLY BE DISCUSSED FACE-TO-FACE.
YOU'RE VERY FUNNY. HOW DID YOU FIND ME?
DO YOU SERIOUSLY THINK YOU COULD HIDE FROM ME IF I WANTED YOU FOUND?
LET'S GET IT OVER WITH.
YOU MISUNDERSTAND. YOU'RE NOT HERE FOR PUNISHMENT-- I JUST WANT TO CLEAR THE AIR BETWEEN US.
WHAT ARE YOU TALKING ABOUT?
THE RECENT INCIDENT AT THE BILBRINGI SHIPYARDS. DON'T DENY IT-- I KNOW IT WAS YOU AND ELLOR WHO DESTROYED THAT UNFINISHED STAR DESTROYER. NORMALLY, THE EMPIRE WOULD EXTRACT AN EXTREMELY HIGH PRICE FOR SUCH AN ACT. HOWEVER, UNDER THE PRESENT CIRCUMSTANCES, I'M PREPARED TO LET YOU GO.
I DON'T UNDERSTAND.
IT'S VERY SIMPLE, CAPTAIN. YOUR ATTACK ON BILBRINGI WAS IN REVENGE FOR THE IMPERIAL ATTACK AGAINST THE SMUGGLERS' MEETING ON TROGAN. BUT NEITHER I NOR ANY SENIOR IMPERIAL OFFICER AUTHORIZED THAT ATTACK.
YOU EXPECT ME TO BELIEVE THAT?
WOULD YOU RATHER BELIEVE I AM SO INCOMPETENT THA I ALLOWED AN INADEQUATE FIELD FORCE TO BE SENT ON A MISSION?
I ALWAYS THOUGHT WE GOT AWAY TOO EASILY.

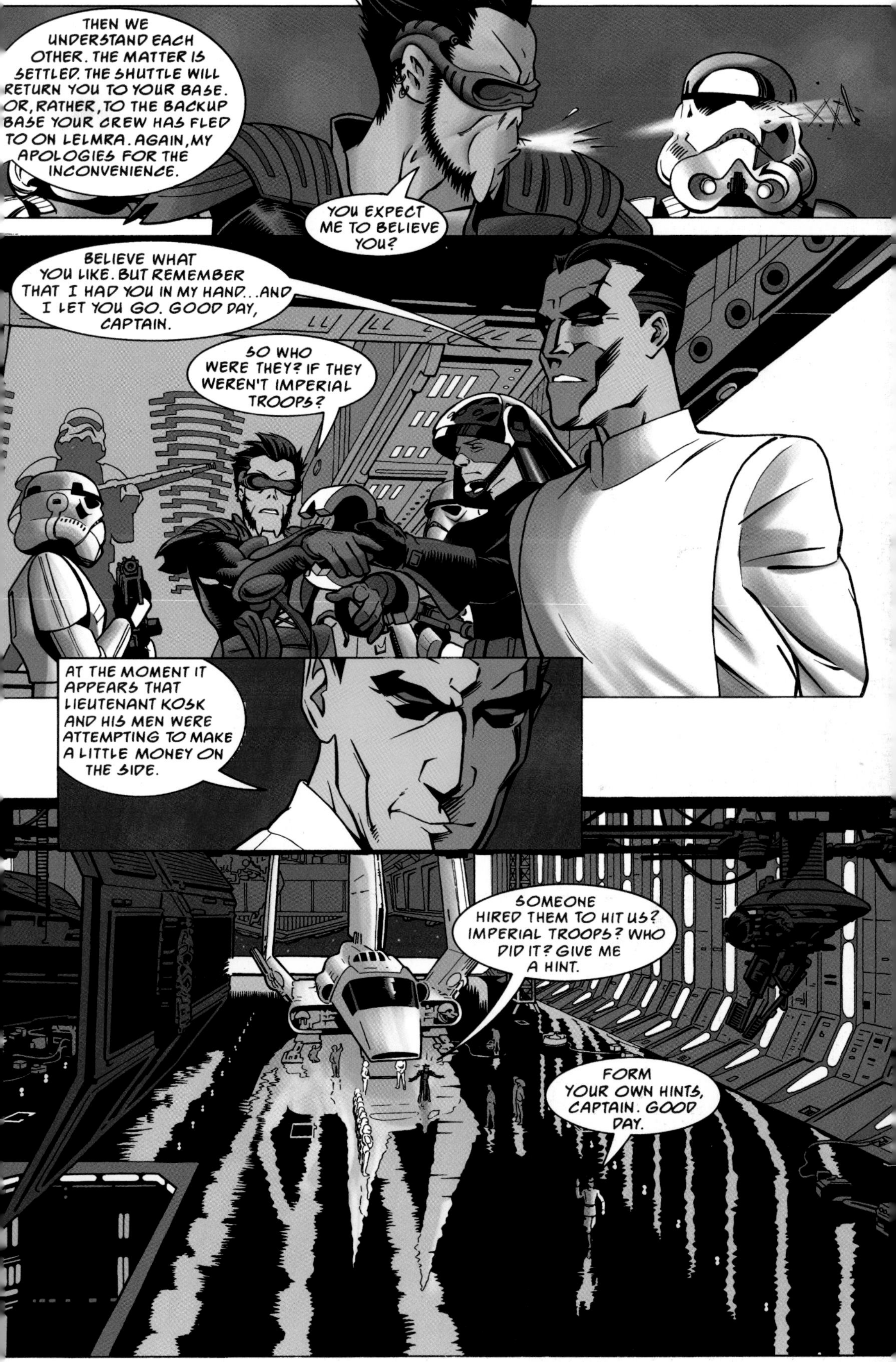
THEN WE UNDERSTAND EACH OTHER. THE MATTER IS SETTLED. THE SHUTTLE WILL RETURN YOU TO YOUR BASE. OR, RATHER, TO THE BACKUP BASE YOUR CREW HAS FLED TO ON LELMRA. AGAIN, MY APOLOGIES FOR THE INCONVENIENCE.
YOU EXPECT ME TO BELIEVE YOU?
BELIEVE WHAT YOU LIKE. BUT REMEMBER THAT I HAD YOU IN MY HAND...AND I LET YOU GO. GOOD DAY, CAPTAIN.
SO WHO WERE THEY? IF THEY WEREN'T IMPERIAL TROOPS?
AT THE MOMENT IT APPEARS THAT LIEUTENANT KOSK AND HIS MEN WERE ATTEMPTING TO MAKE A LITTLE MONEY ON THE SIDE.
SOMEONE HIRED THEM TO HIT US? IMPERIAL TROOPS? WHO DID IT? GIVE ME A HINT.
FORM YOUR OWN HINTS, CAPTAIN. GOOD DAY.

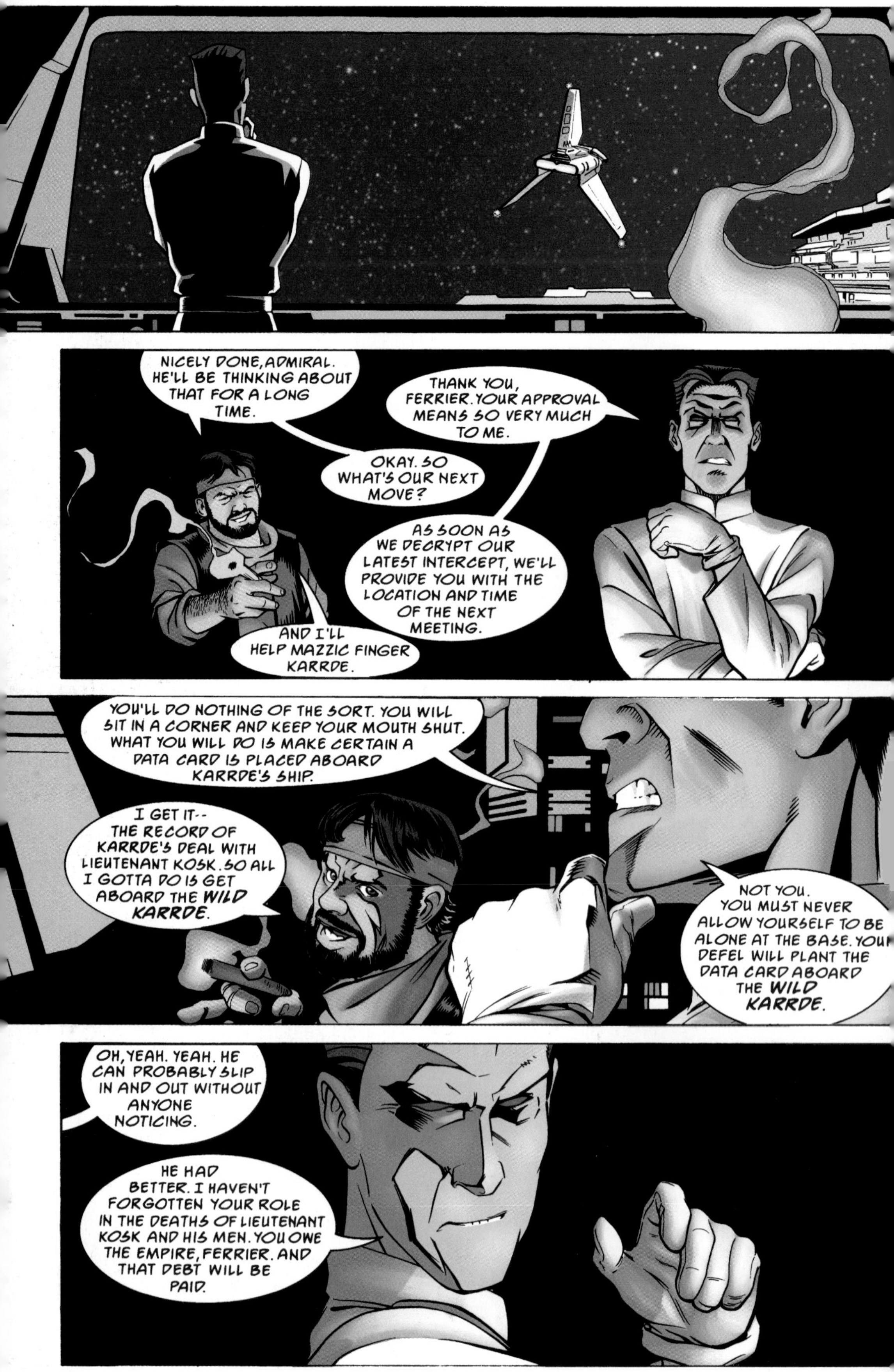
NICELY DONE, ADMIRAL. HE'LL BE THINKING ABOUT THAT FOR A LONG TIME.
THANK YOU, FERRIER. YOUR APPROVAL MEANS SO VERY MUCH TO ME.
OKAY. SO WHAT'S OUR NEXT MOVE?
AS SOON AS WE DECRYPT OUR LATEST INTERCEPT, WE'LL PROVIDE YOU WITH THE LOCATION AND TIME OF THE NEXT MEETING.
AND I'LL HELP MAZZIC FINGER KARRDE.
YOU'LL DO NOTHING OF THE SORT. YOU WILL SIT IN A CORNER AND KEEP YOUR MOUTH SHUT. WHAT YOU WILL DO IS MAKE CERTAIN A DATA CARD IS PLACED ABOARD KARRDE'S SHIP.
I GET IT-- THE RECORD OF KARRDE'S DEAL WITH LIEUTENANT KOSK. SO ALL I GOTTA DO IS GET ABOARD THE *WILD KARRDE*.
NOT YOU. YOU MUST NEVER ALLOW YOURSELF TO BE ALONE AT THE BASE. YOU DEFEL WILL PLANT THE DATA CARD ABOARD THE *WILD KARRDE*.
OH, YEAH. YEAH. HE CAN PROBABLY SLIP IN AND OUT WITHOUT ANYONE NOTICING.
HE HAD BETTER. I HAVEN'T FORGOTTEN YOUR ROLE IN THE DEATHS OF LIEUTENANT KOSK AND HIS MEN. YOU OWE THE EMPIRE, FERRIER. AND THAT DEBT WILL BE PAID.

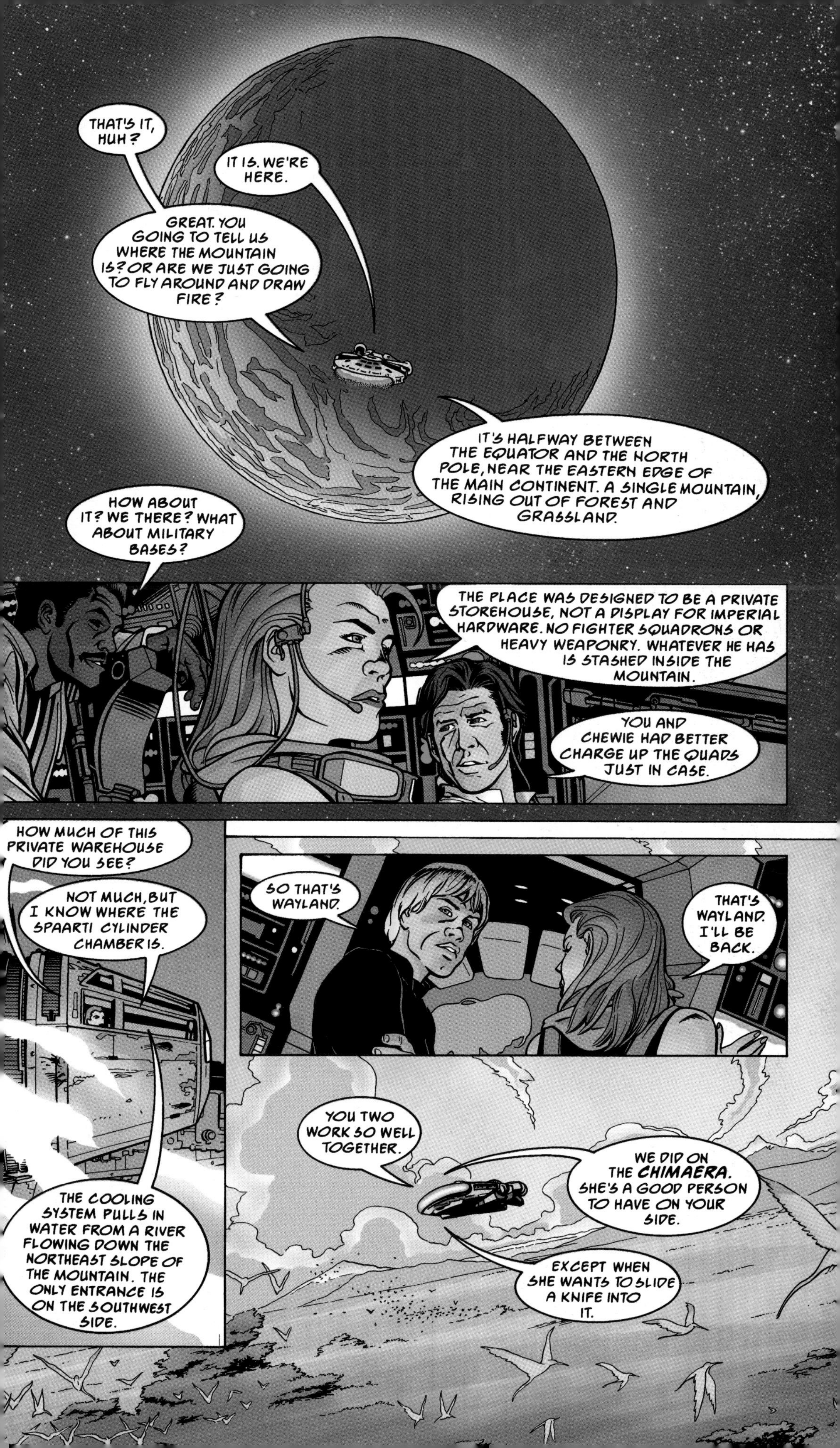
THAT'S IT, HUH?
IT IS. WE'RE HERE.
GREAT. YOU GOING TO TELL US WHERE THE MOUNTAIN IS? OR ARE WE JUST GOING TO FLY AROUND AND DRAW FIRE?
IT'S HALFWAY BETWEEN THE EQUATOR AND THE NORTH POLE, NEAR THE EASTERN EDGE OF THE MAIN CONTINENT. A SINGLE MOUNTAIN, RISING OUT OF FOREST AND GRASSLAND.
HOW ABOUT IT? WE THERE? WHAT ABOUT MILITARY BASES?
THE PLACE WAS DESIGNED TO BE A PRIVATE STOREHOUSE, NOT A DISPLAY FOR IMPERIAL HARDWARE. NO FIGHTER SQUADRONS OR HEAVY WEAPONRY. WHATEVER HE HAS IS STASHED INSIDE THE MOUNTAIN.
YOU AND CHEWIE HAD BETTER CHARGE UP THE QUADS JUST IN CASE.
HOW MUCH OF THIS PRIVATE WAREHOUSE DID YOU SEE?
NOT MUCH, BUT I KNOW WHERE THE SPAARTI CYLINDER CHAMBER IS.
THE COOLING SYSTEM PULLS IN WATER FROM A RIVER FLOWING DOWN THE NORTHEAST SLOPE OF THE MOUNTAIN. THE ONLY ENTRANCE IS ON THE SOUTHWEST SIDE.
SO THAT'S WAYLAND.
THAT'S WAYLAND. I'LL BE BACK.
YOU TWO WORK SO WELL TOGETHER.
WE DID ON THE CHIMAERA. SHE'S A GOOD PERSON TO HAVE ON YOUR SIDE.
EXCEPT WHEN SHE WANTS TO SLIDE A KNIFE INTO IT.

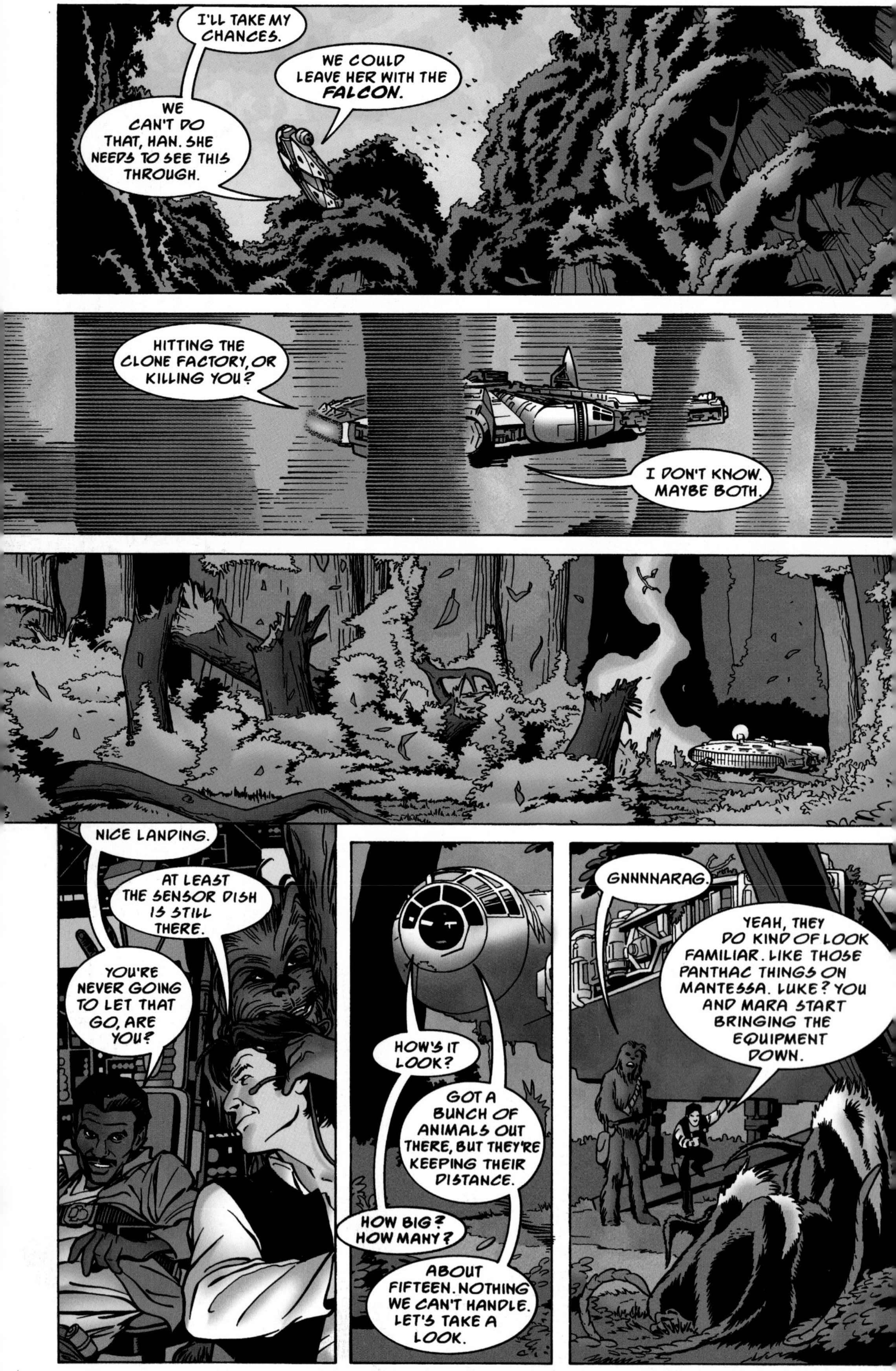
WE CAN'T DO THAT, HAN. SHE NEEDS TO SEE THIS THROUGH.
I'LL TAKE MY CHANCES.
WE COULD LEAVE HER WITH THE FALCON.
HITTING THE CLONE FACTORY, OR KILLING YOU?
I DON'T KNOW. MAYBE BOTH.
NICE LANDING.
AT LEAST THE SENSOR DISH IS STILL THERE.
YOU'RE NEVER GOING TO LET THAT GO, ARE YOU?
HOW'S IT LOOK?
GOT A BUNCH OF ANIMALS OUT THERE, BUT THEY'RE KEEPING THEIR DISTANCE.
HOW BIG? HOW MANY?
ABOUT FIFTEEN. NOTHING WE CAN'T HANDLE. LET'S TAKE A LOOK.
GNNNNARAG.
YEAH, THEY DO KIND OF LOOK FAMILIAR. LIKE THOSE PANTHAC THINGS ON MANTESSA. LUKE? YOU AND MARA START BRINGING THE EQUIPMENT DOWN.

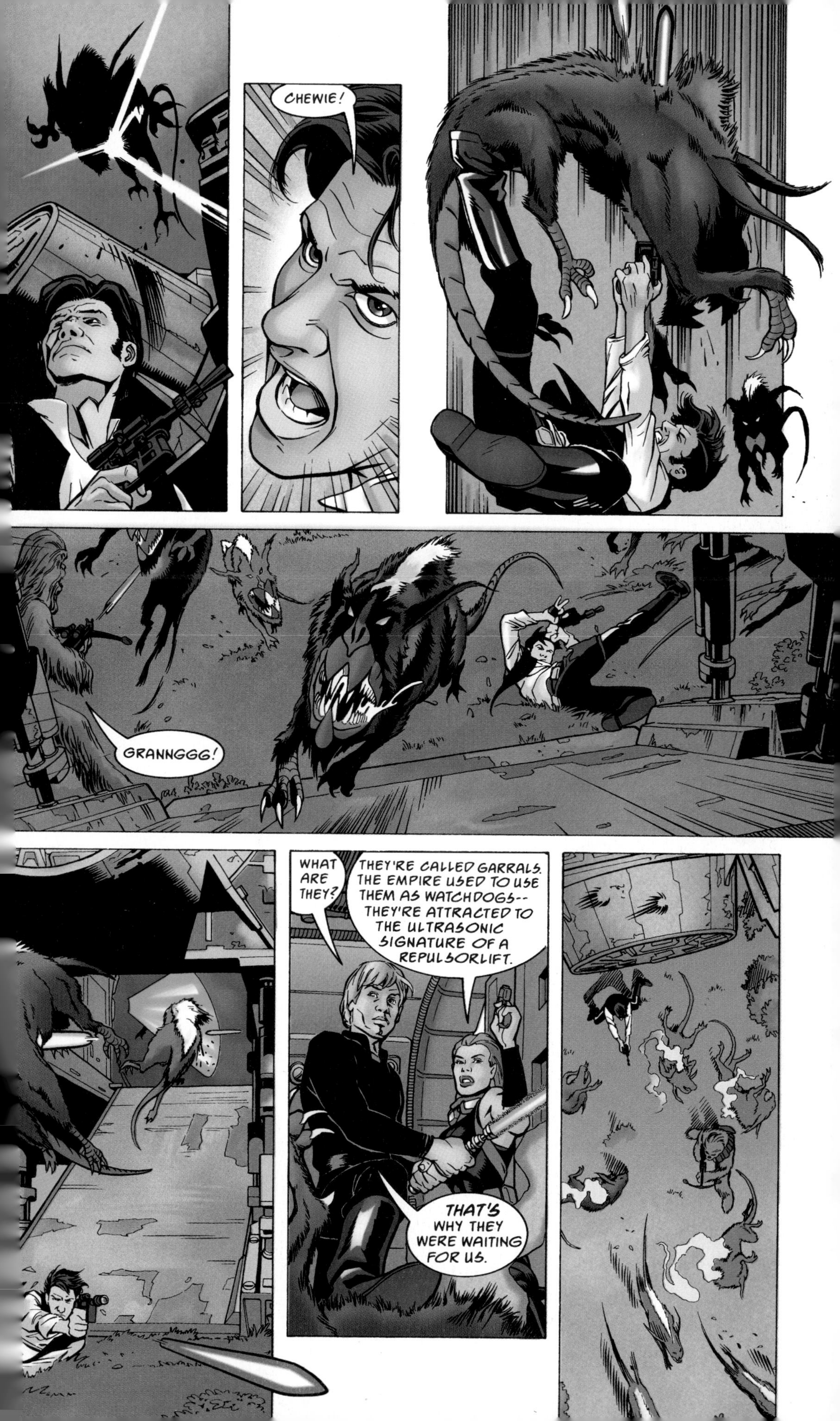
CHEWIE!
GRANNGGG!
WHAT ARE THEY?
THEY'RE CALLED GARRALS. THE EMPIRE USED TO USE THEM AS WATCHDOGS-- THEY'RE ATTRACTED TO THE ULTRASONIC SIGNATURE OF A REPULSORLIFT.
THAT'S WHY THEY WERE WAITING FOR US.

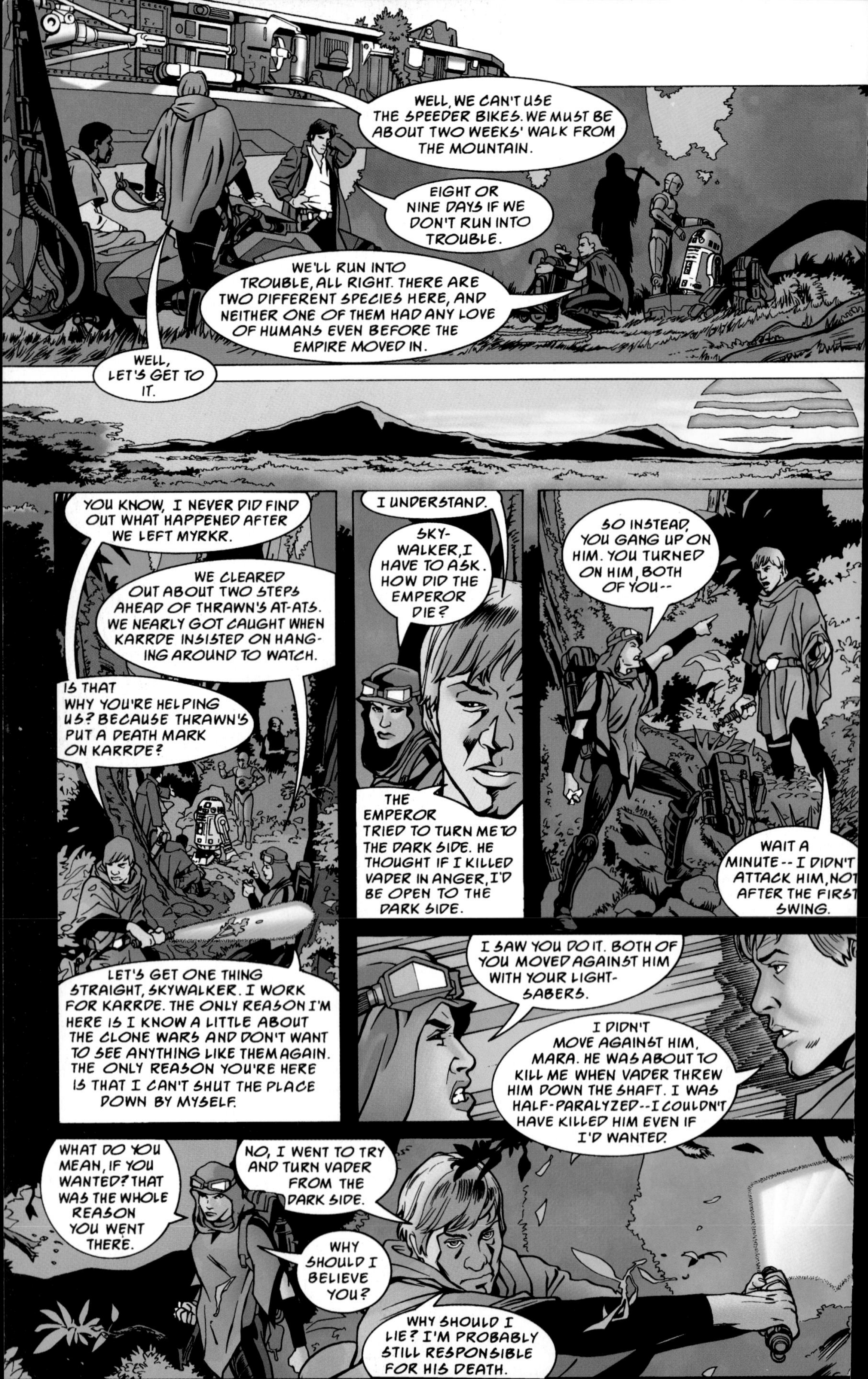
WELL, WE CAN'T USE THE SPEEDER BIKES. WE MUST BE ABOUT TWO WEEKS' WALK FROM THE MOUNTAIN.
EIGHT OR NINE DAYS IF WE DON'T RUN INTO TROUBLE.
WE'LL RUN INTO TROUBLE, ALL RIGHT. THERE ARE TWO DIFFERENT SPECIES HERE, AND NEITHER ONE OF THEM HAD ANY LOVE OF HUMANS EVEN BEFORE THE EMPIRE MOVED IN.
WELL, LET'S GET TO IT.
YOU KNOW, I NEVER DID FIND OUT WHAT HAPPENED AFTER WE LEFT MYRKR.
WE CLEARED OUT ABOUT TWO STEPS AHEAD OF THRAWN'S AT-ATS. WE NEARLY GOT CAUGHT WHEN KARRDE INSISTED ON HANGING AROUND TO WATCH.
IS THAT WHY YOU'RE HELPING US? BECAUSE THRAWN'S PUT A DEATH MARK ON KARRDE?
LET'S GET ONE THING STRAIGHT, SKYWALKER. I WORK FOR KARRDE. THE ONLY REASON I'M HERE IS I KNOW A LITTLE ABOUT THE CLONE WARS AND DON'T WANT TO SEE ANYTHING LIKE THEM AGAIN. THE ONLY REASON YOU'RE HERE IS THAT I CAN'T SHUT THE PLACE DOWN BY MYSELF.
I UNDERSTAND.
SKYWALKER, I HAVE TO ASK. HOW DID THE EMPEROR DIE?
THE EMPEROR TRIED TO TURN ME TO THE DARK SIDE. HE THOUGHT IF I KILLED VADER IN ANGER, I'D BE OPEN TO THE DARK SIDE.
SO INSTEAD, YOU GANG UP ON HIM. YOU TURNED ON HIM, BOTH OF YOU--
WAIT A MINUTE -- I DIDN'T ATTACK HIM, NOT AFTER THE FIRST SWING.
I SAW YOU DO IT. BOTH OF YOU MOVED AGAINST HIM WITH YOUR LIGHTSABERS.
I DIDN'T MOVE AGAINST HIM, MARA. HE WAS ABOUT TO KILL ME WHEN VADER THREW HIM DOWN THE SHAFT. I WAS HALF-PARALYZED--I COULDN'T HAVE KILLED HIM EVEN IF I'D WANTED.
WHAT DO YOU MEAN, IF YOU WANTED? THAT WAS THE WHOLE REASON YOU WENT THERE.
NO, I WENT TO TRY AND TURN VADER FROM THE DARK SIDE.
WHY SHOULD I BELIEVE YOU?
WHY SHOULD I LIE? I'M PROBABLY STILL RESPONSIBLE FOR HIS DEATH.

BY TRACING OUR PLANTED MESSAGES, I SHOULD BE ABLE TO LOCATE DELTA SOURCE. HOW ARE WE DOING, GHENT?

WE'RE DOWN TO ONE HUNDRED TWENTY-SEVEN POSSIBILITIES.

THOUGHT I'D FIND YOU HERE. WE'RE READY TO GIVE THE STAR-DUST PLAN A TRY, IF YOU WANT TO WATCH.

YES, I WOULD. WINTER, I'LL BE IN THE WAR ROOM WHEN YOU'RE FINISHED.

WE'RE STARTING JUST ABOVE THE PLANETARY SHIELD. ANALYSIS INDICATES MOST OF THE CLOAKED ASTEROIDS WOUND UP IN LOW ORBIT.

HARRIER, STAND BY NEGATIVE ION BEAM.

FIRE NEGATIVE ION BEAM.

CEASE FIRE. LET'S SEE IF THAT DOES IT.

THAT SOLAR WIND IS GOING TO BE A REAL NUISANCE.

TURBULENCE!

GET A TRACK ON IT. HARRIER, FIRE AT WILL.

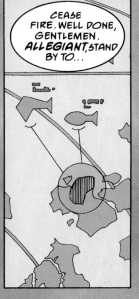

CEASE FIRE. WELL DONE, GENTLEMEN. ALLEGIANT, STAND BY TO...

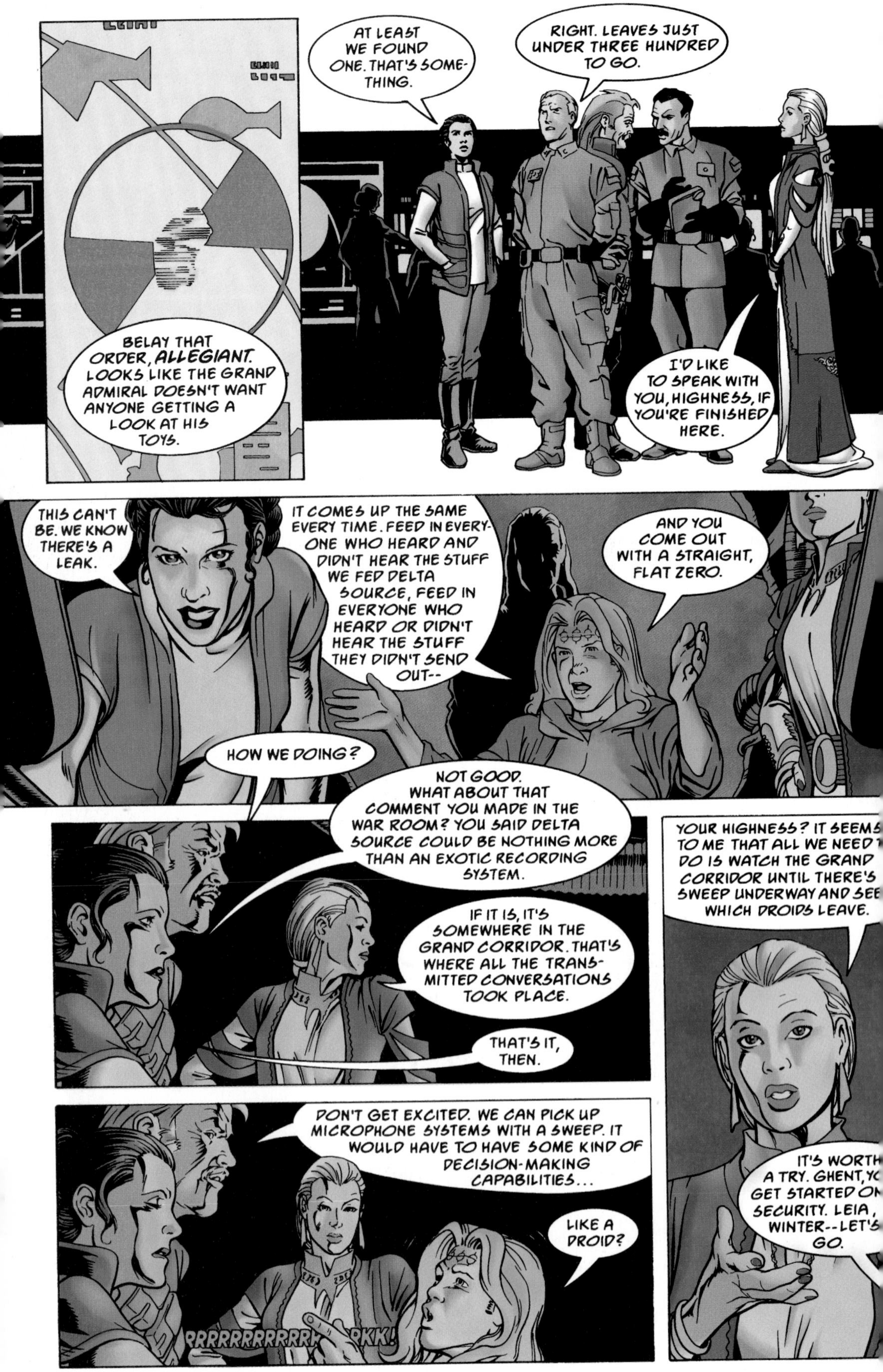
BELAY THAT ORDER, ALLEGIANT. LOOKS LIKE THE GRAND ADMIRAL DOESN'T WANT ANYONE GETTING A LOOK AT HIS TOYS.
AT LEAST WE FOUND ONE. THAT'S SOMETHING.
RIGHT. LEAVES JUST UNDER THREE HUNDRED TO GO.
I'D LIKE TO SPEAK WITH YOU, HIGHNESS, IF YOU'RE FINISHED HERE.
THIS CAN'T BE. WE KNOW THERE'S A LEAK.
IT COMES UP THE SAME EVERY TIME. FEED IN EVERYONE WHO HEARD AND DIDN'T HEAR THE STUFF WE FED DELTA SOURCE, FEED IN EVERYONE WHO HEARD OR DIDN'T HEAR THE STUFF THEY DIDN'T SEND OUT--
AND YOU COME OUT WITH A STRAIGHT, FLAT ZERO.
HOW WE DOING?
NOT GOOD. WHAT ABOUT THAT COMMENT YOU MADE IN THE WAR ROOM? YOU SAID DELTA SOURCE COULD BE NOTHING MORE THAN AN EXOTIC RECORDING SYSTEM.
IF IT IS, IT'S SOMEWHERE IN THE GRAND CORRIDOR. THAT'S WHERE ALL THE TRANSMITTED CONVERSATIONS TOOK PLACE.
THAT'S IT, THEN.
DON'T GET EXCITED. WE CAN PICK UP MICROPHONE SYSTEMS WITH A SWEEP. IT WOULD HAVE TO HAVE SOME KIND OF DECISION-MAKING CAPABILITIES...
LIKE A DROID?
RRRRRRRRRRRK RKK!
YOUR HIGHNESS? IT SEEMS TO ME THAT ALL WE NEED TO DO IS WATCH THE GRAND CORRIDOR UNTIL THERE'S A SWEEP UNDERWAY AND SEE WHICH DROIDS LEAVE.
IT'S WORTH A TRY. GHENT, YOU GET STARTED ON SECURITY. LEIA, WINTER--LET'S GO.

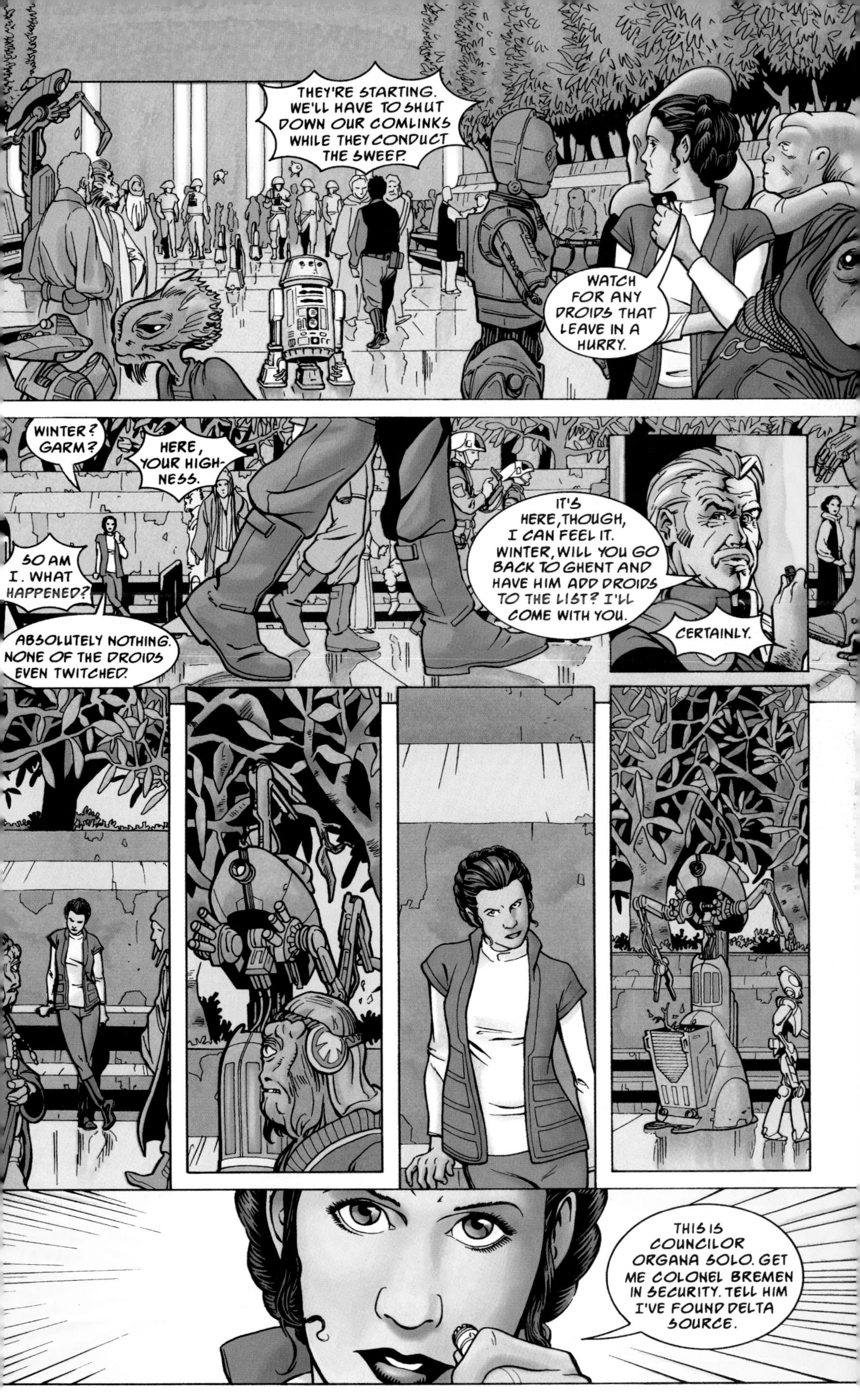
THEY'RE STARTING. WE'LL HAVE TO SHUT DOWN OUR COMLINKS WHILE THEY CONDUCT THE SWEEP.
WATCH FOR ANY DROIDS THAT LEAVE IN A HURRY.
WINTER? GARM?
HERE, YOUR HIGH-NESS.
SO AM I. WHAT HAPPENED?
ABSOLUTELY NOTHING. NONE OF THE DROIDS EVEN TWITCHED.
IT'S HERE, THOUGH, I CAN FEEL IT. WINTER, WILL YOU GO BACK TO GHENT AND HAVE HIM ADD DROIDS TO THE LIST? I'LL COME WITH YOU.
CERTAINLY.
THIS IS COUNCILOR ORGANA SOLO. GET ME COLONEL BREMEN IN SECURITY. TELL HIM I'VE FOUND DELTA SOURCE.

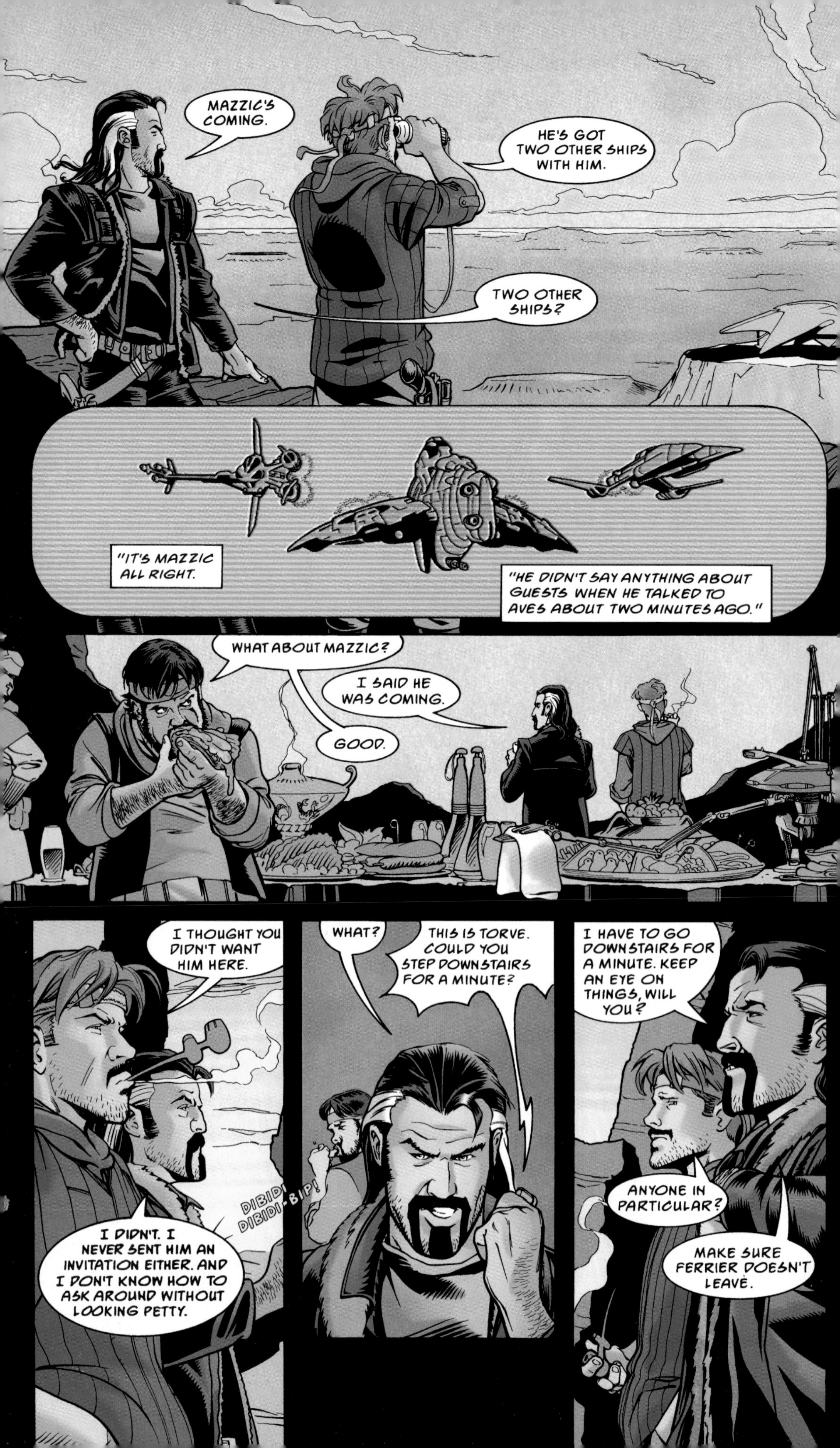
MAZZIC'S COMING.
HE'S GOT TWO OTHER SHIPS WITH HIM.
TWO OTHER SHIPS?
"IT'S MAZZIC ALL RIGHT.
"HE DIDN'T SAY ANYTHING ABOUT GUESTS WHEN HE TALKED TO AVES ABOUT TWO MINUTES AGO."
WHAT ABOUT MAZZIC?
I SAID HE WAS COMING.
GOOD.
I THOUGHT YOU DIDN'T WANT HIM HERE.
I DIDN'T. I NEVER SENT HIM AN INVITATION EITHER. AND I DON'T KNOW HOW TO ASK AROUND WITHOUT LOOKING PETTY.
DIBIDI DIBIDI-BIP!
WHAT?
THIS IS TORVE. COULD YOU STEP DOWNSTAIRS FOR A MINUTE?
I HAVE TO GO DOWNSTAIRS FOR A MINUTE. KEEP AN EYE ON THINGS, WILL YOU?
ANYONE IN PARTICULAR?
MAKE SURE FERRIER DOESN'T LEAVE.

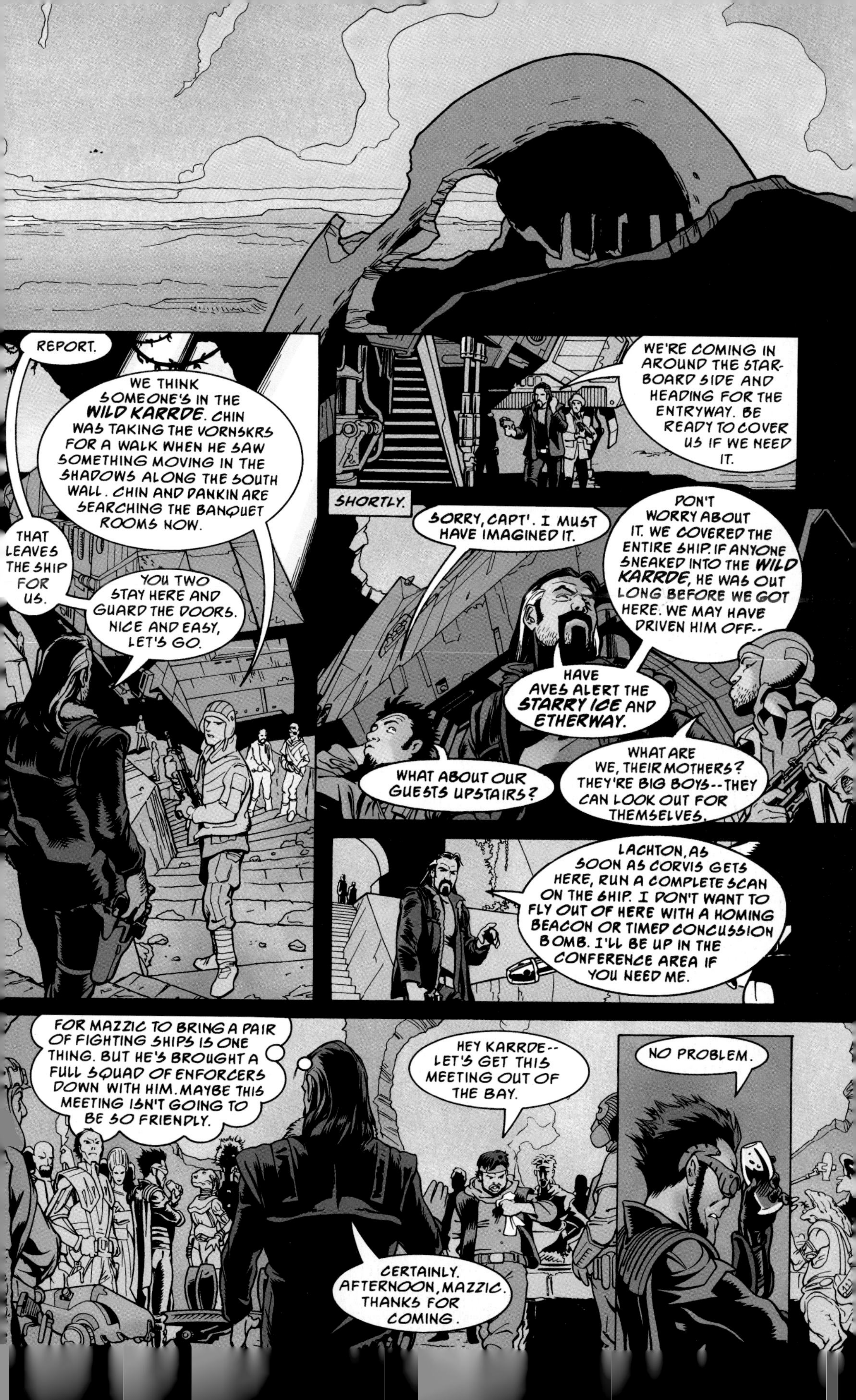
REPORT.
WE THINK SOMEONE'S IN THE WILD KARRDE. CHIN WAS TAKING THE VORNSKRS FOR A WALK WHEN HE SAW SOMETHING MOVING IN THE SHADOWS ALONG THE SOUTH WALL. CHIN AND DANKIN ARE SEARCHING THE BANQUET ROOMS NOW.
THAT LEAVES THE SHIP FOR US.
YOU TWO STAY HERE AND GUARD THE DOORS. NICE AND EASY, LET'S GO.
WE'RE COMING IN AROUND THE STARBOARD SIDE AND HEADING FOR THE ENTRYWAY. BE READY TO COVER US IF WE NEED IT.
SHORTLY.
SORRY, CAPT'. I MUST HAVE IMAGINED IT.
DON'T WORRY ABOUT IT. WE COVERED THE ENTIRE SHIP. IF ANYONE SNEAKED INTO THE WILD KARRDE, HE WAS OUT LONG BEFORE WE GOT HERE. WE MAY HAVE DRIVEN HIM OFF--
HAVE AVES ALERT THE STARRY ICE AND ETHERWAY.
WHAT ABOUT OUR GUESTS UPSTAIRS?
WHAT ARE WE, THEIR MOTHERS? THEY'RE BIG BOYS--THEY CAN LOOK OUT FOR THEMSELVES.
LACHTON, AS SOON AS CORVIS GETS HERE, RUN A COMPLETE SCAN ON THE SHIP. I DON'T WANT TO FLY OUT OF HERE WITH A HOMING BEACON OR TIMED CONCUSSION BOMB. I'LL BE UP IN THE CONFERENCE AREA IF YOU NEED ME.
FOR MAZZIC TO BRING A PAIR OF FIGHTING SHIPS IS ONE THING. BUT HE'S BROUGHT A FULL SQUAD OF ENFORCERS DOWN WITH HIM. MAYBE THIS MEETING ISN'T GOING TO BE SO FRIENDLY.
HEY KARRDE-- LET'S GET THIS MEETING OUT OF THE BAY.
NO PROBLEM.
CERTAINLY. AFTERNOON, MAZZIC. THANKS FOR COMING.

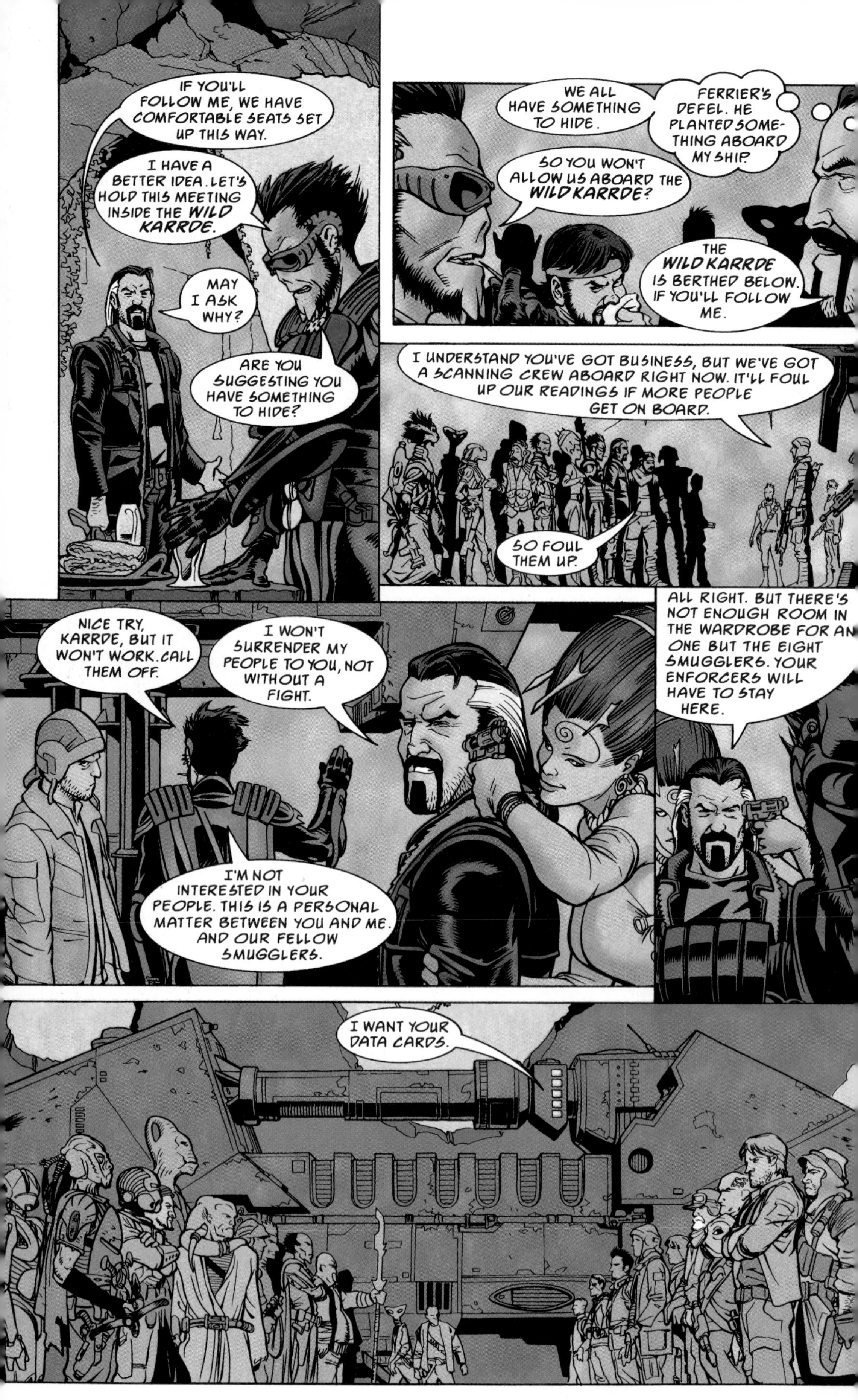
IF YOU'LL FOLLOW ME, WE HAVE COMFORTABLE SEATS SET UP THIS WAY.
I HAVE A BETTER IDEA. LET'S HOLD THIS MEETING INSIDE THE WILD KARRDE.
MAY I ASK WHY?
ARE YOU SUGGESTING YOU HAVE SOMETHING TO HIDE?
WE ALL HAVE SOMETHING TO HIDE.
FERRIER'S DEFEL. HE PLANTED SOMETHING ABOARD MY SHIP.
SO YOU WON'T ALLOW US ABOARD THE WILD KARRDE?
THE WILD KARRDE IS BERTHED BELOW. IF YOU'LL FOLLOW ME.
I UNDERSTAND YOU'VE GOT BUSINESS, BUT WE'VE GOT A SCANNING CREW ABOARD RIGHT NOW. IT'LL FOUL UP OUR READINGS IF MORE PEOPLE GET ON BOARD.
SO FOUL THEM UP.
NICE TRY, KARRDE, BUT IT WON'T WORK. CALL THEM OFF.
I WON'T SURRENDER MY PEOPLE TO YOU, NOT WITHOUT A FIGHT.
I'M NOT INTERESTED IN YOUR PEOPLE. THIS IS A PERSONAL MATTER BETWEEN YOU AND ME. AND OUR FELLOW SMUGGLERS.
ALL RIGHT. BUT THERE'S NOT ENOUGH ROOM IN THE WARDROBE FOR AN ONE BUT THE EIGHT SMUGGLERS. YOUR ENFORCERS WILL HAVE TO STAY HERE.
I WANT YOUR DATA CARDS.

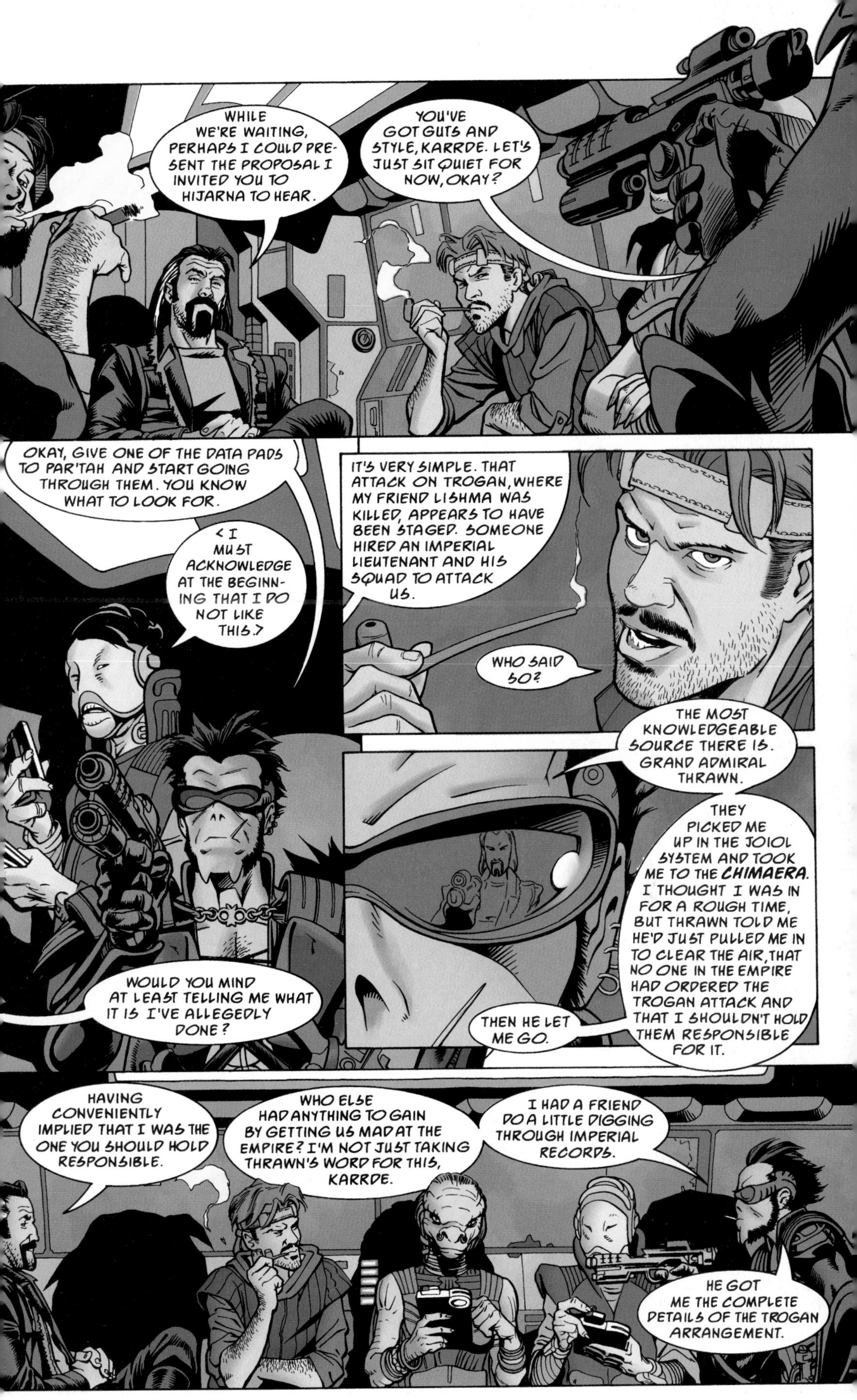

WHILE WE'RE WAITING, PERHAPS I COULD PRESENT THE PROPOSAL I INVITED YOU TO HIJARNA TO HEAR.
YOU'VE GOT GUTS AND STYLE, KARRDE. LET'S JUST SIT QUIET FOR NOW, OKAY?
OKAY, GIVE ONE OF THE DATA PADS TO PAR'TAH AND START GOING THROUGH THEM. YOU KNOW WHAT TO LOOK FOR.
<I MUST ACKNOWLEDGE AT THE BEGINNING THAT I DO NOT LIKE THIS.>
IT'S VERY SIMPLE. THAT ATTACK ON TROGAN, WHERE MY FRIEND LISHMA WAS KILLED, APPEARS TO HAVE BEEN STAGED. SOMEONE HIRED AN IMPERIAL LIEUTENANT AND HIS SQUAD TO ATTACK US.
WHO SAID SO?
THE MOST KNOWLEDGEABLE SOURCE THERE IS. GRAND ADMIRAL THRAWN.
THEY PICKED ME UP IN THE JOIOL SYSTEM AND TOOK ME TO THE *CHIMAERA*. I THOUGHT I WAS IN FOR A ROUGH TIME, BUT THRAWN TOLD ME HE'D JUST PULLED ME IN TO CLEAR THE AIR, THAT NO ONE IN THE EMPIRE HAD ORDERED THE TROGAN ATTACK AND THAT I SHOULDN'T HOLD THEM RESPONSIBLE FOR IT.
THEN HE LET ME GO.
WOULD YOU MIND AT LEAST TELLING ME WHAT IT IS I'VE ALLEGEDLY DONE?
HAVING CONVENIENTLY IMPLIED THAT I WAS THE ONE YOU SHOULD HOLD RESPONSIBLE.
WHO ELSE HAD ANYTHING TO GAIN BY GETTING US MAD AT THE EMPIRE? I'M NOT JUST TAKING THRAWN'S WORD FOR THIS, KARRDE.
I HAD A FRIEND DO A LITTLE DIGGING THROUGH IMPERIAL RECORDS.
HE GOT ME THE COMPLETE DETAILS OF THE TROGAN ARRANGEMENT.

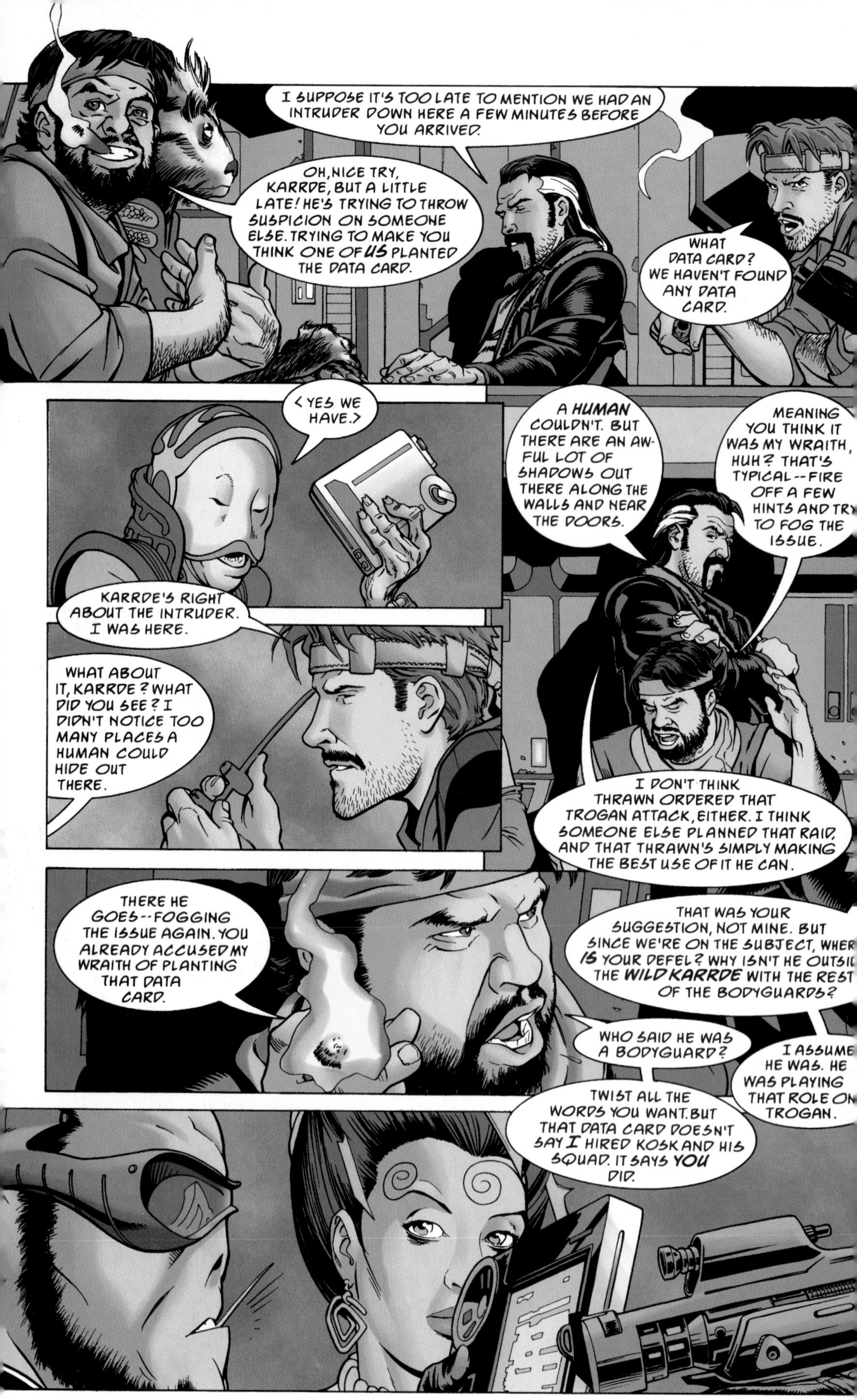
I SUPPOSE IT'S TOO LATE TO MENTION WE HAD AN INTRUDER DOWN HERE A FEW MINUTES BEFORE YOU ARRIVED.
OH, NICE TRY, KARRDE, BUT A LITTLE LATE! HE'S TRYING TO THROW SUSPICION ON SOMEONE ELSE. TRYING TO MAKE YOU THINK ONE OF US PLANTED THE DATA CARD.
WHAT DATA CARD? WE HAVEN'T FOUND ANY DATA CARD.
<YES WE HAVE.>
A HUMAN COULDN'T. BUT THERE ARE AN AWFUL LOT OF SHADOWS OUT THERE ALONG THE WALLS AND NEAR THE DOORS.
MEANING YOU THINK IT WAS MY WRAITH, HUH? THAT'S TYPICAL--FIRE OFF A FEW HINTS AND TRY TO FOG THE ISSUE.
KARRDE'S RIGHT ABOUT THE INTRUDER. I WAS HERE.
WHAT ABOUT IT, KARRDE? WHAT DID YOU SEE? I DIDN'T NOTICE TOO MANY PLACES A HUMAN COULD HIDE OUT THERE.
I DON'T THINK THRAWN ORDERED THAT TROGAN ATTACK, EITHER. I THINK SOMEONE ELSE PLANNED THAT RAID, AND THAT THRAWN'S SIMPLY MAKING THE BEST USE OF IT HE CAN.
THERE HE GOES--FOGGING THE ISSUE AGAIN. YOU ALREADY ACCUSED MY WRAITH OF PLANTING THAT DATA CARD.
THAT WAS YOUR SUGGESTION, NOT MINE. BUT SINCE WE'RE ON THE SUBJECT, WHERE IS YOUR DEFEL? WHY ISN'T HE OUTSIDE THE WILD KARRDE WITH THE REST OF THE BODYGUARDS?
WHO SAID HE WAS A BODYGUARD?
I ASSUME HE WAS. HE WAS PLAYING THAT ROLE ON TROGAN.
TWIST ALL THE WORDS YOU WANT. BUT THAT DATA CARD DOESN'T SAY I HIRED KOSK AND HIS SQUAD. IT SAYS YOU DID.

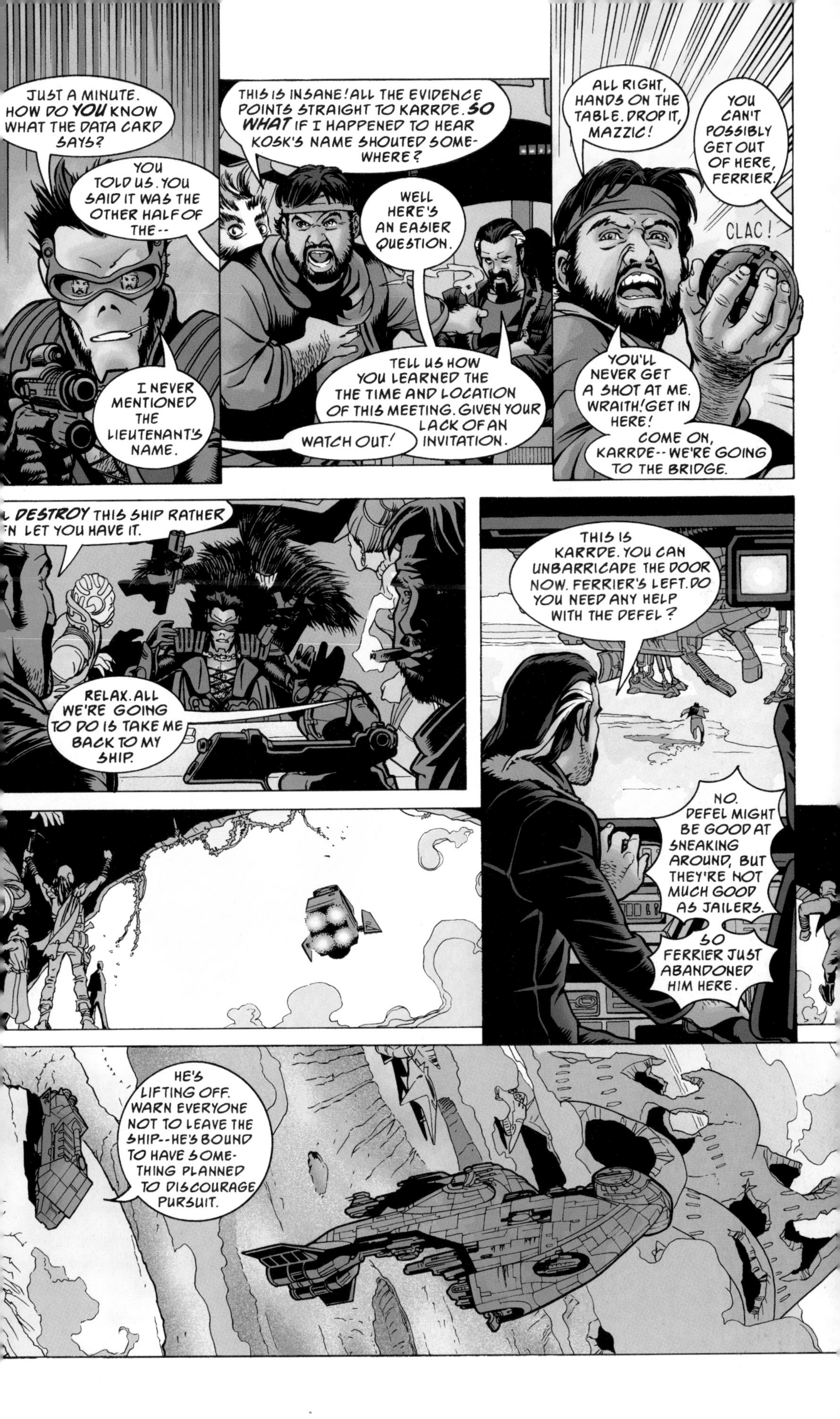
JUST A MINUTE. HOW DO YOU KNOW WHAT THE DATA CARD SAYS?
YOU TOLD US. YOU SAID IT WAS THE OTHER HALF OF THE--
I NEVER MENTIONED THE LIEUTENANT'S NAME.
THIS IS INSANE! ALL THE EVIDENCE POINTS STRAIGHT TO KARRDE. SO WHAT IF I HAPPENED TO HEAR KOSK'S NAME SHOUTED SOMEWHERE?
WELL HERE'S AN EASIER QUESTION.
TELL US HOW YOU LEARNED THE THE TIME AND LOCATION OF THIS MEETING. GIVEN YOUR LACK OF AN INVITATION.
WATCH OUT!
ALL RIGHT, HANDS ON THE TABLE. DROP IT, MAZZIC!
YOU CAN'T POSSIBLY GET OUT OF HERE, FERRIER.
CLAC!
YOU'LL NEVER GET A SHOT AT ME. WRAITH! GET IN HERE!
COME ON, KARRDE-- WE'RE GOING TO THE BRIDGE.
DESTROY THIS SHIP RATHER N LET YOU HAVE IT.
RELAX. ALL WE'RE GOING TO DO IS TAKE ME BACK TO MY SHIP.
THIS IS KARRDE. YOU CAN UNBARRICADE THE DOOR NOW. FERRIER'S LEFT. DO YOU NEED ANY HELP WITH THE DEFEL?
NO. DEFEL MIGHT BE GOOD AT SNEAKING AROUND, BUT THEY'RE NOT MUCH GOOD AS JAILERS.
SO FERRIER JUST ABANDONED HIM HERE.
HE'S LIFTING OFF. WARN EVERYONE NOT TO LEAVE THE SHIP--HE'S BOUND TO HAVE SOMETHING PLANNED TO DISCOURAGE PURSUIT.

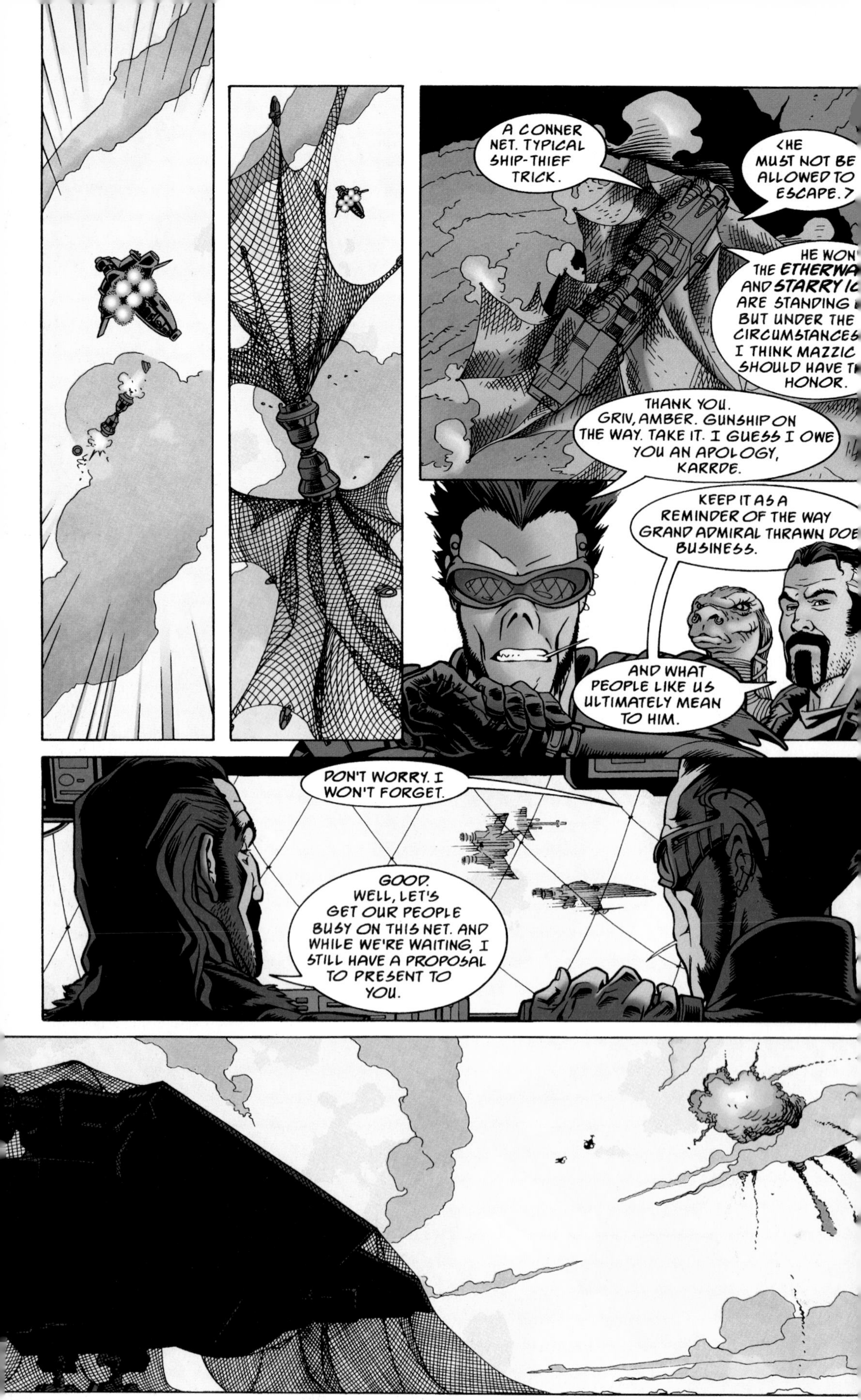
A CONNER NET. TYPICAL SHIP-THIEF TRICK.
<HE MUST NOT BE ALLOWED TO ESCAPE.>
HE WON' THE ETHERWA AND STARRY IC ARE STANDING BUT UNDER THE CIRCUMSTANCES I THINK MAZZIC SHOULD HAVE T HONOR.
THANK YOU. GRIV, AMBER. GUNSHIP ON THE WAY. TAKE IT. I GUESS I OWE YOU AN APOLOGY, KARRDE.
KEEP IT AS A REMINDER OF THE WAY GRAND ADMIRAL THRAWN DOE BUSINESS.
AND WHAT PEOPLE LIKE US ULTIMATELY MEAN TO HIM.
DON'T WORRY. I WON'T FORGET.
GOOD. WELL, LET'S GET OUR PEOPLE BUSY ON THIS NET. AND WHILE WE'RE WAITING, I STILL HAVE A PROPOSAL TO PRESENT TO YOU.

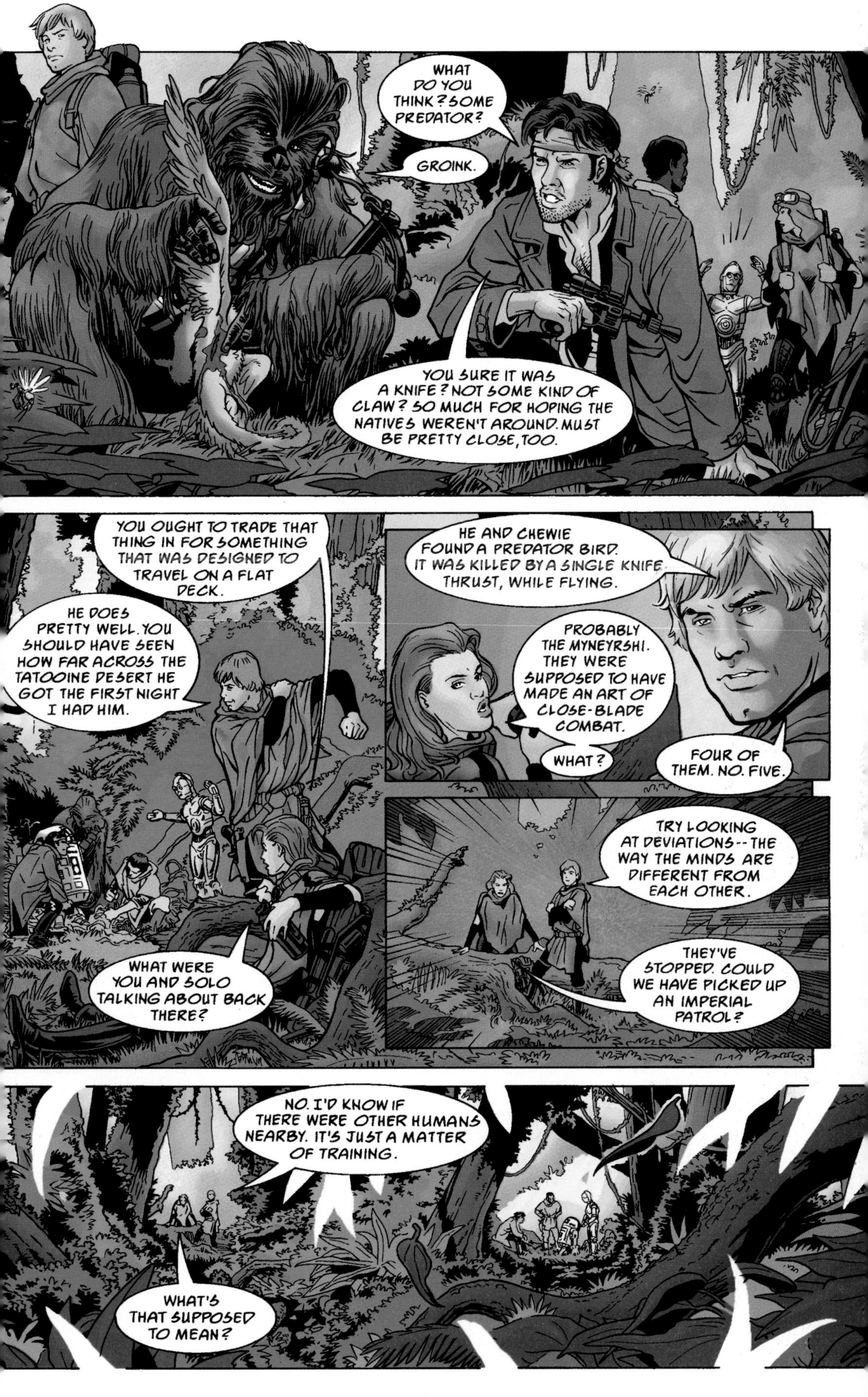
WHAT DO YOU THINK? SOME PREDATOR?
GROINK.
YOU SURE IT WAS A KNIFE? NOT SOME KIND OF CLAW? SO MUCH FOR HOPING THE NATIVES WEREN'T AROUND. MUST BE PRETTY CLOSE, TOO.
YOU OUGHT TO TRADE THAT THING IN FOR SOMETHING THAT WAS DESIGNED TO TRAVEL ON A FLAT DECK.
HE DOES PRETTY WELL. YOU SHOULD HAVE SEEN HOW FAR ACROSS THE TATOOINE DESERT HE GOT THE FIRST NIGHT I HAD HIM.
WHAT WERE YOU AND SOLO TALKING ABOUT BACK THERE?
HE AND CHEWIE FOUND A PREDATOR BIRD. IT WAS KILLED BY A SINGLE KNIFE THRUST, WHILE FLYING.
PROBABLY THE MYNEYRSHI. THEY WERE SUPPOSED TO HAVE MADE AN ART OF CLOSE-BLADE COMBAT.
WHAT?
FOUR OF THEM. NO. FIVE.
TRY LOOKING AT DEVIATIONS-- THE WAY THE MINDS ARE DIFFERENT FROM EACH OTHER.
THEY'VE STOPPED. COULD WE HAVE PICKED UP AN IMPERIAL PATROL?
NO. I'D KNOW IF THERE WERE OTHER HUMANS NEARBY. IT'S JUST A MATTER OF TRAINING.
WHAT'S THAT SUPPOSED TO MEAN?

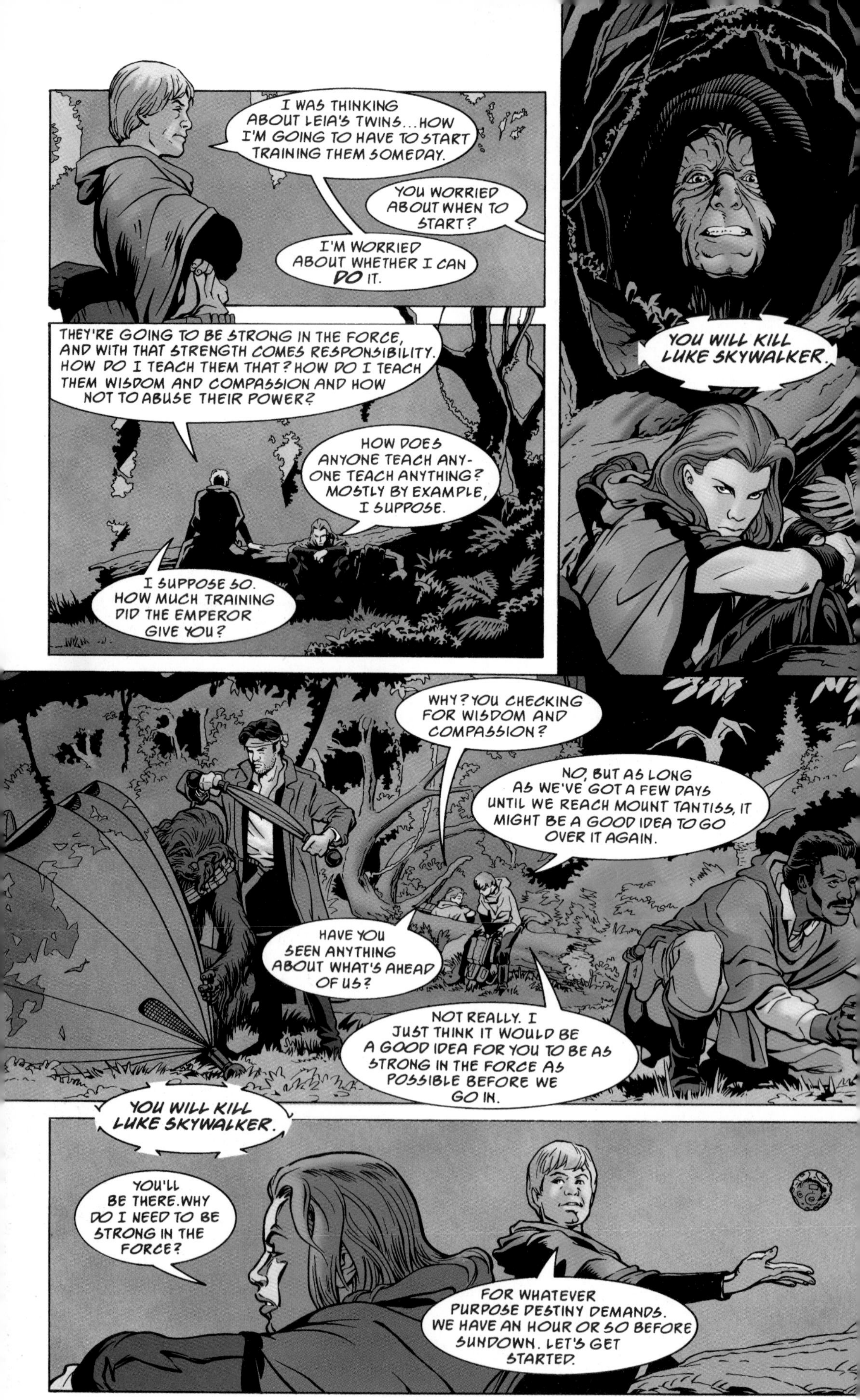
I WAS THINKING ABOUT LEIA'S TWINS...HOW I'M GOING TO HAVE TO START TRAINING THEM SOMEDAY.
YOU WORRIED ABOUT WHEN TO START?
I'M WORRIED ABOUT WHETHER I CAN DO IT.
THEY'RE GOING TO BE STRONG IN THE FORCE, AND WITH THAT STRENGTH COMES RESPONSIBILITY. HOW DO I TEACH THEM THAT? HOW DO I TEACH THEM WISDOM AND COMPASSION AND HOW NOT TO ABUSE THEIR POWER?
HOW DOES ANYONE TEACH ANY-ONE TEACH ANYTHING? MOSTLY BY EXAMPLE, I SUPPOSE.
I SUPPOSE SO. HOW MUCH TRAINING DID THE EMPEROR GIVE YOU?
YOU WILL KILL LUKE SKYWALKER.
WHY? YOU CHECKING FOR WISDOM AND COMPASSION?
NO, BUT AS LONG AS WE'VE GOT A FEW DAYS UNTIL WE REACH MOUNT TANTISS, IT MIGHT BE A GOOD IDEA TO GO OVER IT AGAIN.
HAVE YOU SEEN ANYTHING ABOUT WHAT'S AHEAD OF US?
NOT REALLY. I JUST THINK IT WOULD BE A GOOD IDEA FOR YOU TO BE AS STRONG IN THE FORCE AS POSSIBLE BEFORE WE GO IN.
YOU WILL KILL LUKE SKYWALKER.
YOU'LL BE THERE. WHY DO I NEED TO BE STRONG IN THE FORCE?
FOR WHATEVER PURPOSE DESTINY DEMANDS. WE HAVE AN HOUR OR SO BEFORE SUNDOWN. LET'S GET STARTED.

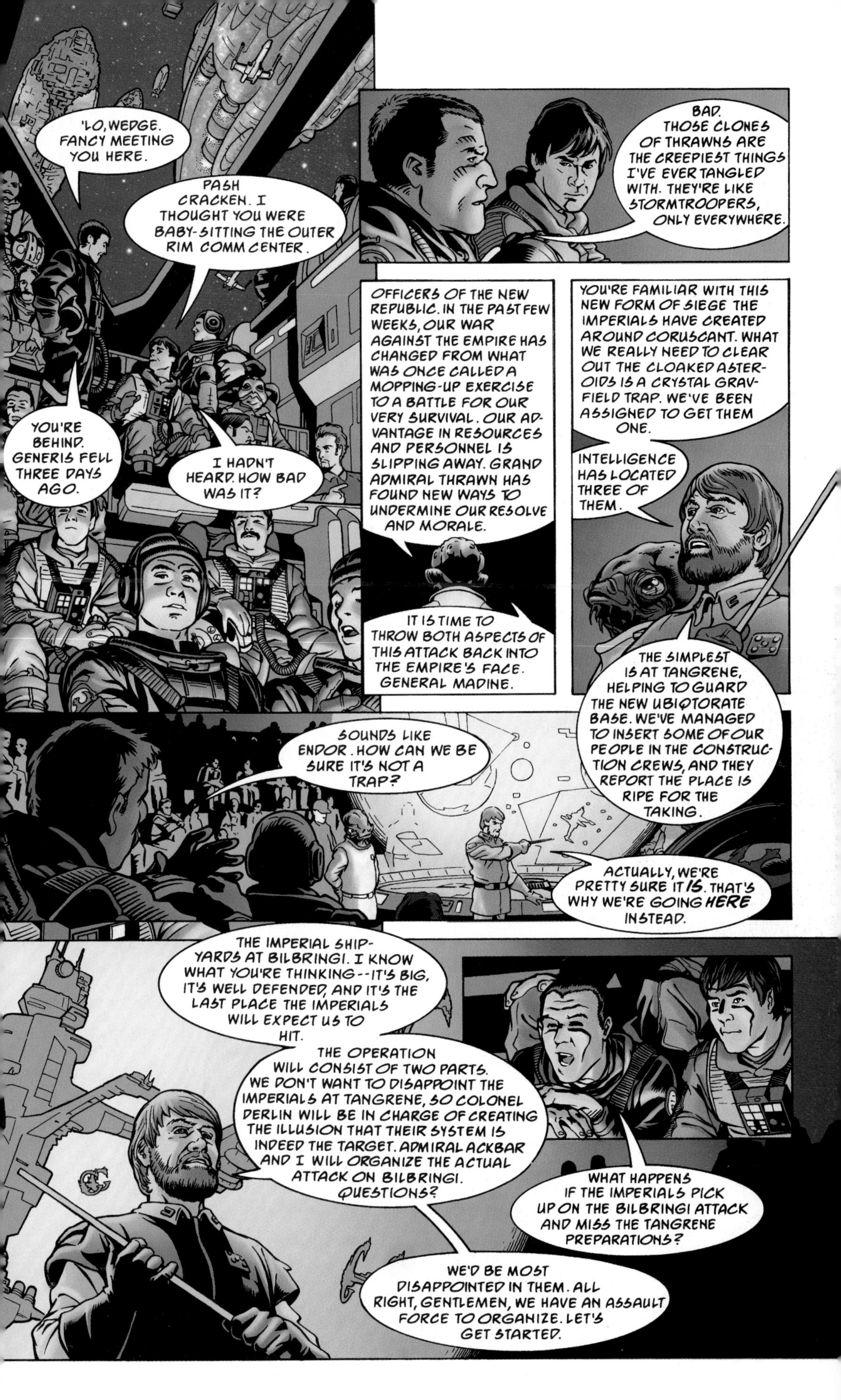
'LO, WEDGE. FANCY MEETING YOU HERE.
PASH CRACKEN. I THOUGHT YOU WERE BABY-SITTING THE OUTER RIM COMM CENTER.
YOU'RE BEHIND. GENERIS FELL THREE DAYS AGO.
I HADN'T HEARD. HOW BAD WAS IT?
BAD. THOSE CLONES OF THRAWNS ARE THE CREEPIEST THINGS I'VE EVER TANGLED WITH. THEY'RE LIKE STORMTROOPERS, ONLY EVERYWHERE.
OFFICERS OF THE NEW REPUBLIC. IN THE PAST FEW WEEKS, OUR WAR AGAINST THE EMPIRE HAS CHANGED FROM WHAT WAS ONCE CALLED A MOPPING-UP EXERCISE TO A BATTLE FOR OUR VERY SURVIVAL. OUR ADVANTAGE IN RESOURCES AND PERSONNEL IS SLIPPING AWAY. GRAND ADMIRAL THRAWN HAS FOUND NEW WAYS TO UNDERMINE OUR RESOLVE AND MORALE.
IT IS TIME TO THROW BOTH ASPECTS OF THIS ATTACK BACK INTO THE EMPIRE'S FACE. GENERAL MADINE.
YOU'RE FAMILIAR WITH THIS NEW FORM OF SIEGE THE IMPERIALS HAVE CREATED AROUND CORUSCANT. WHAT WE REALLY NEED TO CLEAR OUT THE CLOAKED ASTEROIDS IS A CRYSTAL GRAV-FIELD TRAP. WE'VE BEEN ASSIGNED TO GET THEM ONE.
INTELLIGENCE HAS LOCATED THREE OF THEM.
THE SIMPLEST IS AT TANGRENE, HELPING TO GUARD THE NEW UBIQTORATE BASE. WE'VE MANAGED TO INSERT SOME OF OUR PEOPLE IN THE CONSTRUCTION CREWS, AND THEY REPORT THE PLACE IS RIPE FOR THE TAKING.
SOUNDS LIKE ENDOR. HOW CAN WE BE SURE IT'S NOT A TRAP?
ACTUALLY, WE'RE PRETTY SURE IT *IS*. THAT'S WHY WE'RE GOING ***HERE*** INSTEAD.
THE IMPERIAL SHIPYARDS AT BILBRINGI. I KNOW WHAT YOU'RE THINKING--IT'S BIG, IT'S WELL DEFENDED, AND IT'S THE LAST PLACE THE IMPERIALS WILL EXPECT US TO HIT.
THE OPERATION WILL CONSIST OF TWO PARTS. WE DON'T WANT TO DISAPPOINT THE IMPERIALS AT TANGRENE, SO COLONEL DERLIN WILL BE IN CHARGE OF CREATING THE ILLUSION THAT THEIR SYSTEM IS INDEED THE TARGET. ADMIRAL ACKBAR AND I WILL ORGANIZE THE ACTUAL ATTACK ON BILBRINGI. QUESTIONS?
WHAT HAPPENS IF THE IMPERIALS PICK UP ON THE BILBRINGI ATTACK AND MISS THE TANGRENE PREPARATIONS?
WE'D BE MOST DISAPPOINTED IN THEM. ALL RIGHT, GENTLEMEN, WE HAVE AN ASSAULT FORCE TO ORGANIZE. LET'S GET STARTED.

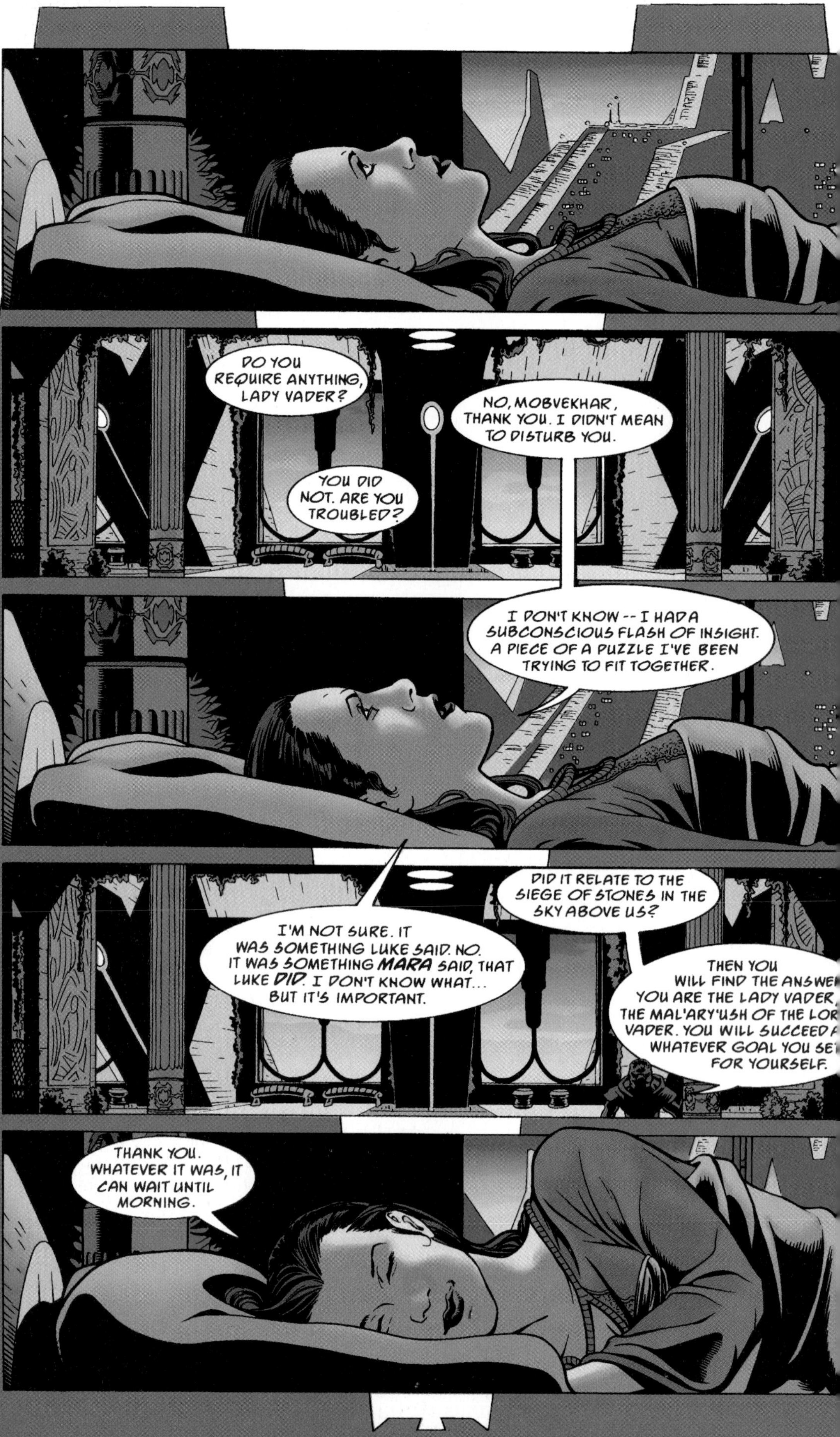
DO YOU REQUIRE ANYTHING, LADY VADER?
NO, MOBVEKHAR, THANK YOU. I DIDN'T MEAN TO DISTURB YOU.
YOU DID NOT. ARE YOU TROUBLED?
I DON'T KNOW -- I HAD A SUBCONSCIOUS FLASH OF INSIGHT. A PIECE OF A PUZZLE I'VE BEEN TRYING TO FIT TOGETHER.
DID IT RELATE TO THE SIEGE OF STONES IN THE SKY ABOVE US?
I'M NOT SURE. IT WAS SOMETHING LUKE SAID. NO. IT WAS SOMETHING MARA SAID, THAT LUKE DID. I DON'T KNOW WHAT... BUT IT'S IMPORTANT.
THEN YOU WILL FIND THE ANSWE
YOU ARE THE LADY VADER,
THE MAL'ARY'USH OF THE LOR
VADER. YOU WILL SUCCEED
WHATEVER GOAL YOU SE
FOR YOURSELF.
THANK YOU. WHATEVER IT WAS, IT CAN WAIT UNTIL MORNING.

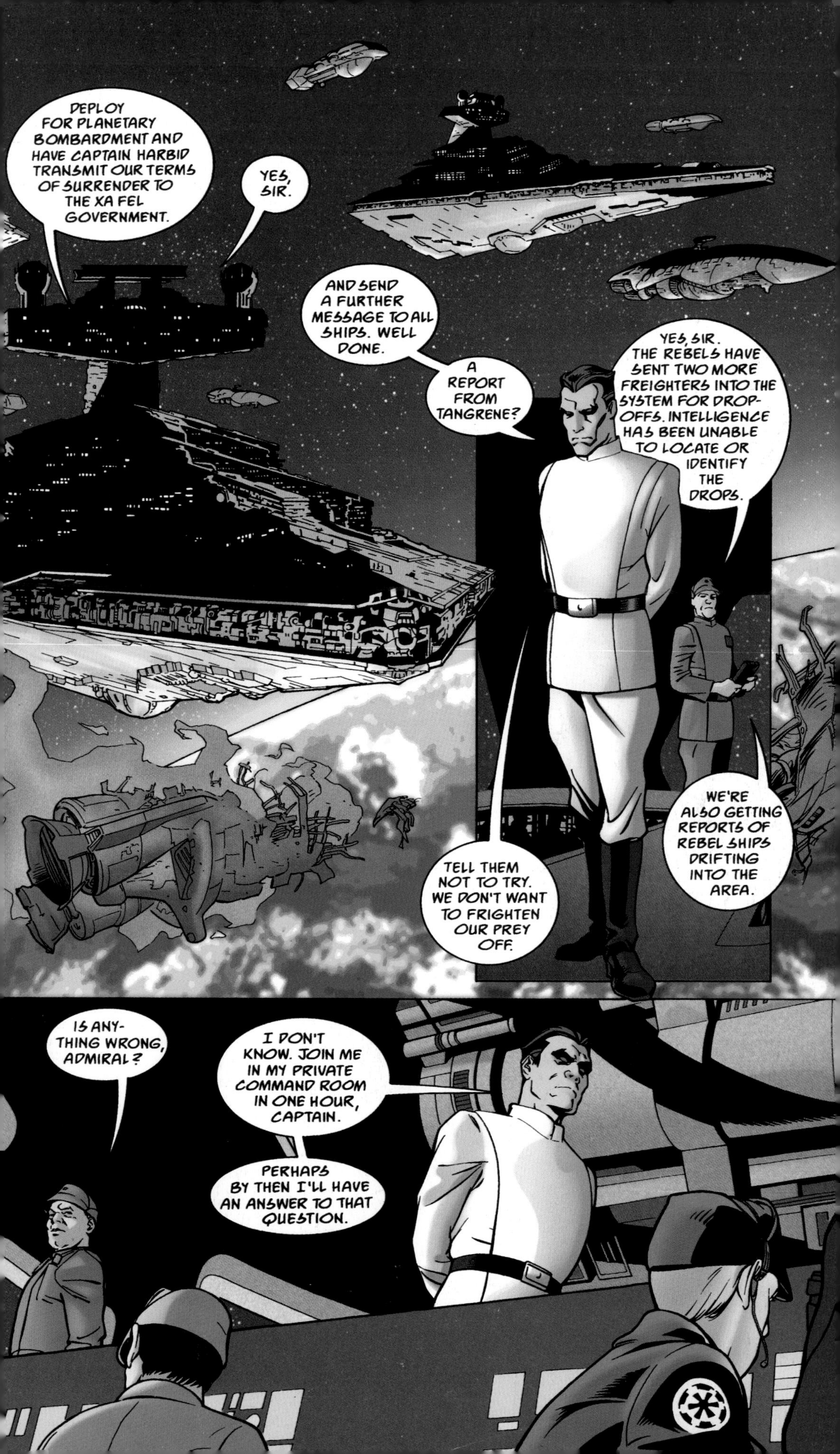
DEPLOY FOR PLANETARY BOMBARDMENT AND HAVE CAPTAIN HARBID TRANSMIT OUR TERMS OF SURRENDER TO THE XA FEL GOVERNMENT.
YES, SIR.
AND SEND A FURTHER MESSAGE TO ALL SHIPS. WELL DONE.
A REPORT FROM TANGRENE?
YES, SIR. THE REBELS HAVE SENT TWO MORE FREIGHTERS INTO THE SYSTEM FOR DROP-OFFS. INTELLIGENCE HAS BEEN UNABLE TO LOCATE OR IDENTIFY THE DROPS.
WE'RE ALSO GETTING REPORTS OF REBEL SHIPS DRIFTING INTO THE AREA.
TELL THEM NOT TO TRY. WE DON'T WANT TO FRIGHTEN OUR PREY OFF.
IS ANYTHING WRONG, ADMIRAL?
I DON'T KNOW. JOIN ME IN MY PRIVATE COMMAND ROOM IN ONE HOUR, CAPTAIN.
PERHAPS BY THEN I'LL HAVE AN ANSWER TO THAT QUESTION.

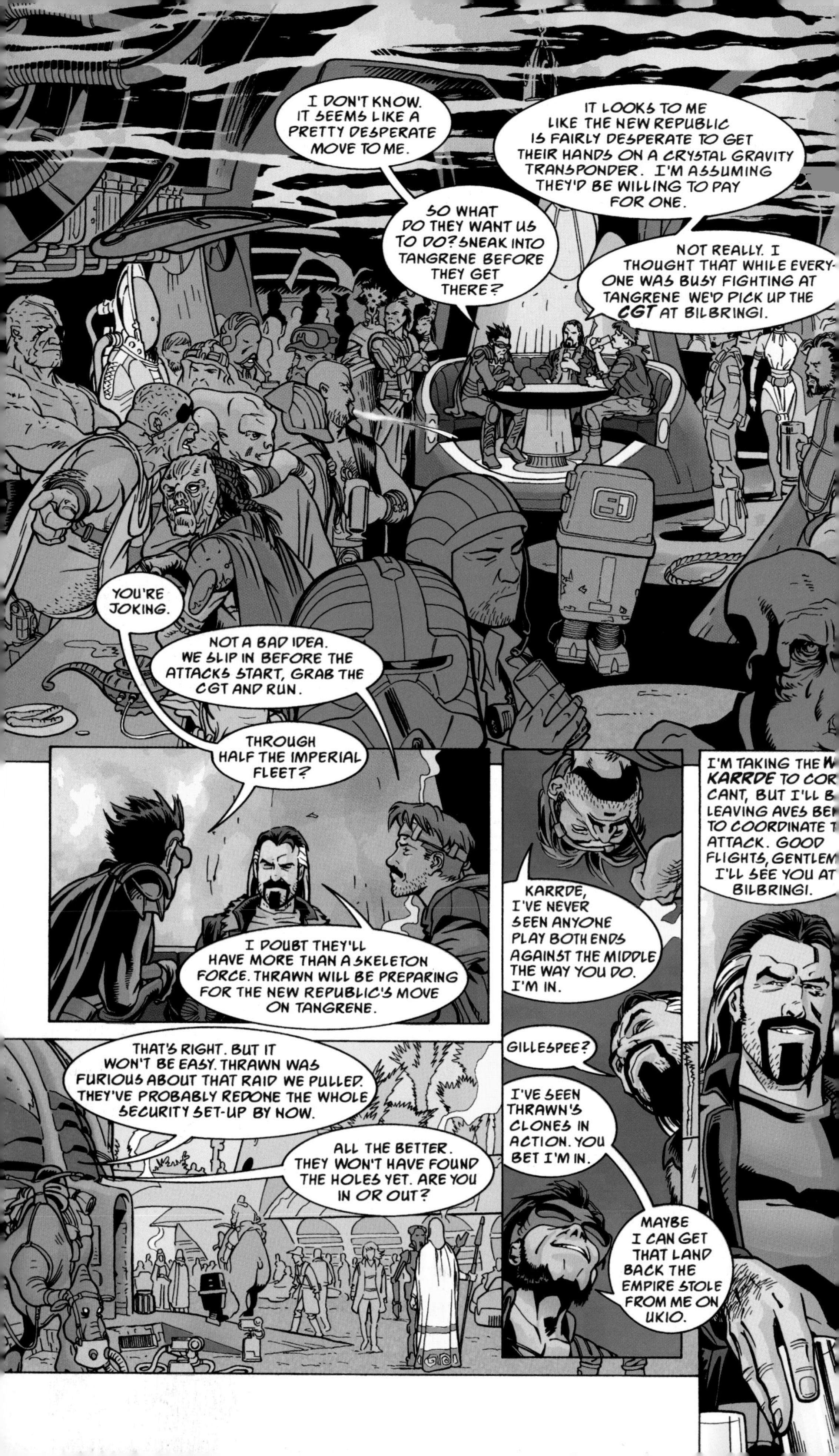
I DON'T KNOW. IT SEEMS LIKE A PRETTY DESPERATE MOVE TO ME.
IT LOOKS TO ME LIKE THE NEW REPUBLIC IS FAIRLY DESPERATE TO GET THEIR HANDS ON A CRYSTAL GRAVITY TRANSPONDER. I'M ASSUMING THEY'D BE WILLING TO PAY FOR ONE.
SO WHAT DO THEY WANT US TO DO? SNEAK INTO TANGRENE BEFORE THEY GET THERE?
NOT REALLY. I THOUGHT THAT WHILE EVERY-ONE WAS BUSY FIGHTING AT TANGRENE WE'D PICK UP THE CGT AT BILBRINGI.
YOU'RE JOKING.
NOT A BAD IDEA. WE SLIP IN BEFORE THE ATTACKS START, GRAB THE CGT AND RUN.
THROUGH HALF THE IMPERIAL FLEET?
I DOUBT THEY'LL HAVE MORE THAN A SKELETON FORCE. THRAWN WILL BE PREPARING FOR THE NEW REPUBLIC'S MOVE ON TANGRENE.
THAT'S RIGHT. BUT IT WON'T BE EASY. THRAWN WAS FURIOUS ABOUT THAT RAID WE PULLED. THEY'VE PROBABLY REDONE THE WHOLE SECURITY SET-UP BY NOW.
ALL THE BETTER. THEY WON'T HAVE FOUND THE HOLES YET. ARE YOU IN OR OUT?
KARRDE, I'VE NEVER SEEN ANYONE PLAY BOTH ENDS AGAINST THE MIDDLE THE WAY YOU DO. I'M IN.
GILLESPEE?
I'VE SEEN THRAWN'S CLONES IN ACTION. YOU BET I'M IN.
MAYBE I CAN GET THAT LAND BACK THE EMPIRE STOLE FROM ME ON UKIO.
I'M TAKING THE
KARRDE TO COR
CANT, BUT I'LL
LEAVING AVES BE
TO COORDINATE
ATTACK. GOOD
FLIGHTS, GENTLEM
I'LL SEE YOU AT
BILBRINGI.

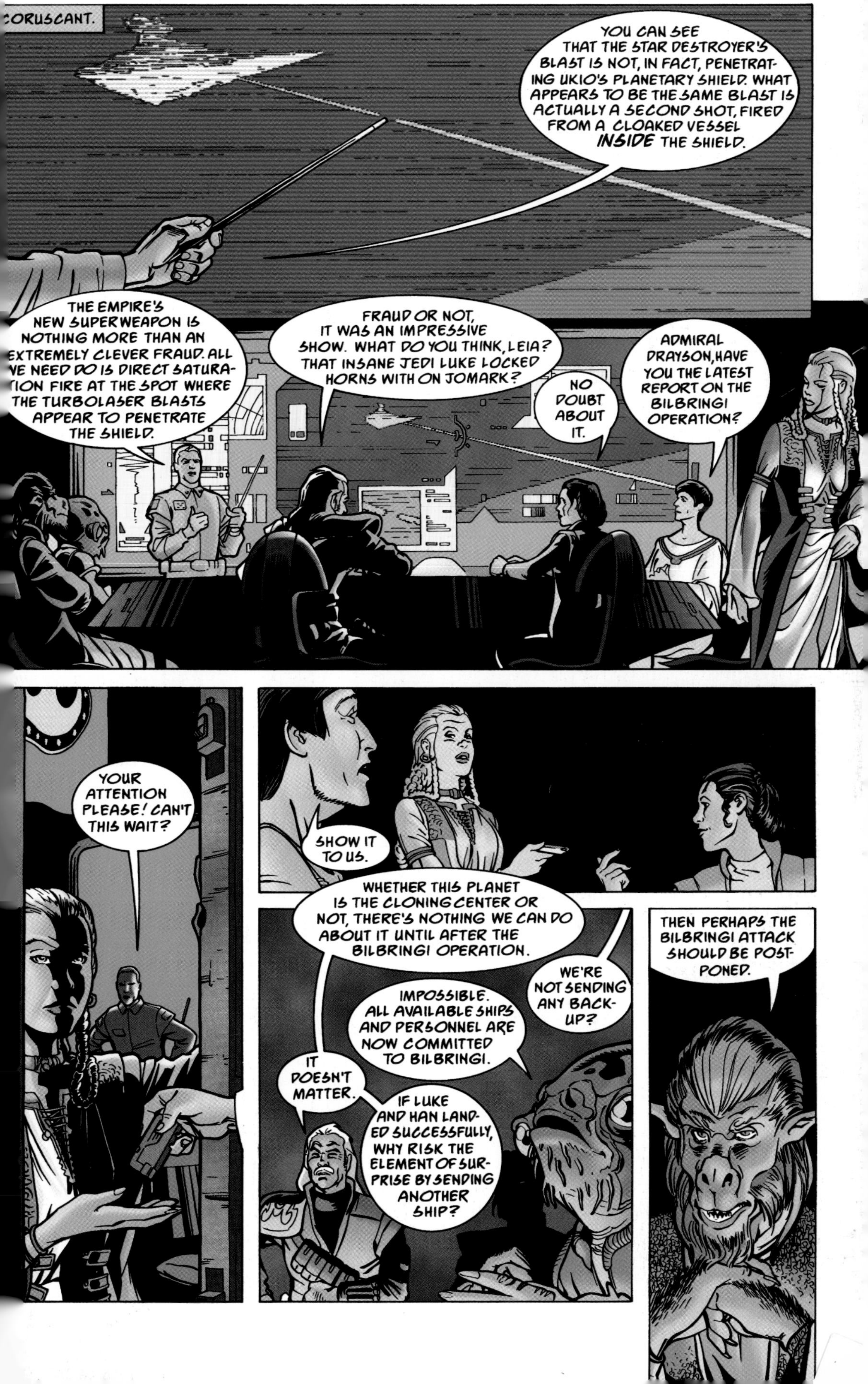
CORUSCANT.
YOU CAN SEE THAT THE STAR DESTROYER'S BLAST IS NOT, IN FACT, PENETRATING UKIO'S PLANETARY SHIELD. WHAT APPEARS TO BE THE SAME BLAST IS ACTUALLY A SECOND SHOT, FIRED FROM A CLOAKED VESSEL INSIDE THE SHIELD.
THE EMPIRE'S NEW SUPERWEAPON IS NOTHING MORE THAN AN EXTREMELY CLEVER FRAUD. ALL WE NEED DO IS DIRECT SATURATION FIRE AT THE SPOT WHERE THE TURBOLASER BLASTS APPEAR TO PENETRATE THE SHIELD.
FRAUD OR NOT, IT WAS AN IMPRESSIVE SHOW. WHAT DO YOU THINK, LEIA? THAT INSANE JEDI LUKE LOCKED HORNS WITH ON JOMARK?
NO DOUBT ABOUT IT.
ADMIRAL DRAYSON, HAVE YOU THE LATEST REPORT ON THE BILBRINGI OPERATION?
YOUR ATTENTION PLEASE! CAN'T THIS WAIT?
SHOW IT TO US.
WHETHER THIS PLANET IS THE CLONING CENTER OR NOT, THERE'S NOTHING WE CAN DO ABOUT IT UNTIL AFTER THE BILBRINGI OPERATION.
WE'RE NOT SENDING ANY BACK-UP?
IMPOSSIBLE. ALL AVAILABLE SHIPS AND PERSONNEL ARE NOW COMMITTED TO BILBRINGI.
IT DOESN'T MATTER.
IF LUKE AND HAN LANDED SUCCESSFULLY, WHY RISK THE ELEMENT OF SURPRISE BY SENDING ANOTHER SHIP?
THEN PERHAPS THE BILBRINGI ATTACK SHOULD BE POSTPONED.

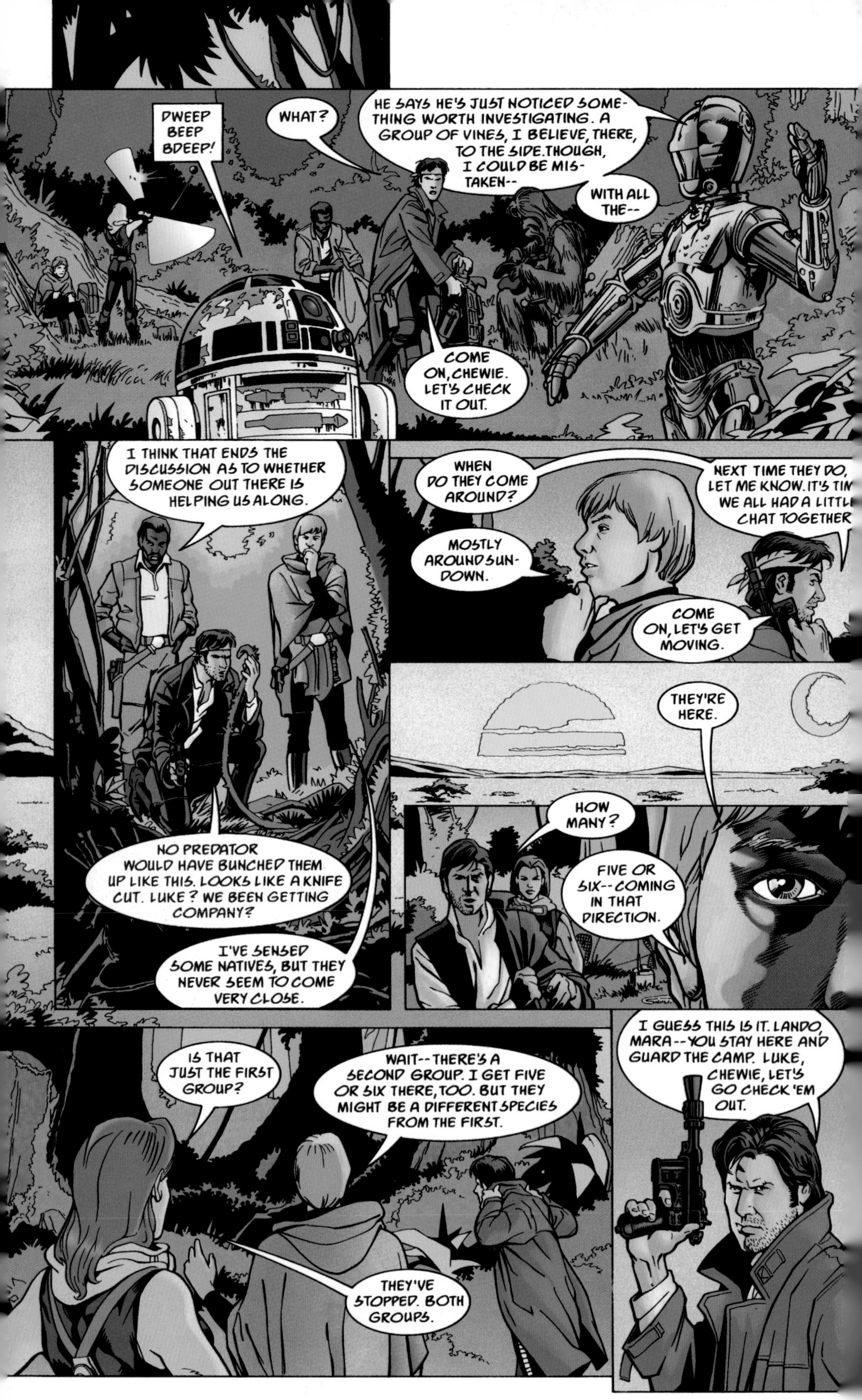
DWEEP BEEP BDEEP!
WHAT?
HE SAYS HE'S JUST NOTICED SOMETHING WORTH INVESTIGATING. A GROUP OF VINES, I BELIEVE, THERE, TO THE SIDE.THOUGH, I COULD BE MISTAKEN--
WITH ALL THE--
COME ON, CHEWIE. LET'S CHECK IT OUT.
I THINK THAT ENDS THE DISCUSSION AS TO WHETHER SOMEONE OUT THERE IS HELPING US ALONG.
NO PREDATOR WOULD HAVE BUNCHED THEM UP LIKE THIS. LOOKS LIKE A KNIFE CUT. LUKE? WE BEEN GETTING COMPANY?
I'VE SENSED SOME NATIVES, BUT THEY NEVER SEEM TO COME VERY CLOSE.
WHEN DO THEY COME AROUND?
MOSTLY AROUND SUNDOWN.
NEXT TIME THEY DO, LET ME KNOW. IT'S TIM WE ALL HAD A LITTL CHAT TOGETHER
COME ON, LET'S GET MOVING.
THEY'RE HERE.
HOW MANY?
FIVE OR SIX--COMING IN THAT DIRECTION.
IS THAT JUST THE FIRST GROUP?
WAIT--THERE'S A SECOND GROUP. I GET FIVE OR SIX THERE, TOO. BUT THEY MIGHT BE A DIFFERENT SPECIES FROM THE FIRST.
THEY'VE STOPPED. BOTH GROUPS.
I GUESS THIS IS IT. LANDO, MARA--YOU STAY HERE AND GUARD THE CAMP. LUKE, CHEWIE, LET'S GO CHECK 'EM OUT.

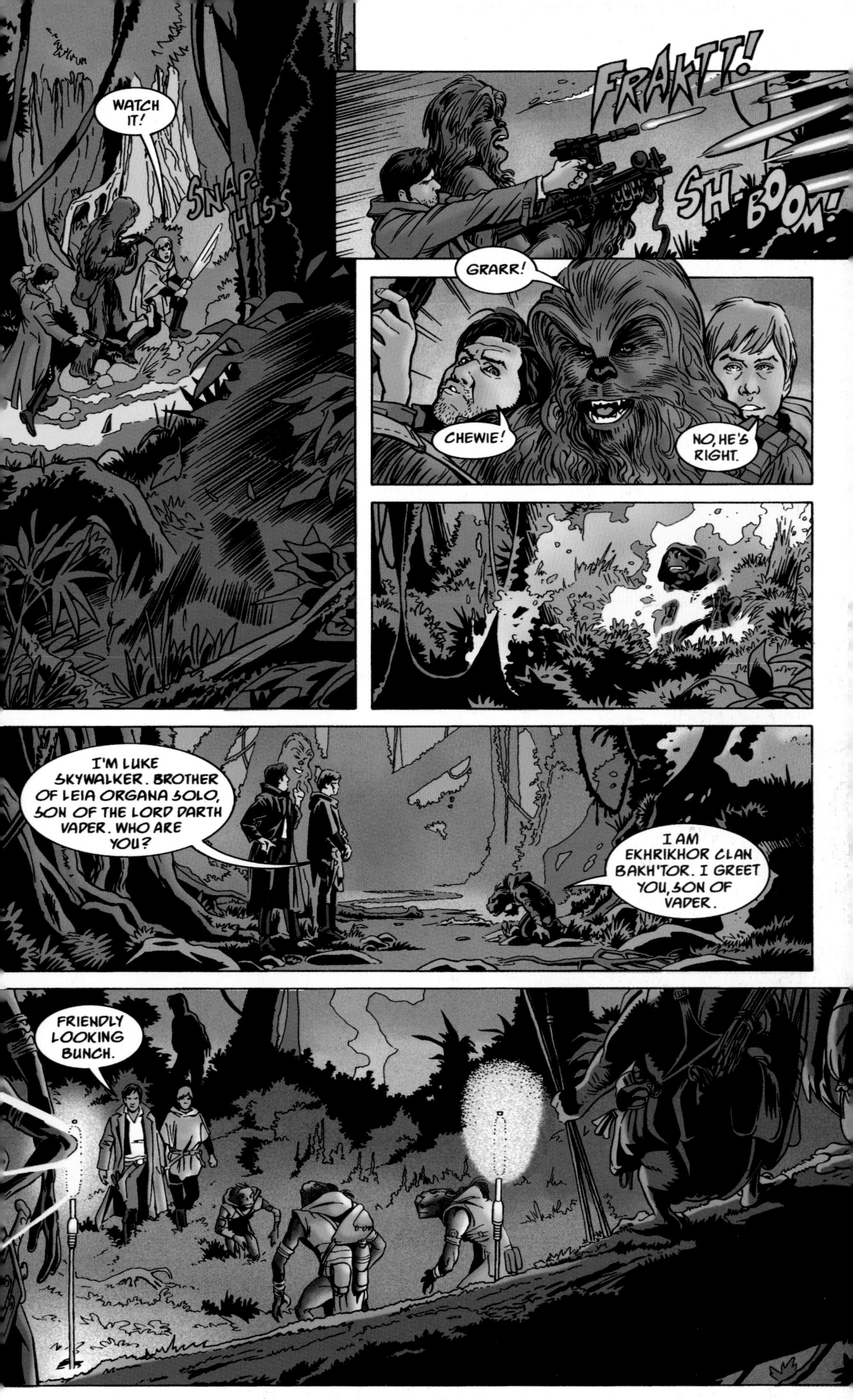
WATCH IT!
SNAP-HISS
FRAKTT!
SH-BOOM!
GRARR!
CHEWIE!
NO, HE'S RIGHT.
I'M LUKE SKYWALKER. BROTHER OF LEIA ORGANA SOLO, SON OF THE LORD DARTH VADER. WHO ARE YOU?
I AM EKHRIKHOR CLAN BAKH'TOR. I GREET YOU, SON OF VADER.
FRIENDLY LOOKING BUNCH.

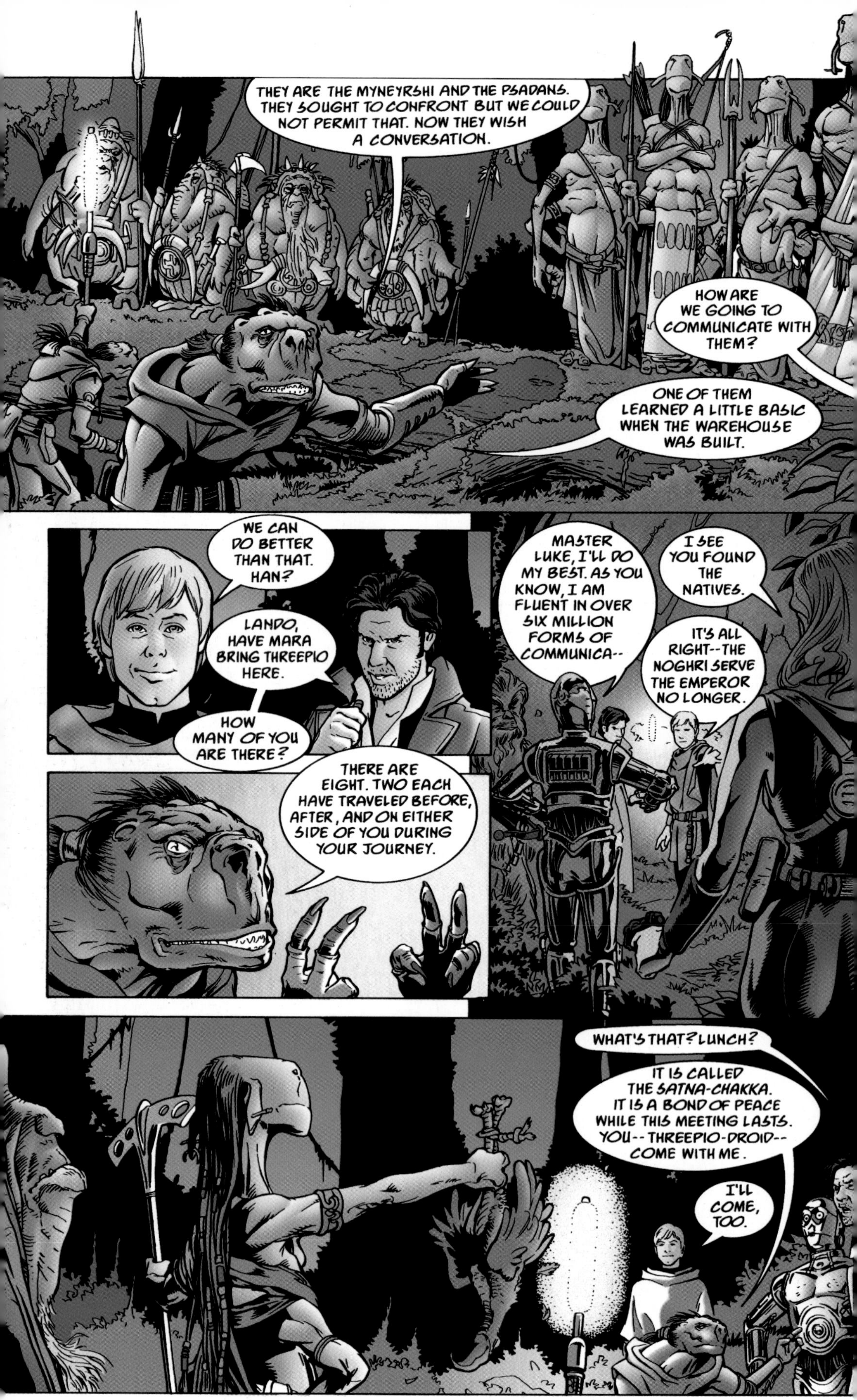
THEY ARE THE MYNEYRSHI AND THE PSADANS. THEY SOUGHT TO CONFRONT BUT WE COULD NOT PERMIT THAT. NOW THEY WISH A CONVERSATION.
HOW ARE WE GOING TO COMMUNICATE WITH THEM?
ONE OF THEM LEARNED A LITTLE BASIC WHEN THE WAREHOUSE WAS BUILT.
WE CAN DO BETTER THAN THAT. HAN?
LANDO, HAVE MARA BRING THREEPIO HERE.
HOW MANY OF YOU ARE THERE?
THERE ARE EIGHT. TWO EACH HAVE TRAVELED BEFORE, AFTER, AND ON EITHER SIDE OF YOU DURING YOUR JOURNEY.
MASTER LUKE, I'LL DO MY BEST. AS YOU KNOW, I AM FLUENT IN OVER SIX MILLION FORMS OF COMMUNICA--
I SEE YOU FOUND THE NATIVES.
IT'S ALL RIGHT--THE NOGHRI SERVE THE EMPEROR NO LONGER.
WHAT'S THAT? LUNCH?
IT IS CALLED THE SATNA-CHAKKA. IT IS A BOND OF PEACE WHILE THIS MEETING LASTS. YOU--THREEPIO-DROID--COME WITH ME.
I'LL COME, TOO.

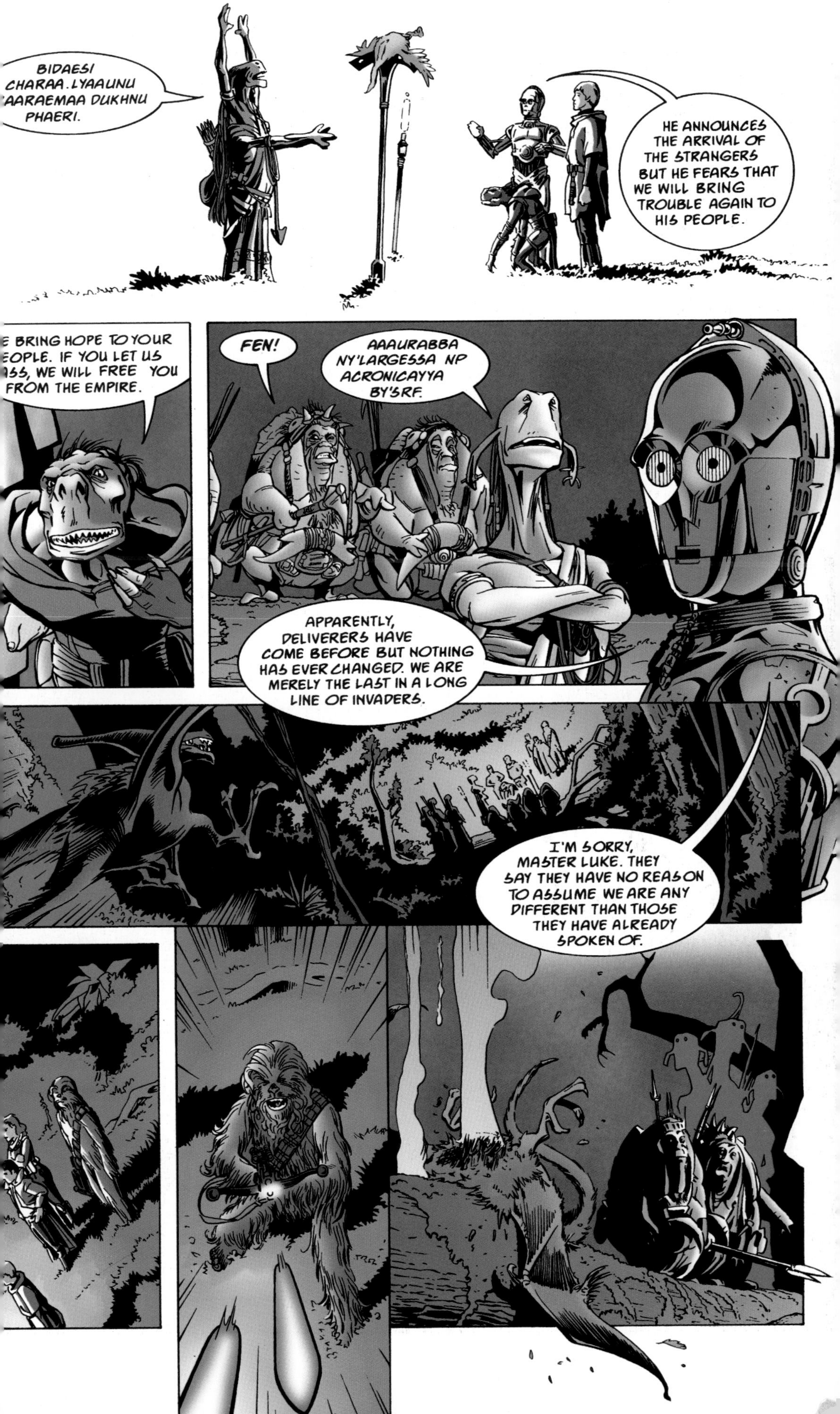
BIDAESI CHARAA. LYAAUNU AARAEMAA DUKHNU PHAERI.
HE ANNOUNCES THE ARRIVAL OF THE STRANGERS BUT HE FEARS THAT WE WILL BRING TROUBLE AGAIN TO HIS PEOPLE.
E BRING HOPE TO YOUR EOPLE. IF YOU LET US ASS, WE WILL FREE YOU FROM THE EMPIRE.
FEN!
AAAURABBA NY'LARGESSA NP ACRONICAYYA BY'SRF.
APPARENTLY, DELIVERERS HAVE COME BEFORE BUT NOTHING HAS EVER CHANGED. WE ARE MERELY THE LAST IN A LONG LINE OF INVADERS.
I'M SORRY, MASTER LUKE. THEY SAY THEY HAVE NO REASON TO ASSUME WE ARE ANY DIFFERENT THAN THOSE THEY HAVE ALREADY SPOKEN OF.

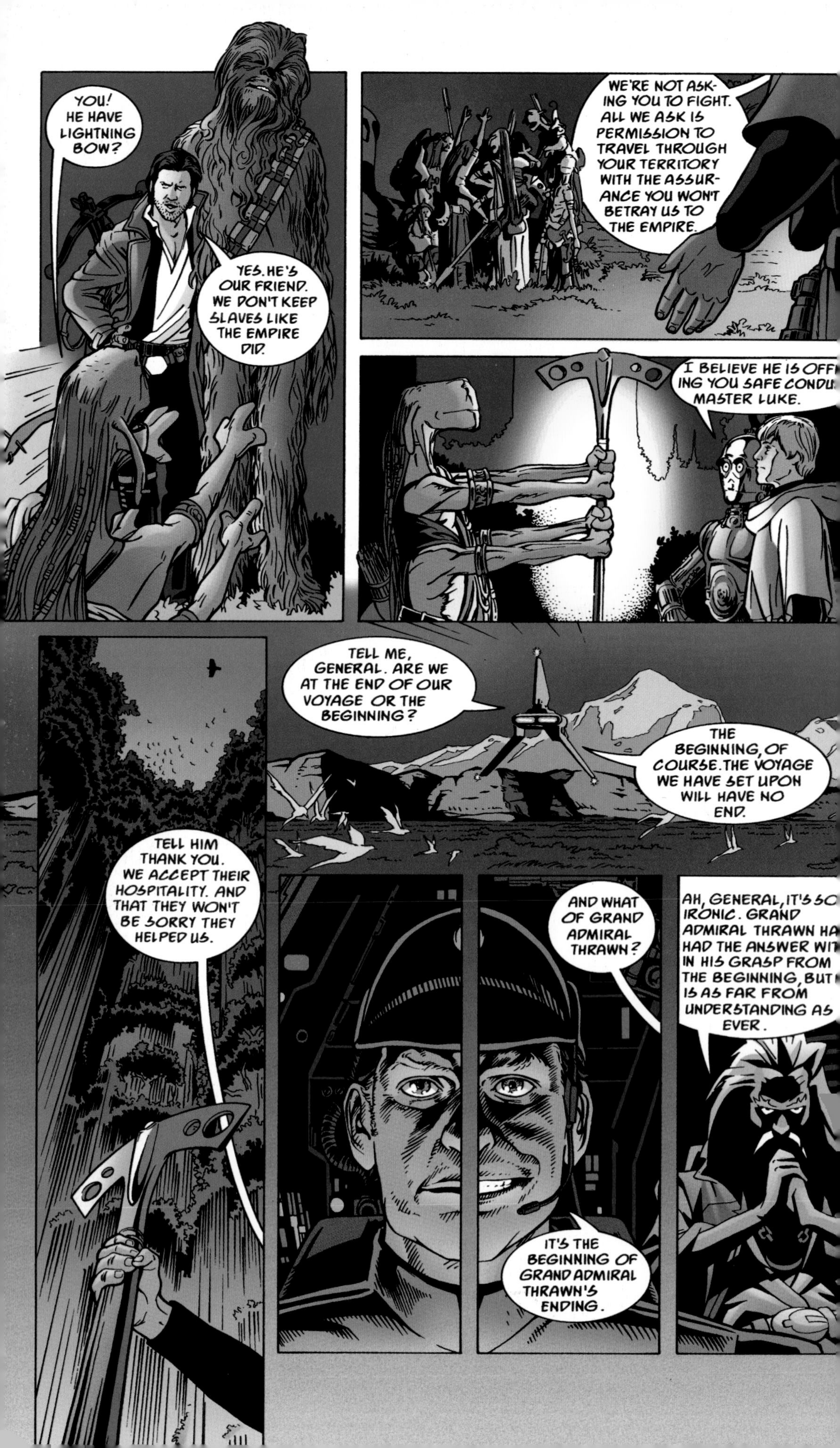

YOU! HE HAVE LIGHTNING BOW?
YES. HE'S OUR FRIEND. WE DON'T KEEP SLAVES LIKE THE EMPIRE DID.
WE'RE NOT ASKING YOU TO FIGHT. ALL WE ASK IS PERMISSION TO TRAVEL THROUGH YOUR TERRITORY WITH THE ASSURANCE YOU WON'T BETRAY US TO THE EMPIRE.
I BELIEVE HE IS OFFERING YOU SAFE CONDUCT, MASTER LUKE.
TELL HIM THANK YOU. WE ACCEPT THEIR HOSPITALITY. AND THAT THEY WON'T BE SORRY THEY HELPED US.
TELL ME, GENERAL. ARE WE AT THE END OF OUR VOYAGE OR THE BEGINNING?
THE BEGINNING, OF COURSE. THE VOYAGE WE HAVE SET UPON WILL HAVE NO END.
AND WHAT OF GRAND ADMIRAL THRAWN?
IT'S THE BEGINNING OF GRAND ADMIRAL THRAWN'S ENDING.
AH, GENERAL, IT'S SO IRONIC. GRAND ADMIRAL THRAWN HAS HAD THE ANSWER WITHIN HIS GRASP FROM THE BEGINNING, BUT HE IS AS FAR FROM UNDERSTANDING AS EVER.

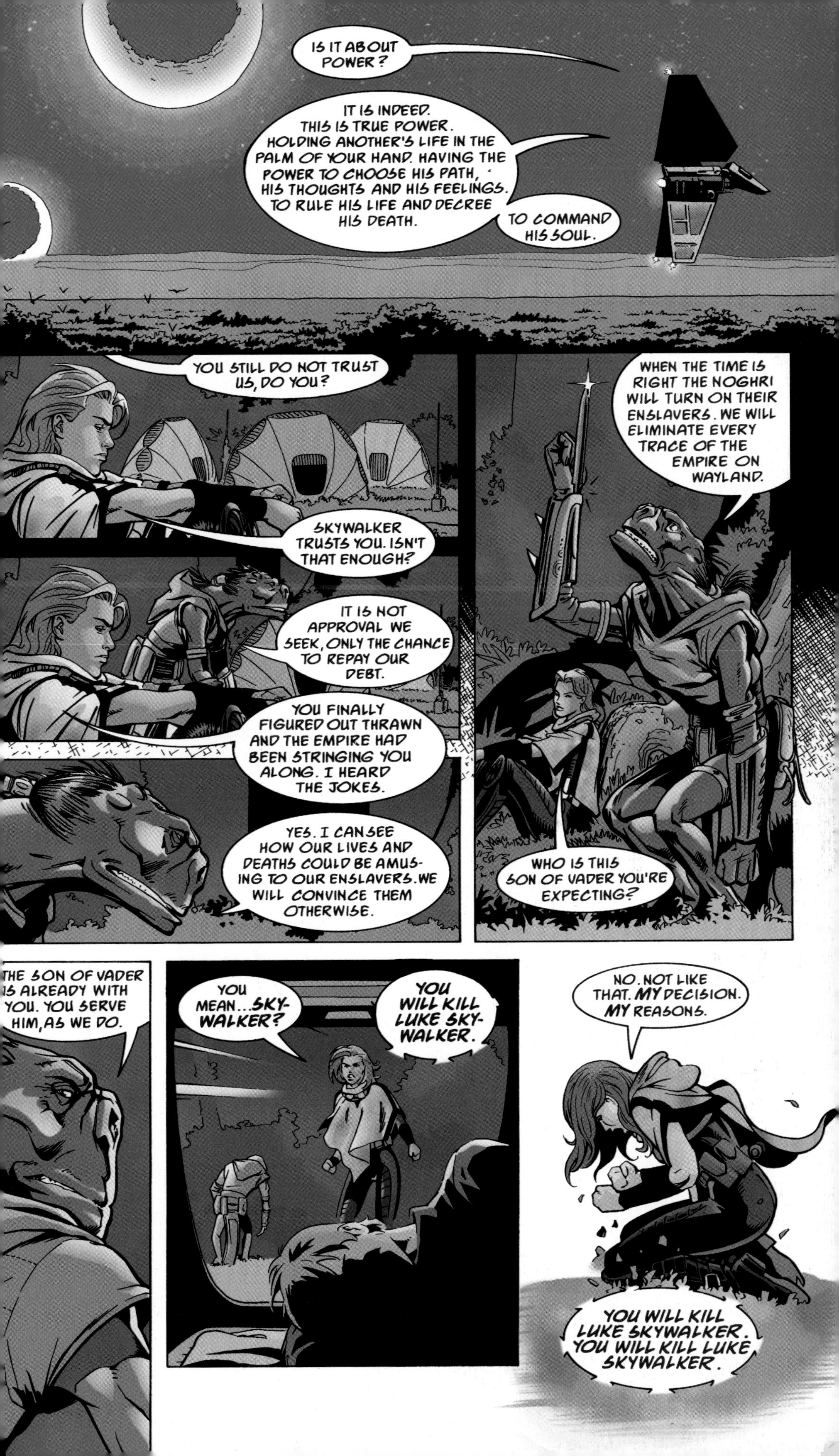
IS IT ABOUT POWER?
IT IS INDEED. THIS IS TRUE POWER. HOLDING ANOTHER'S LIFE IN THE PALM OF YOUR HAND. HAVING THE POWER TO CHOOSE HIS PATH, HIS THOUGHTS AND HIS FEELINGS. TO RULE HIS LIFE AND DECREE HIS DEATH.
TO COMMAND HIS SOUL.
YOU STILL DO NOT TRUST US, DO YOU?
SKYWALKER TRUSTS YOU. ISN'T THAT ENOUGH?
IT IS NOT APPROVAL WE SEEK, ONLY THE CHANCE TO REPAY OUR DEBT.
YOU FINALLY FIGURED OUT THRAWN AND THE EMPIRE HAD BEEN STRINGING YOU ALONG. I HEARD THE JOKES.
YES. I CAN SEE HOW OUR LIVES AND DEATHS COULD BE AMUSING TO OUR ENSLAVERS. WE WILL CONVINCE THEM OTHERWISE.
WHEN THE TIME IS RIGHT THE NOGHRI WILL TURN ON THEIR ENSLAVERS. WE WILL ELIMINATE EVERY TRACE OF THE EMPIRE ON WAYLAND.
WHO IS THIS SON OF VADER YOU'RE EXPECTING?
THE SON OF VADER IS ALREADY WITH YOU. YOU SERVE HIM, AS WE DO.
YOU MEAN...SKYWALKER?
YOU WILL KILL LUKE SKYWALKER.
NO. NOT LIKE THAT. MY DECISION. MY REASONS.
YOU WILL KILL LUKE SKYWALKER. YOU WILL KILL LUKE SKYWALKER.

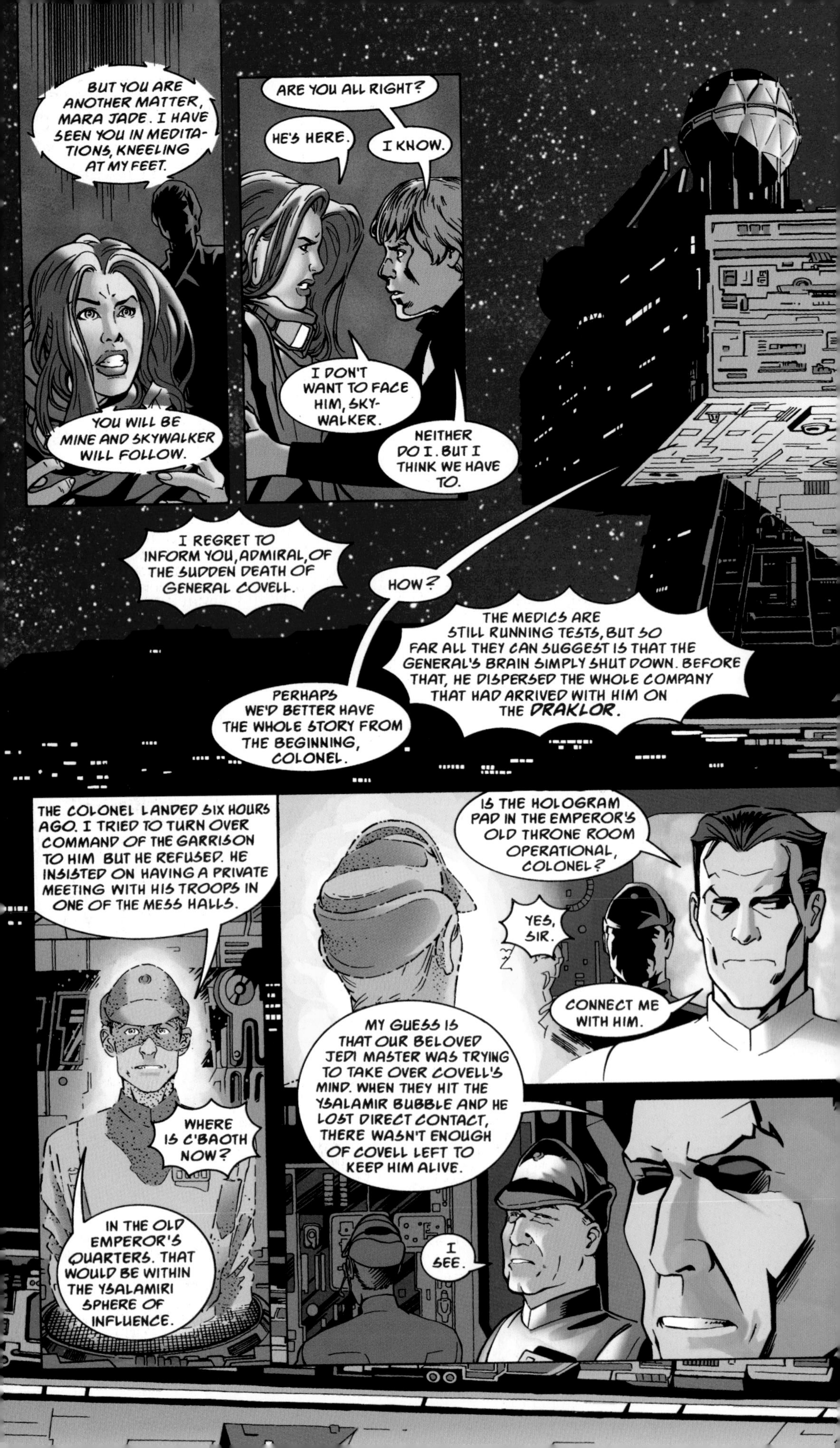
BUT YOU ARE ANOTHER MATTER, MARA JADE. I HAVE SEEN YOU IN MEDITATIONS, KNEELING AT MY FEET.
YOU WILL BE MINE AND SKYWALKER WILL FOLLOW.
ARE YOU ALL RIGHT?
HE'S HERE.
I KNOW.
I DON'T WANT TO FACE HIM, SKYWALKER.
NEITHER DO I. BUT I THINK WE HAVE TO.
I REGRET TO INFORM YOU, ADMIRAL, OF THE SUDDEN DEATH OF GENERAL COVELL.
HOW?
THE MEDICS ARE STILL RUNNING TESTS, BUT SO FAR ALL THEY CAN SUGGEST IS THAT THE GENERAL'S BRAIN SIMPLY SHUT DOWN. BEFORE THAT, HE DISPERSED THE WHOLE COMPANY THAT HAD ARRIVED WITH HIM ON THE DRAKLOR.
PERHAPS WE'D BETTER HAVE THE WHOLE STORY FROM THE BEGINNING, COLONEL.
THE COLONEL LANDED SIX HOURS AGO. I TRIED TO TURN OVER COMMAND OF THE GARRISON TO HIM BUT HE REFUSED. HE INSISTED ON HAVING A PRIVATE MEETING WITH HIS TROOPS IN ONE OF THE MESS HALLS.
WHERE IS C'BAOTH NOW?
IN THE OLD EMPEROR'S QUARTERS. THAT WOULD BE WITHIN THE YSALAMIRI SPHERE OF INFLUENCE.
IS THE HOLOGRAM PAD IN THE EMPEROR'S OLD THRONE ROOM OPERATIONAL, COLONEL?
YES, SIR.
CONNECT ME WITH HIM.
MY GUESS IS THAT OUR BELOVED JEDI MASTER WAS TRYING TO TAKE OVER COVELL'S MIND. WHEN THEY HIT THE YSALAMIR BUBBLE AND HE LOST DIRECT CONTACT, THERE WASN'T ENOUGH OF COVELL LEFT TO KEEP HIM ALIVE.
I SEE.

GOOD MORNING, MASTER C'BAOTH. I SEE YOU'VE DISCOVERED THE EMPEROR'S PRIVATE HOLOGRAM SETTING.

GRAND ADMIRAL THRAWN. IS THIS HOW YOU REWARD MY WORK ON YOUR BEHALF? BY AN ACT OF BETRAYAL?

I HAVE NOTHING TO DEFEND. TELL ME WHAT YOU DID TO GENERAL COVELL.

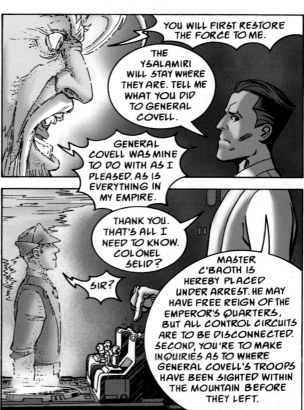

YOU WILL FIRST RESTORE THE FORCE TO ME.

THE YSALAMIRI WILL STAY WHERE THEY ARE. TELL ME WHAT YOU DID TO GENERAL COVELL.

GENERAL COVELL WAS MINE TO DO WITH AS I PLEASED. AS IS EVERYTHING IN MY EMPIRE.

THANK YOU. THAT'S ALL I NEED TO KNOW. COLONEL SELID?

SIR?

MASTER C'BAOTH IS HEREBY PLACED UNDER ARREST. HE MAY HAVE FREE REIGN OF THE EMPEROR'S QUARTERS, BUT ALL CONTROL CIRCUITS ARE TO BE DISCONNECTED. SECOND, YOU'RE TO MAKE INQUIRIES AS TO WHERE GENERAL COVELL'S TROOPS HAVE BEEN SIGHTED WITHIN THE MOUNTAIN BEFORE THEY LEFT.

NONE OF THOSE TROOPS ARE TO BE ALLOWED BACK IN. YOU ARE, OF COURSE, REINSTATED AS GARRISON COMMANDER. ANY QUESTIONS?

NO, SIR.

CHIMAERA, OUT.

MASTER C'BAOTH'S USE TO THE EMPIRE IS RAPIDLY NEARING AN END, CAPTAIN. HOWEVER HE STILL HAS ONE LAST ROLE TO PLAY. HIS INSANITY IS IN HIS MIND, NOT HIS BODY.

WHY NOT? NOT AT THESE FACILITIES, CERTAINLY, AND NOT AT THE NORMAL SPEED. SOMEWHERE ABSOLUTELY SECURE, PERHAPS IN THE UNKNOWN REGIONS.

ARE YOU SUGGESTING WE CLONE HIM?

INSTRUCT INTELLIGENCE TO BEGIN SEARCHING FOR A SUITABLE WORLD AS SOON AS WE'VE CRUSHED THE REBELS AT BILBRINGI.

SIR, ALL OUR EVIDENCE STILL INDICATES TANGRENE AS THE PROBABLE POINT OF ATTACK.

NEVERTHELESS THE REBELS WILL BE AT BILBRINGI. AND SO WILL WE. SET COURSE FOR BILBRINGI, AND LET US PREPARE TO MEET OUR GUESTS.

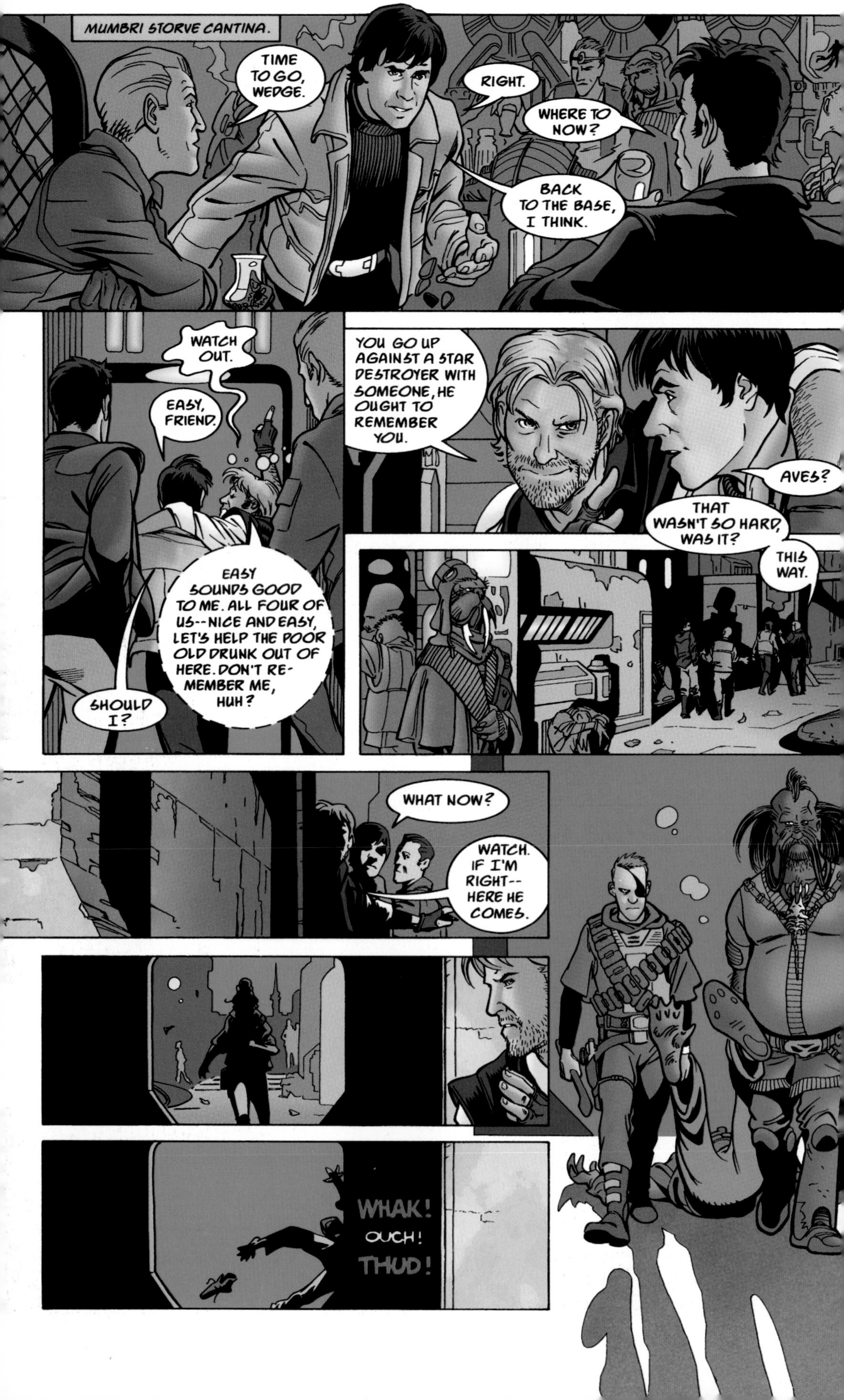
MUMBRI STORVE CANTINA.
TIME TO GO, WEDGE.
RIGHT.
WHERE TO NOW?
BACK TO THE BASE, I THINK.
WATCH OUT.
EASY, FRIEND.
EASY SOUNDS GOOD TO ME. ALL FOUR OF US--NICE AND EASY, LET'S HELP THE POOR OLD DRUNK OUT OF HERE. DON'T REMEMBER ME, HUH?
SHOULD I?
YOU GO UP AGAINST A STAR DESTROYER WITH SOMEONE, HE OUGHT TO REMEMBER YOU.
AVES?
THAT WASN'T SO HARD, WAS IT?
THIS WAY.
WHAT NOW?
WATCH. IF I'M RIGHT-- HERE HE COMES.
WHAK!
OUCH!
THUD!

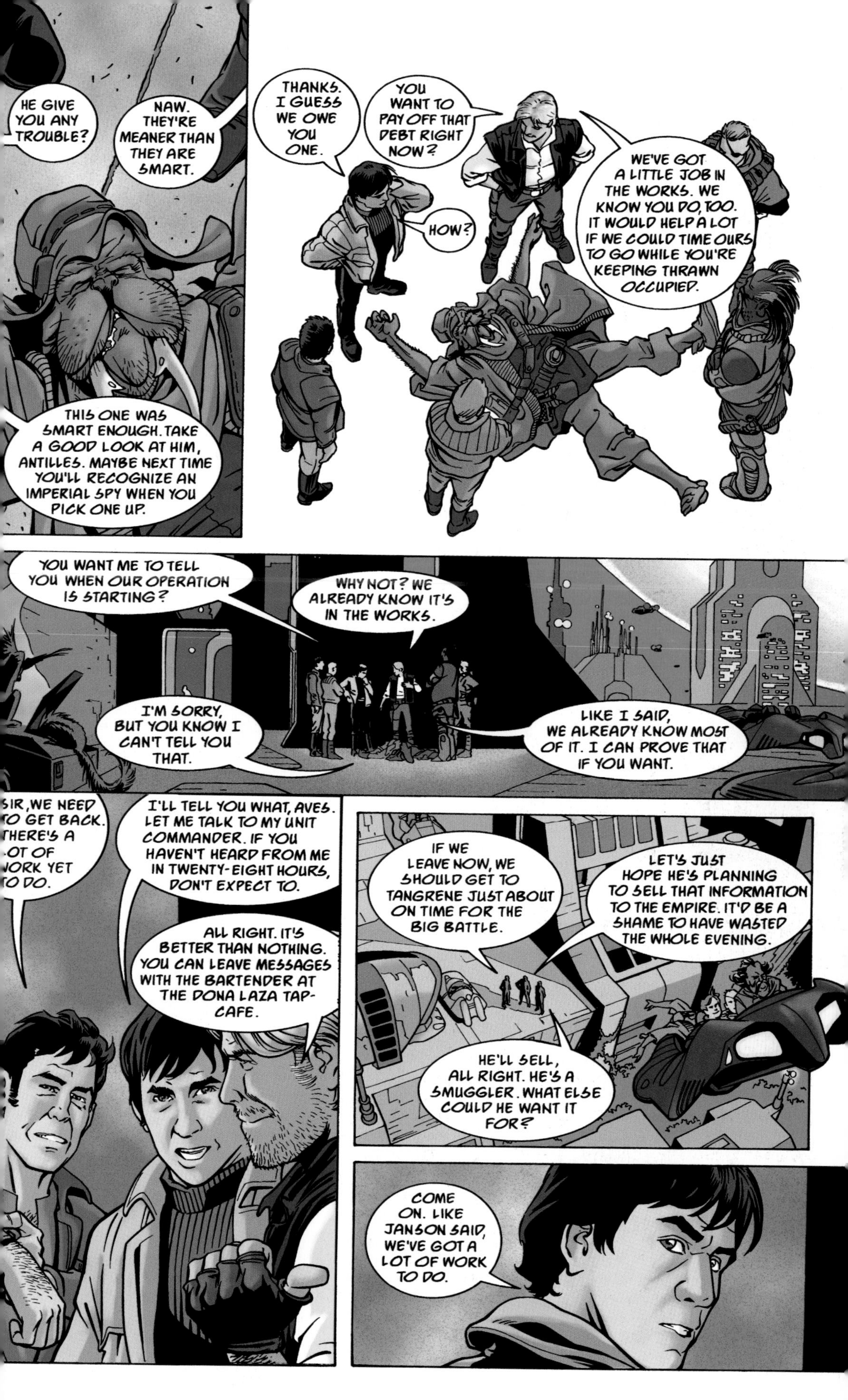
HE GIVE YOU ANY TROUBLE?
NAW. THEY'RE MEANER THAN THEY ARE SMART.
THIS ONE WAS SMART ENOUGH. TAKE A GOOD LOOK AT HIM, ANTILLES. MAYBE NEXT TIME YOU'LL RECOGNIZE AN IMPERIAL SPY WHEN YOU PICK ONE UP.
THANKS. I GUESS WE OWE YOU ONE.
YOU WANT TO PAY OFF THAT DEBT RIGHT NOW?
HOW?
WE'VE GOT A LITTLE JOB IN THE WORKS. WE KNOW YOU DO, TOO. IT WOULD HELP A LOT IF WE COULD TIME OURS TO GO WHILE YOU'RE KEEPING THRAWN OCCUPIED.
YOU WANT ME TO TELL YOU WHEN OUR OPERATION IS STARTING?
WHY NOT? WE ALREADY KNOW IT'S IN THE WORKS.
I'M SORRY, BUT YOU KNOW I CAN'T TELL YOU THAT.
LIKE I SAID, WE ALREADY KNOW MOST OF IT. I CAN PROVE THAT IF YOU WANT.
SIR, WE NEED TO GET BACK. THERE'S A LOT OF WORK YET TO DO.
I'LL TELL YOU WHAT, AVES. LET ME TALK TO MY UNIT COMMANDER. IF YOU HAVEN'T HEARD FROM ME IN TWENTY-EIGHT HOURS, DON'T EXPECT TO.
ALL RIGHT. IT'S BETTER THAN NOTHING. YOU CAN LEAVE MESSAGES WITH THE BARTENDER AT THE DONA LAZA TAP-CAFE.
IF WE LEAVE NOW, WE SHOULD GET TO TANGRENE JUST ABOUT ON TIME FOR THE BIG BATTLE.
LET'S JUST HOPE HE'S PLANNING TO SELL THAT INFORMATION TO THE EMPIRE. IT'D BE A SHAME TO HAVE WASTED THE WHOLE EVENING.
HE'LL SELL, ALL RIGHT. HE'S A SMUGGLER. WHAT ELSE COULD HE WANT IT FOR?
COME ON. LIKE JANSON SAID, WE'VE GOT A LOT OF WORK TO DO.

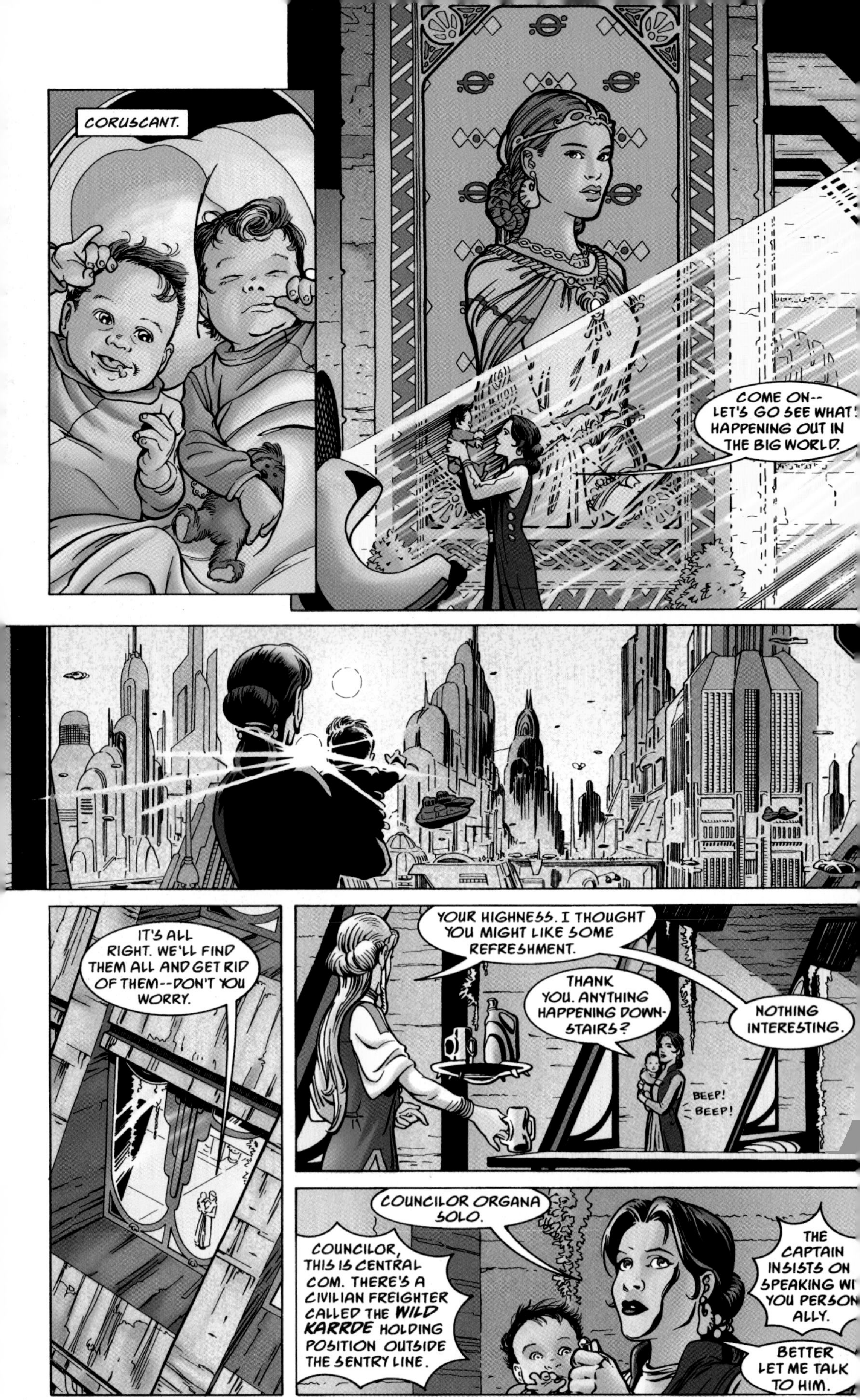
CORUSCANT.
COME ON-- LET'S GO SEE WHAT'S HAPPENING OUT IN THE BIG WORLD.
IT'S ALL RIGHT. WE'LL FIND THEM ALL AND GET RID OF THEM--DON'T YOU WORRY.
YOUR HIGHNESS. I THOUGHT YOU MIGHT LIKE SOME REFRESHMENT.
THANK YOU. ANYTHING HAPPENING DOWN-STAIRS?
NOTHING INTERESTING.
BEEP! BEEP!
COUNCILOR ORGANA SOLO.
COUNCILOR, THIS IS CENTRAL COM. THERE'S A CIVILIAN FREIGHTER CALLED THE WILD KARRDE HOLDING POSITION OUTSIDE THE SENTRY LINE.
THE CAPTAIN INSISTS ON SPEAKING WI YOU PERSON ALLY.
BETTER LET ME TALK TO HIM.

HELLO, KARRDE.

HELLO, COUNCILOR. I TRUST YOU RECEIVED MY PACKAGE.

YES, WE DID. THE REPUBLIC THANKS YOU.

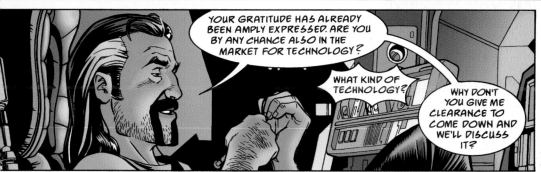

YOUR GRATITUDE HAS ALREADY BEEN AMPLY EXPRESSED. ARE YOU BY ANY CHANCE ALSO IN THE MARKET FOR TECHNOLOGY?

WHAT KIND OF TECHNOLOGY?

WHY DON'T YOU GIVE ME CLEARANCE TO COME DOWN AND WE'LL DISCUSS IT?

I'M AFRAID THAT WON'T BE POSSIBLE. ALL NON-ESSENTIAL TRAFFIC HAS BEEN RESTRICTED.

ONLY NON-ESSENTIAL?

WHAT EXACTLY HAVE YOU HEARD?

ASSORTED WHISPERS, ONLY ONE OF WHICH CONCERNS ME. TELL ME ABOUT MARA. IS SHE UNDER ARREST?

KARRDE, THIS ISN'T THE TIME OR THE PLACE...

DON'T GIVE ME THAT. YOU OWE HER. FIND GHENT AND TELL HIM TO PROGRAM IN ONE OF MY PERSONAL ENCRYPT CODES. THAT SHOULD GIVE US ENOUGH PRIVACY.

I'LL GO FIND HIM.

I'LL BE WAITING.

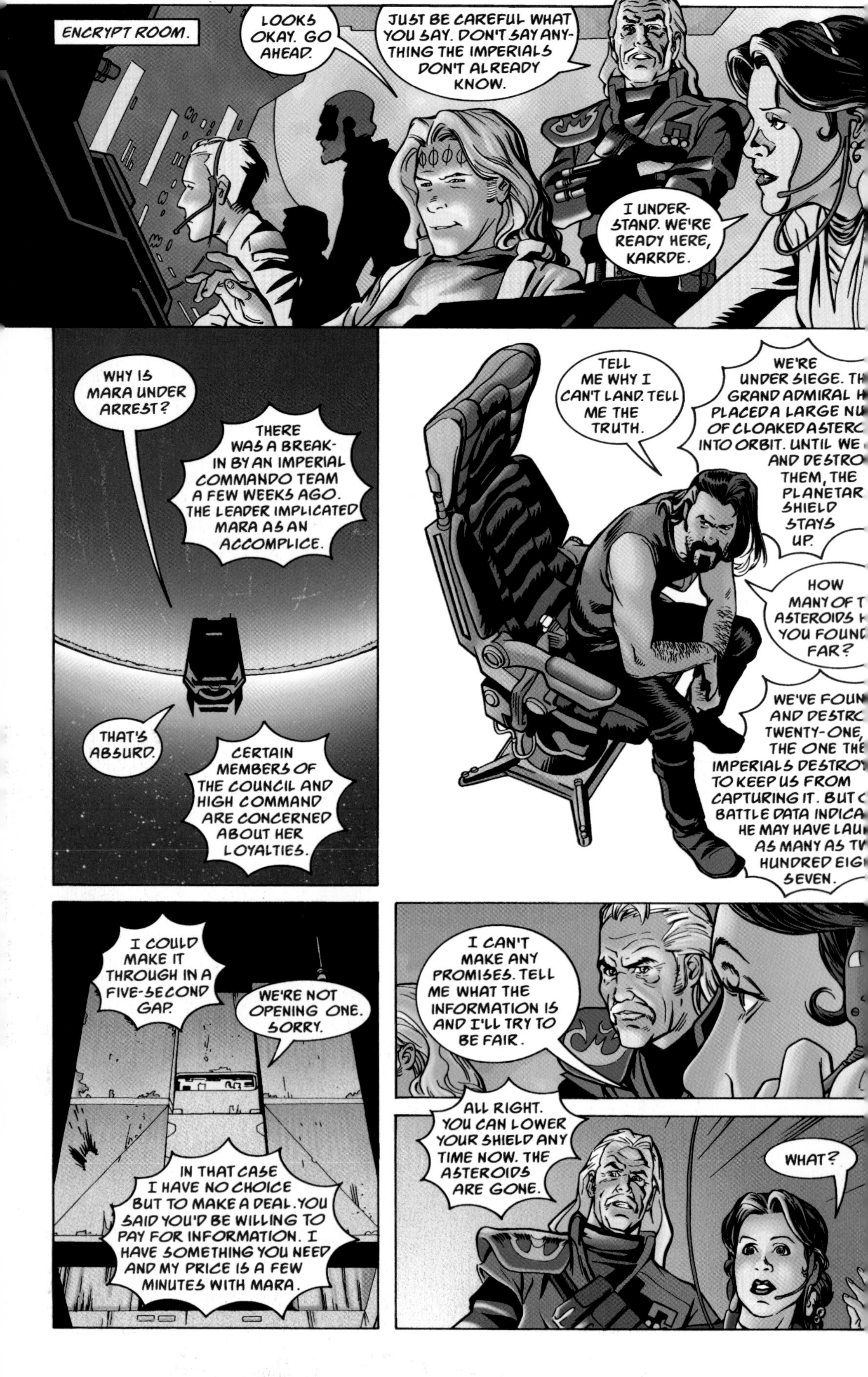
ENCRYPT ROOM.
LOOKS OKAY. GO AHEAD.
JUST BE CAREFUL WHAT YOU SAY. DON'T SAY ANYTHING THE IMPERIALS DON'T ALREADY KNOW.
I UNDERSTAND. WE'RE READY HERE, KARRDE.
WHY IS MARA UNDER ARREST?
THERE WAS A BREAK-IN BY AN IMPERIAL COMMANDO TEAM A FEW WEEKS AGO. THE LEADER IMPLICATED MARA AS AN ACCOMPLICE.
THAT'S ABSURD.
CERTAIN MEMBERS OF THE COUNCIL AND HIGH COMMAND ARE CONCERNED ABOUT HER LOYALTIES.
TELL ME WHY I CAN'T LAND. TELL ME THE TRUTH.
WE'RE UNDER SIEGE. TH GRAND ADMIRAL H PLACED A LARGE NU OF CLOAKED ASTERC INTO ORBIT. UNTIL WE AND DESTRO THEM, THE PLANETAR SHIELD STAYS UP.
HOW MANY OF T ASTEROIDS H YOU FOUND FAR?
WE'VE FOUN AND DESTRC TWENTY-ONE, THE ONE THE IMPERIALS DESTROY TO KEEP US FROM CAPTURING IT. BUT C BATTLE DATA INDICA HE MAY HAVE LAU AS MANY AS TV HUNDRED EIG SEVEN.
I COULD MAKE IT THROUGH IN A FIVE-SECOND GAP.
WE'RE NOT OPENING ONE. SORRY.
IN THAT CASE I HAVE NO CHOICE BUT TO MAKE A DEAL. YOU SAID YOU'D BE WILLING TO PAY FOR INFORMATION. I HAVE SOMETHING YOU NEED AND MY PRICE IS A FEW MINUTES WITH MARA.
I CAN'T MAKE ANY PROMISES. TELL ME WHAT THE INFORMATION IS AND I'LL TRY TO BE FAIR.
ALL RIGHT. YOU CAN LOWER YOUR SHIELD ANY TIME NOW. THE ASTEROIDS ARE GONE.
WHAT?

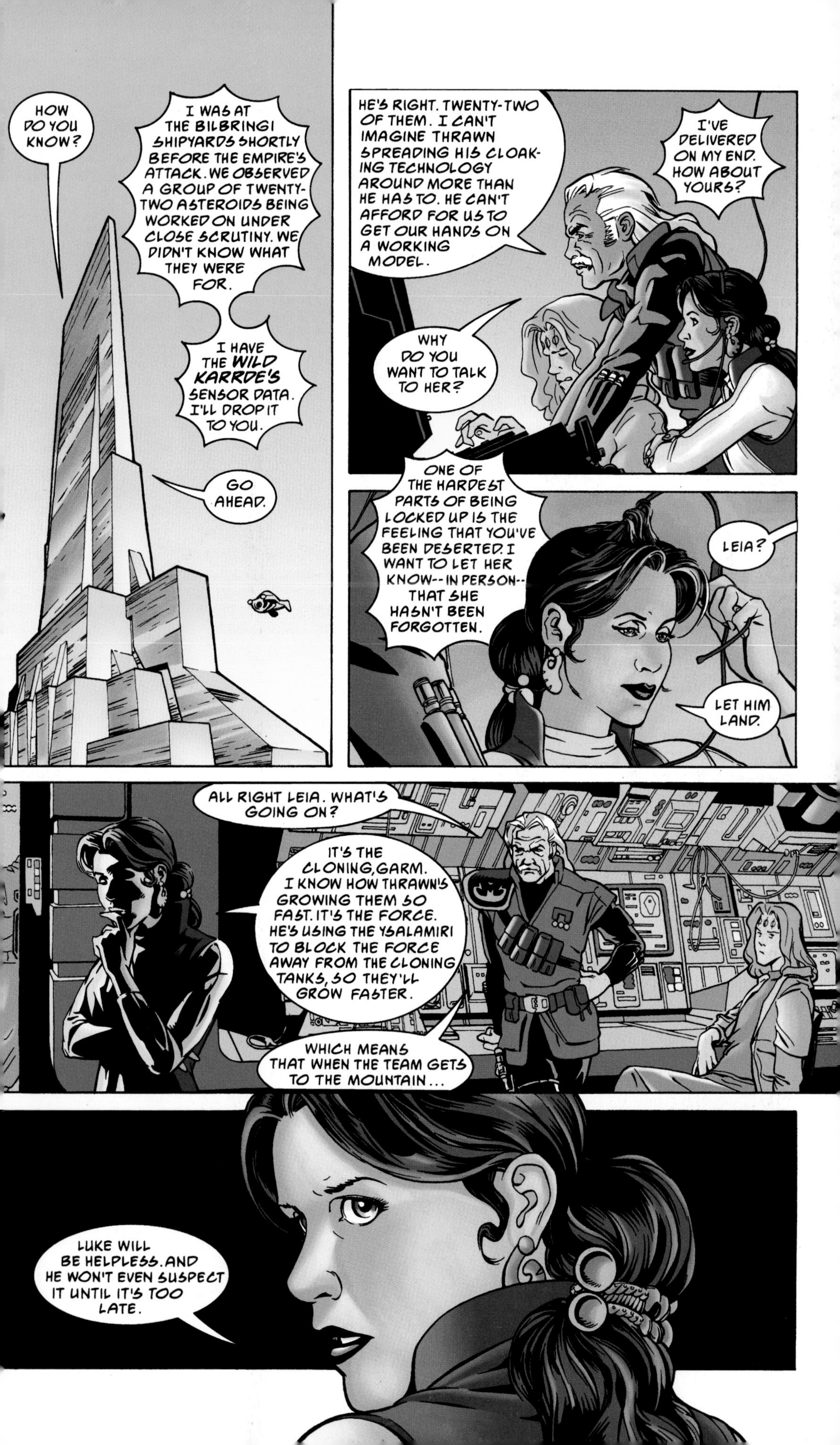
HOW DO YOU KNOW?
I WAS AT THE BILBRINGI SHIPYARDS SHORTLY BEFORE THE EMPIRE'S ATTACK. WE OBSERVED A GROUP OF TWENTY-TWO ASTEROIDS BEING WORKED ON UNDER CLOSE SCRUTINY. WE DIDN'T KNOW WHAT THEY WERE FOR.
I HAVE THE WILD KARRDE'S SENSOR DATA. I'LL DROP IT TO YOU.
GO AHEAD.
HE'S RIGHT. TWENTY-TWO OF THEM. I CAN'T IMAGINE THRAWN SPREADING HIS CLOAKING TECHNOLOGY AROUND MORE THAN HE HAS TO. HE CAN'T AFFORD FOR US TO GET OUR HANDS ON A WORKING MODEL.
I'VE DELIVERED ON MY END. HOW ABOUT YOURS?
WHY DO YOU WANT TO TALK TO HER?
ONE OF THE HARDEST PARTS OF BEING LOCKED UP IS THE FEELING THAT YOU'VE BEEN DESERTED. I WANT TO LET HER KNOW--IN PERSON--THAT SHE HASN'T BEEN FORGOTTEN.
LEIA?
LET HIM LAND.
ALL RIGHT LEIA. WHAT'S GOING ON?
IT'S THE CLONING, GARM. I KNOW HOW THRAWN'S GROWING THEM SO FAST. IT'S THE FORCE. HE'S USING THE YSALAMIRI TO BLOCK THE FORCE AWAY FROM THE CLONING TANKS, SO THEY'LL GROW FASTER.
WHICH MEANS THAT WHEN THE TEAM GETS TO THE MOUNTAIN...
LUKE WILL BE HELPLESS. AND HE WON'T EVEN SUSPECT IT UNTIL IT'S TOO LATE.

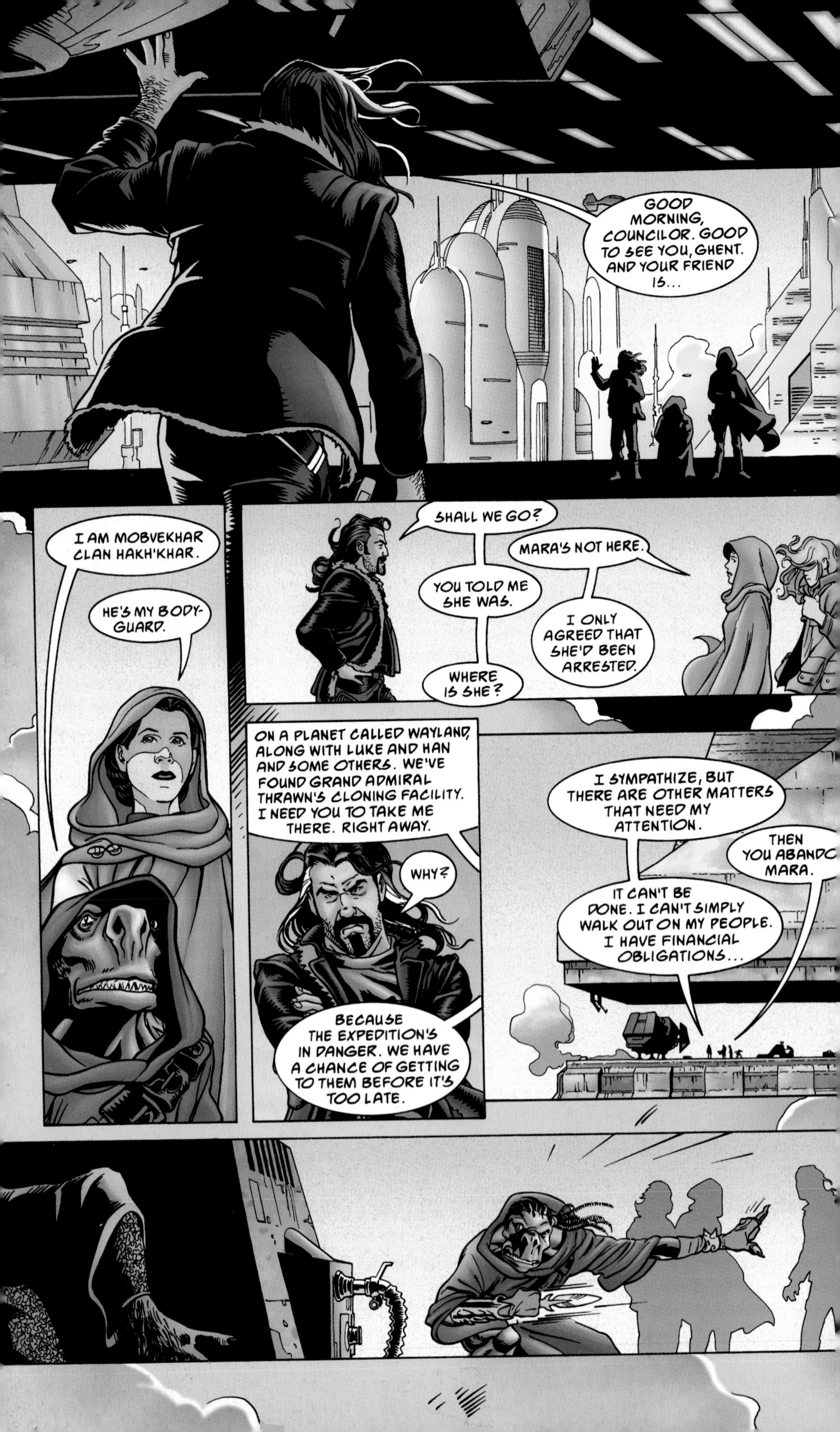
GOOD MORNING, COUNCILOR. GOOD TO SEE YOU, GHENT. AND YOUR FRIEND IS...
I AM MOBVEKHAR CLAN HAKH'KHAR.
HE'S MY BODY-GUARD.
SHALL WE GO?
MARA'S NOT HERE.
YOU TOLD ME SHE WAS.
I ONLY AGREED THAT SHE'D BEEN ARRESTED.
WHERE IS SHE?
ON A PLANET CALLED WAYLAND, ALONG WITH LUKE AND HAN AND SOME OTHERS. WE'VE FOUND GRAND ADMIRAL THRAWN'S CLONING FACILITY. I NEED YOU TO TAKE ME THERE. RIGHT AWAY.
WHY?
BECAUSE THE EXPEDITION'S IN DANGER. WE HAVE A CHANCE OF GETTING TO THEM BEFORE IT'S TOO LATE.
I SYMPATHIZE, BUT THERE ARE OTHER MATTERS THAT NEED MY ATTENTION.
THEN YOU ABANDO MARA.
IT CAN'T BE DONE. I CAN'T SIMPLY WALK OUT ON MY PEOPLE. I HAVE FINANCIAL OBLIGATIONS...

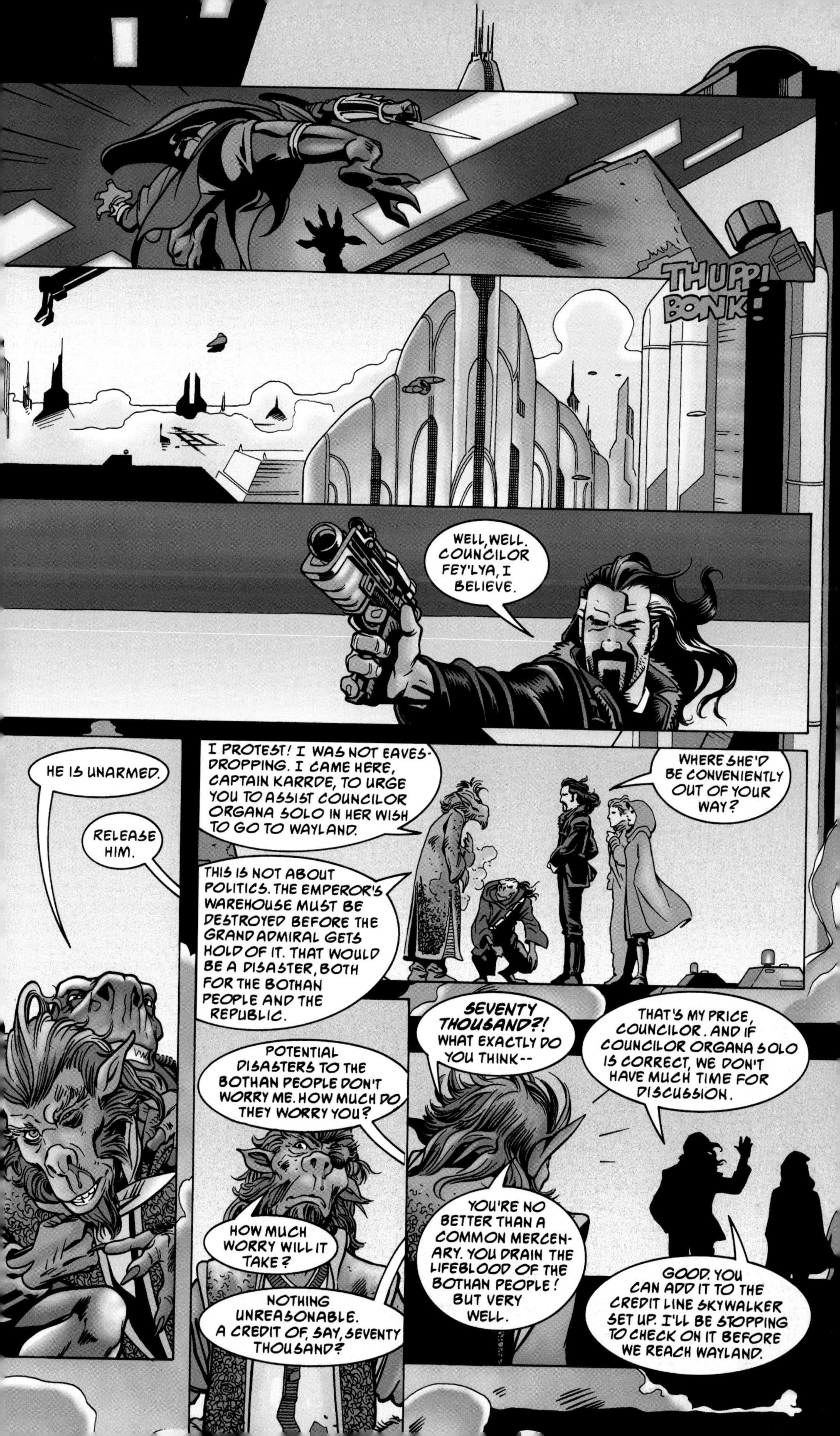
THUPP!
BONK!
WELL, WELL. COUNCILOR FEY'LYA, I BELIEVE.
HE IS UNARMED.
RELEASE HIM.
I PROTEST! I WAS NOT EAVES-DROPPING. I CAME HERE, CAPTAIN KARRDE, TO URGE YOU TO ASSIST COUNCILOR ORGANA SOLO IN HER WISH TO GO TO WAYLAND.
WHERE SHE'D BE CONVENIENTLY OUT OF YOUR WAY?
THIS IS NOT ABOUT POLITICS. THE EMPEROR'S WAREHOUSE MUST BE DESTROYED BEFORE THE GRAND ADMIRAL GETS HOLD OF IT. THAT WOULD BE A DISASTER, BOTH FOR THE BOTHAN PEOPLE AND THE REPUBLIC.
POTENTIAL DISASTERS TO THE BOTHAN PEOPLE DON'T WORRY ME. HOW MUCH DO THEY WORRY YOU?
HOW MUCH WORRY WILL IT TAKE?
NOTHING UNREASONABLE. A CREDIT OF, SAY, SEVENTY THOUSAND?
SEVENTY THOUSAND?! WHAT EXACTLY DO YOU THINK--
THAT'S MY PRICE, COUNCILOR. AND IF COUNCILOR ORGANA SOLO IS CORRECT, WE DON'T HAVE MUCH TIME FOR DISCUSSION.
YOU'RE NO BETTER THAN A COMMON MERCEN-ARY. YOU DRAIN THE LIFEBLOOD OF THE BOTHAN PEOPLE! BUT VERY WELL.
GOOD. YOU CAN ADD IT TO THE CREDIT LINE SKYWALKER SET UP. I'LL BE STOPPING TO CHECK ON IT BEFORE WE REACH WAYLAND.

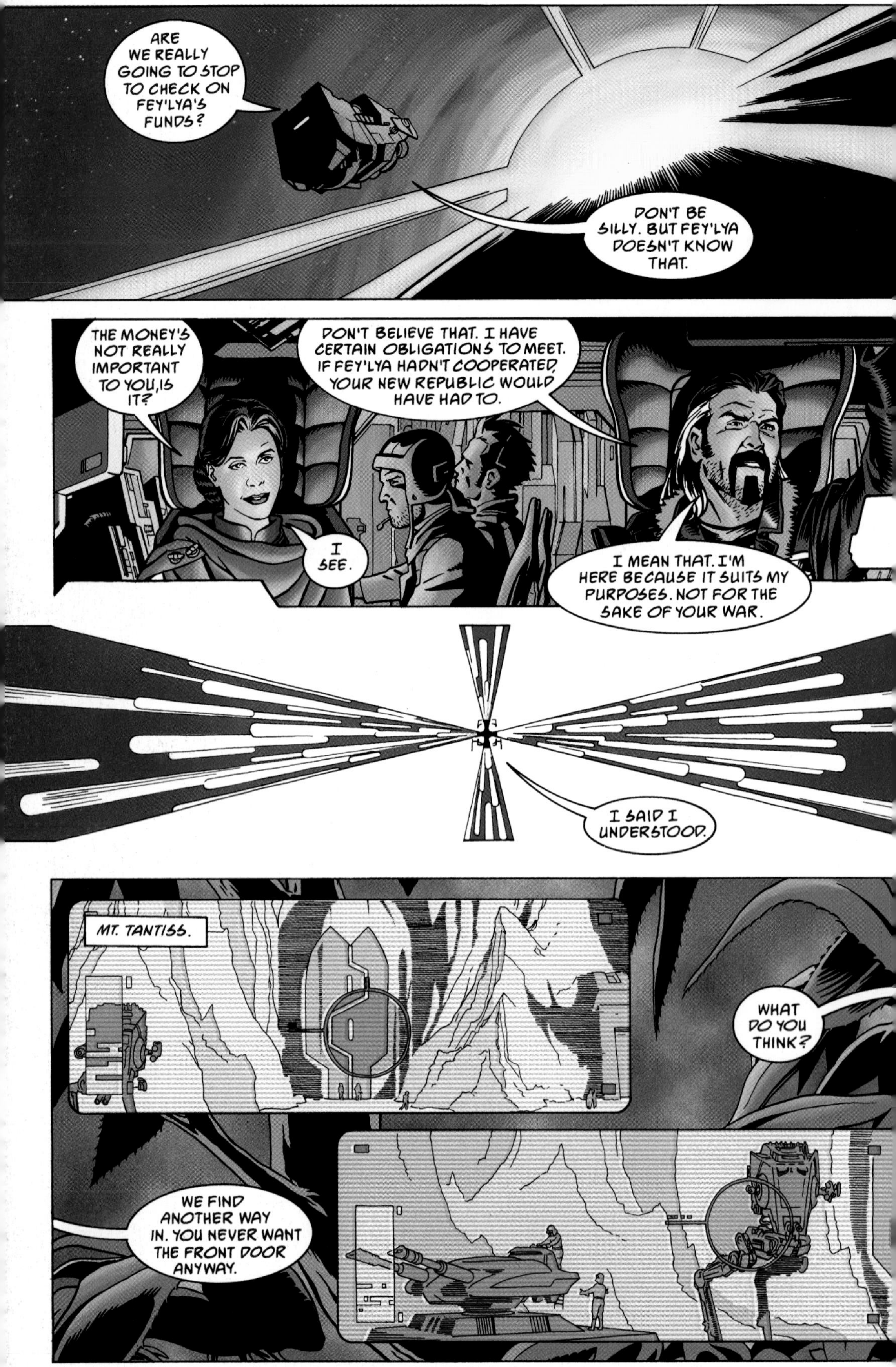
ARE WE REALLY GOING TO STOP TO CHECK ON FEY'LYA'S FUNDS?
DON'T BE SILLY. BUT FEY'LYA DOESN'T KNOW THAT.
THE MONEY'S NOT REALLY IMPORTANT TO YOU, IS IT?
DON'T BELIEVE THAT. I HAVE CERTAIN OBLIGATIONS TO MEET. IF FEY'LYA HADN'T COOPERATED, YOUR NEW REPUBLIC WOULD HAVE HAD TO.
I SEE.
I MEAN THAT. I'M HERE BECAUSE IT SUITS MY PURPOSES. NOT FOR THE SAKE OF YOUR WAR.
I SAID I UNDERSTOOD.
MT. TANTISS.
WHAT DO YOU THINK?
WE FIND ANOTHER WAY IN. YOU NEVER WANT THE FRONT DOOR ANYWAY.

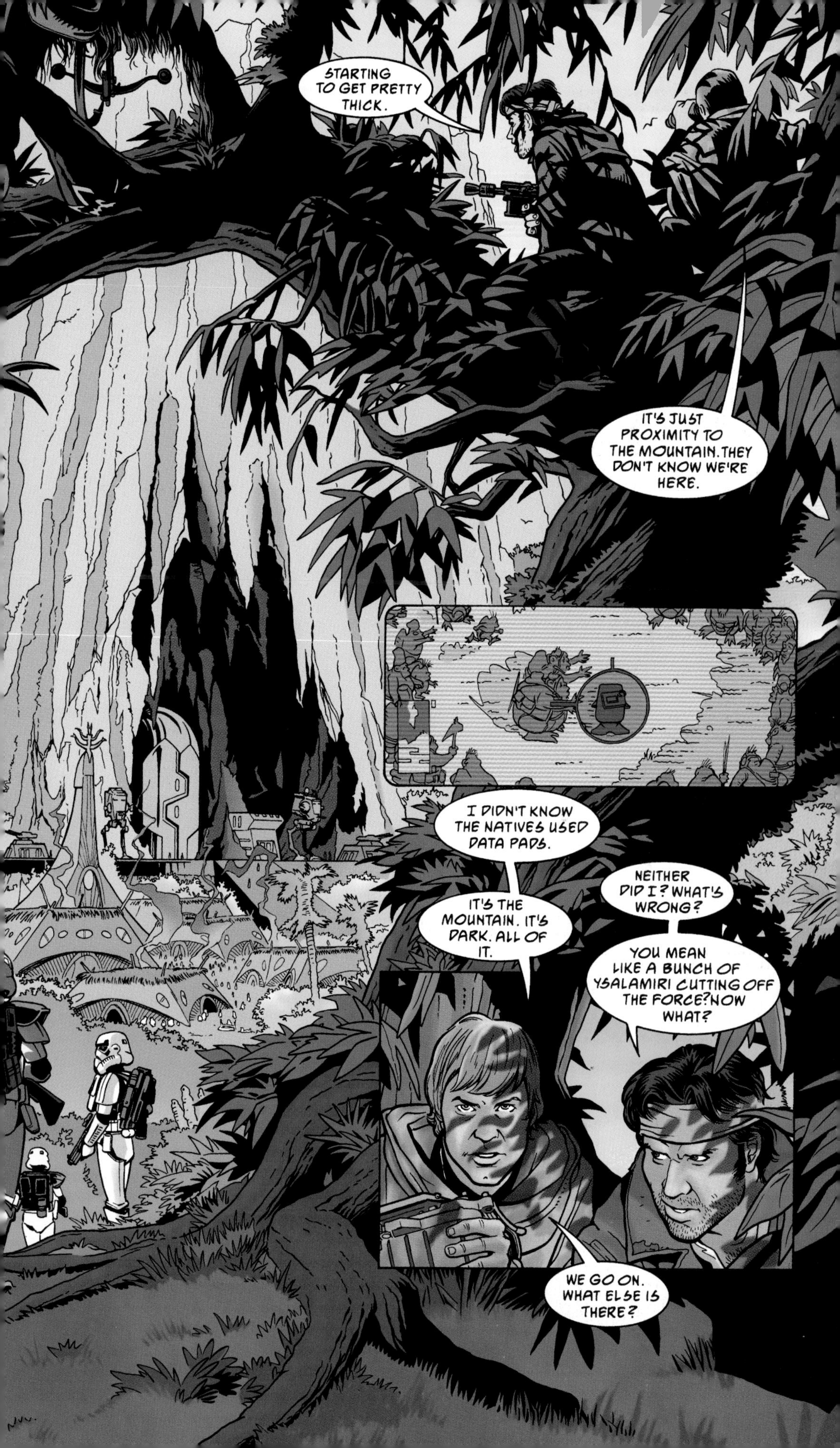
STARTING TO GET PRETTY THICK.
IT'S JUST PROXIMITY TO THE MOUNTAIN. THEY DON'T KNOW WE'RE HERE.
I DIDN'T KNOW THE NATIVES USED DATA PADS.
NEITHER DID I? WHAT'S WRONG?
IT'S THE MOUNTAIN. IT'S DARK. ALL OF IT.
YOU MEAN LIKE A BUNCH OF YSALAMIRI CUTTING OFF THE FORCE? NOW WHAT?
WE GO ON. WHAT ELSE IS THERE?

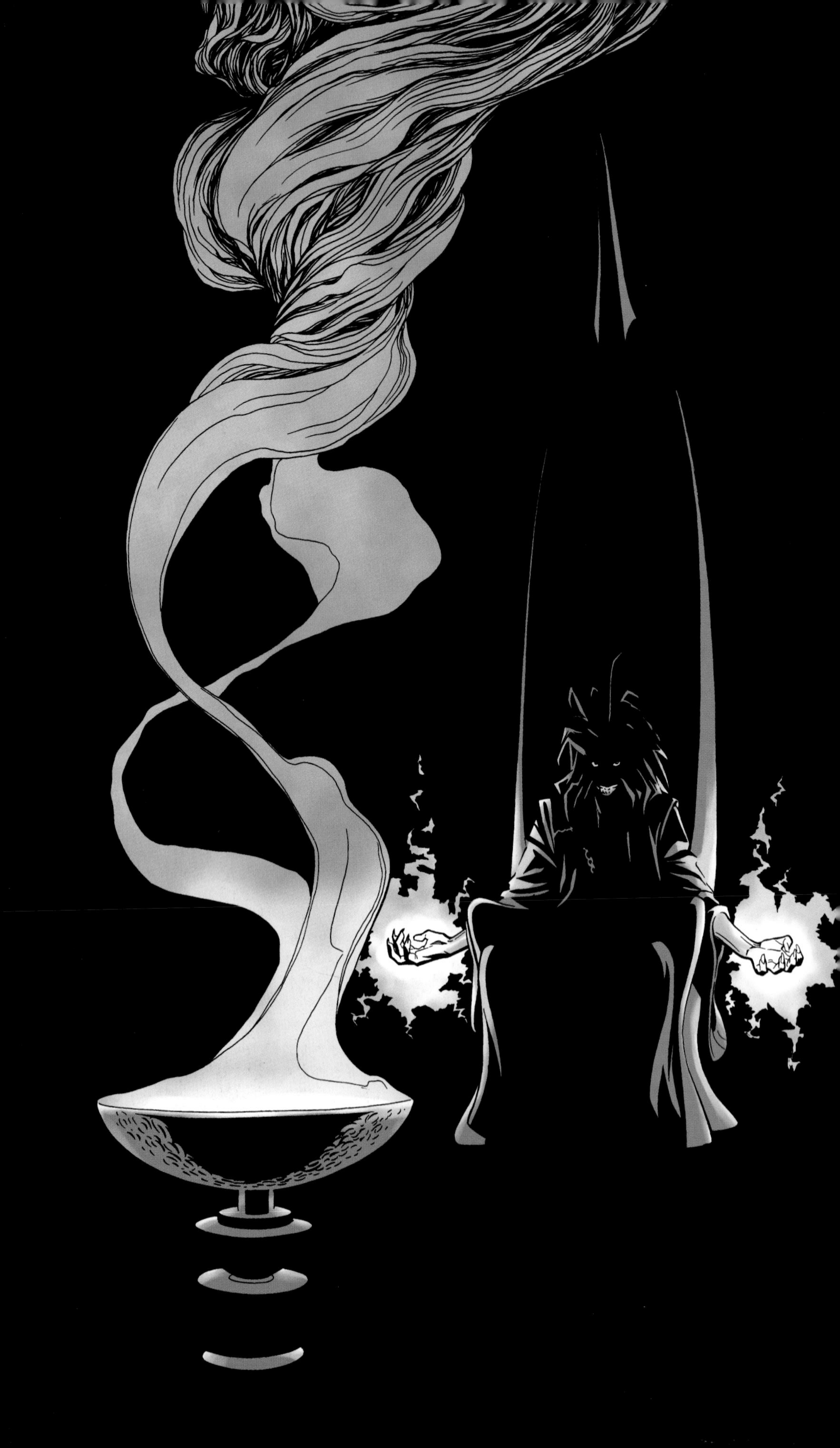

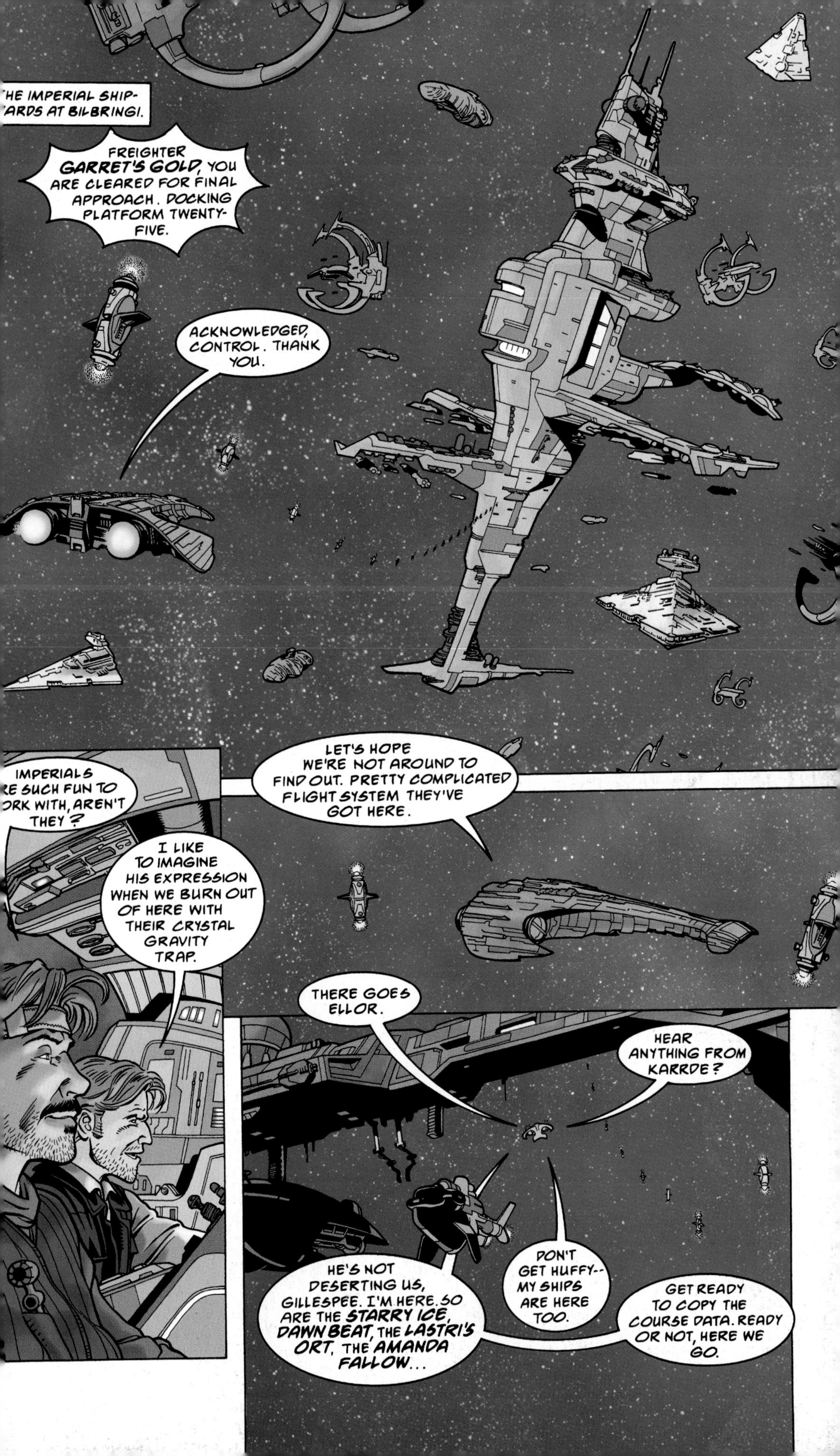
THE IMPERIAL SHIP-YARDS AT BILBRINGI.
FREIGHTER GARRET'S GOLD, YOU ARE CLEARED FOR FINAL APPROACH. DOCKING PLATFORM TWENTY-FIVE.
ACKNOWLEDGED, CONTROL. THANK YOU.
IMPERIALS RE SUCH FUN TO ORK WITH, AREN'T THEY?
LET'S HOPE WE'RE NOT AROUND TO FIND OUT. PRETTY COMPLICATED FLIGHT SYSTEM THEY'VE GOT HERE.
I LIKE TO IMAGINE HIS EXPRESSION WHEN WE BURN OUT OF HERE WITH THEIR CRYSTAL GRAVITY TRAP.
THERE GOES ELLOR.
HEAR ANYTHING FROM KARRDE?
HE'S NOT DESERTING US, GILLESPEE. I'M HERE. SO ARE THE STARRY ICE, DAWN BEAT, THE LASTRI'S ORT, THE AMANDA FALLOW...
DON'T GET HUFFY-- MY SHIPS ARE HERE TOO.
GET READY TO COPY THE COURSE DATA. READY OR NOT, HERE WE GO.

ROGUE SQUADRON, THIS IS ROGUE LEADER. WE'RE GOING IN WITH FIRST WAVE. ALL SHIPS ACKNOWLEDGE.

YOU SUPPOSE THRAWN GOT OUR MESSAGE, ROGUE LEADER?

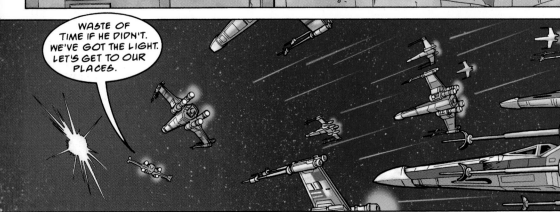

WASTE OF TIME IF HE DIDN'T. WE'VE GOT THE LIGHT. LET'S GET TO OUR PLACES.

TANGRENE.

THEY'RE DOING QUITE WELL, AREN'T THEY, CAPTAIN? A VERY CONVINCING PERFORMANCE ALL AROUND.

SIR, I RESPECTFULLY SUGGEST THAT THE REBEL ACTIVITY IS NOT ANY KIND OF PERFORMANCE. TANGRENE IS THEIR KEY TARGET.

WRONG, CAPTAIN. IT'S NOTHING MORE THAN A CAREFULLY CONSTRUCTED ILLUSION. THE BULK OF THEIR FORCE IS EVEN NOW ON ITS WAY TO BILBRINGI.

YES, SIR.

I VERY MUCH HOPE SO, SIR.

YOU DON'T HAVE TO BELIEVE, BUT BE PREPARED TO BE PROVED WRONG.

THEN PREPARE THE FLEET FOR HYPER-SPACE. AND FOR BATTLE.

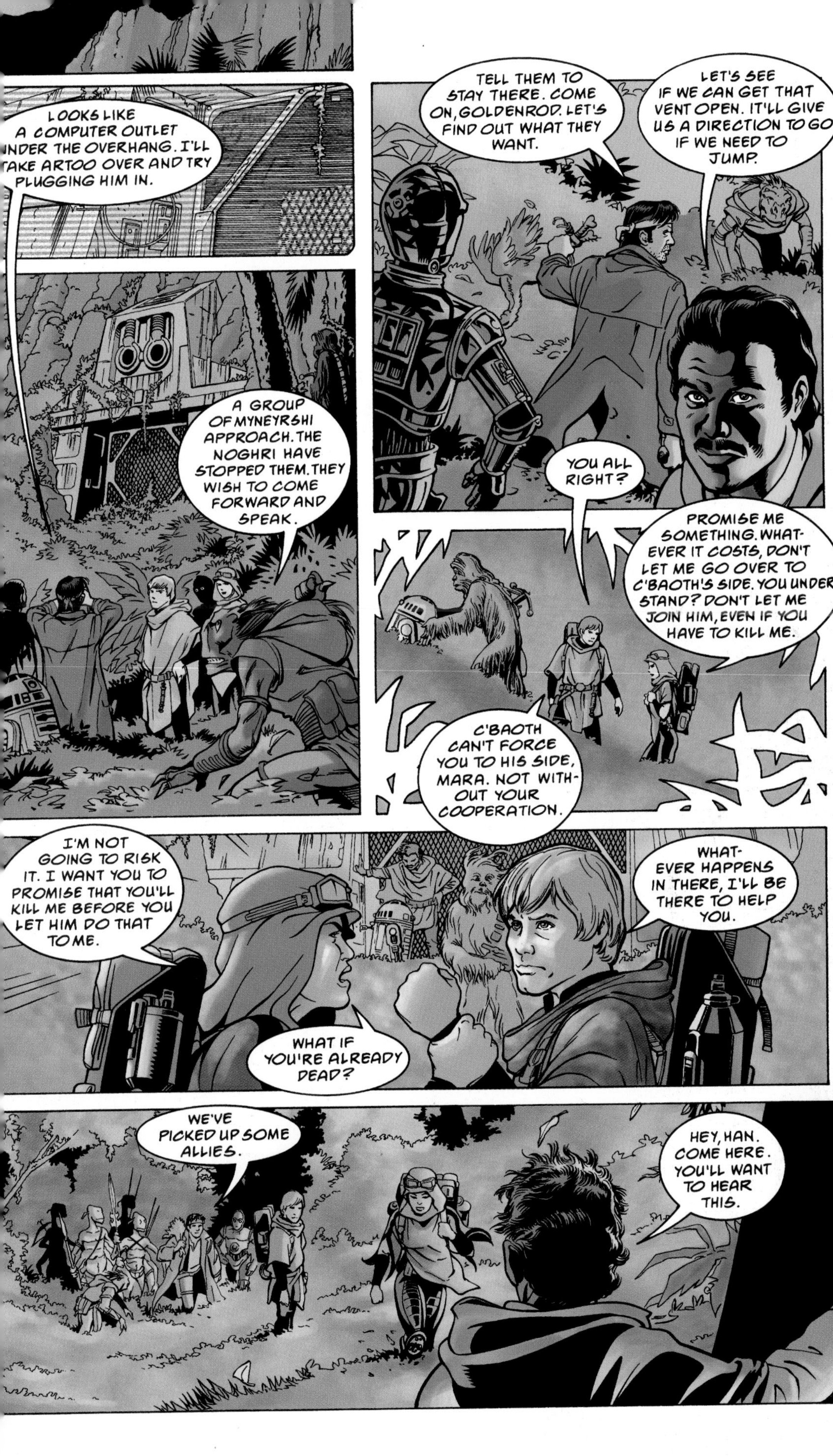
LOOKS LIKE A COMPUTER OUTLET UNDER THE OVERHANG. I'LL TAKE ARTOO OVER AND TRY PLUGGING HIM IN.
TELL THEM TO STAY THERE. COME ON, GOLDENROD. LET'S FIND OUT WHAT THEY WANT.
LET'S SEE IF WE CAN GET THAT VENT OPEN. IT'LL GIVE US A DIRECTION TO GO IF WE NEED TO JUMP.
A GROUP OF MYNEYRSHI APPROACH. THE NOGHRI HAVE STOPPED THEM. THEY WISH TO COME FORWARD AND SPEAK.
YOU ALL RIGHT?
PROMISE ME SOMETHING. WHATEVER IT COSTS, DON'T LET ME GO OVER TO C'BAOTH'S SIDE. YOU UNDERSTAND? DON'T LET ME JOIN HIM, EVEN IF YOU HAVE TO KILL ME.
C'BAOTH CAN'T FORCE YOU TO HIS SIDE, MARA. NOT WITHOUT YOUR COOPERATION.
I'M NOT GOING TO RISK IT. I WANT YOU TO PROMISE THAT YOU'LL KILL ME BEFORE YOU LET HIM DO THAT TO ME.
WHATEVER HAPPENS IN THERE, I'LL BE THERE TO HELP YOU.
WHAT IF YOU'RE ALREADY DEAD?
WE'VE PICKED UP SOME ALLIES.
HEY, HAN. COME HERE. YOU'LL WANT TO HEAR THIS.

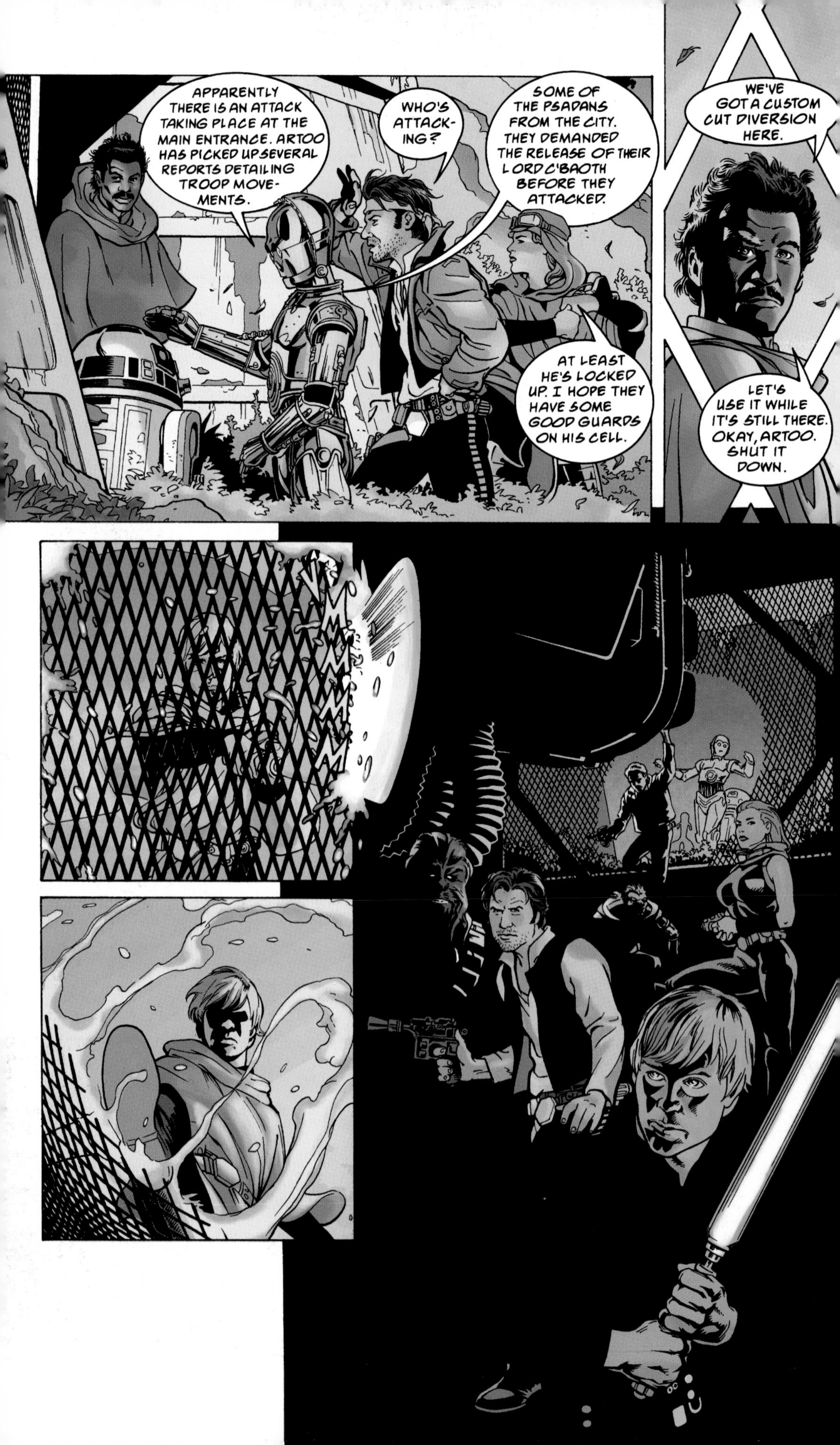
APPARENTLY THERE IS AN ATTACK TAKING PLACE AT THE MAIN ENTRANCE. ARTOO HAS PICKED UP SEVERAL REPORTS DETAILING TROOP MOVE-MENTS.
WHO'S ATTACK-ING?
SOME OF THE PSADANS FROM THE CITY. THEY DEMANDED THE RELEASE OF THEIR LORD C'BAOTH BEFORE THEY ATTACKED.
AT LEAST HE'S LOCKED UP. I HOPE THEY HAVE SOME GOOD GUARDS ON HIS CELL.
WE'VE GOT A CUSTOM CUT DIVERSION HERE.
LET'S USE IT WHILE IT'S STILL THERE. OKAY, ARTOO. SHUT IT DOWN.

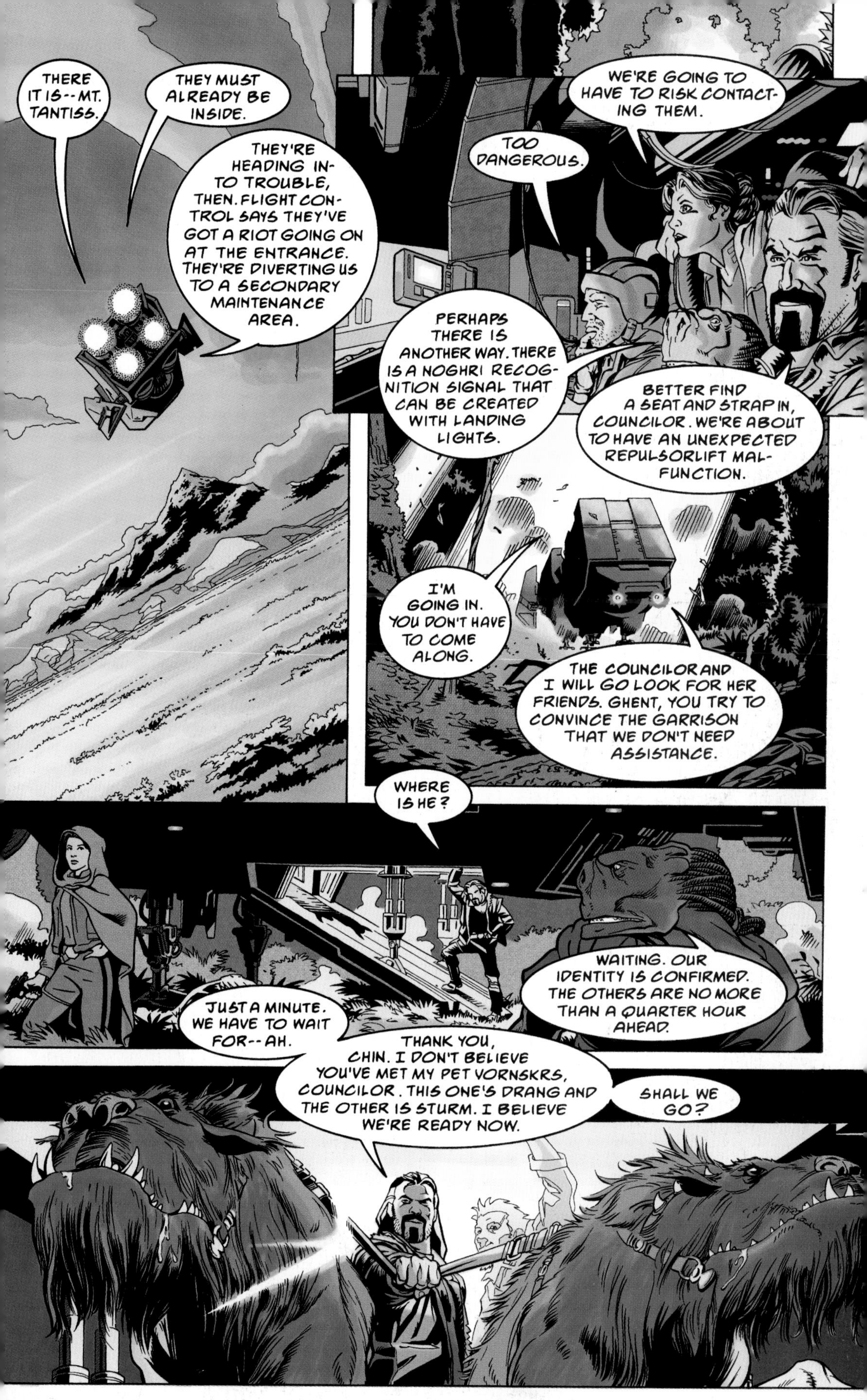
THERE IT IS--MT. TANTISS.
THEY MUST ALREADY BE INSIDE.
THEY'RE HEADING INTO TROUBLE, THEN. FLIGHT CONTROL SAYS THEY'VE GOT A RIOT GOING ON AT THE ENTRANCE. THEY'RE DIVERTING US TO A SECONDARY MAINTENANCE AREA.
WE'RE GOING TO HAVE TO RISK CONTACTING THEM.
TOO DANGEROUS.
PERHAPS THERE IS ANOTHER WAY. THERE IS A NOGHRI RECOGNITION SIGNAL THAT CAN BE CREATED WITH LANDING LIGHTS.
BETTER FIND A SEAT AND STRAP IN, COUNCILOR. WE'RE ABOUT TO HAVE AN UNEXPECTED REPULSORLIFT MALFUNCTION.
I'M GOING IN. YOU DON'T HAVE TO COME ALONG.
THE COUNCILOR AND I WILL GO LOOK FOR HER FRIENDS. GHENT, YOU TRY TO CONVINCE THE GARRISON THAT WE DON'T NEED ASSISTANCE.
WHERE IS HE?
WAITING. OUR IDENTITY IS CONFIRMED. THE OTHERS ARE NO MORE THAN A QUARTER HOUR AHEAD.
JUST A MINUTE. WE HAVE TO WAIT FOR--AH.
THANK YOU, CHIN. I DON'T BELIEVE YOU'VE MET MY PET VORNSKRS, COUNCILOR. THIS ONE'S DRANG AND THE OTHER IS STURM. I BELIEVE WE'RE READY NOW.
SHALL WE GO?

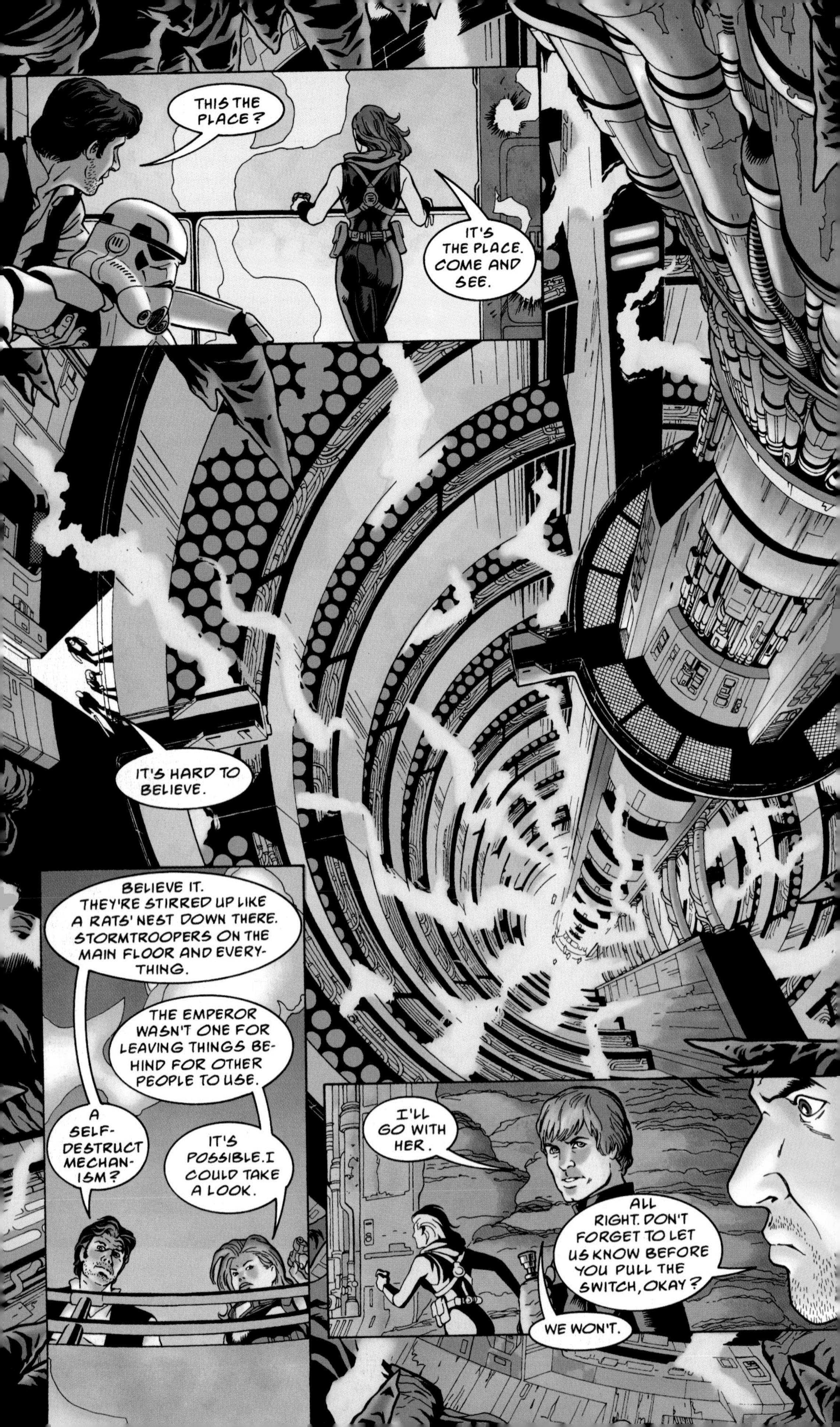
THIS THE PLACE?
IT'S THE PLACE. COME AND SEE.
IT'S HARD TO BELIEVE.
BELIEVE IT. THEY'RE STIRRED UP LIKE A RATS' NEST DOWN THERE. STORMTROOPERS ON THE MAIN FLOOR AND EVERY-THING.
THE EMPEROR WASN'T ONE FOR LEAVING THINGS BE-HIND FOR OTHER PEOPLE TO USE.
A SELF-DESTRUCT MECHAN-ISM?
IT'S POSSIBLE. I COULD TAKE A LOOK.
I'LL GO WITH HER.
ALL RIGHT. DON'T FORGET TO LET US KNOW BEFORE YOU PULL THE SWITCH, OKAY?
WE WON'T.

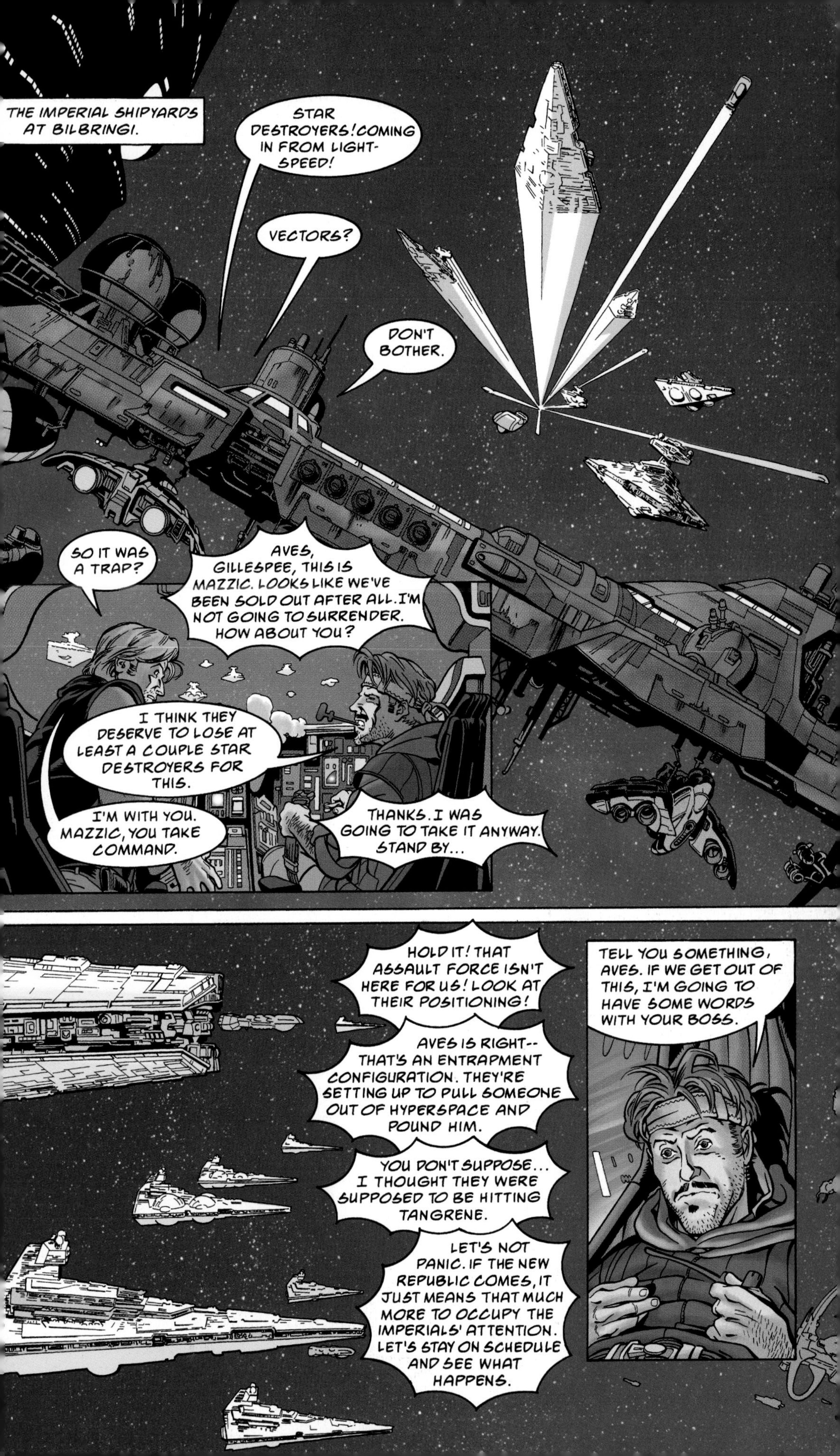
THE IMPERIAL SHIPYARDS AT BILBRINGI.
STAR DESTROYERS! COMING IN FROM LIGHT-SPEED!
VECTORS?
DON'T BOTHER.
SO IT WAS A TRAP?
AVES, GILLESPEE, THIS IS MAZZIC. LOOKS LIKE WE'VE BEEN SOLD OUT AFTER ALL. I'M NOT GOING TO SURRENDER. HOW ABOUT YOU?
I THINK THEY DESERVE TO LOSE AT LEAST A COUPLE STAR DESTROYERS FOR THIS.
I'M WITH YOU. MAZZIC, YOU TAKE COMMAND.
THANKS. I WAS GOING TO TAKE IT ANYWAY. STAND BY...
HOLD IT! THAT ASSAULT FORCE ISN'T HERE FOR US! LOOK AT THEIR POSITIONING!
AVES IS RIGHT-- THAT'S AN ENTRAPMENT CONFIGURATION. THEY'RE SETTING UP TO PULL SOMEONE OUT OF HYPERSPACE AND POUND HIM.
YOU DON'T SUPPOSE... I THOUGHT THEY WERE SUPPOSED TO BE HITTING TANGRENE.
LET'S NOT PANIC. IF THE NEW REPUBLIC COMES, IT JUST MEANS THAT MUCH MORE TO OCCUPY THE IMPERIALS' ATTENTION. LET'S STAY ON SCHEDULE AND SEE WHAT HAPPENS.
TELL YOU SOMETHING, AVES. IF WE GET OUT OF THIS, I'M GOING TO HAVE SOME WORDS WITH YOUR BOSS.

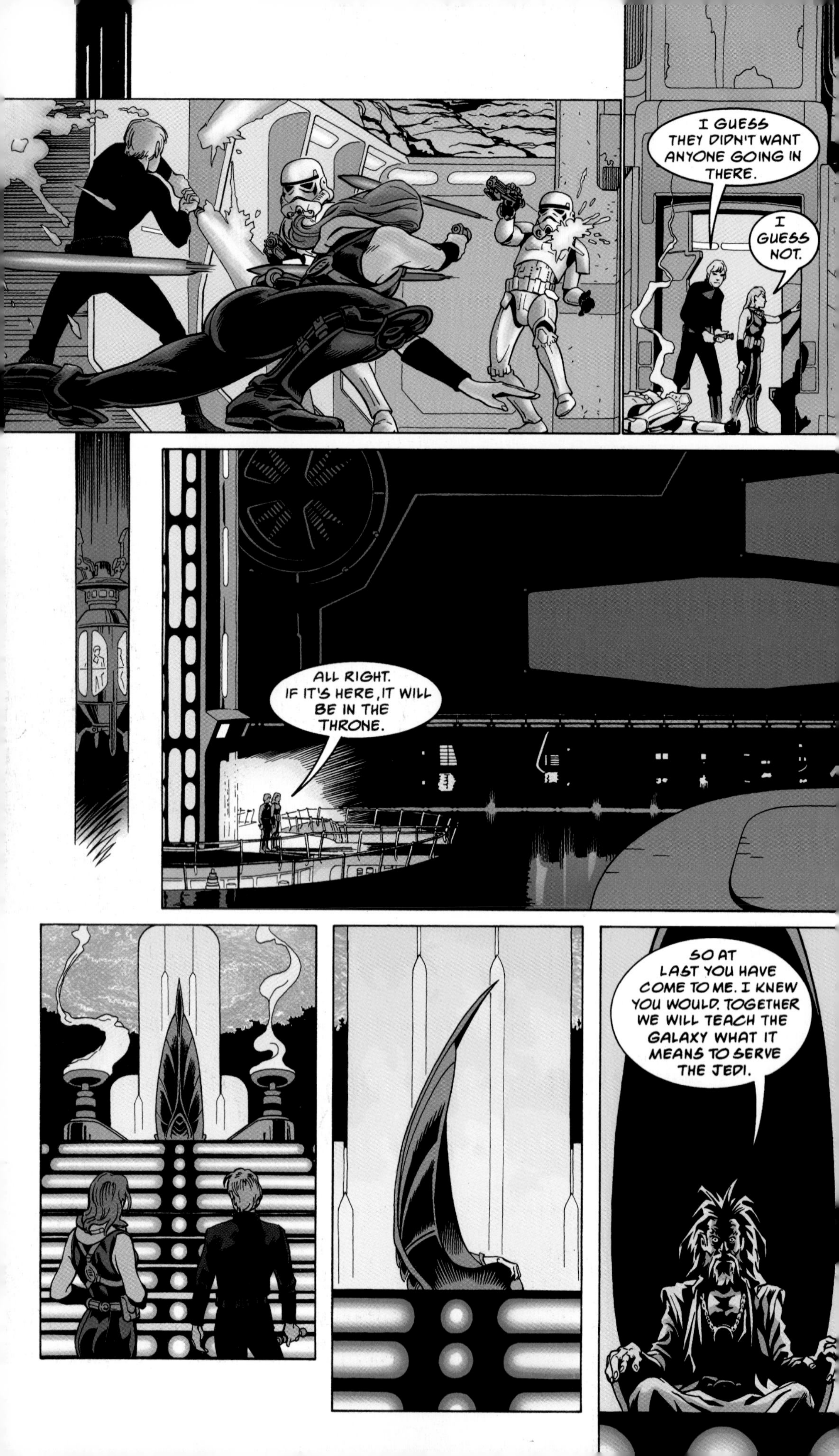
I GUESS THEY DIDN'T WANT ANYONE GOING IN THERE.
I GUESS NOT.
ALL RIGHT. IF IT'S HERE, IT WILL BE IN THE THRONE.
SO AT LAST YOU HAVE COME TO ME. I KNEW YOU WOULD. TOGETHER WE WILL TEACH THE GALAXY WHAT IT MEANS TO SERVE THE JEDI.

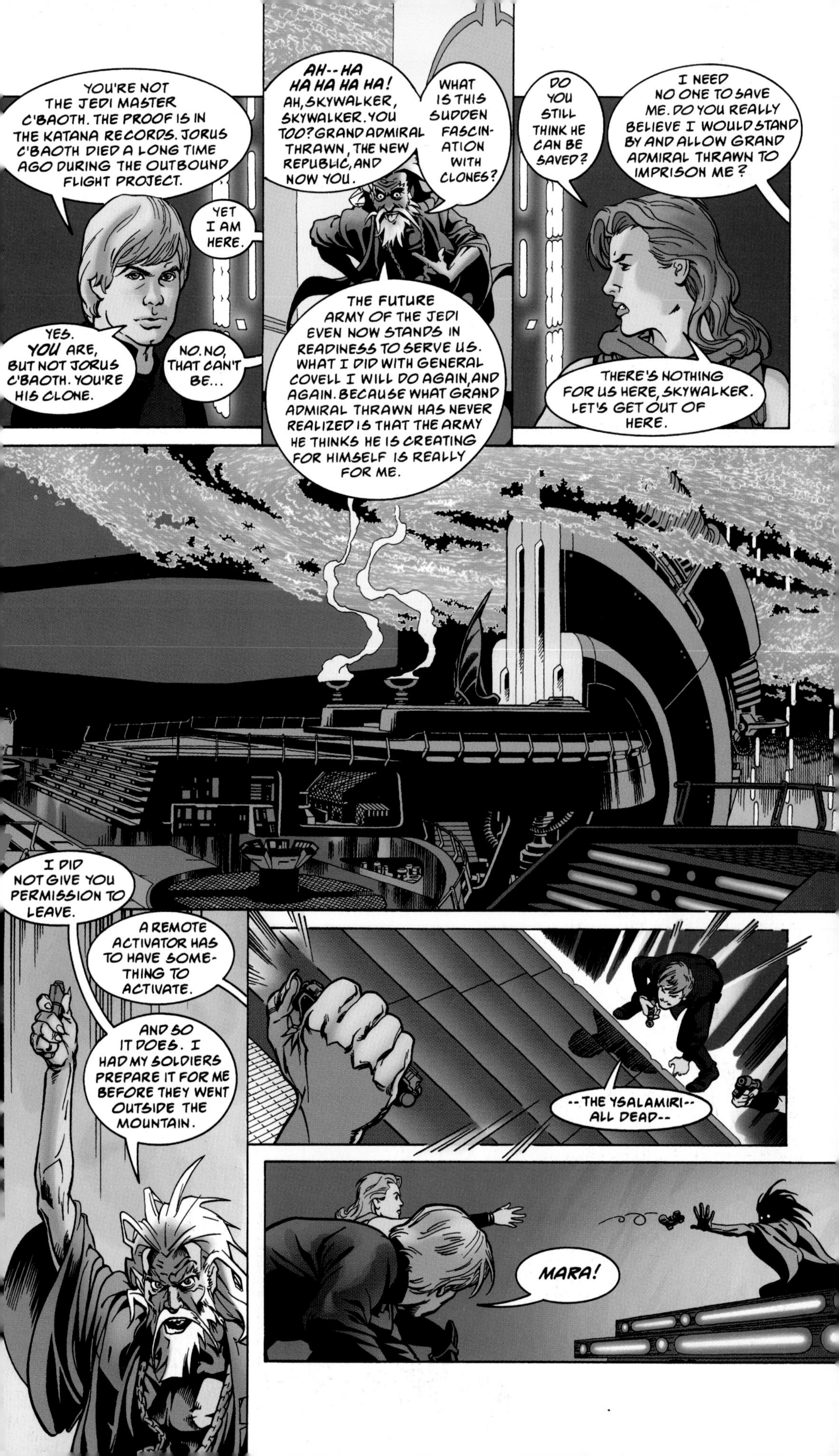

YOU'RE NOT THE JEDI MASTER C'BAOTH. THE PROOF IS IN THE KATANA RECORDS. JORUS C'BAOTH DIED A LONG TIME AGO DURING THE OUTBOUND FLIGHT PROJECT.
YET I AM HERE.
YES. YOU ARE, BUT NOT JORUS C'BAOTH. YOU'RE HIS CLONE.
NO. NO, THAT CAN'T BE...
AH--HA HA HA HA HA! AH, SKYWALKER, SKYWALKER. YOU TOO? GRAND ADMIRAL THRAWN, THE NEW REPUBLIC, AND NOW YOU.
WHAT IS THIS SUDDEN FASCIN-ATION WITH CLONES?
THE FUTURE ARMY OF THE JEDI EVEN NOW STANDS IN READINESS TO SERVE US. WHAT I DID WITH GENERAL COVELL I WILL DO AGAIN, AND AGAIN. BECAUSE WHAT GRAND ADMIRAL THRAWN HAS NEVER REALIZED IS THAT THE ARMY HE THINKS HE IS CREATING FOR HIMSELF IS REALLY FOR ME.
DO YOU STILL THINK HE CAN BE SAVED?
I NEED NO ONE TO SAVE ME. DO YOU REALLY BELIEVE I WOULD STAND BY AND ALLOW GRAND ADMIRAL THRAWN TO IMPRISON ME?
THERE'S NOTHING FOR US HERE, SKYWALKER. LET'S GET OUT OF HERE.
I DID NOT GIVE YOU PERMISSION TO LEAVE.
A REMOTE ACTIVATOR HAS TO HAVE SOME-THING TO ACTIVATE.
AND SO IT DOES. I HAD MY SOLDIERS PREPARE IT FOR ME BEFORE THEY WENT OUTSIDE THE MOUNTAIN.
--THE YSALAMIRI--ALL DEAD--
MARA!

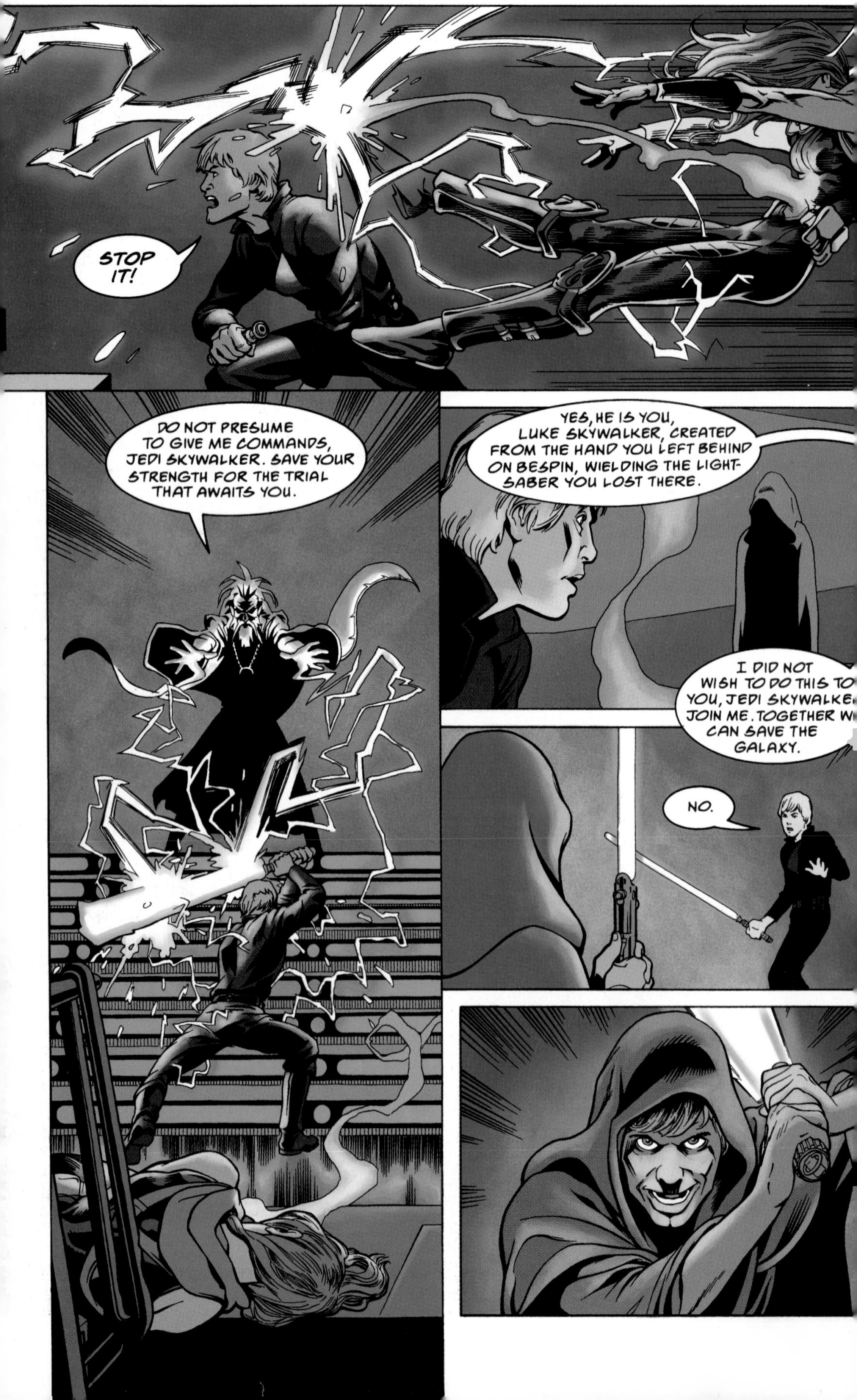
STOP IT!
DO NOT PRESUME TO GIVE ME COMMANDS, JEDI SKYWALKER. SAVE YOUR STRENGTH FOR THE TRIAL THAT AWAITS YOU.
YES, HE IS YOU, LUKE SKYWALKER, CREATED FROM THE HAND YOU LEFT BEHIND ON BESPIN, WIELDING THE LIGHT-SABER YOU LOST THERE.
I DID NOT WISH TO DO THIS TO YOU, JEDI SKYWALKE JOIN ME. TOGETHER W CAN SAVE THE GALAXY.
NO.

JUST MY LUCK TO RUN INTO SOME DESERTERS LOOKING FOR A PLACE TO HIDE...

AAAAAAAAA AAA..?!

HAN! DON'T SHOOT!

LUKE'S IN TROUBLE. HE'S AHEAD SOMEWHERE...

IT'S OKAY-- WE KNEW THE YSALAMIRI WERE HERE GOING IN.

THAT'S JUST IT. THEY'RE NOT. THE FORCE IS BACK.

C'BAOTH.

GOT ANYONE ELSE WITH YOU?

THEY'RE ALL WITH THE WILD KARRDE, GUARDING OUR EXIT.

THEN I GUESS IT'S JUST US. THEY'RE UP IN THE THRONE ROOM.

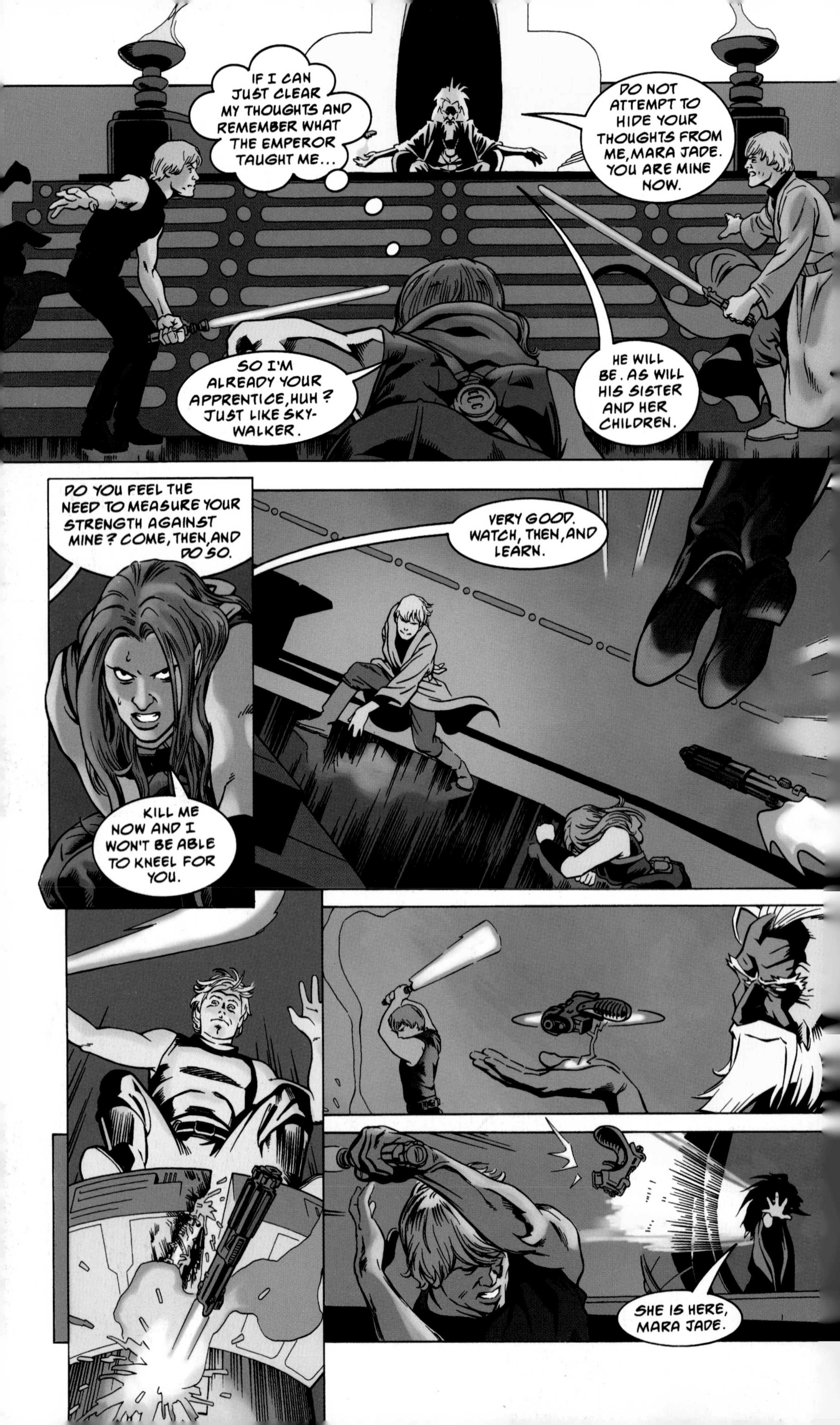
IF I CAN JUST CLEAR MY THOUGHTS AND REMEMBER WHAT THE EMPEROR TAUGHT ME...
DO NOT ATTEMPT TO HIDE YOUR THOUGHTS FROM ME, MARA JADE. YOU ARE MINE NOW.
SO I'M ALREADY YOUR APPRENTICE, HUH? JUST LIKE SKY-WALKER.
HE WILL BE. AS WILL HIS SISTER AND HER CHILDREN.
DO YOU FEEL THE NEED TO MEASURE YOUR STRENGTH AGAINST MINE? COME, THEN, AND DO SO.
VERY GOOD. WATCH, THEN, AND LEARN.
KILL ME NOW AND I WON'T BE ABLE TO KNEEL FOR YOU.
SHE IS HERE, MARA JADE.

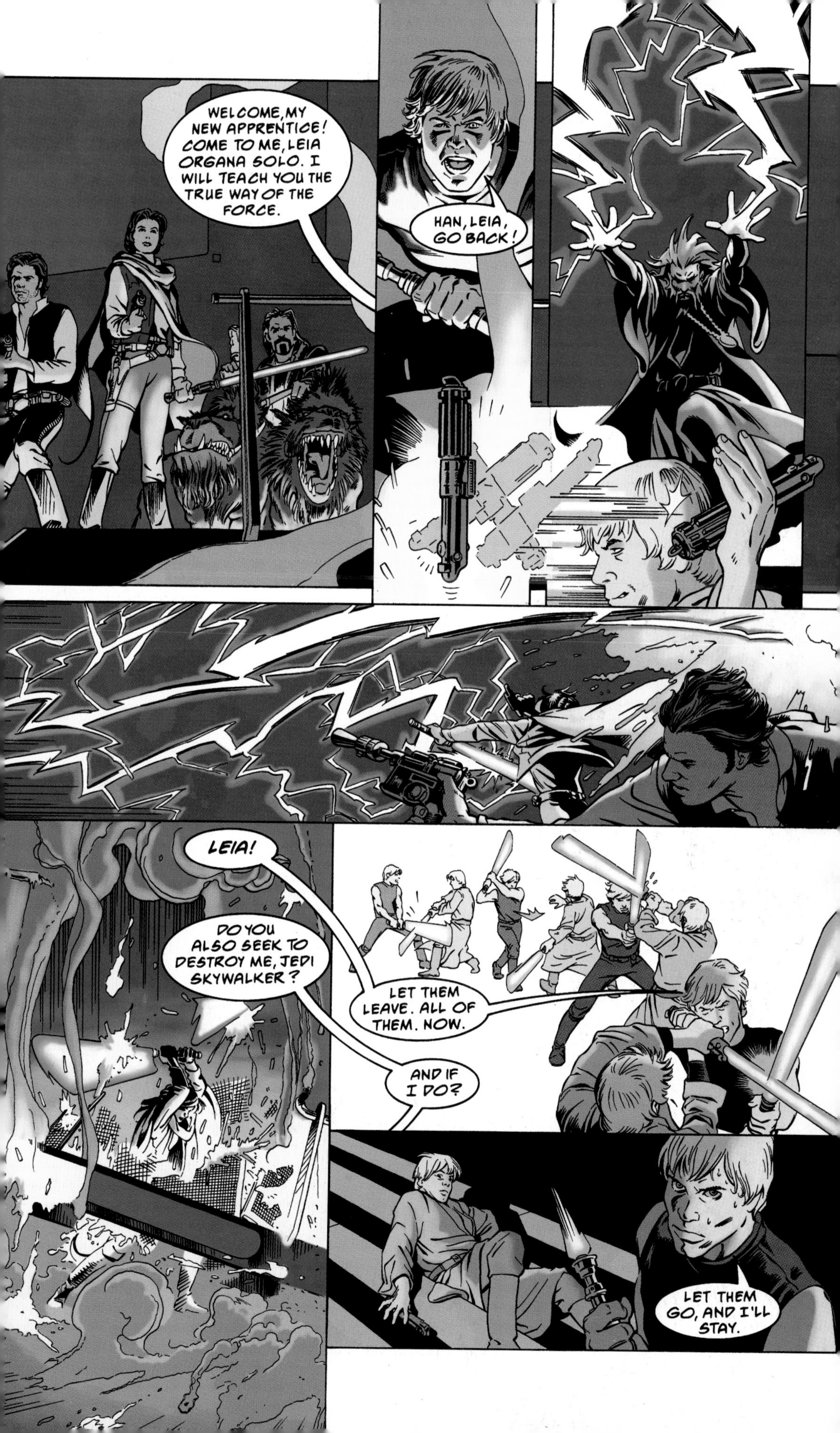

WELCOME, MY NEW APPRENTICE! COME TO ME, LEIA ORGANA SOLO. I WILL TEACH YOU THE TRUE WAY OF THE FORCE.
HAN, LEIA, GO BACK!
LEIA!
DO YOU ALSO SEEK TO DESTROY ME, JEDI SKYWALKER?
LET THEM LEAVE. ALL OF THEM. NOW.
AND IF I DO?
LET THEM GO, AND I'LL STAY.

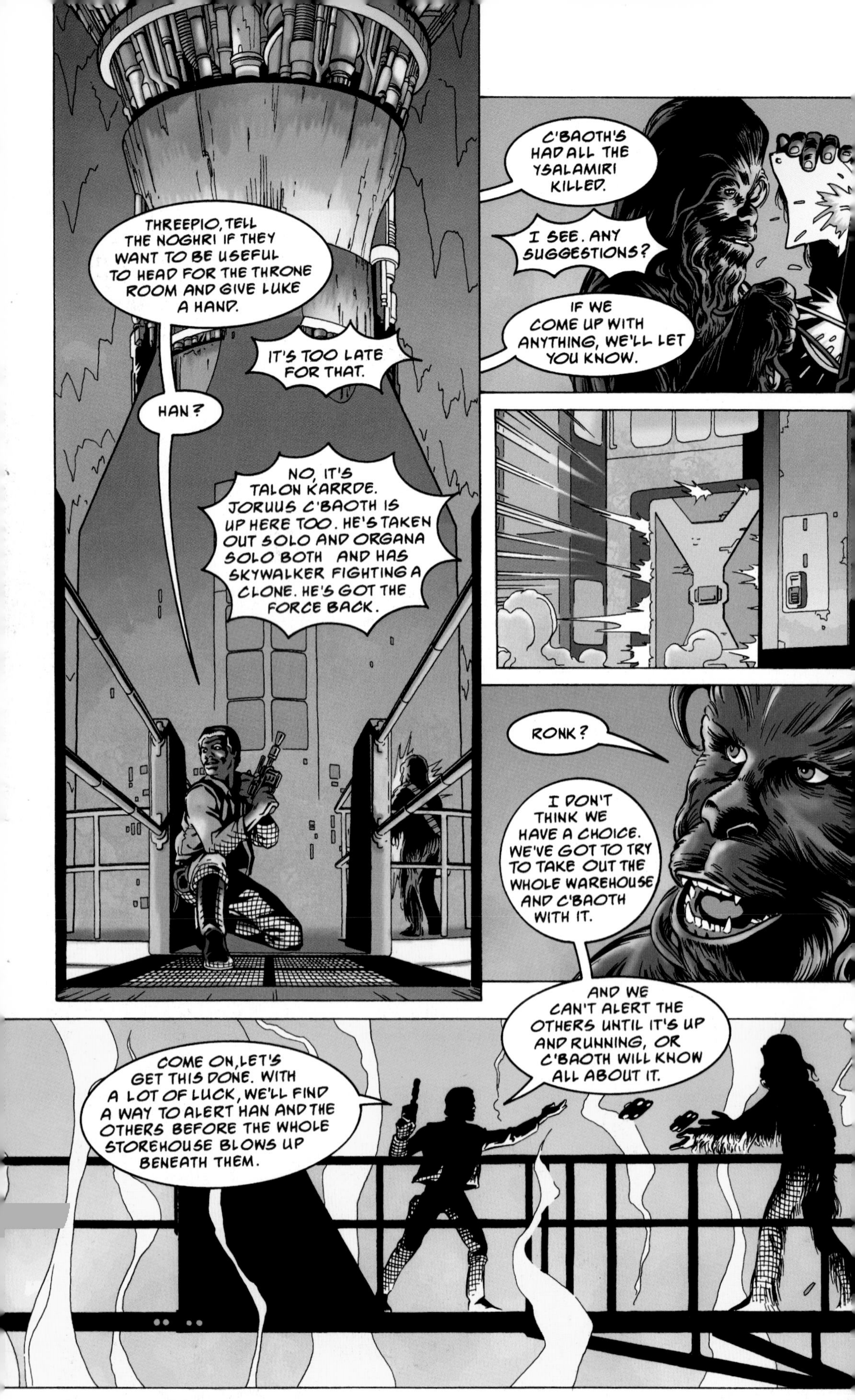
THREEPIO, TELL THE NOGHRI IF THEY WANT TO BE USEFUL TO HEAD FOR THE THRONE ROOM AND GIVE LUKE A HAND.
IT'S TOO LATE FOR THAT.
HAN?
NO, IT'S TALON KARRDE. JORUUS C'BAOTH IS UP HERE TOO. HE'S TAKEN OUT SOLO AND ORGANA SOLO BOTH AND HAS SKYWALKER FIGHTING A CLONE. HE'S GOT THE FORCE BACK.
C'BAOTH'S HAD ALL THE YSALAMIRI KILLED.
I SEE. ANY SUGGESTIONS?
IF WE COME UP WITH ANYTHING, WE'LL LET YOU KNOW.
RONK?
I DON'T THINK WE HAVE A CHOICE. WE'VE GOT TO TRY TO TAKE OUT THE WHOLE WAREHOUSE AND C'BAOTH WITH IT.
AND WE CAN'T ALERT THE OTHERS UNTIL IT'S UP AND RUNNING, OR C'BAOTH WILL KNOW ALL ABOUT IT.
COME ON, LET'S GET THIS DONE. WITH A LOT OF LUCK, WE'LL FIND A WAY TO ALERT HAN AND THE OTHERS BEFORE THE WHOLE STOREHOUSE BLOWS UP BENEATH THEM.

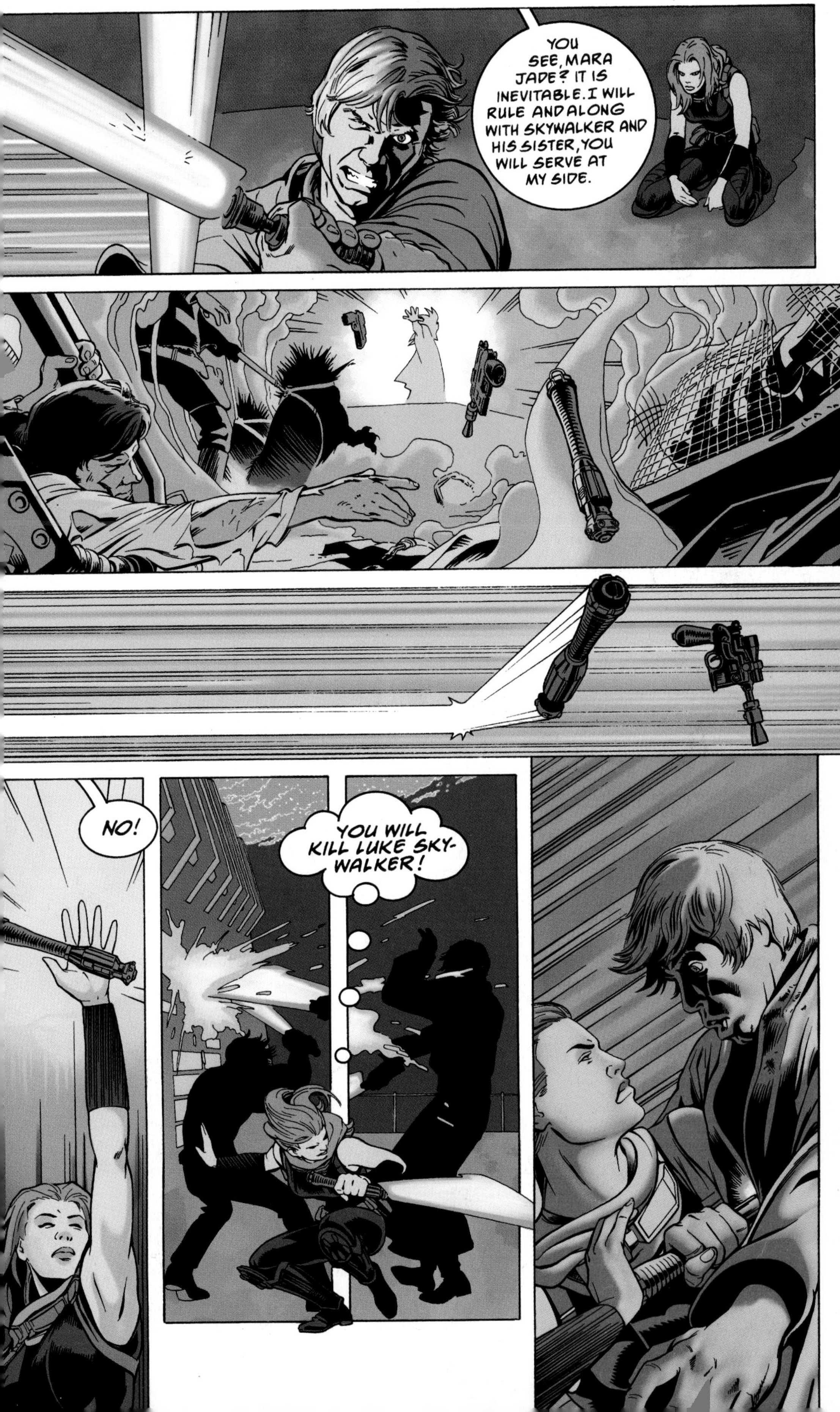
YOU SEE, MARA JADE? IT IS INEVITABLE. I WILL RULE AND ALONG WITH SKYWALKER AND HIS SISTER, YOU WILL SERVE AT MY SIDE.
NO!
YOU WILL KILL LUKE SKY-WALKER!

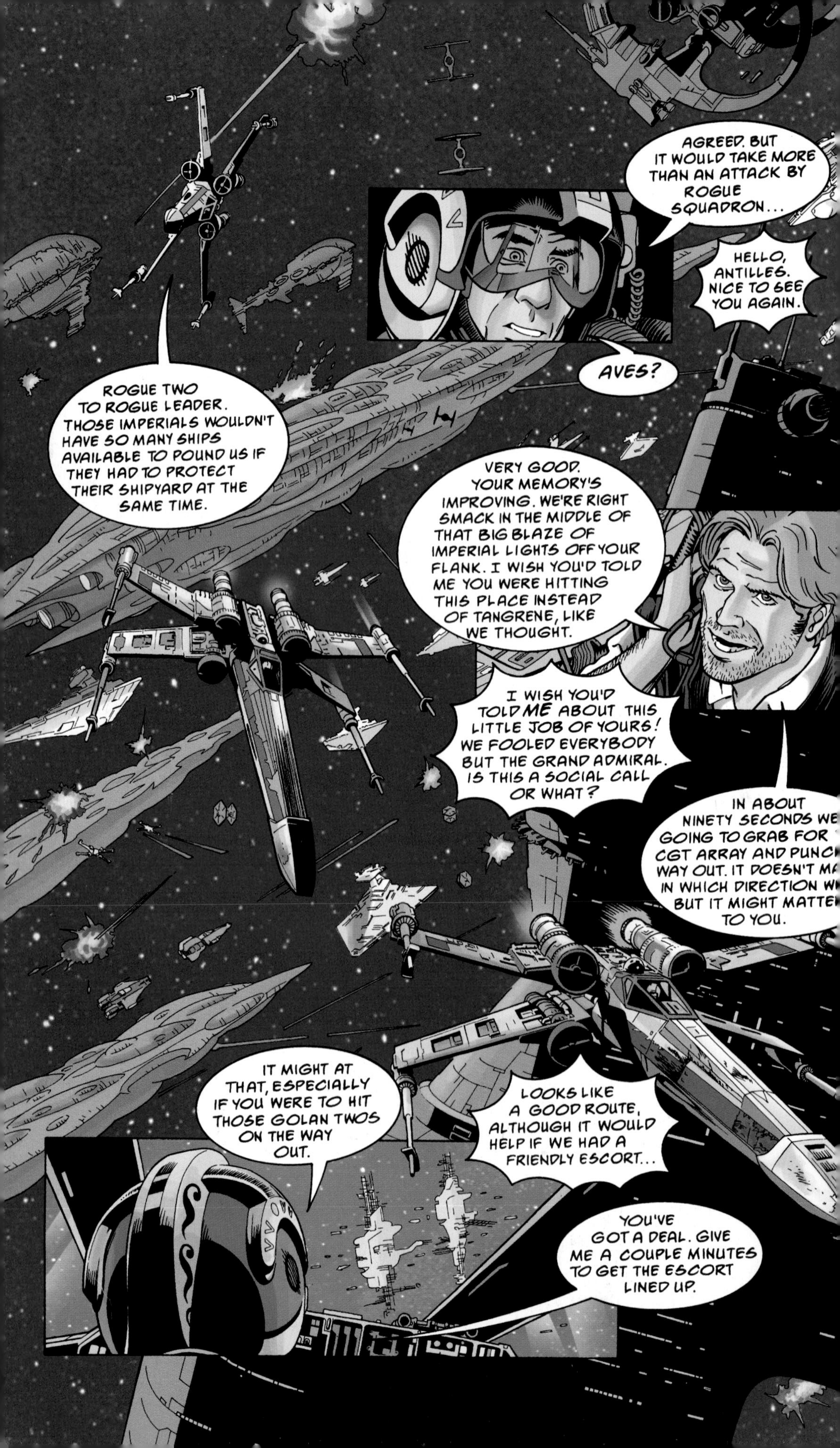
ROGUE TWO TO ROGUE LEADER. THOSE IMPERIALS WOULDN'T HAVE SO MANY SHIPS AVAILABLE TO POUND US IF THEY HAD TO PROTECT THEIR SHIPYARD AT THE SAME TIME.
AGREED. BUT IT WOULD TAKE MORE THAN AN ATTACK BY ROGUE SQUADRON...
HELLO, ANTILLES. NICE TO SEE YOU AGAIN.
AVES?
VERY GOOD. YOUR MEMORY'S IMPROVING. WE'RE RIGHT SMACK IN THE MIDDLE OF THAT BIG BLAZE OF IMPERIAL LIGHTS OFF YOUR FLANK. I WISH YOU'D TOLD ME YOU WERE HITTING THIS PLACE INSTEAD OF TANGRENE, LIKE WE THOUGHT.
I WISH YOU'D TOLD ME ABOUT THIS LITTLE JOB OF YOURS! WE FOOLED EVERYBODY BUT THE GRAND ADMIRAL. IS THIS A SOCIAL CALL OR WHAT?
IN ABOUT NINETY SECONDS WE GOING TO GRAB FOR CGT ARRAY AND PUNC WAY OUT. IT DOESN'T MA IN WHICH DIRECTION W BUT IT MIGHT MATTE TO YOU.
LOOKS LIKE A GOOD ROUTE, ALTHOUGH IT WOULD HELP IF WE HAD A FRIENDLY ESCORT...
IT MIGHT AT THAT, ESPECIALLY IF YOU WERE TO HIT THOSE GOLAN TWOS ON THE WAY OUT.
YOU'VE GOT A DEAL. GIVE ME A COUPLE MINUTES TO GET THE ESCORT LINED UP.

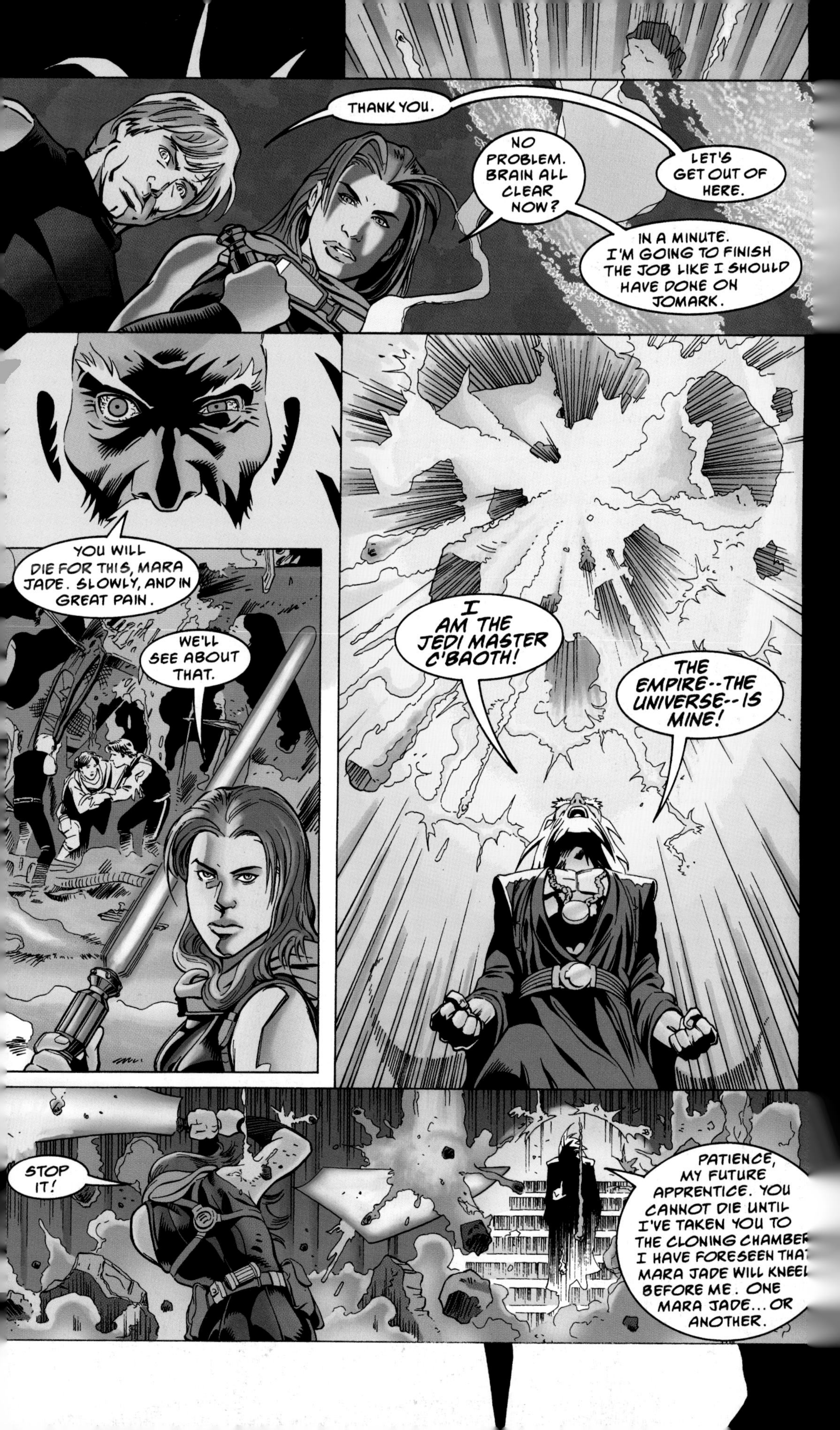
THANK YOU.
NO PROBLEM. BRAIN ALL CLEAR NOW?
LET'S GET OUT OF HERE.
IN A MINUTE. I'M GOING TO FINISH THE JOB LIKE I SHOULD HAVE DONE ON JOMARK.
YOU WILL DIE FOR THIS, MARA JADE. SLOWLY, AND IN GREAT PAIN.
WE'LL SEE ABOUT THAT.
I AM THE JEDI MASTER C'BAOTH!
THE EMPIRE--THE UNIVERSE--IS MINE!
STOP IT!
PATIENCE, MY FUTURE APPRENTICE. YOU CANNOT DIE UNTIL I'VE TAKEN YOU TO THE CLONING CHAMBER I HAVE FORESEEN THAT MARA JADE WILL KNEEL BEFORE ME. ONE MARA JADE... OR ANOTHER.

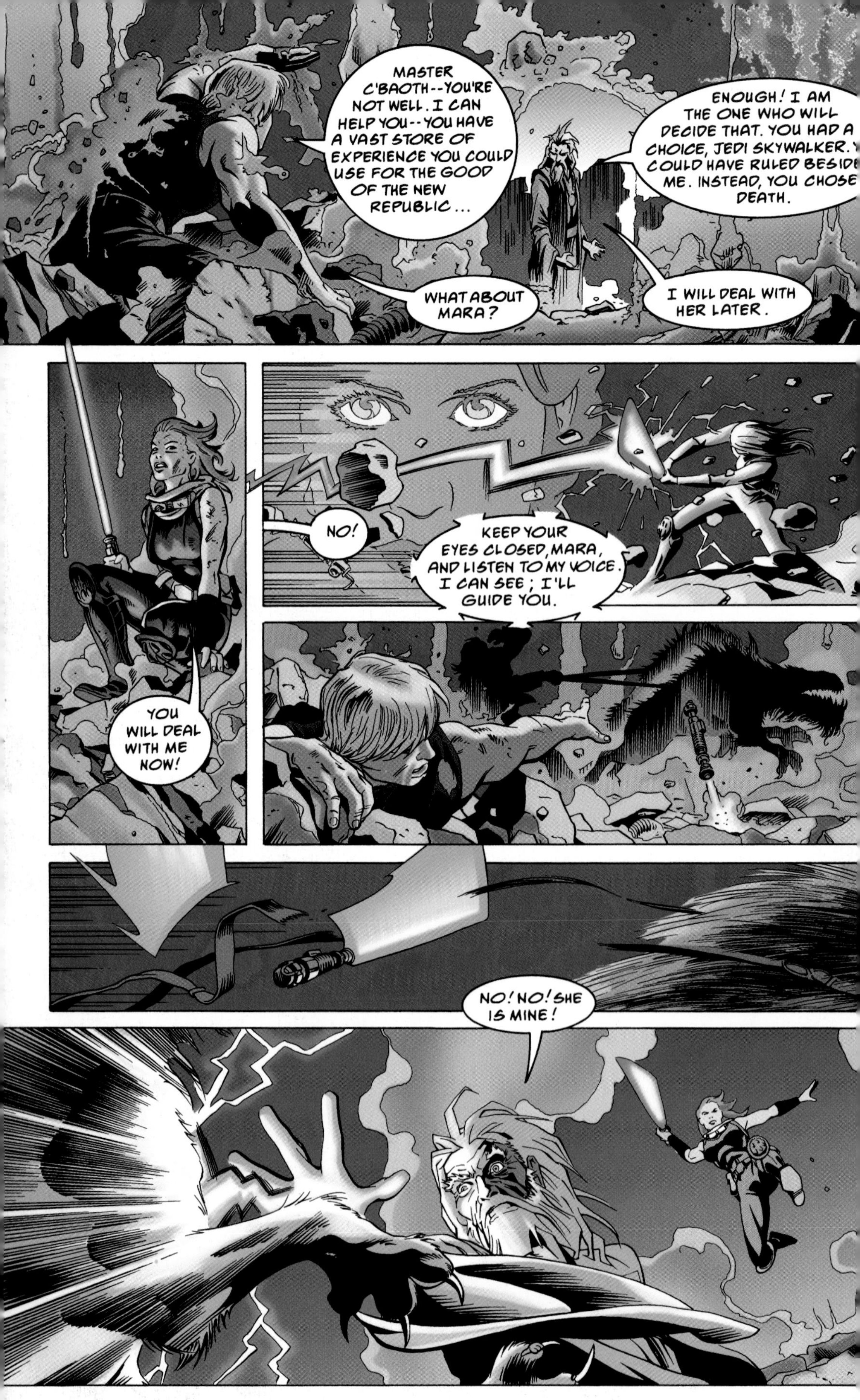
MASTER C'BAOTH--YOU'RE NOT WELL. I CAN HELP YOU--YOU HAVE A VAST STORE OF EXPERIENCE YOU COULD USE FOR THE GOOD OF THE NEW REPUBLIC...
ENOUGH! I AM THE ONE WHO WILL DECIDE THAT. YOU HAD A CHOICE, JEDI SKYWALKER. YOU COULD HAVE RULED BESIDE ME. INSTEAD, YOU CHOSE DEATH.
WHAT ABOUT MARA?
I WILL DEAL WITH HER LATER.
YOU WILL DEAL WITH ME NOW!
NO!
KEEP YOUR EYES CLOSED, MARA, AND LISTEN TO MY VOICE. I CAN SEE; I'LL GUIDE YOU.
NO! NO! SHE IS MINE!

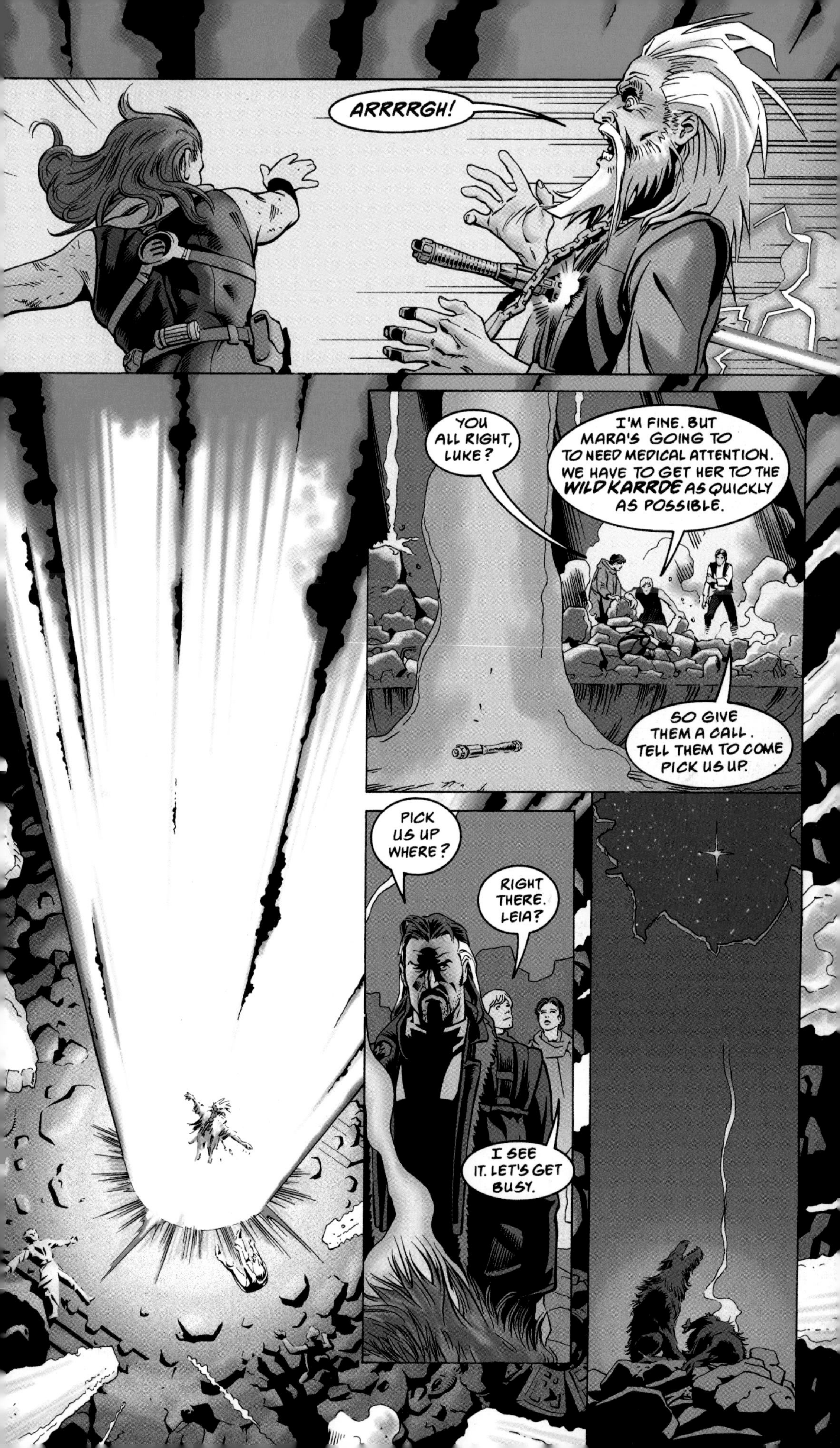
ARRRRGH!
YOU ALL RIGHT, LUKE?
I'M FINE. BUT MARA'S GOING TO TO NEED MEDICAL ATTENTION. WE HAVE TO GET HER TO THE WILD KARRDE AS QUICKLY AS POSSIBLE.
SO GIVE THEM A CALL. TELL THEM TO COME PICK US UP.
PICK US UP WHERE?
RIGHT THERE. LEIA?
I SEE IT. LET'S GET BUSY.

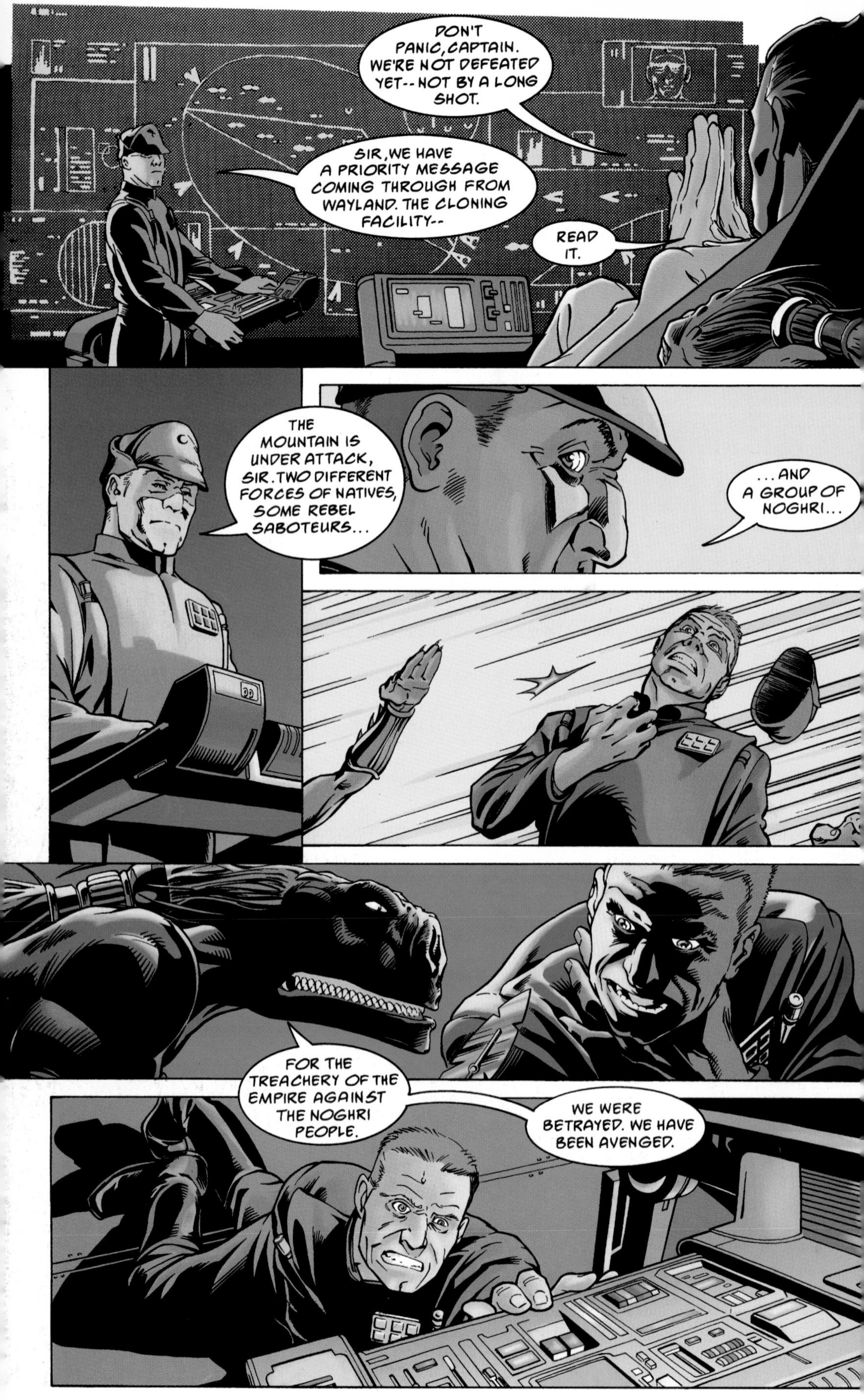
DON'T PANIC, CAPTAIN. WE'RE NOT DEFEATED YET-- NOT BY A LONG SHOT.
SIR, WE HAVE A PRIORITY MESSAGE COMING THROUGH FROM WAYLAND. THE CLONING FACILITY--
READ IT.
THE MOUNTAIN IS UNDER ATTACK, SIR. TWO DIFFERENT FORCES OF NATIVES, SOME REBEL SABOTEURS...
...AND A GROUP OF NOGHRI...
FOR THE TREACHERY OF THE EMPIRE AGAINST THE NOGHRI PEOPLE.
WE WERE BETRAYED. WE HAVE BEEN AVENGED.

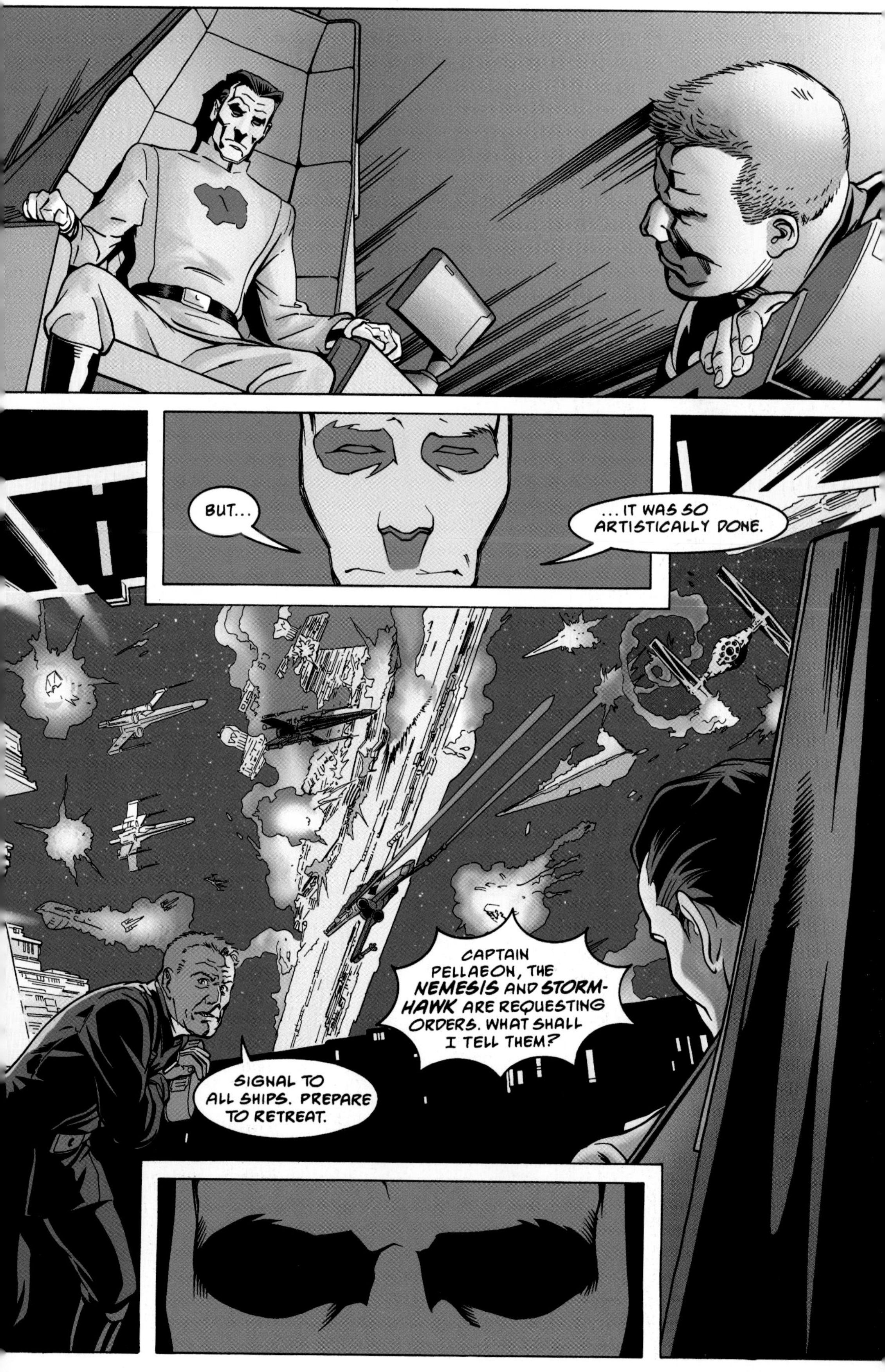

BUT...
...IT WAS SO ARTISTICALLY DONE.
CAPTAIN PELLAEON, THE NEMESIS AND STORMHAWK ARE REQUESTING ORDERS. WHAT SHALL I TELL THEM?
SIGNAL TO ALL SHIPS. PREPARE TO RETREAT.

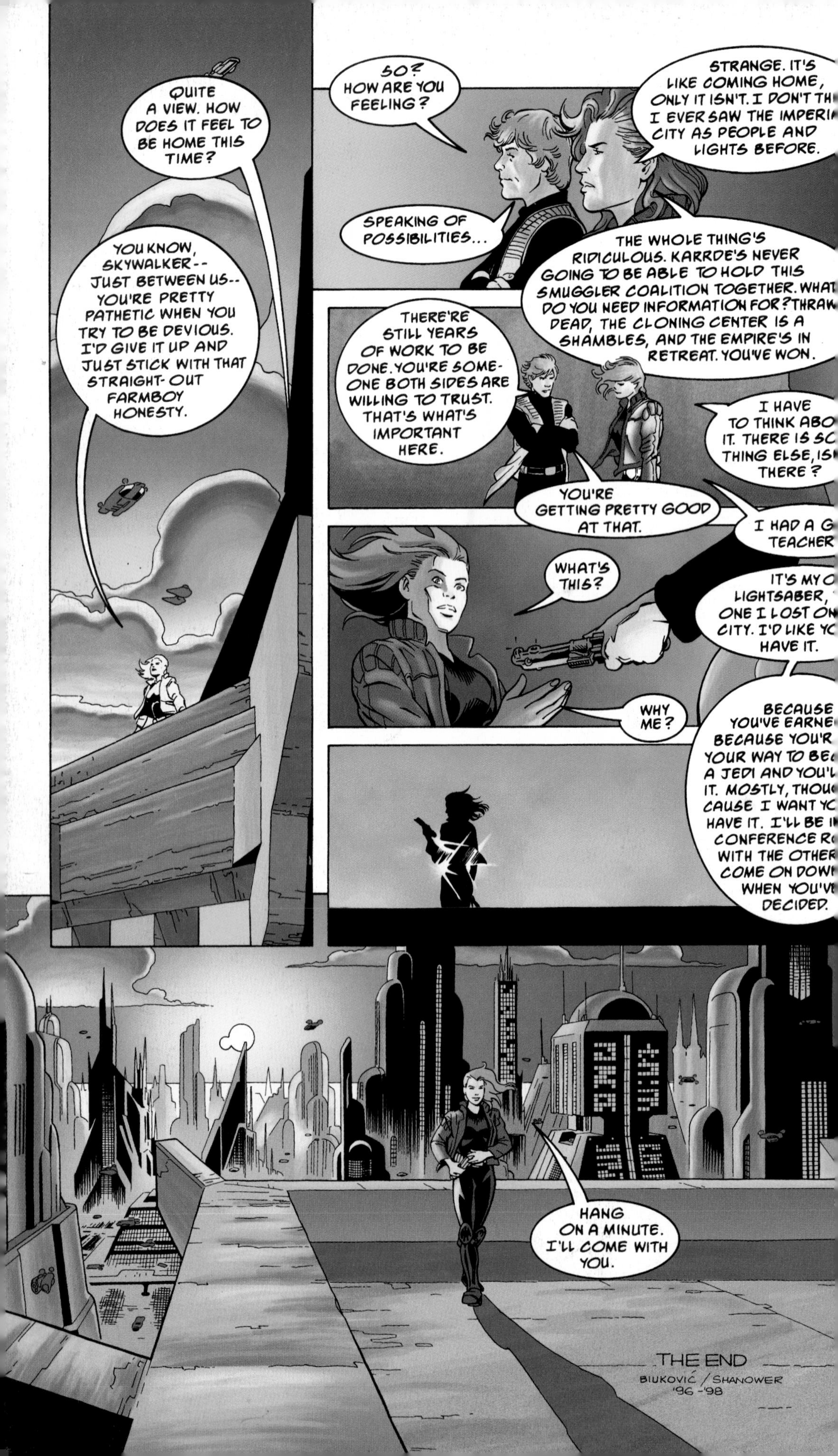
QUITE A VIEW. HOW DOES IT FEEL TO BE HOME THIS TIME?
YOU KNOW, SKYWALKER-- JUST BETWEEN US-- YOU'RE PRETTY PATHETIC WHEN YOU TRY TO BE DEVIOUS. I'D GIVE IT UP AND JUST STICK WITH THAT STRAIGHT-OUT FARMBOY HONESTY.
SO? HOW ARE YOU FEELING?
STRANGE. IT'S LIKE COMING HOME, ONLY IT ISN'T. I DON'T TH I EVER SAW THE IMPERI CITY AS PEOPLE AND LIGHTS BEFORE.
SPEAKING OF POSSIBILITIES...
THE WHOLE THING'S RIDICULOUS. KARRDE'S NEVER GOING TO BE ABLE TO HOLD THIS SMUGGLER COALITION TOGETHER. WHAT DO YOU NEED INFORMATION FOR? THRAW DEAD, THE CLONING CENTER IS A SHAMBLES, AND THE EMPIRE'S IN RETREAT. YOU'VE WON.
THERE'RE STILL YEARS OF WORK TO BE DONE. YOU'RE SOME-ONE BOTH SIDES ARE WILLING TO TRUST. THAT'S WHAT'S IMPORTANT HERE.
I HAVE TO THINK ABO IT. THERE IS SO THING ELSE, IS THERE?
YOU'RE GETTING PRETTY GOOD AT THAT.
I HAD A G TEACHER
WHAT'S THIS?
IT'S MY O LIGHTSABER, ONE I LOST ON CITY. I'D LIKE YO HAVE IT.
WHY ME?
BECAUSE YOU'VE EARNE BECAUSE YOU'R YOUR WAY TO BE A JEDI AND YOU'L IT. MOSTLY, THOU CAUSE I WANT YO HAVE IT. I'LL BE I CONFERENCE R WITH THE OTHER COME ON DOW WHEN YOU'V DECIDED.
HANG ON A MINUTE. I'LL COME WITH YOU.
THE END
BIUKOVIĆ / SHANOWER
'96 - '98

STAR WARS ®
THE LAST COMMAND

COVER GALLERY

FEATURING THE ART OF
MATHIEU LAUFFRAY

ISSUE #1

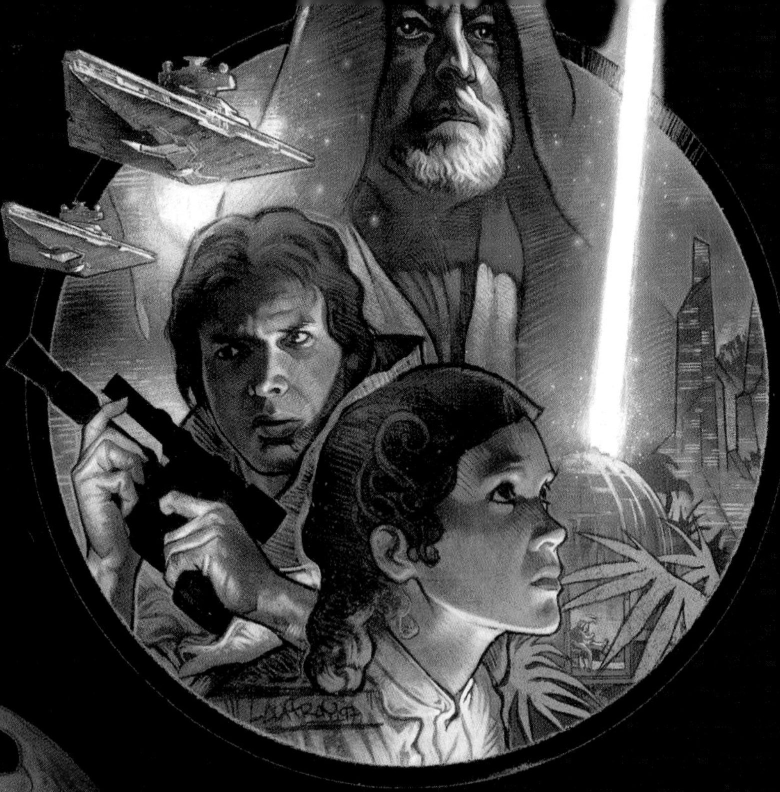

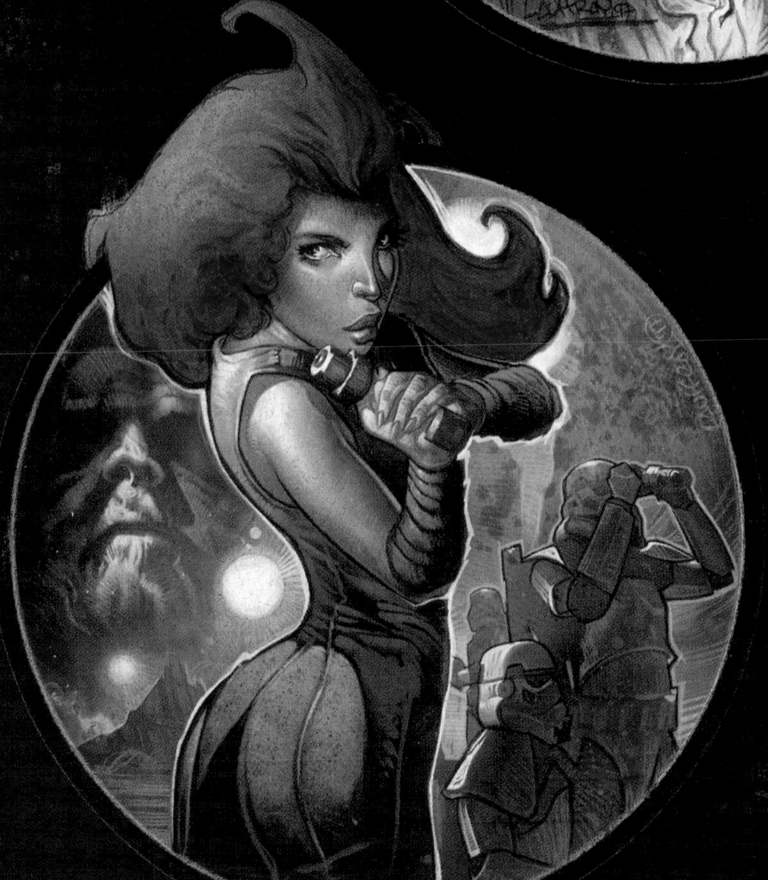

ISSUE #2

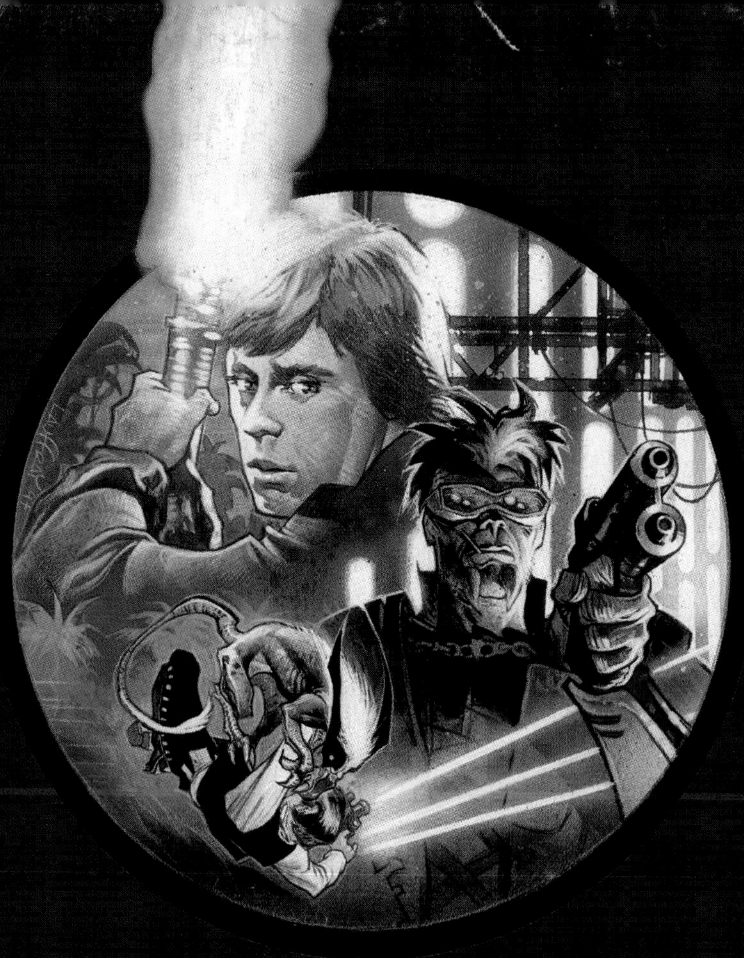

ISSUE #4

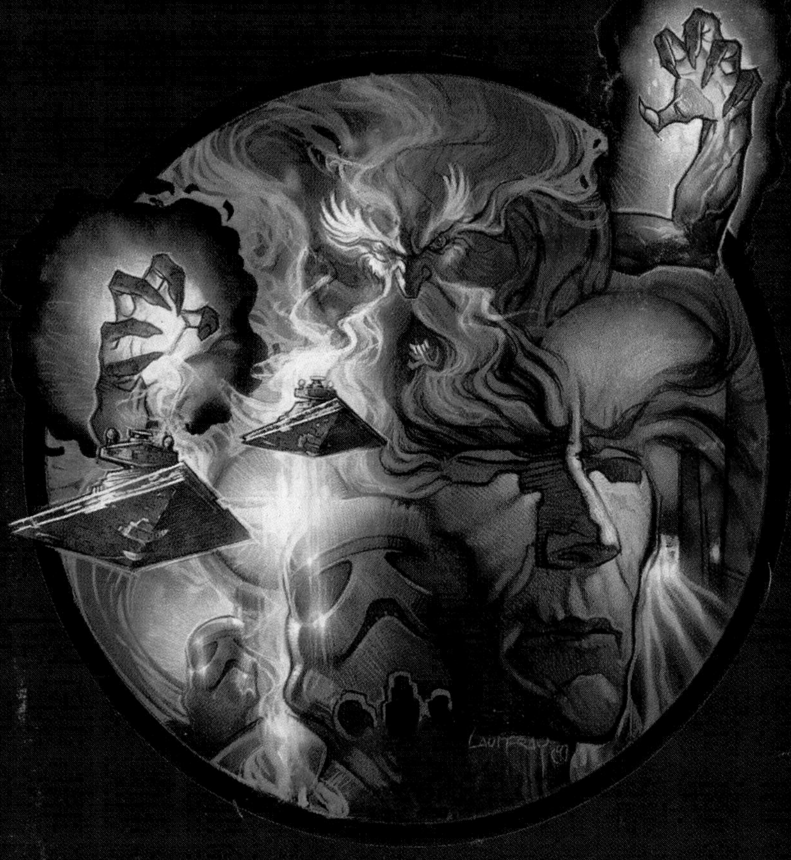

ISSUE #3

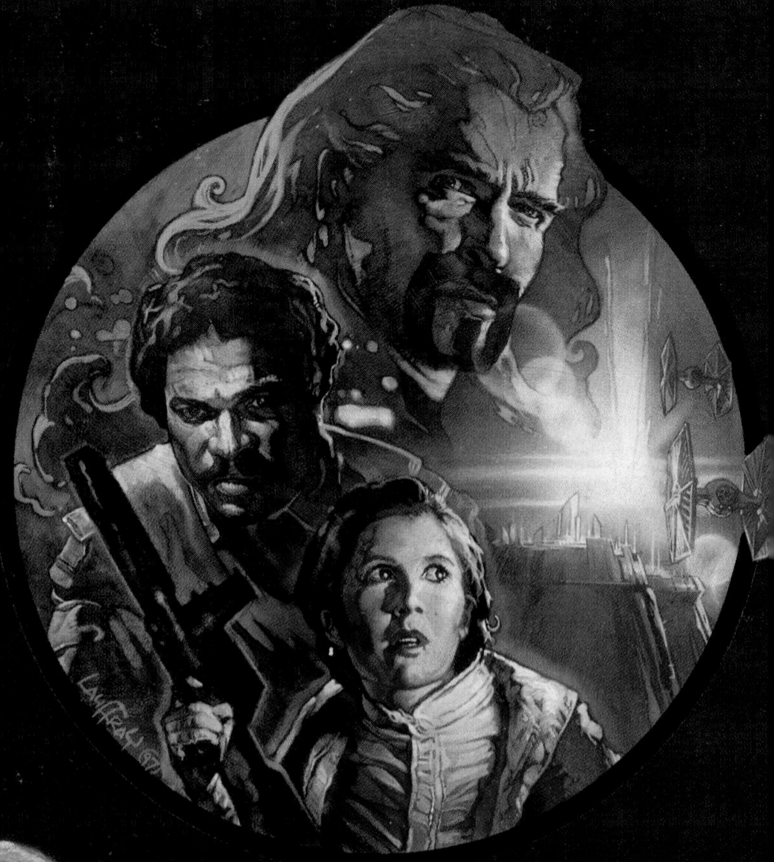

ISSUE #5

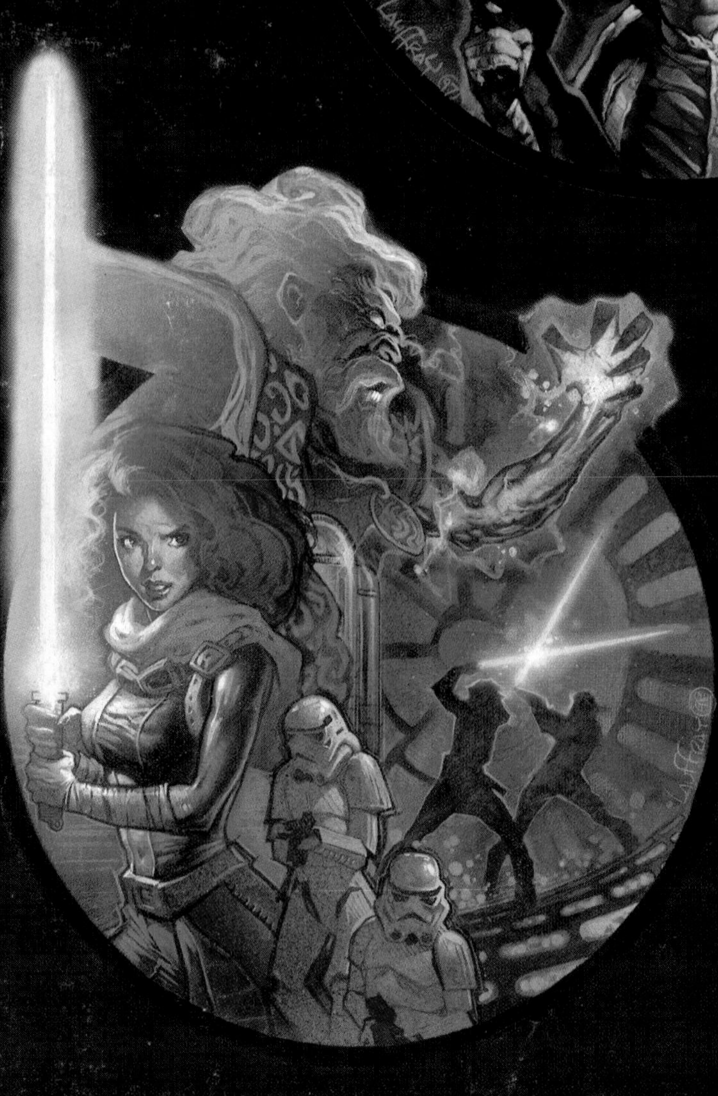

ISSUE #6